HOLDING UP THE SKY

AN AFRICAN LIFE

SANDY BLACKBURN-WRIGHT

PIER 9

PREFACE

THERE ARE THREE THINGS I HAVE ALWAYS BELIEVED: FIRSTLY, THAT I COULD DO ANYTHING I SET MY MIND TO; SECONDLY, THAT I SHOULD ALWAYS BACK THE UNDERDOG AND THE POWERLESS; AND THIRDLY, THAT I WOULD DIE YOUNG. THESE THREE BELIEFS HAVE SHAPED THE WAY I LIVE EACH DAY OF MY LIFE. I HAVE IMAGINED I MIGHT DIE OF A RARE DISEASE, SOME RANDOM ACT OF VIOLENCE OR IN A DEVASTATING PLANE CRASH—SOME TRAGIC END TO A SHORT BUT FULL LIFE. I DON'T KNOW WHICH CAME FIRST, THE NEED TO LIVE LIFE ON FAST FORWARD OR THE BELIEF THAT I DIDN'T HAVE A LOT OF TIME TO WASTE ON THINGS THAT WEREN'T IMPORTANT. I THINK, IN THE END, THEY HAVE FED OFF EACH OTHER.

Oddly, despite placing myself in danger's way sufficiently often to facilitate my early death, I sit writing these words in my forties. I don't know at what age I thought I would die. I just never imagined myself as old. Perhaps the two are not mutually exclusive and in our mind's eye we are eternally young, feeling the age of the soul within us, not the body without. My husband finds my premonition of death somewhat disturbing. I have factored it in when we talk of our future long-term plans, something which I've only started doing in the last few years. At such times I try reassuring him that it was just one of those childhood thoughts that stuck, and he shouldn't take it too seriously, but I think he wishes I would grow out of it. Yet after writing my story, I now see that my premonition of an early death was not literal but, rather, figurative; time and again I have died to one life, one way of living, only to enter a new and different life, as if reborn.

I have one more childhood thought that stuck: I remember as an eight-year-old, growing up in suburban Sydney, becoming completely entranced by the thought of Africa. Then began a binge diet of Tarzan movies, *National Geographic* documentaries, books and TV shows on tribal cultures of East Africa. It was a feeding frenzy that lasted many years. I tossed up between a career as a doctor working in a remote African hospital and a career as a biologist studying endangered lowland gorillas. I remember thinking that friends who planned to marry their childhood sweethearts and buy a little three-bedroom house in an affordable Sydney suburb were somehow limiting their options. Me, I had plans. And along with those plans, heightened by my need for high impact in a short space of time, was an ideological world view the size of Mount Kilimanjaro—one I had been sharpening on my family and friends for years. I think my father suffered badly during my adolescence. Perhaps his appearance towards the end of his life—weary beyond his years—was in no small part due to my teenage pillaging of his emotional reserves, followed by many years of ardent risk taking 10,000 kilometres beyond his reach.

IN MEMORY OF MY FATHER, BRUCE BLACKBURN, WHO PASSED AWAY BEFORE MY STORY WAS COMPLETE. THE WORLD TURNED THAT DAY, NEVER TO BE QUITE THE SAME.

Imbali Township, 'Maritzburg
Photo: Peter Rundle

01
February 1988
Into Africa

AS MY FRIENDS AND I—SIX YOUNG, IDEALISTIC AUSTRALIANS—CROSSED THE BORDER INTO SOUTH AFRICA AFTER FIFTY LONG HOURS ON THE TRAIN FROM HARARE WE WERE ALL AWARE OF A CHANGE, A TENSION THAT HUNG IN THE AIR LIKE STATIC ELECTRICITY, READY TO STRIKE AND BURN AT THE SLIGHTEST SUGGESTION OF FRICTION.

Newly arrived in Africa, nothing we had seen before prepared us for the confrontation with the unimaginable that awaited us here. We had spent the previous weeks in Zimbabwe, seeing black and white families living side by side in middle class suburbs, kids of all races at school together and the relaxed faces of people who were not afraid. In 1988, Zimbabwe was the warm heart of Africa and though that would change a decade later, the extraordinary graciousness and optimism of its people then allows me to believe that the magic will one day return to that now war-torn country.

I had set eyes on Africa for the very first time only three weeks earlier. Flying in from Sydney, I looked down from my window seat and saw the coastline of Mozambique stretching out for miles and miles. I imagined the savannah, the people, the villages, the animals, the cities—the life pulsing beneath my feet. And I cried. I had been waiting for this moment for years, and I was ready to fall in love. I had dreamt of Africa since my childhood, imagined what it would be like to be here: a blonde-haired, blue-eyed, fair-skinned child who would have stood out like a flash of sulphur in a sea of black faces. Africa was my obsession and although I was about to move from dream to reality, somehow the obsession would remain. As the months unfolded, the real Africa would be far more mesmerising for me than the Africa I had read about in books and seen on TV. Its real people lived an unimaginable drama that would drive me deeper into their lives, rather than leaving me disillusioned and estranged from the continent of my childhood yearnings.

Tearful plane journeys would punctuate my life for many years. This flight had begun with tears of farewell. I had said goodbye to my parents at Sydney airport, not knowing when I would return. In the days leading up to my departure, my mother and I had promised each other we wouldn't cry but this time, and every time, my father had to prise us apart. 'Just go', he would say, and I'd turn back to see Mum laughing and crying as she waved me through customs.

Six of us flew from Sydney to Harare, all of us fresh from university or first jobs: myself; Matt, the deep-thinking, kind-hearted man I had dated for over two years until the relationship ended amicably several months before; Bee, actress, journalist, comedian and close friend of mine and Matt's for many years; Chook, a tall red-headed newcomer we got to know after his time in a theatre company with Bee the year before; Charlie, a shy fellow we knew through church who surprised us all by coming along on this adventure; and Liz, Matt's sister's best friend and, more recently, Matt's new girlfriend. Plans had been in place for almost two years to make this trip a reality. We were to spend a few weeks in Zimbabwe working in schools in and around Harare, and then three months in Pietermaritzburg, South Africa, taking part in a youth leadership program with a local church organisation working for change. After that, I was planning to further my studies in Canada for a semester or two before returning to work in Tanzania in 1989. I had a pre-med type of science degree under my belt and would be studying third world nutrition, health and politics in Canada, in an effort to contextualise my studies for the realities of Africa.

As our plane touched down at Harare airport we strained to see what the African landscape looked like up close. To my surprise, I saw rows of gum trees next to the runway: the southern parts of this new continent looked an awful lot like home. Discussing theories of continental shift, we waited by the carousel for Matt's friends to arrive. I was all eyes and ears, thrilled at my first opportunity to sit and observe Africa for a time.

Despite the fact that we were sitting quietly in the arrival area, I soon became aware we were creating a scene. Passengers were staring, heads were popping around corners, porters were gathered in small groups discussing us or, perhaps more specifically, discussing Bee. Ever since I'd known her, Bee had had a fashion sense all her own. We now suspected it was a bit much for Harare. She wore hiking boots, baggy denim jeans with splits on the knees, a thick leather belt, a bright orange checked shirt, a straw bowler hat, brown hair cut short but with a long fringe that covered half her face and a toothbrush hanging as an earring from one ear. Jet lag had stolen our capacity to endure this public scrutiny, so we were enormously relieved when Matt's friends Richard and Venetia arrived and whisked us away in an old, large Mercedes.

Their beautiful house in Marlborough, in the eastern suburbs of Harare, was only slightly larger that my own home in Sydney but the grounds were extensive and well manicured, much larger than the quarter acre block we had all grown up with. I remember nothing of the meal or the dinner conversation, only the moment when I fell exhausted into bed.

My first morning in Africa I was woken by the delicious sounds of a dove outside my window. It was a sound so distinctive—more song than bird call—that each time I heard it thereafter it would take me back to that moment. The sun was rising and the house was still quiet. Bee was not yet awake in the bed across the room. I lay there and drank it all in. I was not reading about it, not looking down from a plane at 30,000 feet: I was finally here in the middle of the great continent. As I listened to the sounds of the garden outside, I felt the expansiveness of Africa spreading out through the suburbs and into the bush that lay beyond. I felt the vastness of possibilities that lay ahead, and at the same time, the stillness of the moment, as if time held its breath, listening with me to the dove calling for a mate: 'do do, da do do do'.

We travelled for a few days before the work began in earnest. On our trip to Fothergill Island on Lake Kariba, I had my first experience of the uniqueness of African light. The light in Africa never ceases to amaze me, particularly in the early morning and late afternoon. It has a quality that makes the air itself seem brighter, bringing the colours to life as the day dawns or fades. It gave our photos a surreal appearance that, looking back, makes me doubt it was ever more than a dream. During three magical days on Fothergill Island my friends and I saw elephants, wildebeest, zebra, hippos ... it was like the Africa of my childhood dreams: lush, fertile and teeming with life. We came away under the false impression that all game viewing in Africa would be like this, yet on only one other occasion would I see so much game in such close proximity.

Back in Harare, we did our first performance at Eaglevale High School which, along with many others in the mixed suburbs of Harare, schooled the children of middle class families, black and white. Though the white students outnumbered the black, it appeared to be comfortably integrated. Our show was a combination of drama, speeches, music, comedy and even a song, which was a brave thing for a bunch of Australians to do in Africa, as we soon found out. But the Eaglevale students loved it, which boosted our confidence for the ten shows we were to do over the next five days and we threw ourselves into them.

Visiting these schools was a fabulous experience for me. As we entered the school grounds, looking conspicuous wearing our civvies and carrying our paraphernalia, a wave of nervous energy would pass through us and the students. Faces would appear at classroom windows and doors, students on errands would stop and whisper. Sometimes they were noisy, thrilled to be out of class, speculating on what the show was about. In other schools, they would file in, sit quietly and wait. Either way, you could feel the energy. Often when we arrived, the students would break into song, hundreds of kids singing and dancing in anticipation of something new. In those moments, we hotly regretted having a song in the show as our strained white voices and halting rhythm put us to shame. In the end, though, what we lacked in talent we made up for in enthusiasm and it all seemed to go over well.

While the performances were fun, the real rush came afterwards in all the conversations they opened up. We would sometimes spend hours talking to kids after the show, hearing about their lives and interests, what they wanted to do when they left high school. There was always a sea of smiling faces, requests for addresses to be exchanged and photos taken. I quickly learnt that having my photo taken with a group of black people never ends well—my sun-bleached hair and white skin makes me look like a ghost in comparison to their rich darkness. Vanity aside, the school encounters were a fantastic opportunity to meet a variety of young Zimbabweans of different races and social standings, and to find out what was important to them. They spoke of plans to be doctors, teachers, to work for the community, to travel abroad, echoing the aspirations of young people all over the world.

To give ourselves a break from performing, we went into Harare to the 'Mini Cini' to see a movie. The only show on was *Cry Freedom*, which was banned in South Africa, so that made it a must-see for us. The story of the South African journalist Donald Woods and black activist Steve Biko is engaging at any time, but seeing it in a cinema just across the South African border made it thoroughly compelling. It turned out to be a preview of the strange, contradictory life we were about to immerse ourselves in.

We had observed a little of the race relations in Harare; while there was more integration than we would see for years in South Africa, still, working-class African communities were living in the sprawling townships that surrounded the city. In previously white suburbs such as Marlborough, middle-class black families and white families now lived happily side by side. Our hosts Richard and Venetia told us that the black families were very pleasant neighbours, but seemed to have no more than passing contact. As with every household in the suburbs, Richard and Venetia also had domestic servants: Bobina, who was their maid, and Wilson, who tended their gardens. Both were Shona speaking. Bobina tried to teach us a few Shona words as she told us a little about her life.

After a couple of weeks in Africa I was starting to experience the common, but rarely acknowledged, white malaise of feeling out of place. I wrote in my diary: 'I really hate being a tourist in Africa. I feel so WHITE. I look white, dress white, talk white, think white. Black people fit in here and whites don't'.

To finally realise my dream and then to feel out of place was difficult. But that feeling was also a strong driver for wanting to immerse myself in the culture and languages of Africa. I realise that not everyone responds in the same way to feeling out of place. Many people, instead of going deeper, create for themselves a life that they could essentially have in England, Europe or America. But I had deliberately chosen to be in Africa and so I wanted more of it, not less.

By the time we set out for Johannesburg, we had knocked some of the kinks out of our own relationships and historical baggage. Our unstated arrangement involved me spending most of my time with Chook and Charlie. Bee fitted easily into the new dynamic with Matt and Liz.

Our time in Zimbabwe proved to be a gentle introduction to Africa. The train from Harare would take us from an independent Zimbabwe to the bloody struggle for self-determination that was raging in the south. Zimbabwe, while burdened with all the challenges of a newly independent nation, still had a lightness that South Africa lacked.

The first leg of the trip took us down to Bulawayo, Zimbabwe's second largest city. We had a cabin to ourselves in second class, with three beds on each side and a table in the middle. Chook disappeared to explore the train and came back telling cautionary tales of third class where people were packed together like sardines and someone had vomited on the floor. From the stares he'd received, he gathered that white people didn't wander down the aisles of the third class cabins very often.

Bulawayo train station is not a must-see travel destination so we were relieved when we finally pulled out, heading for Gaborone in Botswana. But at about six o'clock that night, as the day began to cool, our train ground to a halt in the middle of nowhere. Flat grasslands stretched as far as the eye could see—and yet, not long after we had stopped, some women and children approached the train to barter and ask for coins or keepsakes. I could not see a single village or dwelling across the horizon. These people seemed to have emerged from the earth itself. Wherever they had come from, a train full of people wealthy enough to afford a ticket represented a rare opportunity for momentary relief from the blanket of poverty covering areas as remote as this one. After seven long hours, passengers cheered as the train finally jerked forward, ready to move on. We later heard that a train further up the line had hit a cow and derailed. 'Only in Africa' was a phrase we were quickly to learn. I peered back into the darkness for a final glimpse of the groups of women who had camped beside the tracks, ever-optimistic that while the train stayed, there was bartering to be done. They slowly gathered their few belongings, woke their children and disappeared into the scrub. I was beginning to understand that in Africa, no matter where you are, you are not alone.

Gaborone train station was a delightful oasis in a sea of grass. We had been told that you could rush off the train at Gaborone and buy cold Coca Cola at the nearby store. If you were fast, the train wouldn't leave you behind. I watched as my companions and others leapt from the train and dashed towards the store. The whistle was blowing as they ran back along the platform, fizzy treasures pressed to their chests.

This day, my first on the South African side of the border, our train sped deeper into the lion's den. From Zimbabwe I had brought with me a vision of what was possible, but also the images of what lay ahead, splashed graphically before me in the cinema when I watched *Cry Freedom*. Australians are brought up to support the underdog as a matter of national pride. After seeing this movie and reading such books as *Cry the Beloved Country*, I knew that if sides were to be taken my choice would lie with the black majority, and the African National Congress in particular. Carrying that choice in my back pocket, along with my tendency to be intense and strong-willed in my dealings with people, would prove to be an explosive combination.

Eventually, we disembarked from the train in Jo'burg. After spending several days there with other friends of Matt's, we continued our journey on to Pietermaritzburg, which was to be our home for the next few months. 'Maritzburg, a quiet university town in the Natal Midlands, is sometimes referred to as Sleepy Hollow. But we were soon to discover that nothing could be further from the truth.

02

February 1988
Nonsuch Road

THE PROVINCE OF NATAL, NOW KNOWN AS KWAZULU NATAL, IS PICTURESQUE BEYOND DESCRIPTION. FROM THE DRAMATIC DRAKENSBURG MOUNTAINS ON ITS EASTERN BORDER, YOU TRAVEL THROUGH THE LUSH MIDLANDS, ALL FOREST AND GREEN PASTURE, ON TO THE VALLEY OF A THOUSAND HILLS AND FINALLY THROUGH TO THE PRISTINE BEACHES ON THE COAST WHERE YOU CAN OFTEN SEE DOLPHINS SURFING THE TURQUOISE WAVES.

But its natural beauty belies a bloody past. Towards the end of the eighteenth century, the Zulu warrior Shaka was forcing allegiance from the Nguni-speaking farming communities who had lived scattered through the region for centuries, forming them into the powerful Zulu nation. The first white settlers in the province were the English who established Durban as a trading port in 1824, a few years before Shaka was assassinated. The Zulus tolerated this minor incursion into their kingdom as it provided a useful trading opportunity for them. However, less than fifteen years later, several thousand voortrekkers—farmers and adventurers of Dutch descent—had crossed the mighty Drakensburg ranges and settled in the province. A series of bloody wars followed as each group fought for domination of the land the Zulus called 'heaven'. The small city of Pietermaritzburg, just under an hour from Durban and the coast, was now a city divided. The predominant language in town was English, though Afrikaans was spoken at the many government institutions. The Zulu-speaking descendants of the once great kingdom lived in shanty towns on the outskirts of the city, burdened with the various pass laws and work restrictions that ruled their daily lives. The descendants of the indentured Indian labourers who arrived in the second half of the nineteenth century to work on the sugar plantations along the north coast also now lived in their own segregated townships, as did the mixed race or 'coloured' community who developed their own distinct language and culture. But we were yet to understand the complexity of the situation, and the harshness with which it was enforced.

It was almost dusk as we drove into Pietermaritzburg. We took the first turn-off as instructed and drove along Bush Road as it wound up into the hills. We finally saw the sign, 'Centre for African Renewal', and stopped the car; the tar road gave way to a dirt track with the seemingly appropriate name of 'Nonsuch Road'. As the mist fell, we followed this track through a forest filled with the screeching of monkeys, finally rounding a corner into a clearing. Lights glowed from the windows of a cluster of white-washed Dutch Cape buildings peppered across a sweeping green lawn. We had arrived.

Following the sounds of laughter, we climbed the broad stairs to the dining hall in the largest building, crossed the wide veranda and entered through the French doors that were open to let in the cool evening breeze. The hall contained a number of long wooden tables and around these tables sat the thirty or so people we would be living with in the months ahead. Ernie was the first to jump up and shout a greeting, ushering us over to the nearest table and introducing us to those seated there. Within a few minutes, we were surrounded by people enquiring about our drive down from Jo'burg and inviting us to join them for supper.

Steven, the program director, was at home with his family and we would meet him in the morning. The group of trainee youth workers with whom we would be living and working came from all over southern Africa and from many different communities. They introduced themselves as Vusi, a Zulu-speaking guy from Natal; blonde-haired, blue-eyed Gary who had been studying at Rhodes University; Xhosa-speaking Msizi from Grahamstown in the Eastern Cape; Kedrick from Zambia; Mary-Anne, an English-speaking woman from Cape Town; and Tshidi, another Zulu speaker from the north coast of Natal.

That first night, I found Msizi quite hard to talk to. Whether it was my own self-consciousness or his natural reserve, I'm not sure. The rest of the group was warm and welcoming. Over dinner they told us stories of the first six weeks of the year-long program. Because it was church-based the theory included theology, bible study, prayer and meditation, and the practical component allowed them to engage in community issues, trying to make a contribution. There were, apparently, mixed views in the organisation about the nature of the practical work as some felt it was a little too political. We didn't really understand what was meant by that but Gary assured us that Steve would give us a full briefing in the morning.

After dinner, we were shown to our rooms. Matt, Chook and Charlie would be staying in a cottage near the dining hall, bunking in with one of the many volunteers who came to work with the organisation. Bee, Liz and I would be living with the trainees in the big house up the hill. The trainees' house, once we finally reached it, was almost a kilometre further up the road from the main cluster of buildings, deep in the forest near the home of Steve and his family. The house was newly built, as this was the first year of the program. However, given its remoteness, the electricity was yet to be connected. So we unloaded our gear into a dark house as our new housemates lit candles in each of the rooms. I was shown to a small room in the back half of the house while Bee and Liz opted to share a larger room off the front lounge. I unpacked and fell into bed, very happy to have arrived at last.

I awoke to a morning as misty as the night before and lay snuggled in my warm bed. Within moments, a blood-curdling scream propelled me out into the corridor. Gary was quietly reading in the lounge, seemingly unperturbed. Calmly, he explained that the screaming was a morning ritual in the house.

'You see, it's not only lights we are missing, it's also hot water. Msizi has a theory that if you scream, the water doesn't feel so cold.' Nodding towards the nearby bathroom, he added: 'Seems Kedrick agrees with him'.

A few minutes later, I experienced for myself just how cold water can be in the first week of autumn, even in Africa. While I was tempted to try the screaming theory, I settled for a land speed showering record instead. My mother would have been proud.

I walked down to breakfast with Gary. Of average height and build, with a kind face and demeanour, Gary had a peacefulness about him that put you in the mood to talk. After studying theology at Rhodes University he had taken an extra year to do this program in preparation for his future ministry in the Methodist church. On our walk down to the dining hall I learnt about Gary's interests and the love of his life, Vicky, who was still finishing her studies in Grahamstown. He heard from me about the chain of events that had brought me here, including details of my childhood fascination with all things African.

After breakfast we walked across the wet lawns, leaving our footprints in the dew, past the small lake with a chapel on an island in its centre, and up the gentle slope to the meeting room that was attached to the office block. All staff and volunteers met each morning for devotions. I was surprised at how many people worked at the centre. Some were paid staff, but many, like us, were volunteers from all over the world. Despite its seeming remoteness, it was a surprisingly cosmopolitan environment.

After devotions, we met with Steve for introductions and a briefing. Steve was an impressive character. Originally from England, he met and married Beth, a South African woman, at Bible College.

They had been living in South Africa for seven years. Steve and Beth had two children, an angelic blonde-haired, blue-eyed little girl and a boy, dark-haired and devilish, in whom the trainees invested serious effort trying to avoid. Steve was charismatic and articulate, with a dry English wit. He spoke passionately about the current situation in Pietermaritzburg.

A township is an area on the outskirts of each South African town where 'non-white' families were allowed to live. It is near enough to the town to allow black workers to service its industries, shops and homes, but not so close that white families have to see it. There are also separate townships for each of the other racial groups that call South Africa home. During the apartheid era, each was divided up neatly into its own areas, to live and prosper in what was called 'separate development'. It might have been an interesting social experiment if each racial group had been given the same level of resources to work with. That's where the experiment came undone.

When we arrived in Pietermaritzburg, the townships were like war zones. The two warring parties were the African National Congress, or ANC, whose leader was Nelson Mandela; and the Inkatha Freedom Party, or IFP, under the Zulu tribal leader, Mangosuthu Buthelezi. Steve told us that the South African police were working in partnership with Inkatha to bring down the ANC in the area. Thousands had been killed in the violence to date and thousands more were currently detained without trial. It seemed almost impossible to believe that only fifteen minutes drive from our idyllic community centre in the forest, such events were taking place. But from the looks on the faces of our black fellow trainees, this was real.

Though Buthelezi had once been a member of the ANC, during his student days he revived a Zulu cultural organisation which refused to support sanctions against the South African government or respond to the ANC call for arms. Being of royal Zulu blood, he chose instead to lead the Buthelezi clan and ultimately the IFP down a different road, one that allegedly had close ties with the national government and other foreign governments sympathetic to the apartheid regime. In so doing, he set himself against the ANC and the other liberation movements in South Africa. His Inkatha constituency was largely based amongst the rural, more conservative Zulu people, as opposed to the urban dwelling Zulus in the townships. So the lines were drawn and the blood would flow.

Steve completed the briefing by explaining more about the program and what we would be doing over the next few weeks, before we all piled into the centre's kombis and were driven into town. The director of the organisation, David, was holding a lunchtime prayer meeting in the Town Hall in an effort to bring the attention of the white community to the lives being lost on their doorstep. The media was not covering the murderous events in its own city and most white people had few avenues for finding out what was really going on. At first, I found this almost impossible to believe. How could someone not know what is happening ten minutes from home? Only later did I realise how separate people's lives were. The only black people your average white South African was likely to meet were those who worked in their homes. I learnt that it was rarely in the interests of the blacks to educate their employers about the bloodshed that was all around. It was far safer to smile and say nothing.

At the end of the prayer meeting, David invited all those in the packed hall to take part in a peace march that church leaders were organising in two weeks time. It struck me how different this event was to the prayer meetings I had been to in Sydney. The events that we prayed for here were in our backyard, not safely thousands of kilometres away in some vaguely defined part of Asia or India. I also understood that joining a public march here in 'Maritzburg would put each person under the gaze of the police. Steve had explained on the way into town that the police kept an eye on anyone involved in the peace talks, as David was, or in any cross-cultural or township work, as Steve and the trainees were and we soon would be. It was a sobering thought for a law-abiding Sydney girl who had never even had a school detention.

So from our first day, I realised that South Africa was going to be 'in your face', that I would be constantly confronted with the question: 'What do you stand for?' Not only that, I would have to decide what price I was prepared to pay for standing up for my beliefs. It's one thing to hammer on about what is right and wrong from the safety of the family dinner table; it is another thing altogether to risk your personal safety by taking a public stand on issues in front of a line of armed security police. At that moment, I could have opted to remain a tourist, but like a coffee lover smelling the aroma of the day's first brew, I sniffed a sense of purpose in the air and found it irresistible.

In the days that followed, we fell into a routine: meals in community, drama rehearsals and late nights up at the house. Steve and the team were already doing work in schools and were keen to incorporate the drama performances we had used in Zimbabwe. They also had some music prepared, and a few workshops on different issues as well as opportunities for members of the team to talk about their lives. Steve felt it was particularly important for kids at white schools to hear from the black trainees and understand a little more about them. As Msizi was a particularly gifted speaker, and both Vusi and Tshidi were quite shy, he was often given this role. Sometimes he spoke about his thoughts on hot issues such as conscription of young white men into the army, other times he read some of his poetry. Either way, he always had an impact.

When I first met Msizi, he took my breath away. He was tall, broad shouldered, dark skinned and beautiful. He had a quiet confidence that few of his peers possessed. He was also articulate and intelligent, always ready for a robust discussion on politics, sport, life and love. And lastly, he had a deep commitment to justice and the poor. I was in trouble.

Msizi was given his name by his mother. He was the second born son in his household and she named him 'the one who helps' in the hope that one day he would. His youngest brother, born a few years after him, was named Jonga, 'to look after', though it was mostly Msizi who ultimately did the looking after. He had grown up hard. His mother worked long hours in the homes of white families to support her own. His father was rarely around and if he was, rarely in a state to work. While Msizi grew up very close to his mother, he was frustrated by her tolerance of his father's behaviour. Until he moved to Pietermaritzburg, Msizi had lived with his family in Rini, a small township over the hill from Grahamstown.

The Eastern Cape produced more than its fair share of ANC leaders, the most notable of whom was Nelson Mandela. I have often wondered why this was the case. Some say that it was an old boys' network among Xhosa-speaking men. However, I think it was something to do with the harshness of the region and the harsh characters it produced. Perhaps the extremes turned blood into steel, forging the creation of both uncompromising activists and hard-nosed racists who were often in conflict with one another. Either way, Msizi was a son of the soil and his many childhood experiences of prejudice created a man who was deeply committed to the struggle for change and also deeply angry.

In the years to come, he would go on to be an award-winning film maker and journalist, directing numerous documentaries on the lives of black South Africans, before and after the end of Apartheid. Through his work, he was offered many scholarships, training courses and conference engagements all around the world. However, like a true homing pigeon, he was always drawn back home.

When there weren't programs being run at the centre, the nights were quiet. The other Australians would end up in the guys' cottage, talking with a few other volunteers. Not comfortable there, I would follow the trainees up to the house where someone would build a fire while the candles were being lit. Each night we took turns to tell stories about our lives and the people in them. It was during this nightly story telling that I began to understand the impact of state sanctioned poverty and discrimination, not in an abstract way, but in the lives of people I shared a house with, people I was beginning to care about. It was impossible not to be moved, not to want to be part of working towards a different future. Having said this, they were not always heart-wrenching tales; my new friends also made fun of themselves, telling jokes and lighter stories of their love lives and ill-fated pursuits of the opposite sex.

My ears pricked up whenever Msizi told stories about one conquest or another, as I hadn't yet plucked up the courage to find out if he was seeing someone. It didn't seem as if he was, but he was also a bit of a dark horse so it I couldn't be certain. This, of course, made him even more intriguing to me.

Towards the end of our first week, Steve announced that we were going to visit a few project sites in the township. Both projects were at creches—child care centres—one in rural Sweetwaters and the other in a peri-urban area called Edendale township. Steve and the team had been constructing a new creche building in Sweetwaters and providing education materials and volunteers to assist at the creche in Edendale.

Sweetwaters is utterly picturesque in its physical beauty but also desperately poor. People live in small mud huts scattered over the green hills, connected only by dirt tracks created from years of use by families and their cattle. There is one tar road that runs from Hilton, a leafy white suburb in the hills, through Sweetwaters to the main road in Edendale township below. Sweetwaters was technically part of Kwazulu, the homeland reserved for Zulu speaking people, and not part of South Africa.

We all piled into the program kombi, drove down Nonsuch Road, turned up into Hilton and out the other side. Instead of staying on the main road back to town, we turned right and entered another world. We drove along the tar road for about a kilometre before turning onto dirt. I wasn't sure that the kombi was built for this type of road. It wasn't just dirt, it had ruts and hollows that rocked us from one side of the kombi to the other. I suspect this was Steve's favourite part of the journey, fancying himself as a driver in the Paris to Dakar rally.

Finally, the dirt road gave out all together and we left the kombi to continue on foot. After fifteen minutes of wishing I had worn more appropriate shoes, we arrived at our destination. The creche, which doubled as the teacher's home, was built of mud like all the other dwellings surrounding it. Wattle trees, which were fast growing and in plentiful supply, were cut down and the branches stripped to create a series of poles. The larger poles were sunk into the ground at intervals and the narrower, more supple branches were then woven in and out of the poles until the structure of a wall was built. A small gap for a window was cut into each side of the house and a larger one for the door and frames fitted into place. The women, who do all the building, would then collect mud and slap great clumps of it into the woven wall structure until it was about twenty centimetres thick. Tin sheets were then placed on top and secured as a roof and the structure was complete. If there was enough money, the outside wall would be thinly rendered with a watery concrete mix.

The tiny creche appeared to have been built many years ago, as it was now crumbling away in parts. Lucy, the teacher, and the twenty tiny preschoolers in her care spent the day inside the two-room structure, or playing on the grassy area outside. One room was much larger than the other, the smaller of the two acting as a kitchen and the larger as the classroom itself. On the wall were coloured pieces of card with words and times tables written on them. About twenty metres away from the building was a pit toilet, a hole in the ground surrounded by rusted sheets of corrugated iron.

The children were clean, but dressed in hand-me-down clothing, some with holes, some too small. When we arrived, they were inside sitting in a large circle on the mud floor, which was covered in a variety of patterned blankets. Having no phone, Lucy had not known exactly when to expect us, but was very pleased we had come. The children, on the other hand, looked horrified and started inching towards the far wall in an effort to get some distance between us. Lucy, clearly embarrassed, explained that the only white people they ever saw were the police and they were afraid of them. As we sat down on the ground, she assured the children that we were not the police, but people coming to help build them a new school. From the looks on their faces, they didn't believe her.

Tshidi came into her own at this point. Having some early childhood education training herself, she suggested that she take the kids outside and play some games with them. Before long they were singing and dancing in a circle around her, but still keeping their distance from us. It was over an hour before they would come near. I suspect their curiosity about the cameras and the photos we were taking got the better of them.

This was my first real experience of children living in poverty. I was moved in such a way that, even then, I thought it would be impossible to walk away and go back home to Australia. I thought about all the things I would spend my life doing if I returned to Sydney and none of them seemed more important that doing something practical to improve the lives of these children and children like them. I was never good at staying removed and unattached when it came to the hardship of others. My brother, Jon, an accountant and far more pragmatic than I, would make balanced decisions at these moments and logically weigh up the options – all head. I, however, all heart, would make a decision on a flood of empathy and live with the personal cost later. Sometimes I wondered if I was adopted.

We spent the rest of the morning playing with those children who would let us near. One little boy, sporting a moth-eaten green jumper and a mohawk, captured my heart. He was curious about everything, once he'd summoned the courage to come over. He followed me around, asking rapid-fire questions that Vusi was struggling to translate fast enough for his satisfaction: 'What's your name? Where do you live? What's that? What are you doing now? Can I touch your hair? Do you have any sweets?' On our way out, Steve showed us the site that had been cleared and levelled by the parents of the children in readiness for the wattle and daub structure we would start building on our next youth leadership workshop in April.

We walked back down to where we had left the kombi, abuzz with all that we had seen. I wonder what Tshidi, Kedrick, Vusi and Msizi must have thought of us, fascinated by what was so ordinary to them. We climbed back into the kombi and bumped our way along the dirt track back to the main road and down to Edendale. Along this road, the first built-up area of Edendale you reach is called Caluza (pronounced as if the 'c' is a tisk). In less than two years, unable to resist the desire to make a contribution here, it would be the place that I would call home.

Where Sweetwaters Road intersects with Edendale Road, we turned right, travelled along a few hundred metres and then turned left onto a dirt road that ran parallel to the main tar road. Steve pulled the van up outside a very different creche: a wire mesh fence surrounded the building with a heavy metal gate blocking its entrance. We called out a greeting and entered the yard. Hearing the noise, a teacher emerged, followed by half a dozen curious little faces. The teacher returned our greeting and the children came rushing over, pushing each other aside to be the first to grab a hand. Very quickly, we were pulled over to the playground area, which was composed of a dirt patch with a row of tyres half buried in the ground, and drawn into games of follow-the-leader and other universal playground pastimes.

I looked up to see where the rest of the team was and noticed Kedrick and Vusi had stayed outside and were chatting to someone they appeared to know. I also noticed a small crowd had gathered and were hanging off the gate, watching us play. There were five little boys there, ranging in age from five to ten. All were dressed in what appeared to be secondhand clothes bar one little chap who was wearing a new blue safari suit. Clearly these boys wanted in on the fun. I was unsure if they were neighbourhood kids or street kids, but I did think it odd that they were not at school, or supervised at all for that matter.

Another group of preschoolers were gathered around Bee and Chook and were giving a joyous rendition of 'Jesus Loves Me'. Others were chatting away in Zulu to Matt and Liz while Charlie took their photo, after which they crowded round Charlie chanting 'Photo, photo'. I wondered how many English words they knew. Clearly we weren't the first to come and take their picture.

On the whole the children were better dressed and better nourished than their counterparts up the road. They were housed in a brick building that was at least three times the size of the Sweetwaters creche. Even the atmosphere between the two areas was different. Edendale was full of barbed wire and tension, giving you the feeling that you should keep one eye looking over your shoulder. Sweetwaters was the opposite, having that wonderful relaxed rural feel about it. South Africa was proving to be a country of contrasts: I had assumed they would only be along racial lines. Clearly it was much more complex than that.

The experiences of the day prompted a long discussion with Msizi that night about the struggle for political reform and what the role of white people was in that. He felt that it was important not to simply lobby from the sidelines, that to have a genuine impact, you had to identify with the day-to-day difficulties of black people's lives. I believe his comments were influential in the way I would choose to live my life in the years that followed. Given my initial discomfort at feeling so white and apart in Africa, the idea of being part of a community was very appealing to me. My conversation with Msizi also clarified another question I had. Given the strength of his political views, I was unsure if he would take me seriously, being a white foreigner. I felt he was letting me know that he believed I had something to offer.

In six years, the apartheid system would be abandoned and though the violence in the townships was reaching fever pitch, programs like ours which would have seemed radical ten years before seemed to be tolerated. What I didn't realise at the time was that we were tolerated but still closely watched. While there seemed to be a groundswell of support in the white community for more integration in the country, few were thinking of the political upheaval that would be necessary to integrate at all levels. So while it appeared that protest marches like the one David was organising would include ever increasing numbers of white people, the government and the police were closing a vice on any such organisation in the townships.

A few days later, Steve was uncharacteristically absent from morning devotions. Beth later told us that he had been up most of the night after a phone call had taken him to the township. Through his youth leadership weekend camps, he had come to know many of the local youth leaders in the townships. A call had come through from the family of one such young man: a group of men had attacked his home just after dark, forcing their way inside and locking the family in a bedroom before murdering the young man. I never knew this person's name, only that they hacked him to death with machetes. As no one would come to collect what was left of the body until it was light, Steve helped the family to clean up his remains before returning home covered in blood. Not surprisingly, his attempts to sleep were thwarted by nightmares.

We had ten days left to prepare for our week-long program at Brettonwood High School, a large white school in the suburbs of Durban. The team had never done anything on this scale, so there were quite a few nerves during rehearsals. Mary-Anne, Msizi and I had teamed up to work with five different classes and to run a seminar on fear. I hadn't spent a lot of time with Mary-Anne up until this point, although we were quite alike in looks and temperament. She had trained as a nurse in Cape Town and was doing this year to build her understanding of community work before she moved into a squatter community just south of Johannesburg to live and work. She planned to build a two-room metal shack, with one room acting as a clinic and the other as her home. I was deeply impressed by her vision. She did, in fact, go on to build the clinic and lived in that community for many years. On the back of her amazing work, a substantial community organisation was established that offered a variety of services to the people living there. She later married a doctor and, together with their two sons and adopted black daughter, lived in another informal community outside Pretoria called Winterveld, providing the only medical care to tens of thousands of their neighbours.

As a dry run for Brettonwood, we ran an evening program at St Anne's, a private girls' school in Hilton. We performed five short dramas, Kedrick sang and Msizi read some poetry. The major theme was reconciliation: the things that divide us are not as powerful as the things that unite us. At the time, a message like that delivered by a multiracial group in an Anglican girls' school was quite edgy. Nevertheless, we received positive feedback and were feeling pretty pleased with ourselves.

Steve arranged for us to go away on a team retreat a few days before Brettonwood. We went to L'Abri, a Wilderness Training School set on the side of a cliff in the Karkloof mountain range, overlooking the indigenous forest of the Mshwati River valley. The property is now, not surprisingly, a National Heritage Site.

The days were filled with physical challenges and team-building exercises while the evenings brought us together for barbecue dinners and singing around the fire. It was in those moments, complete with Milo and marshmallows, that my childhood imaginings seemed to come to life.

The retreat to L'Abri was a wonderful escape from our busy preparations. It gave us an opportunity to get to know each other better in an environment that calmed the spirit. It was hard to believe that an indigenous forest existed so close to Pietermaritzburg.

Our return to Nonsuch Road meant rehearsals, rehearsals, rehearsals. We had songs to learn, lesson plans to finish and then more rehearsals. One afternoon, while we waited for the next session to begin, Mary-Anne, Msizi and I were sitting outside the hall on the grass. The conversation came round to the topic of South African dogs. I had noticed that if I walked past a house with a dog in the front yard, it didn't bark at me, but if a black person passed the same yard, the dog would bark hysterically. Msizi said that South

African dogs were as racist as their owners. I suggested that the only way the dogs could tell the difference was by smell. I didn't realise how insensitive my comment was until Msizi excused himself from the conversation. Later, he explained that he wasn't angry with me, knowing I hadn't meant to offend; it was that the concept of being differentiated not only by skin colour but even by smell weighed heavily on him. Sometimes it seemed like there was no way to climb out of it. He was quiet for the rest of the day and did not stay up for our candlelight conversations. I was racked with guilt for having brought this on. I suspect I felt twice as bad as I would have if it was a white friend I had upset. Our black friends' lives were hard enough; to add to their challenges in any way made me feel callous and insensitive.

Finally, Brettonwood arrived. We were all staying at the YMCA, overlooking Durban harbour. Each day of the five-day event we would be presenting a school assembly, as well as individual lessons and an informal coffee shop after school where we could sit and chat with the students. The rehearsals paid off, and I felt incredibly privileged to be part of such a professionally run program. Each of us played our part, but it was Steve who held it all together. We were taking many risks simply by bringing black team members to the school. Woven through the design of the program were two ideas: one, that the personal is political; the other, that to believe in God means to care about what is happening in the lives of people around you. The kids we were talking to believed that politics was about which political party you supported and had something to do with communists and terrorists versus the good guys. We argued that if you went to the beach with a friend and he was not allowed onto the sand because he was black, then the personal became the political. Most of the students saw anything other than party politics as something dangerous and therefore to be avoided. We were attempting to communicate that if you were black you could not avoid politics; and that if you were white, you were still impacted by politics although it felt far less uncomfortable.

The second idea was harder to sell, but we argued that as Christians we could not in good conscience avoid something that impacted so disastrously on others around us. At the very least we were trying to build a simple awareness.

We performed a reconciliation skit we had used in Zimbabwe where Msizi played a character who held all the power and Gary, powerless, was seeking reconciliation. Bee, looking like the chairperson of a Board, played God and sought to broker the reconciliation. It was an impactful skit that allowed the audience to laugh at the stupidity of people living next to each other in complete separateness. Immediately following this skit, Msizi spoke about the cost of reconciliation to him, the cost of forgiving people who had much because his community had little. He spoke about making friends with many of the young white men in the hall over the course of the week, when next year, during their conscription to the army, they might roll into his township in the back of an armoured vehicle and point a gun in his face. Yet if he believed in reconciliation, he would have to get past all those things and be open to building genuine friendships. He told them it would be difficult and it would be costly, but it was the only way to ensure that we had a future to look forward to in South Africa.

This moment was the turning point of the week. At the coffee shop that followed the assembly, there were crowds of people surrounding the black members of our team, asking questions, trying to understand their lives and their points of view. I realised these were probably the first conversations of this nature they had ever had. I also knew that this was the kind of contribution to change I wanted to make. Simplistic as it was, I felt I was making a small difference to a big problem—something I had not felt when I was living in Australia. I knew there were problems back home, but none seemed as enormous as the ones faced by these young people. There seemed, at least, to be a place to start. It was an addictive feeling for me and being part of a team made it even more so. I could feel myself becoming more and more drawn in. South Africa had initially been a stopover on my way to another adventure in East Africa where I had planned to spend a year working in a mission school. But the longer I spent here doing something that seemed to add value, the more I considered that perhaps it was a place where I could stay.

Two weeks after Brettonwood, we invited thirty kids from the school to join us at the centre for a youth leadership camp with forty kids from a school in the township. On the back of our week's work with them, the Brettonwood kids were queuing up to come on the camp. As at Brettonwood, I was teamed up with Msizi and we spent a lot of time together preparing for the five-day camp.

One afternoon, Msizi, Chook, Kedrick and I took a few hours off and went down to the swimming hole in the small river that runs through the forest. It isn't deep, but it holds enough water to cool you off from the hot African sun. While we were splashing around, I waded into the deeper part of the pool, expecting Msizi to follow. He stood waist deep and quietly told me that he couldn't actually swim. In my usual insensitive style, I went a bit overboard in my banter: Msizi seemed to excel in everything he did, and at last there was something I was good at that he couldn't do. Glaring at me, he pointed out that swimming lessons weren't readily available to him when he was growing up as black people were banned from the only public swimming pool in Grahamstown. Yet again, I found myself dredging through the guilt of not knowing when to shut my mouth. I swam over and offered to teach him to swim. He eyed me narrowly and then agreed to let me try. I knew that I was falling head over heels for him and the idea of being physically close while teaching him to swim was certainly the driver behind my offer. However, I was unsure how he felt about me. I seemed to be constantly offending him and wasn't sure what he might see in me. My acting skills certainly weren't alluring; neither was my singing. And there were far more attractive girls around who seemed equally interested in him. Still, he had agreed to me teaching him to swim, so he must at least have trusted me enough to believe I would not let him drown.

The first day of camp arrived and seventy teenagers flooded the normally tranquil centre. When we began the program with some getting-to-know-you games, the two groups were very polarised. We were hoping they would be able to open up over the course of the five days, particularly as they were sharing rooms. After dinner on the first night, we watched a video about a man who comes to town looking very different to everyone else there. The town harasses and rejects him, simply for being unknown to them and different. As he leaves, they discover that it was in fact Jesus visiting them and it was too late to ask him to return. The video opened up all sorts of questions and discussion including—from the Brettonwood group—questions such as: 'Are there any black youths in the township who are Christians?' We hoped that by the end of the camp both groups of teenagers would discover that their lives were more alike than they could have imagined; they just lived in different places.

The next morning, I woke up with a terrible clutching pain on the right side of my back. When I put my hand on the location of the pain, there seemed to be welts there. Bee and Liz had a look and said they could see small flesh-coloured, fluid-filled blisters but didn't know what they were. Halfway through the morning session, the pain was worse so went I to find something in the first aid kit that might help. Steve and some of the others looked at the sores, but couldn't diagnose them either.

Eventually, one of the staff members, Carol, took me to Greys Hospital some five kilometres down the road, and we waited patiently for a few hours before I was shown into an examination area where the shirt lifting began afresh. This time, the person looking did know what it was, but it was so unusual that every other doctor in the hospital wanted to come and have a look. I was the youngest case of shingles they had ever seen. I felt honoured. I also felt humiliated and in a lot of pain. The doctor explained that shingles is usually brought on by stress as it is an opportunistic virus that enters a host when they are run-down and weakened. He explained that there is only one treatment for shingles and it is far from pleasant. Leaving me enough time to contemplate all the ghastly alternatives, he eventually returned holding two enormous syringes full of gamma globulin—one for each buttock, enough to prevent me from sitting for the next four days—plus painkilling injections. It was going to be a fun afternoon.

The painkillers knocked me out for the rest of the day but by evening, I was famished. Carol helped me down to the dining hall, although walking was difficult and sitting down was impossible. The other trainees ran off to find some soft pillows that would cushion my tender behind and then fell about laughing as I perched on top of them trying to eat. Msizi particularly enjoyed this spectacle. If I was worried that I had ever hurt his feelings with my careless words, his teasing over the course of the meal more than made us even.

For the remainder of the camp, I hobbled around accompanied by my faithful pillows and the jokes of all my friends. We ran a mixture of bible studies, simulation games, workshops and outdoor activities during the day, and a different movie each night. We also paired up for a very emotional session where one person washed the other's feet, the washer telling the washee how they had impacted on them during the course of the week. The group was also very moved after watching *Gandhi*. Gandhi's own commitment to change began in 1893 in Pietermaritzburg when, as a young Indian lawyer on his way to Jo'burg to try a case, he was thrown off the first class carriage of the train for not being white.

We also had a few edgier workshops. One reviewed the history of the Church's response to apartheid as outlined in the Kairos Document which had been released three years earlier. Written by an anonymous group of theologians in Soweto, it challenged the Church to take a stand against apartheid. It also criticised the theological justification of racism to which many of the more conservative churches subscribed.

Another session was run by a local community organisation called PACSA, the Pietermaritzburg Agency for Christian Social Awareness. PACSA spent much of their time monitoring the violence in the Natal Midlands area and assisting families who needed support. They came to the camp to raise awareness about what was really going on in the area and what some parts of the Church were willing to do about it. We were very nervous about this session. We felt it was very important but knew that it was the kind of session that could get these camps shut down, deemed too political, especially by some of the Brettonwood parents. These sessions were the heart and soul of my involvement, though, as the people running them demonstrated to me that you could hold onto your faith and still be an activist for change. The system of apartheid was built on the Church and its doctrines, so in many ways, to oppose it seemed 'anti-Church' to the majority of white people and, ironically, to many black people as well.

The camp ended with mixed emotions for me. It was a fabulous time where we did some great work and helped people from different backgrounds gain a better understanding of each other. I believe we also helped people think differently about the interaction between their faith and the world around them. But I was also disappointed that the two groups remained as separate as they did. I saw little openness between individuals from different races. Perhaps my expectations were too high. Still, high expectations are part of who I am—so I was a little disappointed.

That night, my feelings of disappointment took a back seat. The after-dinner candlelit conversations petered out early as people crawled off to bed exhausted. Only Msizi and I were left by the fire. He told me he was glad we were alone as he had been wanting to talk all week. To my great surprise, he told me about the feelings he had held for me ever since we met. When I smiled, he leant across and kissed me. And then he held my cheek tenderly in his hand and kissed me again.

As all new lovers do, we compared impressions. 'When this happened, what were you thinking?' 'When you said that, I was sure you weren't interested.' The biggest question for me was, 'Does it matter to you that I'm white?' He couldn't lie and said it did, which was why he had hesitated so long. He needed to know what kind of white person I was before he could risk opening up to me. We laughed about all the times I had said thoughtless things. He told me that while he was initially angry with me, when he saw how much it hurt me to see him hurt, he realised it was only naivete and not racism. At that moment, our feelings for one another seemed so tender and fragile, as if the slightest breeze might break them. We agreed to keep things between us and not let the others know that we were now together. Looking back, although we were seeking time and privacy, I wonder whether it wasn't crystal clear to everybody that we had feelings for each other. I suspect Steve must have known, perceptive man that he is, and a sucker for a love story.

Given the hectic pace of the last month, Steve gave us all five days off after the camp. Mary-Anne, Msizi and I decided to go down to Cape Town, giving Gary a lift to Grahamstown. Matt and Liz, Bee, Chook and Charlie had decided to take a trip in another direction before heading home to Australia. In four weeks time, I was flying out to Canada, where I had enrolled to study for the remainder of the year. I had no idea when I would see my Aussie friends again. But I knew I would miss their humour, friendship and the occasional shoulder to cry on.

You pass right by the township of Rini on your way into Grahamstown, so we dropped Msizi at his home first. We had planned to stay over in Grahamstown and continue our journey early the next morning. When we arrived at the tiny four-roomed house on a dusty piece of ground that Msizi called home, we all went inside to greet his mother. Jonga, his younger brother, told us she had gone to Port Elizabeth, not knowing we were coming as they had no phone. Msizi looked quite broken-hearted as he hadn't seen his mother for three months. As we drove off, I watched him walking down the dirt road in search of a friend.

We then drove to Jacques and Margie's house. They were good friends with Gary and Vicky as well as with Msizi, as they were active in community development in Grahamstown. Jacques had just become a minister and his church had projects in the township. Margie worked at a local art and craft co-operative that promoted the work of African artists and sold their artwork all over the country. It was my first meeting with this warm and endearing couple who were to become close friends in the years to come, sharing many of my life's milestones and pains.

Over coffee, Mary-Anne took me aside and told me she was so upset about Msizi not being able to see his mother that she wanted to suggest we drive through to Port Elizabeth and try to find her for him. I agreed, but tried not to look overly enthusiastic, given that we hadn't told Mary-Anne about our new relationship. Gary had his graduation ceremony the following night, so he wasn't coming with us to Cape Town. We said our goodbyes and went back to Rini. We were aware that two white women driving alone through the township could attract unwanted attention, so we hoped we found Msizi quickly. He was at the second house we tried, thanks to Jonga's fine directions. Msizi was grateful for the offer to see his mother, so we headed towards the coast. While it's only an hour to Port Elizabeth, it took us a few hours to find Msizi's mother at his uncle's house. His mother's brother was a policeman whom Msizi found little reason to visit, so he had trouble finding the house in the sprawling townships outside the windy city. There were many black policemen in the township, though it was not a popular job as they were often required to act against their own. People usually joined the police force as a way to feed the family. Someone like Msizi, who was often under the watchful eye of the police given his role as a local youth leader, could understand but not support his uncle's decision.

We were offered tea by Msizi's aunt and sat awkwardly around the small living room that was so crammed with furniture that our knees almost touched. It was wonderful to meet Msizi's mother. I watched her watch us and wondered if she could read her son's mind. If she didn't know already, I suspected she might before we came back in the morning. I was unsure what she would think about her son's strange choice. We left after almost an hour of African hospitality and drove through to the beachside suburb where Mary-Anne's brother lived. That evening, we rattled around in the large house overlooking the water and again I was struck by the contrasts that South Africa presented and how my choice of friends took me regularly from one extreme to the other.

We arrived in Cape Town later the next day and drove up the West Coast towards Porterville where Mary-Anne's mother and stepfather lived. He was the local GP and had his surgery in their sprawling colonial-style home. Over dinner, they quizzed us about the work we were doing in 'Maritzburg. I noticed that they were completely unfazed when Mary-Anne arrived with her two friends, without mentioning the colour of one of the guests they were to have in their home. I wondered if Mary-Anne had been surprising them in this way for years, so they had come to expect it, but I was still taken aback that a white couple of their generation was so open-minded. Aside from visiting her parents, Mary-Anne had also wanted to come and swap cars. Up until this point, she had been using one of the family cars, but it appeared to be causing some problems. She explained to her mother that it was the same colour as the yellow cars the police used in the townships and when she arrived to visit friends, she often found them climbing over the back fence to get away. Her mother also took this piece of information in her stride and offered her a respectable metallic green car instead.

We spent two full and fabulous days in the magical city of Cape Town before heading back to Grahamstown. We had dropped Msizi off in Rini before heading into town to fetch Gary. After enjoying Jacques and Margie's hospitality over lunch, we drove back out to Rini to find Msizi. After waiting outside the empty house for about twenty minutes, we decided to fill up with petrol to save some time. As we turned out of the township onto the road into town, an army personnel transport, known as a kasper, spotted us and chased us into town. They hauled us out of the car and questioned us about our business in the township. They doubted our story of fetching a friend, not a common scenario in such a divided country, and warned us of the violent nature of townships and how we were putting our lives at risk. We thanked them for their concern, filled up and headed right back to Rini. They tailed us all the way, with two soldiers carrying automatic weapons perched on the top of the tank-like vehicle. Thankfully, Msizi was home by this time, so he threw his things into the car and we left, waving to his mother as we did.

I would return to Cape Town many times, but only this once would I be here with Msizi. As we had done throughout the trip, Msizi and I snatched moments to talk and be together, enjoying the time away from our busy lives at the Nonsuch Road.

Back at the centre, we continued to keep our relationship to ourselves though finding time together was difficult, living in a community as we did. I was also struggling with the way Msizi treated me in public. In private he was tender and appreciative; however, in public he was distant and would at times run me down with his teasing. I oscillated between thinking I needed to get a thicker skin and wondering whether he enjoyed the arrangement, turning his emotions off and on. In hindsight, the secrecy itself became the higher calling to which everything else, including my sense of wellbeing, was sacrificed. However, in an effort to fit in, I went along with it without question, something I would do many times in the future.

This emerging habit of accommodation would not serve me well. My desire to cause no further injury to those who had been badly injured meant that I opened myself up to being taken for granted and, sometimes, used, whether purposefully or not. As this was the first time I had compromised my own needs, even in a small way, I could not yet see what it would cost me. But I think this is where it began.

One of the masks Msizi wore when he was in the mood for teasing was that of male chauvinist. He knew that Mary-Anne and I, and many others, would get our hackles up when he started to push gender roles, demanding we bring the men food and wash their clothes like proper African women. He took great pleasure in telling us that in traditional homes, the wife would bring the husband's food to him on her knees and then she and the children would eat only after he had eaten his fill. While I knew he was winding us up, the nostalgic look on his face had me a little worried. I later learnt that he and his brothers had done all the work in his home, with both his parents being absent most of the time, so it was not a nostalgia for what he had experienced, but perhaps the one that all men have for the good old days when men were men and women were women. I, however, had no longing for such a time, so Msizi would need to get his own food from the kitchen.

Meanwhile, preparations were well under way for a ten-day mission in Eshowe, a small rural town up the north coast from Durban. The mission was run by a full team this time, not just the trainees as it had been at Brettonwood. We would hold rallies in the community hall, services each night in a large marquee on the football oval in the centre of town, bible studies, prayer meetings and youth meetings. We would be working with a coalition of local churches to host the mission, as they would be responsible for the follow up once it was over. Our organisation ran many such events across southern Africa on a regular basis and had been preparing for this event for almost a year. It was very exciting for me to be part of it, especially with David, the centre's founder, being the keynote speaker. He was currently dividing his time between peace talks in Pietermaritzburg, the Eshowe mission and his many other speaking commitments across the country.

Mary-Anne and I took a break from preparations to visit friends at a local technical high school called Plessislaer, which was located on the edge of Edendale, adjacent to the city's industrial area. Surrounded by high brick walls topped with razor wire, the school looked more like a prison than an institute of learning. We pulled up at the steel gates and went to speak to security. To my surprise, the process felt strangely familiar, somewhat like a border post, as we filled in copious forms to allow us entry to the school. The official stamped memorandum read:

Visit by:
1. Miss M.A van Heerden
2. Miss S. Blackburn
Please allow SCM member D.S Sithole–ID 2862 to meet and accompany them to the meeting in C-28.
Signed P. Zondi

We were required to keep this document on us at all times. Our friends told us that the security was designed to keep the township violence out. Many parents had sent their sons to the school from rural areas and were very aware of the violence in the city, and in Pietermaritzburg in particular; the security was seen as a necessary precaution. My cynical mind wondered whether such measures also kept these young men in, so they could not be influenced by local community groups that were powerfully lobbying against the apartheid government. What I was beginning to learn was that within the black community in South Africa there was not one homogeneous view of the world and how best to live in it. There were diverse views, depending on where you lived, what church you went to and whose company you kept. What was also interesting was that, despite the white community's insistence that there were substantial tribal divides, I was yet to get a sense of that. The divisions seemed to be elsewhere.

In the week before the mission, I took some time out to meet with other local organisations, including World Vision, to explore work options in South Africa. While I was still interested in Tanzania, South Africa continued to grow as a possibility in my mind. As unlikely as this seemed, it had little to do with Msizi. My drive to do something meaningful was powerful, as was my desire to do it in a community or a team. South Africa was appealing simply because I now had a growing network of people that I knew I could work with. In comparison, Tanzania was an unknown entity where I had only corresponded with as yet faceless individuals. My personal drivers of meaning and relationships seemed to be shifting my intention towards continuing where I had begun. My discussions with World Vision were very positive, so yet another avenue was opening up for me to return.

The mission to Eshowe was both exhilarating and exhausting. We were asked to run many of the programs we had offered at Brettonwood and so were often performing in front of large audiences. When we weren't on, we attended other events that different members of the larger team were running. It was a great opportunity for me to hear others speak or run programs. However, one of the strongest memories of that mission was staying with Tshidi and her family, as she was from Eshowe. She lived in the same type of four-roomed house I had seen in every township and she and I shared a mattress on the floor in what was her parents' living room during the day. We were often out late at night with mission events and Msizi would walk us home, the significance of which I suspect was not lost on my host and resident matchmaker. Msizi mentioned that Mary-Anne had also been questioning him about us, and though he felt bad about putting her off, he didn't feel like sharing our relationship with anyone.

During my stay, Tshidi also taught me a very important skill—to wash out of a plastic basin. Millions of black South Africans wash this way each day, but it was the first time I had stayed in a house without running water. Tshidi heated some water on the stove and brought it through in two plastic basins. To my surprise, she then stripped naked and prepared to wash with me in the room. While I had grown up in a household where we were relaxed about seeing each other naked from time to time, this candour did not extend outside the family. For Tshidi, there was no issue. She stood in one bowl and, using a small cloth, soaped her whole body. Next, she rinsed off the soap using the water in the bowl she was standing in. She also took the opportunity to wash her underwear while she had hot soapy water to hand. Next, she stepped into the basin of clean water which she used for a final rinse. She finished by brushing her teeth, spitting the water into the bowl. Lastly, she used a small hand towel to wipe off the remaining water and then dressed, ready for the day. Once dressed, she took the two basins outside and watered the garden with the grey water.

I would wash this way numerous times in following years, always remembering my teacher when I did.

After the mission, there were only a few days before I left for Canada. The whole team was having a short break before the next event, so it gave me a bit more time to be with Msizi, and despite the fact that our relationship was still a secret, we somehow managed to be together without a flood of questions. There was little else to talk about other than my imminent departure and what that meant for us. Despite the intensity of our feelings for each other, there was no real place for the relationship to go. I had options to return, but no solid plans. And even if I did return, we did not see how our relationship could continue outside the relative haven of the centre, where people were kind and interracial friendships were given the space to be normal. Once Msizi returned to Grahamstown, there would be little hope for any kind of normality. My brief visit to his township had taught me that. So we went for long walks, listened to our favourite music, anything just to be in each other's presence a little longer before the bubble burst.

On top of my feelings about Msizi, the thought of leaving South Africa was heartbreaking. Not only was I leaving him, but an entire community of people I had grown to love. I was heading to a country where I knew no one and where, at that moment, I did not really want to be. But plans were made, tickets were booked, and with the term about to start, I could not delay my departure any longer. Msizi and I promised to write, but were unable to commit to any future together.

On my last night at the centre, we all gathered up at the house. Even Steve and Beth's kids joined us to say their goodbyes. After the others had gone to bed, Msizi and I sat by the fire. The words had dried up, leaving only sadness. So he sat with me, his arms around me, and we watched the flames dance until they faded to a dull glow. At the sounds of the first birds, I rose and went to bed.

03

May 1988
Canada

After two days of travelling I arrived at Guelph University near the city of Toronto in Canada feeling lost and tear-stained. Spending my first night in temporary accommodation didn't help, but by day two, things began to look up. My wonderful new roommates, Sandra, an Italian-Canadian and Yuki from Japan, helped me settle in and I was soon fed, unpacked and knew the location of all my lecture halls. I made new friends and found a thriving international community which included many black South Africans who were also studying there. My studies were on nutrition and health care in the third world, which I hoped—on the back of my undergraduate degree—would stand me in good stead for my future work. I spent time compiling a reference library to take back to Africa with me. I read books on South African history, black theology and politics; spent time debating issues with people from across Africa; took part in the university's multicultural festival, the South African Youth Day rally and Mandela's birthday celebrations in Toronto. I was also teaching myself Zulu.

All the while, Msizi and I exchanged long letters, finding new ways each time to describe our longing for each other. He kept me up to date on events at Nonsuch Road, the comings and goings of the volunteers, the workshops they were running, the happenings in 'Maritzburg. I also wrote to Steve about going back to South Africa for the August holidays to participate in a special event they were planning. My parents came to visit and we spent a happy week together in Montreal. With so much going on, my first semester flew by and before I knew it I was on a plane back to Africa.

04

August 1988
Forced Removals

THE SIZE AND THICKNESS OF THE LETTERS MSIZI AND I EXCHANGED HAD RAISED A FEW EYEBROWS WITHIN THE TEAM. MSIZI WAS FORCED TO CONFESS THAT HE AND I HAD FEELINGS FOR EACH OTHER AND THEN ENDURE THE ENDLESS TEASING THAT FOLLOWED. WITH MARY-ANNE, IT WAS ANOTHER STORY. SHE WAS UPSET BY THE NEWS, HAVING HAD HER SUSPICIONS SINCE OUR CAPE TOWN TRIP TOGETHER. I SUSPECT SHE FELT A COMBINATION OF HURT AT NOT BEING TOLD THE TRUTH AND PERHAPS EVEN JEALOUSY THAT IT WAS ME AND NOT HER. SHE AND MSIZI WERE VERY CLOSE SO SHE MIGHT ALSO HAVE FELT THAT OUR RELATIONSHIP WOULD RUIN THEIRS. I DON'T REALLY KNOW. ALL I DO KNOW IS THAT OUR RELATIONSHIP WAS NEVER AGAIN CLOSE AND ALWAYS HAD A SHARP EDGE TO IT. AS MARY-ANNE AND I MOVED IN THE SAME CIRCLES FOR MANY YEARS WE OFTEN HAD OCCASION TO MEET. I ADMIRE HER CHOICES IN LIFE AND GREATLY RESPECT HER COURAGE, SO TO HAVE SOMETHING UNSPOKEN BETWEEN US HAS BEEN A GREAT SADNESS TO ME.

But all this was ahead of me as I jumped into a hire car at Jan Smuts airport in Johannesburg and began the long drive back to Nonsuch Road. In my hurry to return, I was pulled over by the police for speeding but managed (I'm ashamed to admit) to convince the officer that I was a tourist in his beautiful country. He kindly warned me to be more careful and wished me a pleasant journey. Despite the smiles I lavished, my heart was pounding at the sight of a policeman leaping out onto the road and pointing an accusing finger directly at me. My encounters with South African police during my first few months and the stories I had been told made such a sight a little unnerving. This fear of the police worsened considerably over the ensuing years and would take more than a decade to undo.

Finally, I was turning off the tar and up the dirt road into the forest. My heart caught in my throat as the road opened out to reveal once more the rolling green lawns and the white Cape Dutch buildings. As I strolled across the lawn to the dining hall the sounds of lunch drifted out onto the veranda and I felt suddenly shy. I peered in through one of the wooden French doors and saw Msizi, Kedrick, Gary and Tshidi sitting together at one table. Gary, facing the door, saw me first. He tossed a bread roll at Msizi and then came bounding over. I had a flashback to the first time I had entered this hall on a misty night some seven months before. This time it was very different, akin to returning home. The rest of the team and a few of the volunteers were crowded around, welcoming me back with hugs and kisses. I looked across at Msizi, who was still seated, as he smiled his hello. Not one for crowds, he came over after a few minutes and pulled me back out through the door. On the veranda, he wrapped me in his arms and after the longest time whispered in my ear, 'I missed you'. 'I missed you too', I said, letting the tears fall onto his shirt.

Next morning, the team left for a two-day retreat down the south coast, taking me with them. Some friends of the centre, Nigel and Claire, had some land near the beach and we had decided to go and camp there. This sparked some heated discussions within the team. Our black colleagues could not understand why we would opt to be without beds and showers, choosing instead to cook outside and sleep on the ground. We had had a similar discussion once before, late one night up at the house. Msizi wanted to know why white people considered candles romantic when all they did for black people was remind them of their poverty. The camping debate followed similar lines. As it turned out we had a great night under the stars, sitting around a fire, listening to Steve play guitar and solving the problems of Africa and all its peoples. It was the first time Msizi and I had felt relaxed about being affectionate in public, which for me made a nice change from stolen moments.

My relationship with Msizi in those first two weeks proved to be up and down. He had developed a habit of being confrontational and competitive with me when others were around, so as to throw them off the scent of our new relationship. Now that our relationship was out in the open, his persistence with this behaviour put me on the back foot and I was forced to keep my guard up most of the time. Any kind of vulnerability felt like a risk. I knew Msizi loved me and was at a loss to understand why he could not communicate with me as he had in his letters. I knew I was unhappy but was afraid to take him on for fear that I would hurt him. I was also afraid that if I didn't talk to him about it, he would walk all over me. Once or twice when I worked up the courage to address it, he was immediately tender and caring and I quickly forgave him. Finally, after two weeks of feeling like we were a pair of bucks locking horns to see who was the stronger, I remembered something Steve had said about sons repeating the habits of their fathers. I knew I had to say something more definitive.

That night after dinner, I asked Msizi to go for a walk with me. Heart pounding, I told him how I had been feeling and explained that vulnerability and intimacy were part of the same equation in my mind. In the darkness, I could not read his face. After a long silence, he told me that he found vulnerability very difficult, as to survive in his world he had learnt to put away his emotions and be careful about placing his trust in others. Up until this point, the only people he could trust were a few of his closest male friends. He felt that he had opened up with me far more than with any other woman he had dated, having never felt this powerfully for anyone. I was so moved by his words that I almost backed off the issue. But then, consolidating my thoughts, I said, 'What you say and what you do don't match up. I understand that sparring can be like flirting, but you go too far and push me away'. We were nearing the house by this time, so I stopped and turned to face him. He took my hand in his and simply said, 'OK'.

We continued to discuss these issues right through to the end of my stay. Our different experiences and expectations were always on the agenda. However, we began to find a way to make things work.

After our short camping retreat we went down to Sweetwaters to visit the site of the new creche. In my absence, the team had run two youth leadership programs which included some community work. They had brought the groups to Sweetwaters and begun digging up rocks in the surrounding area that could be used on the floor of the creche. They had also dug holes for the creosoted poles that would be used in the walls. Fred, the young English handyman who worked at the centre, had made time on weekends to come out and cement these poles into the ground ready for the roof trusses to be attached, which was the job we were to begin today. As we walked up the same rutted path, carrying shovels over our shoulders, I was glad that this time I had the good sense to wear boots. Fred had been there for an hour already, having earlier directed the truck with the trusses and not wanting to leave them unattended. While this was to be a community creche, building materials were in short supply and the trusses could prove too tempting for many. We spent the day atop ladders, holding the trusses in place while Fred secured them, or digging up wheelbarrowfuls of rocks to add to the floor. It was hot, sweaty work but it felt good to be doing something practical that could make a difference to this community. Under Fred's guidance, it took another eighteen months to finish the creche during which time I became quite a hand at throwing mud walls.

Fred had come out to South Africa a few years earlier, initially as a volunteer at the centre. He was a builder by trade, which was a useful skill in Africa. Fred was about my height, slim, tanned and unashamedly prematurely balding. I loved that Fred was who he was: an honest, nuts and bolts kind of guy. After his initial experiences in Africa, he traded in the cold climate of northern England to stay on in South Africa. We were to become firm friends for many years. He worked at the centre for a few more years, then took a job with World Vision in a remote part of KwaZulu, outside of Tugela Ferry. There he worked with the local women on job creation projects, making and selling mud bricks, wire fencing and the like. I visited him there a few times and was impressed by the way he had made a home in that community, living in a round mud and thatch hut, or rondavel, just as his neighbours did, growing crops, speaking the language. He eventually returned to Pietermaritzburg and opened a successful handyman business in town.

Another volunteer I became good friends with was Charlie. He had finished high school the previous year and while deciding what to do next had come to volunteer at the centre. Charlie was more than 183 centimetres tall and seemed to be all limbs, somewhat like a large puppy who is yet to grow into his body. He had dark hair that spent most of its time in his eyes and a ready smile that spread across his face at the slightest provocation. Charlie was also big hearted and always there to help, listen or chat. Despite the lightness that surrounded him like a halo, he was facing some serious issues. Like all white South African men his age, he had received conscription papers requiring him to serve two years in the army or the police force, stationed either on the border with Namibia or in the townships. He could easily have postponed the call by going to university or travelling abroad. Alternatively, he could have taken six years of community service as a religious objector. He could also have chosen a non-combatant posting, saying that he was a pacifist and therefore not willing to fight. Many young Christians had chosen these routes so as not to compromise their beliefs. Not Charlie.

He argued that he was not a pacifist and did believe that there were times when one had to take up arms. However, he did not believe the army was fighting a just war and therefore he chose to object to having any role in the military.

This was a brave stand for an eighteen-year-old. Not long before, the papers had carried the story of David Bruce who was the second man to be imprisoned for six years for conscientious objection, an act Charlie was now considering. He spent time talking to some of the senior leaders at the centre as well as to two other men in a position similar to his. His other confidant was Msizi. While there were many young black men at the centre, only one or two were as articulate and politically aware as Msizi. Vusi kept his thoughts to himself and Kedrick, coming from Zambia, was himself finding his time in South Africa a revelation. Charlie and Msizi had also become good friends over the year so Msizi tried to help him find a perspective on what he was doing and what he hoped to achieve.

Three months later, on 6 December 1988, Charlie was sentenced to six years in prison. He was not given the status of a political prisoner so was to be housed with criminal prisoners for the duration of his sentence. Though I knew the risk Charlie was taking the judgment jolted me with its harshness. We were all passionate about change but on that day, I knew it was not a game. Charlie was released in 1990 after almost two years in prison, through a deal brokered by Mandela that saw the release of all conscientious objectors. I don't know what Charlie did with his life, but Msizi heard that he struggled for the first few years to find a direction once more.

It was nearing my twenty-third birthday at the end of August as we finalised plans for our time in Lawaaikamp. This was a small black settlement on the outskirts of George, a picturesque town on the southeast coast some five hours drive from Cape Town. As a tourist town at the heart of the Garden Route, a magnificent coastal meander from Cape Town to Port Elizabeth, George had grown over the years. Lawaaikamp was now being absorbed into the tranquil white suburbs of George, a situation that did not please the local white community. While the town needed black labour in order to survive, it preferred to have some distance between the two. The municipality had recently built a new township on an open plain on the far side of the freeway, confident that this would provide enough of a buffer between the two areas. The residents of Lawaaikamp had lived in the same broken down homes for generations; however, they were on the wrong side of the freeway so they had to be moved. The plan was termed a forced removal and many people, including a few of the politically aware white residents of George, were ready to register their protest against such an action. One such resident, Peter, was good friends with Steve's in-laws who lived just outside George. It was through Peter that we were to live in Lawaaikamp for two weeks, hoping that our presence might prevent the forced removal from happening. This kind of political protest was pushing the boundaries of what our Christian community in Pietermaritzburg was comfortable with, but Steve had managed to convince them that it was the right thing to do.

A few days before we were to leave, Lawaaikamp was the topic of morning devotions for the staff and volunteers at the centre. At the end of the hour, Steve pulled the team aside. He asked each one of us to find a quiet spot and take some time to think through the implications of possible detention. He told us that, given what we were intending to do, it was a very real possibility. One look at Msizi confirmed that this was true. The implications would be different for each of us: Msizi, Vusi and Tshidi could be detained indefinitely; Gary and Mary-Anne could also be detained but would find themselves held in far better conditions as prisons, like all else in this strange country, were also segregated; Steve, Kedrick and I would be detained and then deported, unable to return. Steve asked us to meet back at the chapel on the lake in an hour.

With my journal in hand, I sat in sober silence under the trees next to the lake. The thought of leaving South Africa permanently was hard to bear but my gut response was that we should still go. In retrospect, I often wondered why there was no hesitation in these and many other decisions I made. I think I always have been and always will be for the underdog. It is hard-wired into who I am. Even as a young child, I was drawn to befriend those who were different from the rest of the school. I was intrigued by their difference, wanting to understand how they saw the world. If they were treated unfairly, I was the first to come to their defence. In my teenage years, I extended my sense of what was right and wrong beyond my immediate environment to include the rest of the world. When the Ethiopian famine hit the world media in 1984, I was appalled and coordinated my network of friends to take on odd jobs and raise thousands of dollars to be sent to aid relief efforts there. So making the decision to go to Lawaaikamp and protest the forced removals was not, I believe, driven by courage or selflessness but mostly by having a strong opinion and feeling the need to express it. I get this trait from my father. While he, however, would express his strong opinions to friends and family, and usually only when asked, I didn't wait for an invitation.

It seemed that the rest of the team had reached the same conclusion I had, though perhaps for different reasons, for when we all met back at the chapel it was agreed that we would still go.

Lawaaikamp was not like the urban townships I had seen before, nor was it like the rural community of Sweetwaters. Some of the homes were large brick dwellings and though they were in various stages of disrepair they had clearly been there for a long time. Others had old wooden planks for walls and rusted corrugated iron sheets for roofing. They were also larger than the average four-roomed township homes and appeared to have been built by the owners with extensions added over time. There were a few dirt roads that ran through the area but most homes were reached on foot through the long soft grass. The other difference was the trees; there was a whole forest on one side with many established gum trees scattered throughout. The presence of trees and grass reduced the ever-present dust that swirls around most townships, coating every surface as soon as it is cleaned.

Our days in Lawaaikamp were mostly spent visiting homes. A number of churches in the area had donated food, clothing and blankets and our job was to distribute this to families in need. Strangely, I don't recall meeting with any community leaders; we simply got to know the families who lived there. There was one family who lived in what appeared to be the largest and most established home in Lawaaikamp. While I wouldn't have called them community leaders, they certainly knew what was happening and who needed help. They directed us to one family compromised of a grandmother and two small boys, the mother having gone to Cape Town to work. They had not heard from her in weeks and things were very difficult for them, made worse by the grandmother's tuberculosis. Her illness was largely untreated as she had only been able to afford the taxi fare to the clinic once to get the first dose of tablets but had not been able to make her way back. The food and blankets were a blessing, she told us, as George was still in the grip of winter where temperatures would regularly drop below freezing. We also took the two grandsons with us when we visited other homes nearby, allowing their grandmother an opportunity to sleep.

Msizi and I visited another home where the grandmother was ill, though I was not sure with what. Her son showed us into a small annex that was her room, so we could sit and visit her. Hearing a noise, a cry, Msizi asked the old woman if there was a baby in the house. She said there was and pulled back the crusty blankets to reveal a tiny baby, just waking, in the crook of her arm. Apparently the mother of this household was also working as a maid for a white family in Cape Town, having returned to work as soon as the baby was born. Msizi and I exchanged glances and I took the baby from the old woman, wondering if it would catch whatever illness the grandmother was harbouring. Responding to the cries, the son reappeared with a bottle for the baby. It was as filthy as the blankets in which the old woman slept. Ignoring my urge to run and sterilise the bottle, I fed the squawking infant. We agreed to leave some blankets and clean clothes for the grandmother and promised to return.

As we walked away, Msizi told me that the family would not give the blankets and clothes to the old woman.

I turned on him, horrified. 'Why not?'

'They will reason that she doesn't need them the most, as she is old and dying', he explained.

Not believing that anyone could be so callous, I promised myself I would go back the next day.

The next morning I arrived alone. I knocked on the door and the son answered. We greeted each other and he asked me inside. I asked after his family's health and he told me they were all well. I then gave him the baby formula I had brought and asked if I could visit his mother. As I poked my head into the tiny annex, the old woman was awake and beckoned for me to enter. '*Molo*', I said, Hello, how are you? She assured me she was well, though she did not look it. She was wearing the same clothes as the previous day and her bedclothes smelled as if they were still soiled. I quickly scouted the room for the items we had left but they were nowhere to be seen. Reluctantly, I realised that Msizi had been right. I asked her, in a combination of gestures and English words as I spoke no Xhosa, whether she had eaten yet. As she had not, I went to the kitchen to see what I could find. Her son was sitting at the small metal kitchen table with a visiting neighbour. After yet more greetings, I was told there was no porridge, the common breakfast staple, but only leftover pap from the night before. He scraped the contents from the bottom of a pot into a plastic bowl and handed it to me. I thanked him and returned to the annex. Then, sitting next to the old woman, I helped her to eat what little food there was. While pap is quite a bland meal, it is preferred by many as it comfortably fills the stomach, chasing hunger away for many hours. I suspected it would be so with her as well. Before I left, I asked the son for the woollen stockings I had brought the day before, very aware that I was crossing a line with him. He disappeared into another room while I stood awkwardly in the kitchen with the neighbour. After a few minutes he returned with the stockings. I told him that his mother's legs were cold and that I was going to put the stockings on her before I left.

Once out the door, I went to look for Msizi, outraged. 'How could he?' I demanded.

'You don't understand', he replied.

I knew I didn't. I had no idea what it was like not to be able feed and clothe your family and to have to choose between them. I did not know how the son felt having his wife working so far from home, earning only a few rand, or dollars, a day, while he tried to hold it together. In the heat of the moment, my only reference point was myself and I knew I would never let my mother live like that. My moral compass was set too tight to even try to understand, but I was learning that there was no clean line between right and wrong, between victim and oppressor.

We had been in Lawaaikamp a week when the forced removals began. The government had been threatening to demolish homes for the past three months, with the first deadline of 31 May passing quietly. For those few who had given up fighting and agreed to go, a truck arrived to collect their belongings and move them off. The many who would not leave listened anxiously for sounds of bulldozers. They came at night, knocking down only one or two homes each time. Every morning, people would emerge from their homes and gather around each of the new wounds that were opening up in their community. Despite our presence and the protests of those who opposed the removals both locally and overseas, the demolitions continued night after night. One freezing morning we awoke to be told that one old man had refused to leave his house when the bulldozers came and they had demolished the house around him. His granddaughter, who had returned from hospital with her newborn twins a few days before, had spent the night with him in the rubble. Tragically, one of the twins did not survive the cold and died in the night. The community was outraged and I with them, yet somehow we all knew that what was now started could not be stopped.

Towards the end of our second week, Steve went missing. While he had not said he was going to town, we at first assumed that was what he must have done. As the hours went by we began to worry. I suspect we had all put the police out of our minds as there had been no major police presence in the area in that first week. Even when the removals began, the police came at night and we rarely saw them. When Steve had been gone for over five hours without a word we began to talk through what action we should take; clearly, going to the police was not an option. After much discussion we agreed that through Steve's family contacts we could most likely approach a lawyer who could help. Just as we were about to phone Steve's father-in-law, Steve returned. He told us that the police had picked him up on the edge of Lawaaikamp and taken him down to a remote beach road. They questioned him about our presence and the identity of each person in the team. While this was happening, he was running scenarios through his mind, most of them ending badly for him and his family. Finally, the police ended their off-road interrogation with threats of detention and general bodily harm. They then left him on the side of the road and he had spent the last few hours walking back. He was visibly shaken but we all felt he was lucky to get away so lightly.

After two weeks, we left Lawaaikamp, unsure whether we had made a difference to their situation, and made the fifteen-hour drive home. While we had been able to distribute much needed supplies, we knew this could have been done by the local churches themselves. We had taken a stand and thrown in our lot with the community but this had not made their plight any more public, nor stopped the forced removals. I think that sometimes all you can do is be present and say, 'Yes, it happened, I saw it'. Feeling invisible and unnoticed during hard times is difficult enough but having the government, or anyone for that matter, say that it never happened makes the cut deeper still. Miraculously, the forced removals did eventually stop and Lawaaikamp held on until the end of apartheid and finally integrated into George on its own terms.

After we returned to 'Maritzburg, we were in need of a few days off. One night, Msizi and Vusi convinced me to go to a shebeen. A shebeen is like a pub or a bar in someone's home. For decades, the only bars black people were allowed to go to were the government-run drinking houses. While the private manufacture and sale of alcohol was forbidden, a semi underground network of shebeens emerged, mostly run by black women, where traditional maize beer was brewed and sold, along with other store bought varieties. When the police felt inclined, they could sweep in and close down the shebeens but they were virtually impossible to stop, for as soon as the police shut one down, another would spring up somewhere else.

This night, we went with Klaus and Al, two other black volunteers from the centre. Klaus was from a township called Mamelodi outside Pretoria and Al, or Big Al, as we called him, was from Cape Town. While we sat around chatting about our varying school experiences, with a bit of sport and politics thrown in for good measure, Vusi had gone to a friend's house to get a stereo so that we could have some music. He told us he would be ten minutes as the friend was only a few blocks away. We had become so engrossed in our conversation that it was an hour before we began to wonder what was taking him so long. No one was particularly concerned. I was learning that things rarely got done in a straight line around here. There was often an unavoidable detour between intention and action that meant things took two or three times as long as was first imagined. After an hour and a half Vusi walked in with a big smile on his face, carrying the stereo. The police, seeing a black man walking along at night, stereo in hand, had assumed it was stolen and arrested him. It had taken over an hour for him to prove that the stereo was legitimately on loan before they let him go. After a few drinks, this seemed incredibly funny to us so we teased Vusi for being stupid enough to get arrested, put the music on and let the dancing begin.

Having grown up in Australia and not having been in Africa long, my wall of inhibitions when it came to dancing was still quite robust. In the case of my African-born friends, no such inhibitions existed. Msizi eventually convinced me to dance with him and soon everyone was on their feet. I even danced alone to the compulsive rhythms of African jazz. As the night wore on, Msizi pulled me close, still dancing, and whispered to me that he loved me and that I was always his first choice, no matter what happened. There was just a week left before I had to return to Canada and we were both starting to feel the pull of it.

The centre was unusually quiet in my last week, leaving us plenty of time to be together. I was finding it increasingly hard to deal with what was coming next. We would both be finishing our studies at the end of the year. Msizi would return to Grahamstown to look for work and I would return to Australia for Christmas with my family and to plan my next steps. The centre had been a shelter for our relationship but we were aware that once one or both of us left, it would be virtually impossible for us to be together. An Act of Parliament had only recently changed the law that banned mixed marriages. However, the Group Areas Act was still in place, meaning it was not yet legal for mixed race couples to live together: each racial group could live only in the areas designated for it. A number of people got around this by living in so-called 'grey areas' that were either industrial or low income areas—meaning the police received few complaints and did not often enforce the law.

So we began to discuss possible scenarios. At that stage, I was keen to return to South Africa but had no firm arrangements. Msizi had a potential job with the South African Council of Churches in Grahamstown. But it was not these logistical issues that were front of mind; it was the question of finding a community where we could both feel at home. Given how incredibly divided the country was, and in many ways still is, we would be very visible as a couple no matter where we chose to live. There were so few mixed marriages at that stage that they almost took on the status of urban legend. The more we discussed it, the more discouraged he became. I, the eternal optimist, believed that where there was a will there was a way. But Msizi was thinking more long-term than I and couldn't see how we could make it work. We discussed whether we should simply stay together as long as we could, even if it was only for another year or two, until a decision to part needed to be made. To an idealistic twenty-three-year-old, this sounded very romantic and lent an edge of intensity to the situation that it may not have deserved. We still had not reached a conclusion when it came time for me to go. The only thing we could agree on was no more tears.

While leaving South Africa again was a wrench, I was more certain this time that I had a future here, in one form or other. Steve was considering setting up a separate youth organisation in 'Maritzburg, one that was focused more on community development and less on missions and evangelism. After all I had experienced that year, I knew the faith I had brought with me was not the same as the one I was taking away. I needed a more integrated faith that spoke to God's presence in a world of suffering, rather than sermons on how to make time for regular bible study and prayer or how to love a noisy neighbour. I wanted to know where God was when a baby was dying of cold in the rubble of a bulldozed house. Even if the clergy had no answer, I needed them at least to ask the question. I saw that in South Africa there were many people who asked the hard questions, worked in unwinnable situations and yet still had a deep faith. I imagined that working in the organisation Steve was thinking of building would give me a chance to find an expression for my changing faith. I suspected that trying to do that at the centre might put me on the edge of the community there, as it seemed to have done with Steve. What I did not know at the time was that there were factors other than his activism that may have distanced him from the centre leadership.

In a heartbeat, I was leaving again. This time I was flying out of the small airport in 'Maritzburg, with Msizi to see me off. The night before, as I sat crying on my bed not knowing where our relationship was going, Msizi reminded me of our 'no tears' agreement. I had not been able to keep it then, but was determined to appear in control of myself at the airport. When it finally came time to go, he looked at me and said, 'You'll be back'. I hugged him, knowing that he loved me, knowing I was his first choice and not knowing much else, then left without looking back.

On the plane back to Canada I spent much of the time thinking about the other people I had met in 'Maritzburg: Steve, Gary, Tshidi, Kedrick, Vusi, Fred, Klaus, Big Al, Charlie, many of whom I would not see again. Over the years I heard snippets of news about a few. Gary and Vicky married and Gary took up a parish in Johannesburg. Kedrick went back to Zambia and worked for the Church there. Sadly, Vusi died of AIDS. I also realised how naive and trusting I had been when I arrived, something Msizi enjoyed reminding me of. It turned out that Big Al, one of our real favourites, was not Al at all. Msizi bumped into him on a university campus many years later but he did not answer to his name. He would not be drawn on why he used a false name and what, if anything, we knew about him was true. Things happened during the apartheid years and people had to do what they had to do. Another volunteer at the centre was in fact a police agent. But he was also a young man in trouble and Steve had done everything he could to help him. He disappeared shortly after Steve confronted him about his real identity and we never heard from him again.

On that flight, I realised that you either trusted no one or you put your trust in people until there was cause not to; these were the only two choices. I knew my nature was to believe the best about people and if I lost that, I would lose something intrinsic and valuable. I also knew that staying open meant I would be hurt. The choice I made then was to stay open and take each person at face value—and live with the occasional broken heart.

05
September 1988
To Canada and Back Again

RETURNING TO CANADA WAS HARDER THAN I HAD IMAGINED. MANY OF MY FRIENDS FROM THE SUMMER SEMESTERS WERE NOT RETURNING IN AUTUMN. THIS TIME, I HAD TAKEN A ROOM WITH A YOUNG COUPLE WHO LIVED RIGHT NEXT TO CAMPUS—WITH HINDSIGHT, I SUSPECT LIVING ON CAMPUS AMONG OTHER SINGLE STUDENTS WOULD HAVE MADE FOR AN EASIER TIME.

I did make one new close friend, Elaine, with whom I kept in touch for many years. When we weren't in classes, Elaine took me to see the highlights of Toronto, had me over for meals at her parents' house and took me out into the country, generally helping me to feel more at home.

Other than studying and spending time with Elaine and a few of the international students, I marked my time by Msizi's letters. In the top corner of each letter would predictably be: 'From a place in the heart'. In one letter he wrote: 'I have now realised how much of me was in you and how much of you was dug deep into my heart. It is painful for me to think of it'.

What struck me from time to time was how he could open himself up so much to a white person of any nationality, given that he had spent his whole life keeping clear of them. It's no small miracle when intimacy develops between two people, but when one represents discrimination and pain to the other it feels like a such delicate thing.

When writing, we were careful not to talk about the future as that was still so unresolved but kept each other up to date on small events and the emotional highs and lows of our current existence. Nevertheless, the undercurrent was clear: a decision was coming that neither of us was going to be ready for. It hung around me as a mist, colouring my days in shades of grey, like the coming winter.

I also exchanged a few letters with Steve. He had decided to go ahead with his plans for the youth organisation, to be called Sizwe Youth, and was busy fundraising with his old contacts back in the UK. He invited me to consider joining the organisation, if the appropriate visas could be arranged. My work visa would need to be processed outside South Africa so he suggested I should apply in Australia and fundraise there while I was waiting for approval. We both hoped that our time in Lawaaikamp would not prejudice the application.

As I finished the semester, the rich colours of autumn faded and winter descended on the beautiful city of Guelph. I had never lived in a city in snow and as the days got colder, I wasn't sure I wanted to. My Australian body was ill-prepared for even the November weather in Canada, let alone full-blown winter.

My flight home took me via Vancouver and I spent a few days exploring the city on my way through. I also found a production of the South African play *Bopha* by the Earth Players Theatre Company, hosted by the Vancouver East Cultural Centre. The Zulu word *bopha* means to hold, or in the current context, to detain. The play explored, in the powerfully emerging style of black theatre, the stories of young black people striving for a voice in South African society. The thing that, for me, most captures Africa as her true self is her music. African theatre is full of powerful singing that cascades over you in resonating harmonies, its rhythms transforming your emotions so completely that you feel the joy and sorrow as if they were your own. While in Canada, I had read many of the biographies and books that were banned in South Africa at the time. These stories increased my understanding and further galvanised my commitment—but the music and characters of the play lifted me up so that I felt, for a moment, part of the struggle itself.

My hiatus in Vancouver also allowed me some time to read over my travel diary and reflect on the year. It was hard to believe that all my experiences had been squashed into a ten-month period—it felt like years since I had left my parents at Sydney airport. I remembered my naive self walking into Harare airport, imagining the next few months more like a safari than the awakening it was. Growing up in a quiet Sydney suburb and spending my teenage years in the church youth group, the worst I had seen of people was a little vindictive gossiping. Neither I nor my world view were ready for what I experienced in South Africa. Perhaps my response to it was sharpened by the contrast of the two worlds.

One evening, I asked myself whether I would have left Sydney if I'd understood what was to come. In the end, it was a rhetorical question, as at some level I felt that Sydney had not been enough for me, could not engage my passion nor my adolescent ideology and that I had always been looking for something more. What struck me was how different I was to my own brother. Despite our identical upbringings, Jon was still in Sydney focusing all his attention on building what would become a powerful career, only travelling overseas for work or holidays, and struggling to understand why I would not do likewise. He told me many years later that he was proud of what I had done with my life, though I don't think he always understood my motivation.

By the time I left Vancouver to fly home I was confident about the choices I was making. I was looking forward to Christmas with family and to my return to South Africa.

06

December 1988
Home for Christmas

I didn't realise how much I had missed my parents until I saw them—Mum was holding a 'Welcome Home' balloon as she eagerly scanned the crowd. I had long since overtaken my mother's height—she was a respectable 160 centimetres tall, or 161, as she was quick to point out. In the past when we hugged, I tried to tuck her head into my shoulder as she stood on tippy toes trying to evade me. Today, she didn't object and we clung to each other and cried as we had ten months before.

I spent the rest of the day chatting to Mum and Dad, unpacking and just enjoying being home. That night, Msizi phoned and told me he was having a hard time settling back in, now that he was home in Grahamstown himself. He said that he and his mother were arguing a lot, which wounded him terribly. He felt they had both changed over the course of the year and didn't understand each other as well as they had done. I hoped I would not find the same problems awaiting me. Msizi also told me that his friends were ridiculing his feelings for me. They felt he should take what he could get and move on, rather than pining over a future that couldn't exist. The good news was that he had been offered the job with the Council of Churches, to start in February. I suspected he wished it would start straight away, leaving him less time to mull over his feelings.

Once my own initial homecoming flush subsided I also found myself on an emotional roller coaster. I was still waiting for a letter from Steve, formally stating that I was being offered employment with Sizwe, before I could submit my visa application. Then it would take at least three months to process, assuming all went smoothly. I was anxious to get started with the work in South Africa and found the limbo of waiting difficult to manage. Realistically, I couldn't proceed on the assumption that I would get there eventually. If my visa was refused, I would have to change direction completely. I believed I could do anything I set my mind to—so it didn't sit well to know there was nothing I could do to influence the outcome. I had learnt to focus my attention, to work hard for what I wanted, but I had yet to learn patience.

When I was with friends I was happy and distracted, glad to be back with people who had known me for years. But when I was alone my mood would crash and I would sit, brooding with uncertainty. This was my first experience of mild depression, something I would struggle with again in the future.

Msizi's letters and calls, as always, helped me feel connected to the world I had temporarily left behind. Not long after his first phone call, he found some work that kept him busy up until February. I think I gave my father a few grey hairs with the size of our phone bill over that period, but knowing Msizi was happy and settled somehow helped me to find my way out of my own inertia.

Finally, after more than two months of waiting, the letter from Steve arrived and I was able to file my visa application. Because of the Christmas break it had taken longer than expected to process the legal registration of the organisation. The next period of waiting began then, but at least I felt I was one step closer to my goal. At that point, I decided to begin fundraising for the Sizwe. Steve and

I agreed that funding my own salary would be my contribution to the establishment of the organisation but I was confident that, like him, I could also raise seed money to help get the work started. I estimated I would need $150 per month in order to support myself. My local church kindly agreed to put in part of the money and two friends offered to match it. We agreed that I would have funding for the role for the next two years. I was incredibly grateful for their generosity as it meant that any other fundraising I did could go directly to the work. I approached a number of Australian aid agencies and church organisations and managed to raise enough money, once it was converted into South African rands, to make a meaningful contribution. A visual arts company also agreed to produce a promotional video free of charge to help us with our fundraising efforts.

At the end of April, the South African embassy finally issued a visa for me to return. I was excited to be moving on, but very aware that this time I would be gone for years. My flight was booked for early June when Steve felt the organisation, and the property we were to live and work on, would be operational.

During my last two weeks in Australia, I spent all my spare time following my mother around. I wanted to make sure I told her everything I needed to say before distance and phone bills made our conversations short and unfulfilling. I reasoned that if we were in each other's company, I could share thoughts as they popped into my head before they were overwhelmed by the long list of things I needed to do. Mum and I had always been close. I had never felt the need to put up a protective wall around myself to keep her out. Mum was always there to listen but never to judge. From time to time this was annoying as she would never tell me what to do even if I wanted her to. She gave me the freedom to live my own life and make my own decisions. At that time in her life she was always on the go, making the most of every minute. She and Dad ran the bookshop together six days a week, she played golf, was widely read and had a broad circle of friends that included her sister and cousins. Despite all this, she somehow made me feel that she always had time for me. I suspect everyone who knew Mum felt that. So, tapping into Mum's unconditional ear in those last weeks was top of my 'to do' list.

A week before I was due to depart Mum, her best friend Scruffy and I went to see the movie *Beaches*. Mum told us she would use the movie as practice for the airport and not allow herself to cry. True to her word, she remained dry-eyed while Scruffy and I almost had to be carried from the cinema.

Despite her impressive practice run, though, she was a weeping mess in the departure lounge. My father finally managed to drag her away after the third attempted farewell. 'Now, this time, I'm really going', I assured her—but it was I who kept turning back for one more hug. Mum told me years later that this was the hardest period of her life, as my brother moved to London for work two weeks after I left. Though we were both grown, the loss left her heartbroken. Being so self-absorbed at the time, I hadn't thought about how she might be feeling. So I boarded the plane full of ideas for the future, thrilled about being able to work in my beloved 'Maritzburg again and thrilled at the thought of seeing Msizi.

My parents returned home to find a letter that read:

> *You know how much I love you both and I know how deeply you love me, so this day is a hard day for all of us. But it is also a good day. Today you can think of me and be proud because you have done a wonderful job as parents. You have cared for me, made me feel important, taught me to love the truth and to act with justice ...*
>
> *If anything should ever happen to me in Africa, please remember I chose to be there because it fulfilled something in me. It's time for me to grow up and it's nice to love you enough to miss you.*

07 June 1989 Phezulu

SPEEDING ABOVE THE OCEAN, I WAS EUPHORIC KNOWING THAT I WAS GOING TO BE EXACTLY WHERE I WANTED TO BE, AND SOON. AFTER MONTHS OF STANDING STILL, I WAS ON THE MOVE. THE PLANE WAS CARRYING ME TO A PLACE WHERE SIZWE WAS PLANNING TO TAKE ON SEEMINGLY IMPOSSIBLE CHALLENGES WORKING WITH THE TOWNSHIP YOUTH TO BUILD LIFE-LONG LEADERS, LOOKING TO PROVIDE A FRESH START FOR FAMILIES DISPLACED BY TOWNSHIP VIOLENCE, AND GIVING YOUNG PEOPLE SKILLS TO BECOME SELF EMPLOYED. IF I WAS TO LIVE A SHORT LIFE, AS MY CHILDHOOD PREMONITIONS INDICATED, THIS SEEMED TO BE A GOOD SPACE IN WHICH TO DO IT. NO WONDER I FELT FILLED WITH A SENSE OF PURPOSE.

I did not know it at the time, but the next two years would be my most dangerous, and I was fortunate to survive them. The weeks and months were so filled with violence and loss that much of what happened slipped into a black hole, memories lost or hidden with only snatches close enough to the surface to recall. Because of my sponsorship, I sent regular newsletters back to Australia and it has only been through these and the letters I wrote to friends that I have coaxed many of my memories out of the shadows. I doubt whether they will all return.

Arriving back in 'Maritzburg was like a lovers' reunion. Steve picked me up from the small Oribi airport and we drove through Edendale, then Sweetwaters, on our way to our new home, 'Phezulu' (pronounced *pear-zulu*), meaning 'up in the heavens'. It was just after 5 pm as we made our way along Edendale Road and the township was alive with people returning from work. Dust from the many feet and from the car and bus tyres gave the light a reddish haze and the air smelt of coal smoke and the evening meal. The festive mood was infectious; work was done for the day, the English language, the *baas* and madam left behind. People were now free to be their expansive selves, with laughter and conversation crossing roads, fences and yards; no secret words whispered behind closed doors. Community life was at its most visible at dusk and, leaning out the window of the kombi, I was breathing it all in.

The Trust had purchased a 2.2 hectare property near Hilton, only a short distance from the homeland of Kwazulu and the undulating hills of Sweetwaters. The property had an existing house behind which were some old stables and a garage that had been converted into bunkhouses, as well as a small cottage that I was to share with Mama Jenny, our housekeeper. Steve, Beth and the kids were living in the main house, the front room of which was now Steve's office.

Driving through the side gate, we passed the cottage and the carport and swung to stop a in front of the main house. The yellow house lay sprawled out like a dog in the shade. Its many rooms were large and gracious and a covered stoep served as the entrance hall to the house as well as an outdoor dining room. Steve and Beth's offices flanked the glass sliding doors which opened to reveal a sizable room with a sunken floor in the middle. The sunken area was circular and created a ring of seats; there were pillows scattered around its edge. There was also a double-sided fireplace that opened out into this room as well as into the kitchen on the other side of the wall. The door to the left led down a corridor, past the bathroom and bedrooms and into the spacious kitchen. The door to the right was always closed, as this was the family space in what was otherwise a shared house.

The kitchen had a large wooden table running down the centre of the room and windows on three sides that invited the sun. From first glance, you knew that this room was to be the heart and home of the community. Steve had built in industrial stoves on the understanding that we would often be housing displaced families on site and would need to feed large numbers of people. In the back lefthand corner of the kitchen was the door through to the workshop and bunkhouses. An old garage and stables had been converted for our program purposes: bunkhouses for overnight visitors and a workspace for our employment workshops.

After greeting the family I went down to the cottage with Mama Jenny. As she'd never shared a house with a white person before, she was a little nervous about the suitability of our living arrangements. For me, it was an opportunity to learn more about the Zulu language and culture. The cottage was a simple white brick structure with a flat roof, a concrete slab at its front and an awning over the front door. The door opened into a cosy lounge with its own fireplace, then through into the corridor, right towards Mama Jenny's room and left towards mine. Across the hall from me was the bathroom we would share and to the left, the kitchen. Like the main house, the cottage was newly renovated with fresh paint and carpets and shiny kitchen appliances. It was all I would need. Dumping my bags, I started to make myself at home.

After I had unpacked and chatted to Mama Jenny about my trip—which was clearly outside her frame of reference as she had never travelled more than a few hundred kilometres from home—I went outside to explore the garden. Steve and Beth had invited me to join them for supper at seven so I still had some time to spare. Behind the cottage was its old garage that had been converted into the program offices, of which there were two: one for Lee, our project administrator and one for Robbie, my fellow fieldworker, and I to share. In front of the office was a gravel area that served as a carpark. What I had initially thought was the side entrance to the property was clearly serving as the main entrance for all our visitors, with

Lee's office doubling as a reception area. I turned back towards our cottage and up into the main part of the property.

The gardens were park-like—Beth had been as busy with them as Steve had been with the buildings. The cottage was surrounded by established trees and shrubs with a small grassy area off to the side. As I wandered up the gravel road towards the house, the garden changed to include more treeferns and cycads. The road looped out away from the house, opening onto a lush lawn at its front. Keeping to the road, I came upon a fenced-off area that housed a pool and provided a magnificent view of the city below. Beneath the pool area were two terraces, each with grassy paths that meandered through their overflowing garden beds. As the light began to fade I saw that there was still more garden to explore in the morning, but it was time to change for supper.

Mama Jenny had left the cottage when I went off to explore and now laid a hearty pot of stew on the table in the kitchen at the main house, around which we had all gathered. Mama Jenny declined the invitation to join us for supper, saying that she would take some back to the cottage and get an early night. When she joined Steve and Beth a few years earlier, she had struggled to adapt to their more informal style. She had only ever called her previous employer 'Master' and was horrified when Steve told her that a condition of her employment was that she call him Steve and his wife Beth. While she was now able to shyly call Steve by his first name, I don't know how often her confidence extended to joining the family evening meal.

Over Mama Jenny's stew, we took the opportunity to bring each other up to speed on programs, fundraising and the general comings and goings at Sizwe during recent months. Sizwe's inaugural program had been for a group of nine displaced teenagers. Steve helped them think through what it means to take refuge, to be a refugee, and what support they needed to live normal lives again. By the end of the two days, they acknowledged that their lives were now characterised by alienation, dependency, demotivation and vulnerability—these were themes that our programs and support services would need to address. The time not spent on running programs had been taken up by fundraising to cover running costs. We had also sought corporate sponsorship: for example, Toyota donated a Hiace kombi and a bakkie or small truck; and A&W International donated a photocopier.

By the time we finished dessert, my fatigue had overtaken my excitement and I was ready for bed. The whole team would be here at eight in the morning and I was eager to put faces to names. So I thanked my hosts and made my way down to the cottage where Mama Jenny had already turned in for the night. While it was strange lying in my new bed that first night, I knew that it would very quickly feel like home.

The next morning I was back up at the house for the regular Monday morning team meeting. In Steve's office, I found a number of chairs in a rough circle and took one next to Lee, a familiar face. Lee was quiet and efficient in the way of many talented administrators. She had also been Steve's secretary at the Centre for African Renewal; like me, she had been excited by the work Steve was planning to do and was quick to jump on board. Behind Lee's reserve was an adventurous spirit: she was the only female volunteer firefighter in the city and regularly went for long rides on her motorbike on weekends.

Also in the circle was Robbie, about the same age as me, who had the look of a black Santa Claus with a goatee. Robbie and I were to be fieldworkers together, a team. He was round, jolly and kind with a patience that rarely reached its limits. He had also been an activist in the area for many years and I learnt to trust his judgment implicitly in the many difficult situations we would face together. Robbie had been detained for eight months the year before for participating in a peace initiative between the two warring political parties in the area, the ANC and Inkatha. No charges were ever brought against him. Robbie now lived with his sister, Happy, and her husband in a small tin shack out on the outskirts of Edendale. It was a new extension to the township and was, as yet, poorly serviced. The original area had been razed of all its greenery and then a few hundred tin sheds had been dropped onto the sides of the hills, like seeds sown on a terrace. Robbie's contented cheerfulness always stood in stark contrast to the harshness of the valley where he lived. His initial involvement had been through Sizwe's new management committee but Steve quickly offered Robbie a job and, to our great good fortune, he accepted.

Themba was hired to run the self-employment workshops, as well as to look after the maintenance of the property. He was taller than his peers at close to 183 centimetres, lighter skinned than most, with handsome features. He had a gentle spirit, listened often and spoke wisely when he had something to say. Themba lived in Calusa in an outside room behind someone's home. He had no family in 'Maritzburg, having come from the rural areas to study and afterwards find work. Steve had met him through a local technical college and, impressed with his dedication and focus, had offered him a role.

In retrospect, we were incredibly fortunate to find two men of such high calibre to work with. Neither took on the roles for pure financial gain nor to claim the status that being employed offered. They were both selflessly committed to bringing about change in the area and worked tirelessly and with great maturity to do so. We were not so lucky with everyone who came to Sizwe.

Over the next two weeks, Robbie and I spent many hours in the red bakkie driving around the townships, meeting principals, youth leaders, attending community meetings and generally introducing me to the Sizwe network. At that time, few people in townships owned cars so each person who did was known by their car. The whole community appeared to be very familiar with both the Sizwe vehicles, the red bakkie and the green and white kombi, so much so that they acted as a passport of sorts. Sizwe already had such a good reputation in the townships that we could drive anywhere in either vehicle and be greeted by people we met on the way. This was no small comfort as I was fully aware that strange white people in townships often drew unwanted attention, the assumption being that you were somehow connected to the security forces or government departments who were yet to meet people's basic needs. Ironically,

Sizwe's positive reputation led people to believe that we were a much larger organisation than we actually were, and very soon we were struggling to keep up with the demand.

I had arranged with Steve to take a little bit of time off in that induction period as my brother was planning to visit me on his way through to London. After those first two weeks, Jon flew in and we headed off to explore the countryside. I'm told Jon and I look very alike, though he is still cross that I was dished up the blonde hair and blue eyes and he was given brown and hazel. At almost 183 centimetres, he is a good bit taller than me, but we share our family's slim build and our mother's smile.

We began our journey in the nearby Drakensburg mountains which form a ring around Lesotho, the Mountain Kingdom, in the centre of South Africa. We spent two glorious days at the Drakensburg Sun Hotel hiking, riding and talking. Jon and I were born two-and-a-half years apart and though very different in temperament and goals we have always been close, especially in our teenage years and beyond. Jon, like my mother, is a natural peacemaker, often acting as a go-between in the battles of will between my father and I that marked my adolescence. He is also a little more reserved than I, slower to make friends but a generous and committed friend once the bond is formed. I remember on family holidays going out and making new friends in all directions on the first day and bringing them back to meet my brother. Jon also has Mum's action orientation, giving him an efficiency in all he does and bringing him great success in life; he has the ability to do the work of two people in a single day without appearing to be stressed or overrun. But most of all, my brother is a listener and a kind-hearted man, and was therefore a great companion during our journey together. We hired a car which he named the Silver Streak, and spent many hours talking as we sped across the country.

During our stay in the Drakensburg, we went for an all-day horse ride through the foothills of the majestic mountains. Our sturdy mounts had taken us from one breathtaking vista to the next all morning so when we were given a chance to let loose in an open field, we took it. (It is worth mentioning that I was an accident-prone child and that I was unable to cast this affliction aside as I grew older.) In the middle of our wild flight across the open plains, my horse put his leg down a pothole and we both came asunder. Both horse and rider were remarkably lucky not to have broken a bone but I was bruised and the worse for wear for many days after that.

From the Drakensburg we drove to Port Elizabeth, or PE as it is known, my dear brother agreeing to take me to see Msizi on our trip down the coast. Msizi was in PE for work, so we met up for lunch at the beachfront. Despite my heartbursting excitement at seeing him again, it was a little awkward to be reunited in public and in front of my brother, whom he had never met. After an inadequate greeting we found a place to eat. Msizi asked if he could choose the table, my brother recalls, one at the back of the room facing the door, so Msizi could see anyone who entered. Over lunch he told us that things had been quite tense in the last month or two, with many detentions and a lot of harassment. He suspected he was next on the list; one of the reasons he was working in PE at present was that he felt too visible and accessible in the small town of Grahamstown. My brother later told me how surreal this all seemed to him whereas I seemed to be talking it all in as naturally as my next breath. As he cast around for appropriate lunchtime conversation Jon was struggling to see what Msizi and I had in common.

We stayed overnight in PE, with Jon making himself scarce that evening to give Msizi and I a chance to talk. As wonderful as it was to see him, essentially nothing had changed. We still felt as strongly for each other as we always had but saw no way to take the relationship forward—couldn't go forward, couldn't go back. We didn't know when we would next see each other, living so far apart, so it was another heavy-hearted farewell.

The next day, Jon and I headed down the garden route towards Cape Town where we stayed for a few fabulous days. From Cape

Town, I flew back to 'Maritzburg and Jon flew on to London. I was so grateful to Jon for visiting me in South Africa—it was hard to explain what my life was now like and why I had chosen it to be so, without being able to show him around. I now felt I had had that chance. He had met some of the important people in my life and our road trip had given us time simply to be together.

Back in 'Maritzburg, I soon settled down into the workshops we were running. They were a combination of youth leadership programs for young black teenagers and dialogue and development programs which brought together black and white high school groups, one from town and the other from the township, to meet and work together. We also had a constant flow of families with us who had been displaced by the violence in the area. We would feed and clothe them temporarily while assisting them to find more permanent accommodation and new schools, and generally help them to begin the long process of rebuilding their lives. The week after my return from Cape Town a family of six showed up one morning, their home having been torched by a mob the night before. The children, in particular, had been shocked into silence by the experience. Amazingly, their hair began to show patches of grey from the trauma. The situation in the township of nearby Howick was deteriorating and given our involvement with the township's high school in Mpophomeni, we would become the first port of call for many fleeing the area in the weeks to come.

The first dialogue and development program I set up and co-facilitated with Robbie was between Hilton College and Smero High School. We had invited eight boys from each school to join us for the weekend. On Friday afternoon, Robbie and I went to the township to fetch the group from Smero while Steve waited at Phezulu for the bus from Hilton College to arrive. We returned an hour later with a kombi full of nervous lads who had never stayed in a white area, let alone bunked in with white boys the same age. We parked the kombi in the carpark by the gate and began to unload. Each of the young men had brought very little with him, some holding only a plastic bag with a change of clothes. They had begun to make their way to the bunkhouses when the Hilton bus arrived. They turned and watched as out of the bus spilled eight confident young men in their matching sport uniforms, each carrying a large piece of luggage for their weekend adventure. I often wondered what the two groups thought of each other in those first moments with all the deep stereotypes passed on to them by their parents, and their parents before them, swirling around like alcohol in the veins. As we watched the faces we could spot the ones who made an effort to tuck those thoughts away, willing to give this experience a chance. We could also see the white kids who were yet to know that there was anything to be tucked away; they stepped forward with a confidence born of years of being seen, heard and in the right.

Robbie took both groups up to the bunkhouses behind the main house and sorted them into rooms, ensuring there was a good mix in each room. It was clear that some of the Hilton boys took Robbie for a worker on the property and I smiled at the thought of him running the session with them later that evening. We gave them half an hour to settle in and have a look around before we all met up on the stoep. We had planned a bit of an icebreaker to help people get to know each other, our team included. Robbie, Steve and I would run the program with Themba taking charge of the working party on the Saturday.

Soon everyone was assembled, still very much polarised into their two school groups. We took everyone out onto the lawn and asked them to take off their shoes and throw them into a big pile in the middle. Once they had done that, they formed a circle around the shoes. Steve counted to three and unleashed sixteen boys, himself, Thembo, Robbie and I into a mad scramble for shoes—any shoes. With two shoes in hand, we then had to find the owner of each shoe. It was fascinating to watch each of us approach others in the group in an effort to match shoe to owner—who did the grubby shoe belong to, the formal shoe, the tennis shoe? I was very aware of my own assumptions: what matched with black and what matched with white, dirty, dusty, new. By the end of the game, we all discovered that our assumptions were just that, assumptions, as each shoe was finally restored to its rightful place with many surprises along the way.

Next, we wanted to break down some of their physical reserve. We got them to play a game called 'the pretzel', where they once more formed a circle on the lawn, shoulder to shoulder. Each person reached into the circle and grabbed another hand in each of theirs before trying to untangle the pretzel and transforming it back into a large circle. The boys clambered over each other, and me, some laughing, some serious about solving the puzzle, delivering orders to move this way, step that. A number of Hilton boys took the lead and the Smero guys let them, I noticed. Eventually, a large circle emerged among much self-congratulation.

The ice thus broken, we took everyone through to the front room where each found a spot on a cushion somewhere around the sunken circle in the floor; this time the arrangement was a little more mixed than before. Steve asked them to talk about their expectations for the weekend and the reason they had volunteered to come. Some of the Hilton boys were boarders and wanted to get out for the weekend. Some of the Smero guys wanted to get out of the township for a couple of days. Many wanted an opportunity to meet their peers from other schools for the first time. As would often be the case, the average age of the Smero group was older than that of their Hilton peers despite the fact they were in the same year at school. The quality of black education was so poor, each class routinely comprising forty or fifty students, that many repeated a year here or there along the way to graduating. President Verwoerd, when establishing 'Bantu Education' in 1953, had said that there was no place for the black person in white society above certain forms of labour. He questioned the use of 'teaching the Bantu child mathematics where it cannot use it in practice'. Not much had changed in the education system since then.

We arranged a volleyball match before supper where the guys got to rough and tumble it a bit. And I, never wanting to be outdone by a male, rough and tumbled it with them. After a supper of Mama Jenny's famous pumpkin soup and mountains of bread, we once more adjourned to the 'pit', as it came to be called. Robbie led off this session where each person was encouraged to describe 'a day in my life' and then to talk about why those differences existed between boys of a similar age growing up in the same city. Hilton College was one of the top boys' schools in the country, a vast campus set in idyllic parklands in the hills surrounding the city. Its students were drawn from wealthy white families from all over the country. While it was beginning the process of opening its doors to students of other races, its senior years were almost exclusively white at that stage. Smero, on the other hand, consisted of two rows of classrooms resembling abandoned railway carriages dropped on a dusty playground. It had two pit toilets set back from the classrooms, one for the boys and another for the girls, which were visited only as a last resort. As in many other schools across the country, a few neighbourhood women set up informal shops on overturned boxes at the entrance to the school where they sold sweets, fruit and drinks at break times.

Some of the guys described their average school day, others what they did on a normal weekend. Either way, each group surprised the other with the shape and form of their daily lives. Once each person had taken a turn, Robbie led a discussion on why such differences existed. This discussion was always a hard one. Some of the black guys thought white people were rich because they stole their wealth from Africa and cheap African labour; others thought white people had more opportunity and easily walked into high-paying jobs. Some of the white guys thought black people were lazy and didn't want to work; others thought they were too busy making trouble to get an education and find a decent job. Sometimes these thoughts bubbled to the surface, but more often than not they were left unexpressed. Either way, the boys were yet to know each other as individuals and each group still regarded the other as representative of a larger community they had reason to mistrust.

Robbie was usually happy to leave some loose ends and finish the evening with a briefing for the next day. Breakfast would be at 7 am and we would depart half an hour later. For most of the white students, this would be the first time they had set foot in a township; with all the stories they had heard about black people being terrorists, I suspect there were a few restless sleepers in the bunkhouse.

Bright and early the next morning, we took the two vehicles down the road to Sweetwaters and wound our way along that familiar dirt road to the creche site in Imbutshana. We parked the kombi and the bakkie at the usual spot and unloaded people and equipment in quick order. The Hilton boys were keen to see what life was like in the township and I think the Smero guys were happy to be authorities on the topic and show their new friends the ropes. What they weren't so happy about was the day of hard work ahead of them. As for me, I intended to prove my worth. I was the only woman on site and perhaps they were expecting me to make lunch and pass drinks around. But never wanting to be stereotyped, I planned to work harder than any of them. I was constantly frustrated by the sexism that existed in South Africa, regardless of race, and took it on as my own personal mission to be equal in every way. So when we arrived at the creche and Themba began to allocate tasks, he knew better than to give me a light job.

The creche was a bit further advanced than the last time I had seen it. The basic wall structures were up, ready for a layer of mud literally to be thrown onto them to make a thick mud wall, and there were now sufficient rocks to throw a slab. Today, the task was to collect and prepare mud to finish the wall on one side. Themba had us working in four crews, each with their own wheelbarrow and shovels. We followed a small path down the gully to the stream where we could dig up some mud. We would then take the wheelbarrowful of mud back up the path, mix it to the right consistency and pack it onto the walls.

Given this was normally women's work, one of the local experts was on hand to show us how it was done. Steve stood back and laughed as a handful of reluctant young black men worked with a couple of keen young white men to throw mud at a wall under the instruction of a black woman, who spoke to everyone in Zulu. It was quite a sight in our South African context, and he told us so. But soon our team got the hang of it and we fell into a routine of fetching, mixing and throwing mud, no small amount of which ended up on each other. The morning passed quickly and soon we saw Beth and the kids walking up the road with Mama Jenny, bringing us all a packed lunch. My arms felt boneless with fatigue and I suspect it was the same for many others, but as we all sat around eating lunch, we talked about how much more work we would get through in the afternoon.

At about 3.30, we downed tools and reviewed our progress. Between us, we had managed to complete more than half the wall on one side. I did notice that a number of local parents had joined the work party in the afternoon, speeding our progress as the young men's enthusiasm waned. But we were mud-spattered and satisfied as we limped back to the kombi and headed back to Phezulu.

I loved the community work component of our programs as much for its impact on the community as for its impact on the group. Less than twenty-four hours earlier there had been two groups of young men politely sizing each other up; now they were forming themselves into a single group, moving from 'them' to 'us'. Toughing it out together helped them to see the individuals behind the stereotypes, to substitute the name of a friend in place of the descriptor of 'black' or 'white'. I also saw that each time we took them out together in public over the course of the program, they began to identify more and more with each other as a single group, as the broader public became the 'them'. Steve, of course, was well aware of this dynamic and therefore built it into the program.

Once we were back at Phezulu, a trail of muddy shoes and shirts was scattered between the kombi and the pool as everyone braved the cold water to wash off sweat and mud. I left them to it and went in search of a hot shower. An hour or so later, everyone was in clean clothes and part of the soccer match that had broken out on the lawn. Once more, the Smero guys had a chance to be the experts as Hilton College was a rugby school and soccer was the favourite game of every township boy. No matter where we went across the country, small boys would be kicking a ball around a dusty field on the edge of a township. Often, the ball would be made of plastic bags or some other leftovers shaped into a small globe and kicked until it was disembowelled from overuse. On the front lawn, the guys had divided themselves into two teams, mixing up the schools as they did so. Robbie and I joined in, Robbie displaying superior ball skills while I had only speed to recommend me. The game was fast and furious and, lacking an umpire, almost came to blows a few times between two enthusiastic township players until Robbie, the natural peacemaker, stepped in to settle the dispute. Before long Mama Jenny was beating the large triangle to call everyone to supper and the game was declared a draw.

After supper, we took the group to the drive-in for a night out. This time it was the Hilton boys who were in their comfort zone and they enjoyed sharing the novelty with their Smero friends. Though drive-ins were now desegregated, very few black people chose them as their evening entertainment—they lacked the vital ingredient of a car. When we arrived the young, white gate attendant gave us steely-eyed condemnation along with our tickets. We found a spot at the back and sixteen eager teenagers hastily disembarked from the two vehicles. They split up into twos and threes to explore all the drive-in had to offer, the groups now well mixed between the two schools. Robbie and I stayed with the cars while keeping an eye out for our charges. As the movie was about to start each group reappeared, some taking seats inside the kombi, others on the deck chairs we had spread out around the loud speaker. A mixed group such as ours was such a rare sight that it seemed everybody in the drive-in had one eye on us for signs of trouble.

But it wasn't until interval that trouble began. About half a dozen of the boys went to the shop to buy supplies for the second half.

Apparently some other teenage boys had questioned the presence of the Smero guys in the queue, saying they should wait until everyone else had been served. Their new Hilton friends took offence and by the time Robbie and I arrived, the shouting was about to erupt into a brawl. We exchanged glances, quickly assessed the mood and got everybody out of there. Both of us knew that Hilton College would not take kindly to its boys being in a public brawl while under our care, so we decided to cut short our evening entertainment and take everyone back to Phezulu.

All the way back home in the kombi the boys replayed the scene, full of bravado and testosterone. However, later on over coffee at Phezulu, the Smero guys explained that they often avoided town simply to save themselves that kind of harassment. A few of the Hilton boys were stopped short by this—their backgrounds had provided them with easy access to any public space—and they began to ask questions about their friends' lives and what it was like to be black in South Africa. I took this as my signal to head off to bed, the hard labour of the day suddenly hitting me after the drama of our evening had subsided.

As I lay in bed, my mind drifted over the last day and a half. It was amazing to think these teenagers had so little contact with each other that it was like introducing people from different countries. I remembered when I had first arrived in 'Maritzburg, thinking all white people heartless for doing nothing to challenge the situation that was unfolding before me. By now I had realised people were kept apart to such a degree that it was possible not to know. The media was censored and the only black person you were likely to meet in your white world would be cleaning your home. Not surprisingly, it would be most unwise for someone in your tenuous employ to start challenging your world view. And if you did want to find out, it was not as straightforward as driving into the townships to see for yourself. The only way was to be invited, and that required knowing someone who would trust you enough to tell you the truth. I saw that our program would provide a touch point for many young South

Africans, allowing them to talk to each other and see a glimpse of each other's lives. With these thoughts in my mind, I drifted off to a well-earned sleep, believing I had done a good day's work.

Steve, being a church minister, was frequently asked to preach on a Sunday. When these requests coincided with a program, we often took the group along. So by 8.30 the next morning, the guys were clean and well presented as they gathered outside a suburban church that, like the drive-in, rarely saw a mixed congregation. As we entered, all eyes were on us, something I was fast becoming used to. The church service was the same as any suburban service the world over. However, the singing this day certainly benefited from a few well-placed tenors in the congregation. I am often asked if black people are natural singers or possessed of innate rhythm. While it may be a genetic gift, what I have seen is that people simply do a lot of it. Song and movement are so much a part of family and community life that I suspect people improve with practice regardless of their natural talent or lack thereof. On this particular morning, it was clear that I and some of the Hilton boys could have done with a little more practice. When it was time for the service Steve stood up and, instead of taking to the pulpit, stood on the stairs in front. Steve spoke, as he always did, in a masterful way that blended the designated bible reading with the challenges that we faced in our daily work. He told stories of the individuals we met and asked where God was in their suffering. He suggested that God was big enough to accommodate each one of us in this divided country and that our responsibility was simply to engage. I always loved hearing Steve speak. He had a way of helping me stay connected to both my faith and my work without feeling the need to 'switch off' one commitment in order to believe in the other. Looking at the faces of the young men around me, I suspected they had been similarly affected and they seemed pleased to be part of what we were trying to achieve.

After church we returned home to run our next session of the program. This was to be facilitated by me on the topic of democracy and leadership. These issues had very different connotations in the white and black communities and my job was to help the boys thrash out their ideas on the subject, allowing them to build a common understanding of what democracy and leadership would look like in South Africa in future.

I had been facilitating groups since I was fifteen through my local church youth group, though I found this work much more complex in workshops such as these. I struggled to find the right balance between stretching and coaxing, pushing and pulling. Often the black participants would feel I didn't go far enough and the white participants, that I'd gone too far—and both would tell me so. There was always a risk of being labelled 'too political' by the white schools in town and having them withdraw their participation. Alternatively, the township youths could perceive us as having sanitised the issues to protect the white participants, and label us irrelevant. It was a fine line and I regularly found myself crossing it, or not going quite far enough. Thankfully, Robbie was always there as a backup for me if things were starting to unravel. His calm demeanour gave him a credibility that I lacked and I found he was equally impactful with both black and white kids. Over time, slowly, slowly, I learnt to hone my craft, reading the room for its undercurrents. In all honesty, though, my passion for the underdog meant that if I erred on one side it was to be too hard on the white participants, something for which Robbie would often pull me up.

During the session, some of the bonds of new friendship that had been forged began to creak and strain as the group debated democracy. The Smero guys were understandably passionate about the right to have their say on how the country was run, despite at this time having no right to vote. As a result, they saw red when the Hilton boys explained that politics was not an issue and they didn't care whether they voted or not. A heated debate ensued on the nature and value of politics, with the black guys explaining that everything that happened in their lives was political, including getting harassed by racists at the drive-in, or being stared at when they went to a suburban church, or the fact that they couldn't go to a school like

Hilton with all its privileges and wealth. Naturally, this put the Hilton guys on the defensive and it took all my facilitation skills to bring the debate to a productive close.

Not surprisingly, lunch was somewhat subdued. From the looks on people's faces, I suspected they were wondering how to make it work, both between themselves after the program ended and in the country generally when there was such a chasm between them. These thoughts were carried through into the afternoon session as we debriefed the last two days. One of the Smero guys, Mavuso, in answer to the question, 'What was most striking about this weekend?' said, 'Yesterday I saw a woman work like a man'. Gratified as I was by this backhanded compliment, I rolled my eyes at the thought of the work still to be done on issues of gender. But most of the comments were positive ones where each person expressed how they had come to the weekend with one set of beliefs about other people and were leaving with another. While they were unsure what to do with this new knowledge as they returned to their old lives, they all felt that something special had opened up for each of them.

Between them, the guys had agreed to arrange a school exchange where they would each spend a day at the other's school. We agreed to support them with this idea but I secretly wondered if it would not be salt in the wounds for the Smero guys to see Hilton College for themselves. Still, it was clear from the debrief that the program had been a real eye-opener for all. They appreciated seeing something of each other's lives, but most of all they valued meeting people from a different race and finding friends among them. This was clearly something they had not expected.

Robbie, Steve and I watched them say their goodbyes as the Hilton bus drew away and remarked on the stark contrast to their arrival two days before. Now, only the Smero guys were left and Robbie and I loaded them into the Sizwe vehicles for the convoy home. Given that many boys lived far from the school, we usually dropped them at their homes one by one. For me, this further emphasised the gulf between the lives of the two groups as we dropped each boy off at a tiny shack or a small brick four-roomed house. Driving away, I wondered how they would explain their weekend to their family and friends.

Generally, I found this afternoon drive somewhat depressing—saying goodbye to each new friend burst the bubble of possibility that had existed for me during the program. While the programs were always tiring, I also found myself completely taken up into the delicate relationships that were forming, both between people and also between the individual and a new way of looking at the world. It was engaging stuff and when it was over I often found that the cottage felt particularly empty. Steve and his family tended to keep to themselves after an event, Robbie and Themba would have gone home, and Mama Jenny often took the opportunity of having the next day off to go visiting overnight in the township.

I am, at heart, a gregarious soul and the return to Phezulu was like coming down off some kind of pharmaceutical high. I would often spend my own day off in the township so as not to be alone. I had few friends in town and the few I did know were friends of Steve's and therefore mostly married with children. In hindsight, it is clear to me that part of my need to make valuable use of my time was also to do with my fear of being alone. Some kind of grey mist lay there for me and I did what I could to avoid it.

My first program was a thrill for me from start to finish, which was a good thing as we would run two or three a month until the Christmas holidays. When I wasn't doing set-up or follow-through on programs, I was getting to know people in the township through my connection with Robbie and the members of Sizwe's management committee. I got to know Sipho and Mdu through Sizwe and through them, some other high-profile young leaders in the area, such as Skhumbuzo, Thami and others. My own community contacts began to grow, as well as my relationships with people who ran organisations that worked in the area.

One of those organisations was PASCA, the Pietermaritzburg Agency for Christian Social Awareness. I had first met them when we ran a program at the centre in Nonsuch Road where they took a session briefing our participants on the situation in the township. I became friends with Monica, an amazing German woman whose own son spent more time in detention than at home. She and her husband had moved to South Africa years before with their young family and over time they had all become deeply committed to the struggle against apartheid while still remaining members of the local Lutheran church.

Monica introduced me to a group that she was part of called the Imbali Support Group. The intention was to support families in Imbali who were affected by the violence there. Whether politically active or not, many families were being attacked in their beds as they slept. It was quoted to me more than once that year that Imbali had become the most dangerous place on earth. Murders and assassinations were commonplace and a running tally was kept by each side of the conflict. In a strange way, it was monitored like a daily share price by those living and working in the community.

In the late 1980s, politics in South Africa had such a viciousness to it after decades of more covert violence, that it was inconceivable to imagine that the following year Mandela would be released and the worm would turn. In 1989, the townships were boiling cauldrons and Imbali was one of the worst. We supported those families who were high risk by being visible in their homes by day and by night, in the hope that the presence of a white skin would deter attackers. We also hoped that when we as white people called for help, it might come. As an idealistic twenty-three-year-old I enthusiastically launched myself into the thick of it, completely disregarding the danger of such work. I became fast friends with Sipho during this time as his family frequently offered their hospitality to members of the support group.

Sipho wasn't classically good-looking but clearly had something as there was always a bevy of eager young women following him around. He was about my height, rather thin, and had a very round face which seemed slightly too large for his body. He had no features that could be described as handsome but he had intelligence and wit, and a mouth that was constantly getting him into trouble. When Sipho wasn't charming some beautiful girl, he was deeply involved in the community politics of the area. While he was too young to be in the senior ranks of the leadership, he was taken seriously by them. In another life, he would have been a philosopher or a political scientist; in this one, he was a United Democratic Front activist. The UDF was closely affiliated to the then banned ANC and though Sipho's family, many years before, had had cultural ties to the Zulu political party Inkatha, they were now actively UDF. The lines were drawn.

As a prominent UDF activist, Sipho had both Inkatha and the police to worry about. The police would regularly detain young activists, as they had done with Robbie, taking them out of circulation for a time. At one point, this practice became more sinister when an unmarked red minibus was regularly seen patrolling the streets of Imbali and hauling people away. These people rarely returned. Inkatha was also accused of targeting the homes of young activists for their nightly raids.

One Saturday night, another member of the support group and I were staying over with Sipho's family. They lived in a typical four-roomed township home in a busy part of Imbali. They had lived there for many years and knew all the neighbours intimately. We arrived in daylight so that anyone watching the house would see we planned to stay over. I was nervous as darkness fell but could only imagine how much worse it was for the family night after night. Sipho's mother gave each of us a meal of pap and meat that we ate off plates on our laps, the house not being large enough to contain a dining room table. After supper, we sat chatting in front of the TV until it was time for bed.

As we were working out how to sleep nine adults in a two-bedroomed house, we heard shots outside. A hand immediately dimmed the lights and we all dropped to the floor. A second round of shots cut through the screams, one bullet breaking the window of the lounge room we were sheltering in. We then heard a car screech off down the road, firing more shots as it went. After a few minutes of frozen silence, each of us straining to hear sounds of a return, we slowly got to our feet and looked outside. After a few more minutes had passed, we went outside to see if anyone was hurt. Neighbours were cautiously emerging up and down the street, each one checking on the welfare of the other. We quickly discovered that the next door neighbour had been shot in the arm. Perhaps we were not the target tonight. The police and the ambulance were called but we anticipated a long wait for either to arrive. We also called Monica, who arrived quickly with a few other members of the support group. The neighbour was taken to hospital while the others searched around for spent bullet shells and signs of damage. I saw that a few homes surrounding Sipho's house were pockmarked by bullets but I was unsure whether it was the result of this attack or a previous one.

While I was shaken by the events of the last hour, I found that the adrenalin rush gave me an ability to step outside myself and watch what was happening almost dispassionately. It was only much later that the shock of it set in and I was weak-kneed and teary at the thought of it. Still high on adrenalin, I had convinced Monica that I was fine and wanted to stay the night with the family. We were awake for hours afterwards, hashing and rehashing what had happened. Monica returned in the morning to check on us all and took me back to the cottage where, exhausted, I slept until lunchtime.

Mdu was another supporter of Sizwe with whom I was to form a close friendship. He worked for the South African Council of Churches and lived in Imbali with his family. His father was a minister and they lived in a large manse near the seminary at the top end of the township. Like Sipho, he was deeply committed to the struggle and, like Sipho, had a string of adoring women at his beck and call. Where Sipho drew them in on his wit, Mdu drew them with good looks. He was tall, well built and had a smile that blew the cobwebs out of the coldest heart.

Mdu came to Sizwe each month for management committee meetings. Not long after I joined the Imbali Support Group, which

Mdu saw as an unnecessarily risky pastime, he invited me to come to an Imbali Youth Organisation Peace Rally. Both Mdu and Robbie were still involved in the peace initiative despite having been in detention together for their efforts the year before. The rally was intended to bring the local township youth together and encourage an end to the violence. At some point, someone had to stop taking revenge. That Sunday, thousands gathered at the local soccer stadium. Skhumbuzo, Thami, Mdu and others addressed the crowd, calling for peace to return to the area. The atmosphere was tense as gatherings of this size, regardless of the purpose, always drew the attention of the police. After the speeches, which were interspersed with powerful songs and dancing or *toi toi*ing, the rally ended on a high note and the crowd made their way home, mostly on foot. It was the first rally I had attended in the township and I found it exhilarating. It was surreal to have seen such scenes in movies and then to be part of one, a white face in a sea of blackness. Mdu and I stayed on at the stadium until most people were gone, to make sure that everyone left safely and without incident with the police, then I dropped him home on my way back through Sweetwaters.

The next morning, Mdu phoned to tell me to stay out of the township. Two young men had been shot on their way home from the rally and all hell had broken loose. One of those who died was the cousin of a friend of mine, Nhlanhla, whom I had come to know well through the school dialogue program. The days that followed were tense as news filtered through about more deaths. I was worried about Robbie and Themba driving through on their way to work, and I was worried about Mdu and the others who were most likely targets given their role in the rally. It was not clear whether it was Inkatha and the police who were responsible, but someone did not want to see an end to the violence and had the resources to send armed gunmen to churn things up.

There has been much said about the relationship between Inkatha and the Police in Natal. Many believe that Inkatha was built up by the apartheid government as an alternative to the ANC. It has been claimed that the government was also arming Inkatha and fuelling the violence in Natal to overthrow the ANC in the province.

By the end of the week, there were eleven dead in Imbali and Sipho was missing. My stomach was in knots. It was one thing to read about 'black on black violence' in the international press, it was another thing altogether when it was your friends who were being shot at. All else fell away and it was almost impossible to concentrate on the day-to-day business of life, which seemed trivial in comparison. I didn't eat enough or sleep enough and not surprisingly, my shingles returned. To my huge relief, I heard from Sipho on the Friday. He was in hiding, but alive.

Two funerals were planned for the weekend and we were expecting trouble. The Council of Churches and PACSA asked for monitors to observe and record what happened, providing detailed statements for the lawyers who often represented those who were detained. Mdu and I volunteered. The presence of monitors, acting a little like UN peacekeepers, sometimes helped to keep the police in check. Monitors also tried to keep the mourners calm. Political funerals were emotional events where the frustrations of living under apartheid could often bubble over on both sides. Young policemen were often intimidated by the crowds who sang and *toi toi*ed as if it was a rally and not a funeral, and could become aggressive and confrontational. The mourners possessed a smouldering rage against the police for their involvement in the violence and the slightest spark could set that fire ablaze. It was our role to keep communication channels open and to keep everyone calm. If things exploded, we would then bear witness and give the lawyers enough information to pick up the pieces.

The two funerals were eerily alike, giving the weekend the feel of a Groundhog Day. I made a statement on the events of each to give to the lawyers and kept a copy in my diary.

On 31 August 1989, I arrived at the Imbali Anglican Church at 11.30 am with M and N. A large crowd had already gathered in the street outside the church, numbering between 300–400 people. I parked the van adjacent to the main gate of the church compound, amidst half a dozen police vans. Before long, several other police vans pulled up and I was parked in. After locking the van, M approached M, a local lawyer, to be updated on what had taken place before our arrival. The lawyer told us the police had informed him that only 200 people would be allowed inside the church and the rest would be given five minutes to disperse. He warned us that when the word was given to disperse, we should do so immediately, as the police 'meant business'. Approximately ten minutes after this discussion, the crowd withdrew down the street to meet the hearse at the corner. At this time, the police surrounding the church numbered approximately forty. An undetermined number were also positioned at the corner and when the crowd moved back towards the church, some ten to fifteen armed policemen escorted them on foot, followed by two more police vans in the rear and one in front, with several armed officers riding on the back of each.

In this fashion the crowd, now numbering up to six hundred, returned to the church. The crowd, consisting mainly of sixteen- to twenty-year-olds, toi-toied *as they approached. Some twenty-five policemen positioned themselves in front of the gate, armed with rifles and a few sjamboks. The hearse reached the gate and reversed to allow the coffin to be removed and taken into the church. At this point, the officer in charge, Van H, called to M and M to mediate between the crowd spokesman and the police. The crowd was silenced by its leaders to the calls of* 'bopha' *or hold. Several minutes passed without the coffin being moved. There was a group of some twenty-five relatives, mostly women, in front of the gate who had previously been denied entrance. At this point, they were ushered through the gate, followed by friends of the deceased, until they numbered two hundred. As soon as this group was inside, shouting broke out around the hearse and after several minutes, the hearse was ordered to move off and the crowd to disperse over the loudspeaker. We were given five minutes to do so. The lawyer negotiated in vain to stop the hearse leaving with the coffin still in it. He was told to 'leave the scene or he would be shot'. He complied with this directive and left. M was forced to monitor the scene alone from this point. When the word was given to disperse, half the crowd ran towards the two buses that had arrived to transport them to the cemetery. There were also many private cars and kombis present and the remainder of the group crowded into these.*

When we arrived at the cemetery, several of the cars that were following the hearse were permitted inside. At this point, M noticed five young men in the back of police van A19. He approached the police surrounding the van and asked why these boys were being detained. He was given no reply. When he asked the boys for their names, he was chased away. Their names were recorded a few minutes later from a young friend who was with them but not arrested. We were told that these boys, in their early teens, had been at the back of the crowd as it gathered outside the gates of the church. This section of the crowd, at an undetermined time in the proceedings, had been sjambokked and these five arrested. M went to the main gate several times to speak with the officer in charge. He was unresponsive and refused to communicate with M. After a small proportion of the crowd was permitted to enter the cemetery and approach the grave, the officer in charge addressed the remainder of the group over a loud speaker. We were told that this was an illegal gathering and we had three minutes to disperse. M approached the large group of policemen at the gate once more, but was told that if he did not disperse, he would be shot.

The remainder of the crowd reboarded the buses, cars and kombis. As the second bus moved off from the main gate, it was stopped by several police vans. Eighteen young men were dragged off and

> *thrown against the side of the bus. They were frisked and allowed to re-board. After we had observed their safe return, we left the cemetery and made our way directly back to town to inform lawyers of the proceedings and the names of those detained. We were told that many others had been detained in Imbali while we had been at the cemetery.*

I have no memory of monitoring either funeral that weekend, despite having made such detailed statements about the chain of events. Rereading the statement brings it all flooding back, though still in quite a surreal fashion. Other than that, I simply remember what a funeral was like, as I would attend so many, many more funerals than weddings in the years to come. I have always been troubled by my moth-eaten memory of this time, by not knowing what else has been tucked away out of reach.

The following weekend, we had a dialogue and development program scheduled so I was forced to switch my attention. I also watched in awe as Robbie continued to function effectively despite having lived in the township through the violence, and I felt I had no right to be so emotionally undone. We pulled it together and got on with the business of reconciliation, keeping our group well away from Imbali that weekend.

08 SEPTEMBER 1989
I THEE WED

THE PLEASURE OF YOUR COMPANY IS REQUESTED AT
THE WEDDING OF

SKHUMBUZO NGWENYA OF 2147 MBUBE ROAD
THE ONLY SON OF
MRS. L. NGWENYA AND MR. S. MBATHA
TO
ZONKE FAITH SHANGE OF 744 SIKHAKOTHI ROAD
THE ONLY DAUGHTER OF
MR. AND MRS. O. B. SHANGE

ON 16 SEPTEMBER, 1989
VENUE: ST. MARTIN'S ANGLICAN CHURCH (NEXT TO THULANI'S GARAGE)
TIME: 10H00
LUNCH: THUTHUKA HALL (NEXT TO NICOLS EDENDALE)

BRIDE AND GROOM TO PROCEED TO PAULPIETERSBURG FOR THE
TRADITIONAL PART OF THE WEDDING.
YOU ARE ALL INVITED TO ACCOMPANY THEM.

After the horrors of the last month, I was looking forward to attending a wedding. It was not the first traditional wedding I had been to since my return. Robbie, in my second week back, had convinced me to go with him to a wedding far from the city. As usual, I was the only white person there and despite not knowing the bride or groom, had been quickly elevated to the status of honoured guest and featured in every wedding photo that was taken that day. Robbie explained that white people were so very rarely the guests of black people that the couple took it as an honour I had joined them for their wedding. Possibly, my presence gave them some kudos in the local community. I felt like a fraud—that the colour of my skin added status to an event made me itch to get out of it.

Despite the embarrassment of being firmly wedged in the unknown bride's grasp for a full eight hours, I found the wedding itself fascinating. The most remarkable element for me was that the groom appeared to have cerebral palsy and no one treated him any differently in his rite of passage into manhood. The state of marriage in African society is a very important one. Until you marry you are seen as a child in your family and your community, regardless of your age. There is a great deal of consensus decision making done at the extended family and community level and until you marry, your opinions carry no weight. It was clear that the groom, despite his physical limitations, would take his place as a man in his community. I wondered if he would have been accorded such respect in my own culture.

Skhumbuzo and Zonke's wedding was special. They had been together for many years and shared a child, Nkhululeko, meaning 'freedom'. As Skhumbuzo was such a high profile activist, he had spent many of their years together in detention or in hiding, leaving Zonke to cope as best she could. Now, finally, with *lobola* or the bride price paid and with hope for the future, they planned to wed. The only problem was that Skhumbuzo was still restricted, which involved a form of night-time house arrest and travel restriction. He had applied to the police for a variation in his restriction and that of half the bridal party as well, as there were a number of the guests who were also restricted. After a nervous wait, permission was granted the day before the wedding.

Mdu, as one of Skhumbuzo's closest friends, was to be one of the groomsmen and had offered to be my date for the wedding but as Robbie was also going, I thought I would hang with him and be a little less visible. Thankfully, I would not be the token white person at this wedding as a number of white people including Monica and her family had been invited. I had learnt that a ten o'clock start means anywhere from 10.00 onwards, so Robbie and I arrived shortly afterwards and set about catching up with friends.

At 11.30, the bridal party was said to be on its way so we all filed into the church. It was a rendered brick building, painted a lemon yellow many years before. Inside were simple rows of wooden benches facing the pulpit at the front of the church. Above the altar, taking the place of stained glass, was a wall hanging. But what the church lacked in infrastructure the congregation made up for in enthusiasm. The front rows were filled with female relatives of the bride and groom dressed in their colourful finery. Among them was an occasional husband recognising that he was well out of his depth. The rest of the church was packed full of the township's youth, the young men dressed in T-shirts with freedom slogans blazing, the young women relishing the rare opportunity to dress to impress. Given I was not on the lookout for a new love, I felt underdressed in comparison.

Skhumbuzo, Mdu, Thami and the other groomsmen filed into the front of the church looking polished and shining. The music for the bridal procession was quickly drowned out by the women's joyous ululating, '*e le le le le le*'. The crowd broke into one of the many Zulu wedding songs, ushering the bride towards her groom. As always when a crowd sang, it began to move, this time not to the marching rhythms of *toi toi*ing, but rather in a swaying, swirling, tipping figure-of-eight movement that began at the hips and flowed through to the shoulders. Given that today was an especially joyous wedding long anticipated by all, the singing went on, leaving a blushing bride and groom standing at the front of the church soaking in the goodwill.

Eventually, the minister drew us down into our seats and greeted family and friends. He said a few words on the sanctity of marriage and its importance in our community life. He then asked Thami to step up. Thami was a large man, well over 183 centimetres with a wide girth and a powerful personality to match. He was also unusually fair skinned, leaving me to wonder about his distant parentage but not brave enough to ask. Thami turned and faced his friend and comrade. I was expecting a political speech of some nature but instead Thami began to sing. The delicate sounds of 'Ave Maria' flooded the hushed church as he sang with passion and authority. Africa was truly a place of surprising contrasts.

After Thami took his seat, Skhumbuzo and Zonke stood in front of the minister, ready to sanctify their years together. As with all the weddings I would attend, both bride and groom looked sombre: despite the celebratory mood in the church, bride and groom are required to demonstrate the seriousness of the task before them by not smiling. With the appearance of people swearing an oath of allegiance to God and State, they stood and made promises of love, obedience and fidelity before family and community.

There are three parts to an African wedding: the church ceremony, the reception and the traditional celebration the following day. What struck me about the church wedding was the way it mimicked a traditional white wedding. The brides' dresses at African church weddings were often the lacy-bodiced, full-skirted gowns of old wedding magazines, complete with long veils and flowing trains. Zonke's dress was no exception. The bridesmaids wore pastel satin dresses with puffed sleeves and tight waists, with the groom and his groomsmen looking stiff in their new tuxedos, replete with all the trimmings. I saw no need to copy Western/European rituals as African traditions have their own richness, but Robbie explained later that it was a status thing: the wedding was not a 'proper' one unless there was a white dress, a suit and a church service. Despite my own musings during the ceremony it was taken very seriously by the family, especially the women, so I kept my thoughts to myself.

It was afterwards that the wedding felt truly African. As the bridal party filed out of the church with the congregation in close pursuit, they were welcomed by those who had gathered outside. Some had intentionally arrived later, favouring the reception with its huge feast over the formality of the church service. Others had simply arrived late and had decided to wait outside, catching up with friends and neighbours, enjoying the day. Either way, the size of the wedding had more than doubled as it spilt out onto the streets. On sighting the bride and groom, the crowd outside burst into song and dance, making a narrow channel to allow the bridal party to pass through onto the street. Robbie and I joined the throng as we danced our way down the road. This felt more like it. Africa is a jubilant place where, at the slightest provocation or none at all, music and dance burst forth. This day the crowd was singing wedding songs that were both joyous and, fortunately for me, repetitious so I was soon singing along with the best of them. We danced up and down the street for almost an hour until the bridal party was herded into waiting cars to be driven to the reception hall a few kilometres away.

Robbie and I made our way back to the Sizwe bakkie followed by twenty hopeful wedding guests. Robbie made his selection of seven older women whom he believed could be squeezed into our small van. Six of these robust women, in all their wedding finery, clambered into the back and sat three abreast, facing each other. It was a tight fit, but nothing compared to the moulding of human flesh that was required in the cab between myself, Robbie and the last of our hitchhikers. Being the slimmest of the three, I sat in the middle while Robbie drove, manoeuvring the gearstick as delicately as possible between my thighs. We drove slowly and carefully along the potholed road towards the hall, the bakkie successfully bearing its burden without major complaint. The large woman sitting next to me took the opportunity to find out, in a mixture of English and

Zulu, how a young white woman finds herself at a black wedding. She had seen me before—clearly my blonde hair and fair skin were hard to miss in a township—and she was curious to know where I had come from and what my family thought about me being here. I pondered for a moment; technically, my family didn't know I was here. Since my return, I had kept many of the details of my life from them. My parents were planning to visit at Easter the following year and I felt it would be much better to show them my life rather than have them imagine it from 10,000 kilometres away. But I took the liberty and I told the woman that my parents didn't mind me being in the township and I planned to bring them here when they came to visit. My presence was one thing, but the idea of bringing my parents to visit the township seemed to really surprise her. She had a point—you didn't often see sixty-year-old white couples on social visits to the township. She just shook her head and laughed, saying things were certainly changing.

After unloading the bakkie with great care and being thoroughly thanked by our fellow travellers, we found some shade underneath a tree. The sun was at its full height and though we were only into the first few weeks of spring it was strong and punishing. Having spotted a large bull's carcass still cooking on a sheet of corrugated iron around the back Robbie told me it would be a while before lunch was ready. I suspect Robbie would have preferred to cast me off at this point and join the group of men overseeing this work but, being Robbie, he stayed with me under the tree and introduced me to members of the community that I hadn't yet had a chance to meet.

The size of the crowd seemed to have doubled once more. Robbie explained that weddings are always open affairs in townships. While invitations are sent, it is understood that anyone is welcome. Many of the poorer families rely on this generosity to feed their families over the weekends. There is always meat to be had: an African definition of a good meal. So weddings, graduations and even funerals are full community affairs where all bear witness to the events in the lives of their neighbours. I was touched by the deep sense of generosity that feeding a crowd of this size would require. The more I saw of African culture, the more I liked it. Everyone had a place in the community if they wanted one, and the investments people made seemed to be less about their individual material wellbeing and more about each other.

As the bridal party began to circulate, Mdu came to find me, cutting a dashing figure in his dark suit. He was clearly excited about the wedding of his close friend, so long in the making. I teased him about his apparent enthusiasm for weddings, but he assured me he was in no rush to attend his own. I suspected he would have a hard time choosing between the beautiful young women who orbited him. He brushed off my teasing and stated the purpose of his mission: to get me something to eat while we waited for lunch. Waving goodbye to Robbie, I followed Mdu through the crowd until we arrived at the barbecue pit. He greeted the chefs who allowed him to take a knife to their charge and, cutting a slice of meat, handed it to me. I hesitated before eating it as Msizi had long ago explained that it was rude to eat in front of others who were not themselves eating. I raised an eyebrow at Mdu who seemed to catch my meaning, saying, 'Don't worry, you're white'. It was not the first time, nor would it be the last, that I was to be excused from cultural practices. However, I wasn't sure if it was hospitality—as it clearly was in this case—or an assumption that, being white, I was a bit stupid about things and could not be expected to know how to behave. Once out of earshot of our kind barbecuers I proposed this line of thinking to Mdu, who laughed open-mouthed at my interpretation but neither confirmed nor denied it.

Mdu and I swam through the crowds for a while, finding familiar faces and chatting. Sipho was there and in good form as always. He was entertaining a group of listeners, mostly nubile young women, on the topic of recent community events. Upon seeing me, he switched to English and began to tell tales of the community development work we were doing at Sizwe. I appreciated his gesture of inclusion but reading the cold looks on the faces of the women, I told Sipho I would catch up with him a bit later. We also saw Themba with his mates Bonani, Nhlanhla and his girlfriend. We chatted briefly with the bride and groom before stumbling upon Monica with Peter and his wife, all colleagues from PACSA. We spent the final half hour before lunch was served chatting with them about some recent PACSA projects, including the Imbali Support Group work.

Mdu disappeared to join the bridal party at their table while the rest of us queued up to eat. A long line was already snaking from around the back of the hall where plates of food were being dished. Our conversation on local issues continued for a further ten minutes before Robbie reappeared. He had been asked by the family to take the four of us through to the tables. Around the bridal party were a cluster of other tables clearly reserved for family and special guests. As with the wedding I had attended with Robbie when I first arrived, I suspected the colour of our skin was the sole criteria for our inclusion and I once more felt shamed to leave my place in the queue. It seemed, however, that none of our fellow queuers held it against us as Robbie was receiving approving nods, particularly from the older women who appeared to think it was proper that we should be seated. We were served excellent cuts of beef as well as a kind of shredded meat that Monica told me was cooked until it separated into strands. Both were delicious. Along with the meat was the obligatory pap made into a paste from cornflour as well as a variety of coleslaw-style salads, mashed pumpkin (my favourite), beetroot and cabbage. We were also given pitchers of a ginger drink specially made for weddings. For dessert, we were served canned peaches and home-made custard. I caught glimpses of the army of women working in the kitchen to provide us with all our non-meat delicacies. Monica told me they would most likely all be relatives of the couple, as was tradition.

This was where my wedding experience to date had normally ended. However, this time I was going to attend the second day of festivities as well, something I was eagerly looking forward to as it was the traditional African part of the wedding. It was to be hosted by Zonke's family who lived in Paulpietersburg some two hours or so to the north. Paulpietersburg is in the middle of the popular tourist area of the battlefields where the British fought the Zulus in 1879. Despite the images projected in the movie *Zulu*, the British forces were repeatedly punished by the superior military abilities of the Zulu army up until the capture of King Cetshwayo. However, I doubted that tourists would have visited the rural village outside Paulpietersburg where we would be spending the night.

It was almost dark before Robbie and I met up at the bakkie, ready to head north. Once more we were surrounded by a group of hopefuls. Robbie made his choices, which were, thankfully, fewer this time as we had much further to go. We loaded up our fellow travellers who were each clutching a plastic shopping bag which I assumed contained their overnight essentials and headed off. For this trip, it was just Robbie and me in front so we had a good chance to chat.

As we headed north, we talked of our families and our plans for the future. Happy, Robbie's sister, and her husband were childless, so Robbie had no plans to move on from where he was. I adored Happy for she was just that. Whenever I dropped in to visit, her warmth and generosity gave her tiny home an abundance that many large ones can lack. Despite her childlessness, which must have caused her a great deal of pain in a culture where men can return a woman to her parents for such an inadequacy, she and her husband were very much in love and content in their lives together.

Eventually Robbie turned to the difficult topic of Msizi. I told him we spoke on the phone every three or four days and were still very close, but it was clear that despite our feelings for each other, Msizi would not pursue a future with me. While Robbie understood Msizi's position, he suggested that we could think about leaving the country to be together. Msizi and I hadn't discussed this option directly, but I think we both knew that neither one would be happy to be anywhere else in the foreseeable future. We left it there and drove on in silence for a while.

The discussion had brought back my feelings of being in limbo concerning my relationship with Msizi. I wasn't even sure that we were still together. We certainly still had strong feelings for each other and couldn't seem to go for more than a few days without being in touch. However, we were floating in murky uncertainty, not willing to make a move either way. I pushed these thoughts aside and asked Robbie about his love life. He told me there were a few women around. As with most of the black men I knew, Robbie did not seem to confine himself to one woman, nor was he expected to by the women themselves. I have to admit to a moment of doubt about Msizi as we drove along in the darkness. Was he stringing me along while seeing another woman or two in Grahamstown? After a moment's hesitation, I decided he was not: he had such intensity and honesty that he would have told me if he were. But the point was not lost on me that I had never thought to question his fidelity.

Before long we arrived in Paulpietersburg and from there we followed directions until we arrived at the village itself. Zonke's family had no idea how many people would be coming so I was unsure that we would find a bed. Robbie assured me that there would always be space, especially in a rural area, and that I in particular should not be worried as the neighbours would be queuing up to host the 'special guest'. I sent a sneer in his direction but knew he was right.

We pulled up outside the yard of Zonke's home and helped our stiff travellers out of the back of the bakkie. They thanked us profusely before calling out to the house to notify them of our arrival. Given all the noise in this quiet, peaceful place, I was sure they knew. Zonke's mother and aunties soon emerged to greet us and usher us inside. Their eyes widened a little when they saw me; clearly no one had mentioned that I was joining the traditional part of the wedding as well. But their surprise quickly transformed to delight and they took me by the arm and escorted me into the house.

It was much larger than the township homes I was used to and appeared to be made of the same wattle and daub construction we were using for the Sweetwaters creche—but completed with much greater skill. There was no electricity and so the house was lit with candles and paraffin lamps, the latter giving off their telltale odour.

The lounge room was packed with wedding guests, some sitting down to tea, others like ourselves newly arrived. After all the introductions and greetings were complete, which took quite a while, one of the aunties took Robbie aside to discuss arrangements for the night. He was given directions to her home a few houses down the road, where I was to stay the night. Robbie told me we would have supper here before retiring. We were then taken through to the kitchen where large pots of food were bubbling away on the coal stove. One of Zonke's cousins dished a plate each for Robbie and I and offered us a seat at the kitchen table. It had been quite a while since lunch at the reception hall and I was ravenous. The food was very similar to our lunchtime feast with a little less meat and a little more pap. I thought, not for the last time, how much a wedding must cost the family. No wonder they were often planned up to two years in advance.

After thanking our host, Robbie drove us down the road to Zonke's auntie's home. This household seemed as busy as Zonke's parents' home, so I wondered whether I would be in a bed or on the floor. As it turned out I was offered a bed that I was to share with two older female relatives. At this point, I was glad for any place to lie down, so sharing was not a problem. What I hadn't factored in was that these were endurance wedding guests, well used to a two-day affair and happy to chat about the events of the day far into the wee hours of the morning. I'm not quite sure when but eventually, at some point, I fell asleep.

The next morning, the house woke early. There was more cooking to be done for lunch and all those not cooking seemed to be making a start on washing and dressing for the big day. I feigned sleep for as long as I could, reluctantly dragging myself from the bed at about seven o'clock. I realised my mistake when the queue for hot water from the stove already seemed to be seven people long. Robbie was nowhere to be seen and I was told that he had in fact not slept here. Feeling a little lost despite the many friendly offers of breakfast, I decided to wash my face and brush my teeth at the tap outside and then go in search of a familiar face. Even with my gregariousness, lacking a good night's sleep and operating in a second language can make me a little grumpy—so I needed the space.

It was beautiful outside in the freshness of the morning's smells and sounds. There must have been a little rain during the night as the air smelt of fresh earth. The early morning is far and away my favourite time of day, so full of possibilities. In contrast, I sometimes feel a sense of regret at dusk: 'Have I made the most of the day?' The early morning light thrills me, the colours seem fuller without being harsh, and the soil and sun optimistic.

Having arrived in the dark, I had no idea of our surroundings. The village was situated on the gentle slope of a hill overlooking a broad valley. I met and greeted a few people as I strolled up the road, taking the long way round to Zonke's parents' house, enjoying the moment and its peacefulness.

By the time I entered Zonke's yard, I had spotted both our own little red bakkie and Mdu's work car. Robbie was sitting outside the house on a wooden bench having breakfast with a few of the men when I came up. He asked if I had slept well. I lied. Robbie then asked if I had eaten, but as I didn't fancy the pap and sour milk that he was holding, I lied again. I suggested we could go into town a bit later and, taking my meaning, he agreed. I then sat on the bench next to Robbie's and let the men's talk wash over me as I soaked up the early morning sun, my head resting comfortably against the wall. Some time later, I woke to Mdu calling my name. I opened one eye and peered at him before closing it again.

'Rough night?' he asked.

'Hmph', I said, hoping he would leave me in peace.

'Robbie tells me you want to go into town.'

My need for sleep was by now warring against my need for food. 'Maybe.'

'I'll take you now if you want to go.'

As we pulled into town, I reminded myself that I was with a black man in a small rural town. 'Maritzburg, being a university town, was used to occasional socialising between the races; Paulpietersburg was not. We pulled up outside a small shop that boasted a variety of tasty treats. Knowing that cereal, my favourite breakfast food, would be out of the question I was hoping for a bacon and egg burger or some close relative. The stares from the owner and fellow patrons as we entered the store made me regret coming to town but, given my hunger, there was no turning back. I went up to the counter and began reading the board, my eyes quickly settling on the burger I desired. I placed my order amid stony silence, then turned to ask Mdu what he wanted. His work at the Council of Churches put him in contact with all types of people and so, unintimidated by our reception, he looked thoughtfully at the board for some time before replying that he would have the same as me. Not wishing to push our luck, we decided to wait in the car, the man behind the counter and his customers watching in silence as we left the store. Once in the car, I lost my nerve a bit: I hadn't had enough sleep for this. After a few minutes, despite feeling a little shaky, I suggested it was best if I went back in alone. Though Mdu was not put off, for my sake he agreed. When I returned to the car with our brunch, Mdu told me I shouldn't let it get to me. 'People can think what they will', he said. I agreed with his sentiment in principle but still insisted on returning to the village straight away, feeling visible and exposed in town.

Given the nature of my work and the skin colour of my friends, I was beginning to experience the threat of violence like a gathering storm. I could hear it thundering off in the distance, gaining momentum, but had no idea when it would strike. I feared violence at the hands of the police as well as at the hands of members of the public. As I began to move regularly between town and township, city and village, it became clear to me that I only felt the threat of violence at the hands of white people. Though I knew there were community workers who had been attacked in the townships, I had no sense of danger from those around me. The murder of Amy Biehl—a visiting American Fulbright scholar and community volunteer who was killed in a township outside Cape Town two days before she was due to return home—would not take place for another four years. While the news of her death would shake me, I still believed the chances of violence against me from other quarters was far more likely.

As we pulled up near Zonke's house, it was clear that the festivities were under way. The yard was swarming like a beehive, some people intent on cooking, others on eating and a third group on some serious catching up. We entered the yard and the auntie who had housed me overnight spotted me and took me inside. I was given a seat in the lounge room and offered tea and biscuits. Female relatives spent weeks before a wedding cooking special biscuits to serve to all the well-wishers who would visit the house during the wedding week. While I was now neither hungry nor thirsty I didn't wish to appear rude so I gratefully accepted the offer.

As I sat with my tea and my plate of biscuits, watching the general flow of events, I saw a small stream of women going in and out of a particular room. As I peered around one of the women sitting opposite, I caught a glimpse of Zonke inside. She had cast aside the white gown and was now dressed in dazzling traditional African attire. Given how magnificent she looked today, I wondered why she had bothered with the white dress at all. Keen for a better look and the company of women more my own age, I got up off the couch and tried my luck at gaining entry to the bride's room. A young cousin opened the door and peered out. '*Ngi ya cela ukubona*' (I'd like to see) was as far as my language skills would take me, but it seemed to do the trick as she happily ushered me inside.

Zonke was dressed in a patterned gold and green gown with a matching headcloth and, while not the most beautiful among her peers, today she looked regal. Her bridesmaids had also lost the pastels and were now attired in strong primary colours and bold African designs. Surprisingly, it was hard to find traditional attire in South Africa and such outfits were often purchased from West African seamstresses who visited the country regularly for this purpose. I smiled at the bride: 'Zonke you look beautiful, *ubuhle kakhulu*', and she smiled back. It looked as if I had arrived just in time as she and her bridesmaids were getting finishing touches done to their make up. A few minutes later we all swept out of the room.

As Zonke made her entrance, all the women broke into loud, approving ululation, '*e le le le le le*'. The sound must have carried to the yard, as before long the sounds of ululating were heard outside as well. It was a sign that the formal part of the day was to begin. There was a sudden crush in the lounge room when Zonke's female relatives surged forward and drew her outside to the waiting crowd. On catching their first glimpse of the *makoti*, or bride, the crowd began singing. Once more they moved as a single being, urging Zonke in the direction of the neighbour's house where her groom was waiting. Skhumbuzo and his groomsmen emerged and were carried along by an excited crowd of their own. As with yesterday's wedding, people seemed to come from everywhere to enjoy the singing and dancing. I loved the idea that the celebrations were public and exuberant, not hidden away inside a stuffy golf club, stiff and formal in comparison. As the two groups merged into one, the bride and groom were brought together in its centre. The father of the bride appeared from nowhere just in time to place Zonke's hand in Skhumbuzo's and, I assume, let him know his duty of care, before the singing unbelievably cranked up another notch and we were off down the street like a huge mardi gras, all colour, movement and song.

We danced in the street for what seemed like hours. I was determined to embrace the experience, as in my own upbringing such abandon was rare. I loved feeling part of a bigger whole where there was no question of shyness or having to impress.

Finally, we exhausted ourselves and delivered our charges safely back to Zonke's house where the tables for the feast were waiting. Just as they had yesterday, the whole community flocked to join the family for a celebratory meal. I was thankful that this time I wasn't singled out for any special treatment and when I was finally handed a plate heavy with food, I was able to find a quiet spot where I could eat and enjoy the moment. Robbie found me not long after and we sat in companionable silence for a time. Dessert followed with more tea and wedding biscuits and before I knew it, it was time to start thinking about heading back. My energy was spent and I was sorely in need of some serious sleep but I felt privileged to have been invited.

I knew it was impossible to up and leave African hospitality quickly, so I began slowly 'asking the way' of the various hosts, indicating our intention to leave some time in the next hour. Each member of the family I spoke to asked if I had enjoyed myself, whether I'd had enough to eat, and wished me a safe journey and a speedy return. Once all the formalities were complete and we had collected a bakkie full of guests, we headed back to 'Maritzburg. It was very symbolic to all of us that Zonke and Skhumbuzo were finally married. Many were surprised he had lived this long, and their marriage represented a level of faith in the future. Robbie and I chatted about this and a great many other things as we headed south towards home.

On 8 February 1992 Skhumbuzo Ngwenya was gunned down outside a Pietermaritzburg restaurant in the centre of town.

At the time, he was working for a local community development organisation and had taken some international funders out to dinner to talk about funding reconstruction and development programs in Imbali. Mandela was free and negotiations were under way for a new constitution that would facilitate the first multiracial elections in the country's history. The worst now appeared to be over. Yet Skhumbuzo was gunned down as he was leaving a restaurant. It was as shocking to me then as if it had happened on the streets of Sydney. Zonke and her children were alone again. Inkatha were accused of carrying out the assassination but no one was ever charged.

09
Late September 1989
Deadly Orders

THINGS IN THE TOWNSHIP WERE TENSE WHEN I RETURNED TO 'MARITZBURG. AS IF THE WEDDING HAD BEEN THE EYE OF A STORM, A MOMENT OF NORMALITY FOR US ALL, SIPHO AND A FEW OTHERS WENT UNDERGROUND. HE HAD BEEN ON THE RUN FOR ABOUT A WEEK WHEN I GOT A CALL TO COME AND COLLECT HIM. I DROVE INTO THE TOWNSHIP TO THE AGREED MEETING POINT, PICKED HIM UP AND DROVE BACK TO PHEZULU. IT FELT SURREAL—BUT I DIDN'T DOUBT THAT WE NEEDED TO TAKE CARE. THAT EVENING WE KEPT THE LIGHTS OFF IN THE COTTAGE AND WAITED, LISTENING FOR THE SOUNDS OF TYRES OR FEET ON THE GRAVEL OUTSIDE. SIPHO SPENT THE NIGHT UNDER THE BED IN THE SPARE ROOM, JUST IN CASE. HE STAYED WITH ME FOR TWO DAYS, SLEEPING AND STAYING OUT OF SIGHT DURING THE DAY, WATCHING AND LISTENING IN THE EVENINGS. WHEN HE ASKED ME TO TAKE HIM TO ANOTHER SAFE HOUSE I WAS CONCERNED AND RELIEVED IN EQUAL PARTS. I DROPPED HIM OFF, HOPING TO SEE HIM AGAIN SOON.

In the days that followed, rumours spread about the police increasing their presence in the township. To this day, I can't explain why Sipho went home, but he did. The next day I received another call, this time asking me to come to the hospital.

Edendale hospital was located on the main road that swept through the township on its way out to the rural areas beyond. The urban townships were predominantly ANC and rural areas predominantly Inkatha. All traffic, ANC and Inkatha alike, came along Edendale Road right past the hospital. Likewise, the hospital serviced both communities.

I made my way somewhat conspicuously through the hospital grounds, the only other white people being the few foreign doctors on staff. In the men's ward I began moving from bed to bed looking for Sipho. A few beds down, my search ended—not because I had seen him but because I had spotted the two black policemen guarding him. As I'm not known for being able to hide what I'm thinking, my face must have told him that he looked as horrific as he felt. Sipho was unrecognisable. He had been shot and badly beaten. His face had ballooned to twice its size and he was covered in bruises. His eyes were swollen almost shut and his lips split and bleeding. There was a tube in the side of his chest that was draining bloody fluid from his body. I had no words and struggled to manage my feelings, flipping between rage and compassion. With the police watching me carefully—clearly, mine was an unlikely face to find in the middle of a black township hospital—I sat down and asked Sipho to tell me what had happened.

He told me a few fragments then, and more later. After a week, as soon as he could be moved, we took him back to Phezulu to recuperate. He told me that he feared for his life in hospital as many of the staff were Inkatha; somehow, Steve arranged for us to get him out. Perhaps they thought their goal of removing him from circulation was sufficiently achieved, I don't know. Unknown faces regularly appeared at his bedside and he was unsure whether they had come to finish him off or just to gloat.

Because he was unable to walk or care for himself we moved him into the cottage so that I could look after him. Over the next few days, he told me more of his story. Exhausted and hungry, he had stayed at his parents' home that night, arriving well after dark. After taking some food, he had slept and was woken at dawn by the police hammering down their door. Since the police raided the homes of activists regularly perhaps they were just lucky to find him this day. More likely, one of the many informers in the neighbourhood had earned their money the night before. Hearing the noise Sipho leapt out of bed, fully clothed as always, and ran out the back door of the small four-roomed house. He vaulted over the wire fence and ran down the narrow lane behind a row of identical houses.

He could hear the police giving chase behind him, two maybe three men, shouting for him to stop and then firing. He clambered over a corrugated iron fence at the end of the lane and as he lifted his body up, was shot by the policemen waiting on the other side. They shot at his chest five times and the others shot from behind, one bullet lodging in his lung and the other sliding in under his chin. He fell forward into the road and they pounced on him. Then they beat him and took him away, thinking that they had killed him. He remembers them discussing it over his body, saying he was dead. He doesn't know where they took him in the van except that it wasn't the police station. Wherever they took him, he said that they tortured him once they realised he was still alive. But he would not speak of it beyond that. He had been tortured before and told me of it, so I knew this was worse.

Alleged torture at the hands of the South African police has included beatings, electrocution, being sprayed with water while a bag is over your head suffocating you, and being made to stand for days on end or be beaten should you fall over. They were said to have other methods if they wanted you dead. Whatever they did I will never know, only that he emerged from it alive but changed.

Later that day, they dragged him into hospital and put two guards on him while staff tried to assess the extent of his injuries. To their surprise and later to mine, they found the five bullet holes in the front of his shirt, neatly clustered around the pocket over his heart. Yet when they peeled the shirt back, there were no corresponding wounds. The only wounds he had were from the two bullets in his back and head and the terrible beating he had received which left him essentially crippled.

Sipho's mother was a deeply religious woman who attended church services and prayer meetings on a weekly basis. Sipho featured daily in her prayers, and not without reason. As he fled the house that day, she prayed fervently for his life. She heard the shots, begged God to save his life and then ran out into the street. There she heard the policemen telling each other that Sipho was dead. She would not believe it and continued her silent vigil. Then one policeman bent over to check the body and shouted that he was still alive. As they loaded him into the van, Sipho's mother was thanking God, knowing her prayers had been answered but also knowing that he would still need her prayers. She later told me it was her prayers that protected Sipho from the bullets—a miracle. Despite having grown up in the Anglican church myself, I was struggling to fathom what had happened. While Sipho didn't doubt his mother's version, he had another explanation.

Like many black South Africans, he lived in the space between the old and the new. Many people were equal parts traditionalist and Christian, respecting ancestors and traditional medicines as well as biblical teachings. They would go to the *Sangoma*, or traditional healer, on Saturdays and church on Sundays. Sipho and a number of other young men had been going to a local *Sangoma* to ask for protection in the conflict. They believed firmly in the powers of ritual and *muti*, or herbal medicines, to keep them safe. They had sought a particular kind of protection this night, one that was rendered useless unless combined with their own courage. The *Sangoma* splashed the *muti* over them, muttering prayers of protection to the ancestors, before they leapt through the flames of a fire that had been built a little earlier. They repeated this exercise a number of times to ensure the protection was complete. This *muti* only worked from the front: if they ran from their enemies instead of having the courage to face them, they would be unprotected from behind.

Therefore it was no surprise to Sipho that the bullets which had entered his body did so from behind—into his lung and neck. Doctors had removed the bullet from his chest but had left the one lodged under his chin. Sipho wore it as a good luck charm, lifting hand to jaw to feel the lump there. My good luck charm was the shirt he had been wearing that day. As we sat discussing *muti* versus prayer, I would put my fingers in the holes in the front pocket, counting each of them in turn.

This was the first of a number of strange incidents that happened during my years in Africa. When I arrived, I was firm in my faith and world view. Over time, I simply learnt to hold it all more lightly.

After the shooting, Sipho needed another miracle. He had been so badly injured by the beating and torture that he was forced to re-learn simple tasks. He had a severe tremor in his right arm and struggled to feed and dress himself. He needed help to learn how to walk again and for many months after, could only walk with a cane. His speech was also affected, slower than before, as he struggled for the words he wanted. He had been reduced to both a baby and an old man in the same broken body.

In the weeks that followed, we spent many hours in each other's company. Some days, Sipho was light hearted and would joke about needing to be able to walk again so as to chase pretty girls. Other days, he was quiet and seemed deeply humiliated by his dependence on me for the simplest things.

Slowly, Sipho's body healed, but the spark was gone. He lived with me for many months and after he finally moved out of the cottage, he began tentatively casting around for ways to pick up the threads of his life. He was asked to work as a counsellor for young people in a similar situation of loss and damage. He did this sporadically, but spent most of his time at home despite the very real danger of re-detention. I think in the end it was out of a combination of concern for his physical and psychological well being that Monica organised a scholarship for Sipho to study in Canada. We needed to get him out, but I was afraid that a separation from everything familiar would not help his spirit heal. He left all the same and I never saw him again.

10

October 1989
Think of England

JON WROTE TO ME FROM LONDON, OFFERING TO FLY ME OUT FOR CHRISTMAS. I HAD TOLD HIM MUCH OF WHAT WAS GOING ON AND HE KNEW I NEEDED A BREAK, SO I WAS QUICK TO AGREE. SIPHO'S PRESENCE HAD BEEN A CONSTANT REMINDER OF THE SERIOUSNESS OF LIFE IN SOUTH AFRICA. SOMETIMES THE FIGHT AGAINST THE APARTHEID GOVERNMENT FELT LIKE A GAME, LIKE RUNNING THE GAUNTLET IN SOME ADOLESCENT RITE OF PASSAGE—BUT IT WAS NOT. JON'S OFFER WAS A WAY FOR ME TO FEEL SAFE, EVEN FOR A FEW WEEKS, AND I WAS SO GRATEFUL FOR IT. I WAS ALSO AWARE, HOWEVER, THAT ROBBIE, MDU AND SKHUMBUZO HAD NO WEALTHY BROTHERS WHO COULD GIVE THEM A HOLIDAY IN LONDON. FOR THEM THERE WAS NO ESCAPE, NO DETOUR; THE ONLY WAY WAS STRAIGHT THROUGH.

Despite looking forward to seeing Jon in a few months, I began to realise I was no longer just visiting South Africa as I had done the year before; I was now living here. I needed to make a home for myself. In an effort at normality, I went to the local animal shelter and bought myself a pet. There were already two dogs at Phezulu and Beth did not want a third, so I chose a cat to keep me company. As it was one of my Mondays off, I decided to call her *Msombuluku*—Monday in Zulu—and *Sombu* for short. She was a tiny thing even though she was almost a year old. She looked as if she had walked under a ladder causing paint to splatter on her white coat. Sipho wasn't as fond of her as I was—few people in the township had pets. Township animals were purely functional. Guard dogs for the most part, they were often scrawny and underfed and chained up near the gate to bark at passers-by or potential intruders.

Msizi told me early on how much he resented white people's pets which were often treated better than the family's black employees. I, on the other hand, had grown up with family pets and so the cottage didn't really feel like a home without one. Mama Jenny was hopeful that our new addition would catch any mice and rats that planned to take up residence in the cottage, so while she was happy to have Sombu, she preferred her to be underfed in order to drive her to hunt. Somehow, my little cat found her way as part of our growing household. At night, she would return from wherever she had been all day and curl up on my lap as I sat reading in the lounge. She was also something of my own, not something that I shared, and in a strange way her presence gave me a stake in our community life.

We had two other additions to our community towards the end of the year: Barry and Rags (Rags being short for the fine Scottish name Morag). They had just returned from a year at a bible college in London. Barry was a white South African who grew up in Johannesburg and Rags a white Zimbabwean whose parents still owned and ran a farm there. They knew Steve through the Centre for African Renewal and were keen to do a month's volunteering at Sizwe before returning to Johannesburg to live and work in the sprawling township of Tembisa. They were hoping to learn more about combining Christian activism and community work from the way we were doing things.

Barry and Rags were like a cleansing southeasterly wind that blew the smog out of our lives for a time. Their humour and compassion lifted the heaviness of the last few months. Rags set to work making curtains for the bunkhouses, the offices and the pit. Barry took up as Themba's apprentice, helping him set up the self-employment workshops. These workshops had come about through Beth's sister and her husband who lived in Lesotho, the small mountain kingdom in the middle of South Africa. They knew of a local there, Big Boy, who was willing to train Themba in tin craft. Big Boy recycled used oil cans into a variety of useful products and handicrafts and Themba had spent four days with him learning how it was done. He returned with hands covered in cuts and endless enthusiasm for the products. Barry was the first person Themba trained to help him, but soon we all wanted to learn. With my own hands covered in cuts, I proudly held up my first small suitcase made from an oil can.

Given the huge levels of township unemployment and the growing market in indigenous arts and crafts, the demand for Themba's workshops was immediate. Barry, not yet passing Themba's strict quality control criteria, was put to work growing the market for the workshops' products and soon we had a strong demand for products as well as participants. The self-employment arm of our work was born. Nine months later, Themba outgrew the old workshop at Phezulu and we rented a larger factory and training space in the industrial area. Many other items soon joined the product range and are still seen in craft shops all over the country and overseas.

By the end of their month with us, Barry and Rags had clearly demonstrated the value of 'associates'. As a result, the door was opened for a number of my Australian friends to come over and do volunteer work the following year. Their time with us also laid the foundation of a friendship between Rags and myself that still endures. Rags has a wonderful pragmatism: she is one of those rare people who needs very little sleep and would rather fill their days with activity. Rags can fix anything with a needle and thread, get a car moving again with a toothpick and piece of gum, build a house, tile a bathroom and make you feel better all at the same time. She never seems to get flustered and has been a shoulder for me more times than I care to remember. Rags is also a fabulous example of the spirit of the Zimbabwean people: resourceful, forgiving and quick to see the positives in daily life. In recent years, when things have become hard in that magnificent country, instead of whining when queuing days for bread, the ever-optimistic Zimbabweans have been heard to say, 'It's wonderful the people you can meet in the bread queue'.

With the school year coming to a close, we were planning to ramp up our youth leadership programs and run ten in the two months leading up to Christmas. These were run exclusively for young people in the townships and while they presented different challenges from the cross-cultural work of the dialogue and development programs, they were equally stretching for me. We talked about the consequences of good leadership and bad leadership, how to motivate others, organisational skills and time management, analytical skills and social analysis. We did a simulation exercise on power and we gave participants a project to work on over the three days that allowed them to apply what they were learning.

Many teenagers in the townships organise themselves into youth organisations in an attempt to take on local community issues. Each area within the township had a youth organisation, so we simply offered our leadership course to each group in turn. It made the organisation of the events far easier and it also meant that across Edendale, youth organisations were being equipped with a similar skill set. The work was fulfilling and I was glad to see more and more young women being involved in training that was initially almost exclusively male. It seemed that word had got out and the young women didn't want to be left out of the opportunity to further their skills.

The only downside was that I was utterly exhausted. Ten three-day workshops in eight weeks is a tidal wave of work and emotional investment, and looking after Sipho's rehabilitation on top of that took every last drop of my reserve. It was not that I resented Sipho's presence: he participated in the workshops, much to the participants' delight, as he was a bit of a legend in the area. He was still a comedian and philosopher and therefore good company. It was just that he physically needed so much support in those early months that I was constantly on my feet. By the time December rolled around, I was longing to take a break, longing for family. I was booked to fly out from Jo'burg and, as was to become my habit, stayed with Barry and Rags for a day or two to unwind before leaving.

I arrived in London three days before Christmas. My brother had spent the last few months working in Geneva on a large bank fraud investigation and was in need of a holiday himself. I found Heathrow airport disorientating as I stood waiting for Jon's familiar face to appear among what looked like a swarm of bees. Relief surged over me when I saw him and I felt close to tears. I had held back the tears for months now, not feeling that I had a right to cry; other people's funerals, other people's shootings, other people's pain, not my own. But seeing my big brother's smiling face was like a licence to feel it all and the tears began to flow. It was early evening and he took me back to the large apartment he shared with a friend who, fortunately, wasn't at home. We had some time for a quick catch-up but he already seemed to understand that I was fragile and needed looking after. So he disappeared to the small supermarket across the street and returned bearing a ready-made meal for us to share.

The following day was Jon's last at work for the year and I was happy to relax until he finished up for the day. After no more than half an hour's sleep on the plane, I didn't surface until almost noon. The chill of the night before compared to the African summer I had left behind made me reluctant to venture outside. But I also felt a need to stay safely indoors with no demands on me, no need to watch my back nor worry about anyone else. So I tucked myself up on the couch with a book all afternoon and waited for my brother's return.

At about 5.30, he breezed in to say that I should get dressed as we were going out for drinks with his workmates at a pub on the Thames. Pubs had never held much attraction for me, as someone who never smokes and rarely drinks, but I did want to be with my brother. So I changed and we jumped into one of those big black English taxis that I had only seen in the movies. That night, the tables were turned from our childhood holiday routine, with Jon being the talker and myself uncharacteristically shy.

After spending a few hours at the pub, we went on to a nearby restaurant with about half a dozen of Jon's friends who had no reason to go home. As we sat around the table chatting, I listened to the conversations of these young professionals a few years older than myself and felt a world away. They were all accountants and spoke about the world of business and finance in a way that I could not fathom, partly because the technical terminology sounded like a foreign language and partly because the things they were passionate about seemed completely unimportant in the reality I was immersed in. But his friends were kind and tried to include me, asking questions about what I was doing in Africa and about our holiday plans. Seeing my discomfort at the thought of small talk about township violence in an English pub, Jon steered the conversation to our trip. After Christmas with his girlfriend's family, we were off to the Lakes District and then on to Stirling Castle for Hogmanay, Scotland's New Year's Eve celebrations.

We called it a night at about 11.00 and took the train back home. The next day, Jon showed me a little of London and I found it oddly claustrophobic. As we walked down the narrow streets, it seemed to me that the houses and buildings bent towards each other to meet like a canopy of trees, blocking out the sky. A striking aspect of Africa is the sense of space. The sky is stretched high and blue, with cities and towns mere anthills on the rolling savannah. Everywhere there is space and an openness that pulls you out of the city landscape and into the landscape beyond. London seemed completely opposite, with its majestic buildings and urban landmarks drawing you ever deeper into the city.

After walking the streets all morning, we met up with Helen, Jon's girlfriend, for a late lunch. Jon had dated a bit towards the end of high school and through university, but I mostly remember him having a circle of close female friends who all came to him for advice on a wide range of subjects—including other men. As Jon had never had a long-term girlfriend that I knew of, meeting Helen was a new experience for me. I don't believe it is an easy thing for a sister to see a beloved brother develop a closeness to another that will, by necessity, exclude you. However, on meeting Helen, I saw that she was both generous and grounded and that there would be space in my brother's life for both of us. Helen had short dark hair surrounding a square, pretty face, and a flawless English complexion. I liked her immediately and saw that my brother did too. I knew Jon was built for marriage, for faithfulness and that he had the ability to compromise that was so necessary for a long-term relationship. I wondered whether Helen might be the one he chose.

The following day, we drove north to Helen's parents' house for Christmas. I was hoping for my first white Christmas and while it felt cold enough to herald a new ice age, the family assured me it was not cold enough for snow. Helen believed we would see some when we headed north the following day. For lunch, we sat around the family table and enjoyed a traditional English feast with Helen's parents, her younger brother, Helen, Jon and myself.

It stood in stark contrast to our Aussie Christmases at my uncle and aunt's house on the northern beaches of Sydney. All the kids would be wearing whatever new clothes we had found under the tree that morning, more often than not shorts and T-shirts with new swimsuits underneath. My aunt would put on a vast spread: seafood, cold ham and turkey, salads and breads. Between courses, there would be time for a swim in the backyard pool and the opening of more presents. Other relatives and family friends would pop by later and the adults retired to the lounge room to sip wine and chat. We kids would wolf down dessert before returning to the pool for the rest of the afternoon, playing water polo with our cousins. Our parents would eventually find their way down to the pool to referee a match and perhaps, if they succumbed to our begging, our fathers might join in. At sunset, we would be dragged from the pool, prune-like, and doze on the thirty-minute drive home, presents stashed protectively under our arms.

For my English Christmas, I was dressed a little more warmly than shorts and a T-shirt and instead of retiring to the pool, we retired to the local pub where friends and neighbours had all gathered to enjoy a lazy afternoon together. I was persuaded to try my hand at darts, with Jon and I losing the England vs Australia match in a whitewash. We returned from the pub to pick off a few leftovers before bed, Helen's parents having kindly offered to put us up for the night.

A day later, the three of us set off for the Lake District. Jon had hired a small cottage on the edge of a country town in the centre of the District, allowing us to explore its delights on a number of day trips. That first afternoon, Jon and Helen went walking alone. After the buzz of London and the containment of a family Christmas, the tranquil expanse of the Lake District allowed me to unwind and, with that unwinding, the stress of the year surfaced. I didn't want to leave the cottage, content to rest and read on the couch.

In reality, I felt safe being inside. No police, no violence, no gunshots, no red minivans, no death. While my childhood premonition of dying young strangely allowed me to find peace with the thought of a short, full life, having death surround me as it had—violent, raw and messy—had filled me with fear. In the safety of that quiet cottage, the shock of the last six months emerged, jagged and rough, tearing through my defences, leaving me feeling completely exposed.

Without explanation, Jon understood and tried to convince Helen that what I needed was space and some time to recover. However, I think my behaviour offended her, as she felt somehow responsible for showing me the wonders of the District. I know this created tension between them, with Jon trying to protect me and Helen, believing that I was having a breakdown, urging me outside as a way of helping me pull myself together.

On the third day, I agreed to an afternoon drive and a walk around a nearby lake. To my surprise, I felt weary despite a few days with my feet up and so we took a slow stroll around the lakeside. We watched the colours of the day change to purples and pinks as the light faded over the dark lake. There was even snow on the ground. We hardly saw another soul but the air was crisp and fresh enough to remind me that I was alive. The colours of the land—browns and greens, the grey of the rocks—unchanged in centuries, convinced me that wars come and go but the earth is steadfast. Perhaps the struggles of people around the world for freedom and self-determination were just a shadow that passes fleetingly over the surface of the land, soon forgotten as the earth slowly turns, millennium after millennium.

Jon had planned for us to meet up with ten other friends from work and celebrate Hogmanay at Stirling Castle. I don't remember much about Stirling itself, just that it was old beyond all my points of reference, with stone walls and cobbled streets. Of the evening at the castle, I remember long tables full of food, the music, red and black tartan, highland dancing, the presentation of the haggis. I remember my brother looking fine in full Scottish regalia, and the beautiful gowns and tuxedos of his friends, and I remember feeling incredibly grateful that Jon had brought me here, as I was not likely to experience such a thing again.

After our return from Scotland, I planned to catch up with my dear Canadian friend Elaine, who was now married and living in Paris. She had married an engineer whose latest role was to build the castle at Euro Disney. She had offered to have me come and stay for five days. Feeling a little recovered after our trip north and therefore more able to handle the thought of travelling alone in a foreign country, I boarded the train to take me to the ferry that crosses the channel. From there, I caught another train to Paris and then on to the station near Elaine's work.

The journey itself was peaceful and scenic, giving me plenty of time to read and stare out the window at the passing world. I managed to find the right platform when I changed trains in Paris, though I was truly lost when I arrived at Elaine's station only to find that my French currency was useless on all the phones. I would need to buy a phone card. No problem, I thought: six years of schoolgirl French should see me right with the fundamentals at least. Jon's last words of advice to me were to speak French, not English, as the French don't take kindly to foreigners who don't make an effort. Each time I opened my mouth to ask for assistance, however, the last language to enter my head, Zulu, was the first language to leave my mouth, causing great embarrassment on my part and confusion for the good Samaritans who were trying to help me. Ultimately, after resorting to the universal language of smiles and charades, someone kindly gave me their phone card, though I suspect it was the shortest route to put some distance between them and a somewhat emotional me.

I encountered the same language problems when I phoned Elaine's work, but was eventually told that Elaine was on her way to fetch me and we would all meet up at a nearby restaurant for dinner. It was with a rush of relief that I hugged Elaine twenty minutes later and poured out the story of my misadventures. Soon enough, she had me ensconced in a cosy restaurant with half a dozen of her friends from work, laughing about the trials and tribulations of building an American icon in France.

Elaine and I spent the next five days sightseeing, shopping, visiting museums and galleries, eating at cafes for lunch and dining in restaurants at night with Anthony, her husband. We drove down Paris's narrow streets, risked the traffic circle in the Arc de Triomphe just for fun, and could never seem to find a place to park. After the first two days, my Zulu retreated and my French returned. To celebrate, I spoke to anyone who would stop and chat along the way. I loved Paris. Most of all, I remember that heart-stopping moment when, following a tourist map of the city, I turned a corner and in front of me was Notre Dame. I wept for the sheer joy of seeing this magnificent cathedral that my teacher had spoken of so often and with such love. I spent hours devouring every inch of the monument and all it had to offer, each stained glass window, each gargoyle, each statue. I loved it all.

Too soon it was time to head back to London. Being with Elaine and Anthony in Paris was another step in the healing process and I felt my old self returning. The journey back to London was uneventful and I soon found myself in Jon's apartment. We had one last night together before I flew out to Africa—but now I was ready to go back.

11

January 1990
Mandela and the Marquee

MY RETURN TO 'MARITZBURG WAS OCCASION FOR MUCH JUBILATION, MY FRIENDS BEHAVING AS THOUGH I'D BEEN AWAY THREE MONTHS, NOT THREE WEEKS. I SUSPECT THEY THOUGHT I MIGHT NOT COME BACK. DESPITE THE ROCKY START TO MY HOLIDAYS, I RETURNED FEELING REFRESHED AND AS PASSIONATE AS EVER ABOUT THE WORK I WAS DOING. I ALSO KNEW THAT TWO VERY DEAR AUSTRALIAN FRIENDS WOULD BE ARRIVING THAT SAME WEEK TO DO SOME VOLUNTEER WORK WITH SIZWE.

The first was Pete whom I had known since high school. I attended North Sydney Girls High and Pete went to our brother school, North Sydney Boys. While they were academically separate schools, we shared a number of extracurricular activities including school musicals and Scripture Union. Pete was tall and lanky with a mop of auburn hair and a wicked sense of humour. He was also blessed with huge dollops of empathy, giving him a great way with people. During the three months he worked at Sizwe, he was able to cross cultural and language divides and made friends wherever he went. On more than one occasion we would be visiting someone in the township and at some point, Pete would disappear. When I finally managed to find him, he would somehow have organised all the kids in the street into a fast and furious game of soccer despite not having a word of Zulu to his name.

Outside of cricket and soccer, Pete's passion is teaching. He spent two years teaching in a remote area of Tanzania and is now, many years later, Head of the Maths Department at one of Sydney's prestigious private schools. But first and foremost for me, Pete was one of my best mates and I was so delighted that he was here with me in Africa.

The other volunteer was Anne, a close friend through one of the youth groups I led at church. Anne matched me in intensity and was quickly drawn into events in South Africa, particularly as we had spent many hours discussing the political situation when I was back in Sydney. She had now finished her law degree and wanted to do some volunteer work for a month or two before starting her career.

Having two dear friends with me at Sizwe was a perfect start to the year which began with a team conference to plan the events we would run. We also spent some time reviewing the previous year and how we had worked as a team. Over those five days, we had a rare opportunity to build our commitment to each other by spending unrushed time in each other's company. We saw that the high levels of stress we worked under were the greatest threat to our team and our work, so we agreed to build some team 'away days' and counselling sessions into our working year. But that would have to wait; two days after our conference we ran our first dialogue and development weekend of the year, with Girls High and Siyahlumula High. We briefed each school group on what they could expect and headed back to Phezulu to prepare.

In the early hours of 2 February, the day of Prime Minister F. W. de Klerk's famous speech announcing the unbanning of the ANC and the release of Nelson Mandela, a vicious attack was launched on an outlying area of 'Maritzburg called Table Mountain. The normally peaceful community of Maqongqo, under the Zulu Chief Maphumulo, was known as the only area where ANC and Inkatha supporters lived in relative harmony. Maphumulo had offered to take any refugees from the strife-torn townships, 'anyone who loved peace' from any political persuasion, and to give them land so that they could build a new life in this quiet rural community. Maphumulo paid for this generous middle ground that night when the community was attacked by an *impi*, or army of Zulu warriors, from the neighbouring area of KwaNyavu. The police were informed of the attack but told callers it was simply a faction fight among the clans that had been going on for hundreds of years. (A year after the attack, almost to the day, Chief Maphumulo was shot in the driveway of his home. There were rumours that a Security Police hit squad had paid for his assassination but the official inquiry was unable to determine the identity of the assailants and no one was ever charged with his murder.)

The first we knew of the Table Mountain slaughter was when hundreds of people flooded into downtown 'Maritzburg later that day. Many of those who had walked into town were children who had fled in panic, not knowing where their parents were or whether they were still alive. Calls went out immediately for help and in the absence of any state response, we agreed to postpone the program (scheduled to begin in an hour) and do what we could.

I had learnt to flick a switch in situations like this. There would be time later for the shock to sink in. Right now, people needed us to act quickly and calmly and not add to their panic. On the inside, I didn't know how I could bear more killing, more loss. Putting these thoughts aside, Robbie, Pete and I jumped in the two vehicles and headed down to the Congress of South African Trade Unions (COSATU) House, where the survivors had gathered. We found hundreds of angry and traumatised people, all needing food, clothes and a place to stay. We had agreed with Mdu, who was coordinating the response for the Council of Churches, to take the very young and the very old and begin ferrying them back to Phezulu. While we were in town, Themba, Anne and Sipho had made up as many beds as they could find; Mama Jenny added more water to the soup; Beth went to buy as much bread as the local store had in stock; and Steve organised a huge marquee for the front lawn and began phoning schools and churches for help.

By the time we returned with the first load of refugees, the girls from Siyahlumula and Girls High had arrived and refused to be sent home, saying they wanted to stay and help. They were prepared to sleep on the floor if they had to, but they wanted to be of use. So we put them to work settling each load of refugees as we dropped them off, giving them soup and bread, bedding, and finding clothes to fit from the storeroom. We had over eighty people bedded down on site that first night; some slept, others were afraid to or were woken with nightmares. We sat with them in the darkness and listened to their stories of what had happened.

In my journal I wrote:

We found 46 children who had been separated from their parents, some as young as two and three years old. Many were so acutely traumatised that a strange face, particularly a white one, would cause them to burst into hysterical tears.

I listened to story after story of tragic loss and police brutality inflicted on some so aged that even they had forgotten how old they were. There was something in the back of my mind as I sat listening: though my Zulu was still inadequate, I was understanding most of what was being said to me. The area and the circumstances in which I am learning this language mean that the vocabulary of violence and death is well known to me. Words such as 'shot', 'burnt', 'murdered', 'death' and 'fear' are quickly learnt. What this is doing to my mind, and the minds of those around me, I do not know.

Our initial plan was to house the refugees over the weekend while longer term plans were made for their care. However, government officials were busy with other issues. By the middle of the following week, Steve received a letter from the municipality: they were threatening to take legal action against Sizwe for contravening the Squatter Act and endangering public health. They also wanted assurances that Steve would not respond in this way to such crises in future. We had brought refugees into a middle class white suburb and the municipality saw red. Soon the local papers were splashed with headlines: 'Priest at the centre of the storm', 'Refugee camp set up in city', 'Row over refugees'. The more open-minded papers challenged the lack of response by the city council or the department of health and questioned the ethics of attacking those organisations who stepped in to help. There were still 450 refugees at COSATU House, and with only four toilets, public health was a serious issue.

While the issues were fought out on the front pages, we continued to look after those refugees who were staying with us. We prepared and served three meals a day, constantly washed dirty clothes, nappies and bedding, kept the children entertained and continued the search for missing parents. Each of the team seemed to have one or two children who became their favourites, but whether we chose them or they chose us, I'm not sure.

There was one little girl called Thando who stole my heart. She was one of the children who were stunned into silence by the time she arrived, but with gentle coaxing over a few days, she found her voice. She told me she was five years old and lived with her mother and brothers and sisters in Maqongqo. None of them had found their way to Phezulu, so she was here alone. Soon, she became my shadow, big eyes curious about all the newness surrounding her. She had never ridden in a car, never seen internal plumbing or a flush toilet, never touched white skin or blonde hair. I couldn't understand every question she asked, but understanding her curious nature, explained as best I could how everything worked and what it was for. There was another little boy who spent half the day on my hip and the other half trying to get there. His name was Xolani and he looked to be two years old. We knew nothing about him and simply hoped that one day soon his family would find him.

Pete was constantly surrounded by a troupe of young boys wanting him to play soccer, handball and simply wrestle them to the ground. Sipho tried to join in some of the games, as much as his limited movement would allow. We also welcomed a new fieldworker to the team that week, Mondli. I'm sure he wondered what on earth he had signed up for. But he piled in and did what he could to help our small charges.

What we thought would be a three-day exercise turned into a twelve-day marathon. After the shock of the first few days wore off, our extended community seemed to settle into a rhythm, making it easy to forget why they were here as relationships began to form. Anne watched with some concern as my attachment to the kids, Thando in particular, grew. She knew I was getting too close to Thando, making the inevitable separation hard for both of us to bear. I wanted Thando to come and sleep in the cottage with us as I felt guilty sending her to sleep in the marquee. I was too close to see the implications, but Anne was right: I was making it worse, not better. Thando, whether she found her family or not, would return to a lifestyle similar to the one she had left. I was building expectations in Thando's mind that this life was what the future looked like and that I would be in it—none of which I could promise. I think my response in a crisis was to concentrate on the individuals I could help, rather than be overwhelmed by those I couldn't. The danger was in investing so intensely in the people I was caring for that I created dependencies I could not sustain. It helped no one: not them, not me.

A week into the refugee crisis, we all gathered around the TV that Steve had set up on the lawn, connected to a lead that ran from Beth's office. It was 11 February 1990 and we all eagerly awaited the first pictures of Mandela as he was released from prison after twenty-seven years. We watched as he walked along the fence line, hand in hand with Winnie, waving at the crowds of well-wishers. All the old women crowded around the TV to see if he was still the dashing young lawyer they had loved in the early sixties, and they wept. They wept to see him once more, never thinking they would, and they wept for what the years had taken away. While his unusual height and carriage continued to speak of his royal bloodline, he was now an old man, grey-haired, with a slight hesitation in his gait. Despite the change in him, we were all still very aware that we were watching one of the world's greatest living icons return to public life. I turned to Pete and Robbie, with gooseflesh rippling up and down my arms, and tried to hold the memory of this moment. Here we sat in a marquee, surrounded by refugees, watching Mandela walk to freedom.

Everything and nothing had changed.

We continued to watch as Mandela made his way into Cape Town and gave his first speech, thanking all those who had worked for an end to apartheid and reaffirming his support for the ANC and all their work through the years of their banning. He called for unity to speed the work that would now need to be done to repair the stain wrought by apartheid. We sat glued to the TV for hours while children ran to and fro, soaking up the carnival atmosphere without understanding its source. When the speeches were done and the TV turned off, we sat together in the growing darkness and knew that we had shared a moment in history. But we were under no illusions that the worst was over.

Our makeshift refugee camp continued. The legal threats eventually blew over, with the government shamed into turning its attention to the issue of rehousing people. We had been busy at COSATU House in an attempt to locate the parents of the children we were looking after as well as the families of our elderly visitors. In the days that followed Mandela's release, we brought parents to Phezulu to be reunited with their children. We watched tearful scenes as parents searched the marquee for their children whom they had feared dead, and found them safe and well, ready to leap like small frogs into their arms.

The day came when Thando's mother arrived at the gate, having heard that we were housing lost children at Phezulu. Her husband was killed in the attack and she had hidden in the bush for days before feeling it was safe to walk to town. When she arrived at COSATU House asking about Thando, she was directed to us. She set off on foot immediately, rather than waiting for our daily visit. Now she stood over Thando, catching the child up in her skirts, head bowed down to her daughter's. She held her and wept, thanking us through her tears for looking after her little one. While I was deeply relieved that Thando's family had been found, I knew it was time to say goodbye. Relationships forged in crisis run deeper than linear time would suggest. I was profoundly bonded to this child, as caring for her had seen me through the crisis itself. I watched her as, wide-eyed, she told her mother about all the things she had seen and done while with us: from electricity and showers to TV and toys. Her mother sighed and shook her head as she smiled at me, perhaps unable to comprehend the difference between what she imagined had happened to her child and where in reality she had been. As with each family, Thando and her mother were given a parcel of clothes and food to get them started when they moved on.

We were told that the government had allocated Mason's Mill, a vacant site in the industrial area between the township and town, as medium-term accommodation for the refugees. After being reunited, the families stayed with us for a few days until the new site was opened. After twelve days of round the clock care, we began the process of shuttling families down to Mason's Mill. Some families found space inside the vacant buildings, others made their homes in the rows of tents the government had provided.

We said a sad goodbye to each family whose children or grandparents we had cared for, including Xolani and his brother who were back with their father. There was no way to know what the future might hold for these families: whether the community would re-establish itself or be lost. We did know that no one was willing to return as yet, and that people would need to rebuild their lives from Mason's Mill for now. I watched Thando and her mother as they walked away to one of the buildings. Thando turned and waved, giving me one of her dazzling smiles—a row of perfect white teeth against her dark skin. I so wanted to steer the course of her life towards something better than this shaky start might suggest, but was ultimately powerless to do so.

Our tribe of over eighty had dwindled to just a few. Where parents could not be found, other members of the extended family took the children with them. Those who remained were old women who had no one to claim them and, due to the destruction of their homes, nowhere to return to. Keeping them with us was not a real option, so after some discussions with the Chief and community organisations, they too went to Mason's Mill.

Then it was over. The marquee was dismantled leaving a brown stain on the front lawn where people's lives had been. Beds were stripped, plates put away, letters of appreciation written. We had been flooded with clothes, blankets, food and volunteers from the schools and churches we worked with, black and white. We even had students from Hilton College who had offered to act as life savers and watch over the children who swam in the pool from early in the morning until late at night. I was overcome with the generosity of our community and how they had worked together to support strangers—our community who, a year ago, were individuals and groups who only peripherally knew of each other's existence. Not only had we made a difference to the lives of the refugees but we had also become a vehicle for others to show their care and support in a time of crisis.

After the packing up was done, I sat for a while at the table on the front stoep with my journal. The table was a large wooden hexagon with sturdy logs for legs and benches all around; a table that hosted our team lunches each day, all our meals during programs and now where the children of Table Mountain had been fed and cared for.

In my journal I wrote:

The refugee crisis will become one of those experiences that improve with age. Soon we will forget the long hours, fatigue, stress and the endless washing of plates, clothes and children. We will remember the laughter and the faces of the children we love. One of the ironies for Pete and Anne is that they managed to win the undying affection of scores of children without ever saying a word to them that they understood. It must be true that actions speak louder than words.

Too tired to stand, I sat at the table and looked out over the empty lawn. I had neither slept enough nor eaten enough over the last two weeks and now I felt the physical strain on my body. The emotional strain was heavier still. It is one thing to read about such a crisis in the local or international papers. It is another thing altogether to meet the people whose lives have been fragmented; those who have seen a parent or a child hacked to death before their eyes. The horror etches itself into your bones.

Given the strength of our relationships with the families from Maqongqo, we visited Mason's Mill every other day. The joyous reunions were a constant source of amazement and delight to those who had been accommodated elsewhere. Their experience had been one of neglect, living in the shanty that COSATU House had become. While community organisations had done what they could for the 450 people crammed into the building, these refugees knew that government departments had refused to help, fighting among themselves to place the responsibility at someone else's feet. At Mason's Mill, they saw white people who had responded to the need of another community and had not forgotten them when the crisis seemed to have passed. I was proud to be part of that group, where I was able to be the kind of person I always hoped to be.

Outside of social visits to Mason's Mill, we were also able to pass over the clothes and food that continued to find their way to Phezulu. It soon became clear that our response needed to be more long-term. So Themba organised to run a few tin craft workshops to give some of the young men a skill they could take with them. To my delight, a group of mothers—having seen what the young men had produced—

approached Themba to run the workshop with them. It was this group of women who ultimately built a sustainable business out of tin craft as a way to support their families.

In the midst of this follow-up work more bad news reached us. One night, a group of armed men gathered outside the home of a friend I had made through the leadership program. She had become a powerful youth leader in her community and the men had come for her. They called out to the family in the darkness: 'Give her to us and we will leave you alone'. Her parents and two younger brothers blew out the few candles that lit their small home and sat together on the mud floor, fearing what was to come. With no response from the house, the men burst inside, dragged the young woman's father out and shot him instead. My friend, having heard there might be trouble, had slept elsewhere that night. Now she was unable to forgive herself for what that decision had cost her family.

Robbie, Pete, Anne and I attended the father's funeral that weekend in the same church where we had celebrated Skhumbuzo's wedding a few months earlier. Many of the same people were there, including Mdu, Zonke and Skhumbuzo. During the service, one woman became hysterical with grief. She was the mother of one of four young men who had been shot in another incident the night before. She begged us all to tell her why these things keep happening. 'Where was God?' she cried. The minister rose to his feet and spoke of the snake in the hearts of the few who, to increase their own power, made enemies of neighbours and forced us to bury our children. He told this mother that if we listened, we could hear God weeping with us.

There was one moment of normality for me in the river of loss that swept over us in February. Through Sizwe, we had come to know a few organisations attached to the 'Maritzburg campus of the University of Natal. One of those was ETHOS, the Evangelical Theological House of Studies. It was both a program and a residence that facilitated access to tertiary training for black men and women who wanted to become ministers and church community workers. All the applicants for the ETHOS program were people who could not gain access to university through the standard points system. Jacques and Margie, friends I had met through Msizi and Gary from Grahamstown, were moving to 'Maritzburg to live in the residence with the students and lead the community that was to be established there. Given his academic background, Jacques would also teach part of the curriculum. The principal of ETHOS, Tony, was a good friend of Steve's, as were Jacques and Margie, so the entire Sizwe team was invited to the opening.

On the Sunday night following the funeral, a *braai* was held at the new residence which was a large converted two-storey house opposite the main gate of the campus. The other partners in this venture were from CE, Concerned Evangelicals, a non-denominational organisation that represented the voice of the black evangelical churches on issues of justice, democracy, poverty and growth. CE's director was a man by the name of Moses, or Moss to his friends. With him came another CE representative by the name of Teboho. They both lived in a Johannesburg township on the far side of Soweto called Mohlakeng. Over the course of the evening, I found myself talking to both of them for quite some time. Moss was married with a baby son and I assumed Teboho's circumstances were similar. They told me of the work they did in Jo'burg and the issues around which they were lobbying the government. I enjoyed hearing more examples of work that integrated faith and social activism, as they seemed to be few and far between. What I did not know as I stood there, plate in hand, was that these two men would become important figures in my life in the years to come.

February had one more surprise in store: Mandela was coming to Durban for his first rally since his release and we were going to hear him speak. Robbie, Themba, Pete, Anne and I commandeered the Sizwe kombi and, picking up a few of the new ETHOS students on our way through town, headed off to Kings Park stadium in Durban.

It was and still is famous for the rugby matches that have been played there over the years. That day, more black people flocked to the field than ever before or since. In fact, there were so many people that the stadium could not hold us. Over 100,000 gathered on the lawns outside and waited patiently for hours for Mandela to appear.

Pete took photos of the crowd, a sea of faces to the horizon, all black except for our own. But there was nothing intimidating about a crowd that size on this day: it was akin to a rock concert, the air electric and festive in equal parts. Our entry past the marshals at the gate triggered mass head-turning and eyebrow raising that was to recur throughout the day, but our presence was also welcomed with smiles and good humour once the initial shock subsided. My growing command of the Zulu language also allowed me to chat to those around us, explaining who we were and why we were here. There were many nods of understanding when people realised we weren't white South Africans. While today, most white South Africans feel a deep kinship with Mandela and what he stands for, prior to his release he had been portrayed to the white community as a communist and a terrorist; therefore, his visit to Durban was a matter for concern rather than celebration for its white residents.

After a few hours in the sun, we were told that Mandela was on his way. The crowd erupted, 100,000 people leaping to their feet and singing liberation songs to herald his arrival. Pete, Anne and I did the same, doing our best to keep up as I was the only one even vaguely familiar with the words. ANC banners and flags were raised into the air, having not been seen since the ANC's banning decades before. Three hundred years of pent-up frustration and despair were transforming into hope like fire moving across oil, igniting the toxic liquid into dancing flame. They danced, they sang, they raised their arms in the air, they celebrated the pure joy of gathering together without the guns of the police to their heads. They called for the man who symbolised the possibility of a different future to take to the stage. As he did, the sounds of celebration, which already seemed to be at fever pitch, doubled.

It was impossible to not be caught up in the moment. Mandela towered above the other people on stage and waved his acknowledgment to the sea of joy that stretched out before him. One hundred thousand people returned his greeting. Mandela waited for the cheering to quieten and when, after almost fifteen minutes, it did not he once more raised his hands and motioned for us to sit. To a person, we did as he asked. Then the crowd held its breath and waited for him to speak, waited to hear the words of a leader that the vast majority had never seen, having been born after his imprisonment twenty-seven years before. But the power of the man and his steely commitment to freedom had been spread across generations, passed from father to son, mother to daughter, neighbour to neighbour over the decades. And now each one waited to hear him speak. I imagined that the spirits of those who had died at Sharpville, in Soweto, in the killing fields of Natal, were here with us, also waiting.

And so Mandela spoke.

'Friends, comrades, and the people of Natal, I greet you all.' The crowd erupted once more. 'I do so in the name of peace, the peace that is so desperately needed in this region.'

He went on to acknowledge all those who had worked for change, dead and living, male and female, black, white, coloured and Indian, all those whose actions had brought us to this moment in history. He then turned to the conflict in Natal, the blood-letting that had undermined the unity of black South Africans, making murky the waters of change.

'In Natal, apartheid is a deadly cancer in our midst, setting house against house and eating away at the precious ties that bound us together. This strife among ourselves wastes our energy and destroys our unity. My message to those of you involved in this battle of brother against brother is this: take your guns, your knives and your *pangas*, and throw them into the sea. Close down the death factories. End this war now!'

He then spoke of the history of Natal and all those who had worked for change. He went to the knife's edge when he gave his opinion on the role of traditional chiefs in a democratic future and the role of Inkatha itself. Outside of those hostel dwellers in Johannesburg, Natal was the only province in the country that had an Inkatha presence. And it was in Natal that the bloodshed had been the most widespread. Many chiefs had strong alliances with their traditional Zulu structures which were, for the most part, led by Inkatha members. Ironically, Chief Albert Luthuli, one of the Zulus' greatest chiefs, was also the ANC's President-General. So the lines in Natal were not clear and the roles of chiefs in a democratic future would require a respect for tradition coupled with a desire for change. As I listened to Mandela speak, I believed that there were few men who could run the gauntlet of this topic as he was now doing and still emerge with a message of unity.

'Our struggle has won the participation of every language and colour, every stripe and hue in this country. These four strands of resistance and organisation have inspired all South Africans, and provide the foundation for our struggle today.'

Listening to him speak in a rally of this size that had the permission of the government, it was easy to believe we were entering a new future. I had to remind myself that two weeks earlier, I had been living in a refugee camp and then attended funerals where 'house had turned against house'—the guns were yet to be thrown into the sea. The future Mandela spoke of was still to be created and it needed to be created here in the killing fields if it was to be possible at all.

'The ANC offers a home to all who subscribe to the principles of a free, democratic, non-racial and united South Africa. We are committed to building a single nation in our country. Our new nation will include blacks and white, Zulus and Afrikaaners, and speakers of every other language. ANC President-General Chief Luthuli said: "I personally believe that here in South Africa, with all our diversities of colour and race, we will show the world a new pattern for democracy. I think that there is a challenge to us in South Africa, to set an example for the world".'

Looking back, it's clear that we were in the presence of the only man—Nelson Mandela—who was capable of bringing the rest of the country along with him in this audacious dream. He did it when he quietly drove into the countryside to have tea with the widow of the man who had put him into prison. He did it the day he donned the Springbok rugby jersey at the World Cup and danced to the success of the South African team. He is a man who understands both the power of forgiveness and the power of symbols and his personal integrity was strong enough to bring the rest of the nation along with him on his quest to forgive and start again. Sitting in the crowd that day, we wanted to believe that it was possible; we wanted to believe that the losses that had been suffered, and those that still awaited us all, could be forgiven. But even in the short time I had been living in Natal, I saw what it was that he was asking and hoped that it could be given. What I did not know as I sat there on the grass was that the worst was still to come.

'We condemn, in the strongest possible terms, the use of violence as a way of settling differences amongst our people.'

We did not know it, but another meeting was soon to get under way a few hours to the northwest in the heart of Zululand, also discussing what would be tolerated.

'Great anger and violence can never build a nation', Mandela continued.

Meanwhile, the Zulu King was saying to his chiefs, 'Whenever there was a threat to the nation, the *Amakosi*, the chiefs, acted swiftly and decisively'.

'The apartheid regime uses this strife between us as a pretext for further oppression', said Mandela, switching from English to Zulu, his translator doing the opposite.

The Zulu King went on to denounce the behaviour of the militant youth and the action of the trade unionists, such as COSATU: 'I want to know as your King whether you approve of these patterns of behaviour so foreign to our society. If not, what are you going to do about it?'

'Let us now pledge ourselves to peace. Join hands all of you and raise them up for all to see', exhorted Mandela. Hands were joined across the crowd until each held the hand of another and raised them into the air.

'Must we allow this fire to destroy the future of our children and their children's children? Do you mean to tell me that you cannot mobilise your people in your area to stop this raging fire of anarchy?' asked the King.

'It is only the united action of you, the people that will ensure that freedom is finally achieved', Mandela said in closing.

But the King had called his chiefs to defend his kingdom and the flames began to roar. Soon, fire and ash would rain down on all of us, myself included.

12

March 1990
Seven Day War

As February turned into March, we all hoped things would settle. Because Pete and Anne were leaving later that month, we took a few days off and headed up to Umfolozi Game Reserve, a few hours up the northern Natal coast. It was a welcome break for the three of us to pretend we were simply Aussie tourists looking for a safari experience in Africa. We stayed in a small thatched rondavel in a fenced-off area of the park. In the early mornings and late afternoons, we piled into the cab of our bakkie and drove through the park.

I was hoping to recapture the magic of my game-viewing experiences in Zimbabwe, but this part of the world had a very different look and feel. The area was far larger, with the game more spread out. There were also violent afternoon thunderstorms each day that caused both the animals and ourselves to take cover. Each day, after the storm, we would all emerge, animals and people alike, and lift our heads to smell the wet soil, feeling invigorated and alive. Then we saw giraffe, rhino, zebra and impala nibbling on the rain-soaked grass, frisky in the coolness. Outside of the game viewing, it was wonderful to sit with friends in companionable silence waiting out the heat of the midday sun, friends who required no translation of meaning, no explanation of context. While it was thrilling to be living in the richness of another culture, I could not deny that it was also tiring.

We headed back to 'Maritzburg refreshed and ready to run the dialogue and development camp that we had postponed. In our team meeting later that day, we decided that instead of taking the group to church on the Sunday we would head out to Table Mountain. During the week, a few families had returned to the area to assess the damage and begin the process of rebuilding. We thought, given the role the girls had played in the first weekend of the crisis, they might like to see where these children had come from. We also debated the risk of taking the girls there if the situation was still unstable. Robbie had checked and apparently things were quiet—but we knew how quickly that could change and agreed that if there were any signs of trouble, we would turn around and come home.

The next afternoon, the girls arrived. The usual hesitant start to a new program was replaced by the reunion of old friends. As they sat around the wooden table on the stoep and recalled the events of that weekend, albeit through a shinier lens, I knew this weekend would be different from the others we had run. This group could start where most others finished and I wondered where the advantage would take us over the course of the workshop.

Early the next morning we set out for Sweetwaters. After leaving the bakkie and the kombi, we headed off on foot towards the creche. It was now recognisable as a building. The outer walls were finished, the corrugated iron roof was on and the concrete slab was laid. The slab had been a major piece of work that we began with one of the groups and continued with Fred and some of the local men the following day, laying it in two sections. Today, we were throwing the internal mud wall that separated the main room from the kitchen and storeroom. Despite the girls' enthusiasm for the task, very little mud seemed to find its way onto the wall, with most of it being plastered onto the girls themselves.

After returning to Phezulu to wash and eat, we retired to the pit to brief them for the events of the following day. We spent some time formally debriefing the whole refugee experience, something which we had done before they left to go home on the Sunday evening of that first weekend, but which now needed to be revisited. They had been watching the papers and were outraged at how Sizwe, and Steve in particular, had been treated by the council. I took the opportunity to ask them what they would have thought if they had read those articles without having been there. The white girls grudgingly admitted they would have trusted the council's actions and their parents' responses. Many of them told stories of arguments with their parents when the headlines appeared a few days after their return from Phezulu. There was hot debate on what would happen if such things were allowed to continue, with the girls trying to defend the needs of the children and their families in an attempt to humanise the word 'refugee'. Up until this point, the Siyahlumula girls were quiet and so I asked them for their thoughts. They explained that their experience of government had always been an unhappy one. They believed that the black community was always given leftovers and their needs were never taken into account.

This was a difficult concept for many of the white girls to take in. White South African society at the time was quite cut off from the rest of the world and in many ways they believed themselves to be protected from countries who didn't understand them and, within their borders, from communists who wanted to disrupt their way of life. With this was an abiding trust in the government and the police to take care of them, to act in their best interests. They were beginning to see that their black friends' experience had been the complete opposite. Had this been a normal weekend, the conversation could well have fractured the group, with the white kids refusing to believe that black people where deliberately kept down. They would have argued, as their parents often did, that it was a lack of initiative, a lack of discipline that caused black people to squander the opportunities given to them; and because of this difference in the mindsets of the races, separate development was better for all. This group of girls saw something different, something that allowed them to touch on the taboo of politics with a little less fear. The black girls saw the gap and spoke more freely into it. They talked of the poor quality of their schooling, police brutality and ongoing violence.

When they had had their say, in the silence that followed, we asked them if they would like to visit Maqongqo in the morning to see for themselves. I saw the hesitation in all the girls, black and white, but they agreed they wanted to try and find the children and their families, and to see for themselves what had happened.

Early the next morning, we were on our way out to Table Mountain. As we drove along the dusty roads, I suspect we were all wondering how the refugee children had made the walk alone in the dark. It took us an hour in the kombi. What must it have been like for them? We turned off the main road and headed for the chief's house. Culturally, it would be wrong to visit an area without first asking the permission of the chief. Steve and Robbie went inside the chief's kraal, a cluster of large rondavels surrounded by a low mud brick wall. This was the chief's rural home, though he also kept a house in 'Maritzburg. Robbie knew Chief Maphumulo through a political structure called Contralesa, a meeting of the Zulu chiefs who supported a democratic solution to the problems of the country. The chief also knew of Sizwe and our work with the refugees, so he was more than happy that we had come to visit and brought with us some of the young people who had offered their help.

From the chief's kraal, we made our way down to the local store. It was like a small general store in a country town, in both trade and purpose. It was a hub of the community, with information being bartered like eggs and fruit on the front stairs. We all got out of the kombi and sent the girls inside to boost the local economy. Meanwhile, Robbie had a chat with a few of the men sitting outside, while Pete, Anne and I wondered up the road to a small hillock for a better look at the area. We had seen a few burnt out houses along the road on the way in, but it was only from this hill that we could see the extent of the damage. We saw home after home in blackened ruins and approached one home only 50 metres away from where we stood to get a closer look at the destruction. As we came nearer, we realised that sticking out of what was left of the doorway was a burnt crutch. Pete saw it first, an image that would stay with him forever, he told me many years later. We had heard of homes being burnt with the sick and elderly inside, but to see the evidence of it was horrifying. We turned back quickly in case any of the girls had followed.

As we approached the store, we saw an army truck, or kasper, coming up the hill, now only 100 metres from where the girls stood. I knew this was what Steve had feared. It was an armoured vehicle with three soldiers carrying automatic weapons sprouting from the top like flowers in a vase. It pulled to a halt next to our kombi and the sergeant climbed down from the passenger seat. Steve walked over to meet him, I suspect to keep the conversation away from the girls who now stood silently on the stairs watching. After a few minutes Steve came over and told us that the army wanted us out, saying the area was still volatile. They had questioned Steve on what business he had bringing white schoolgirls out here like this. When he told them where he was from, they recognised the organisation and told him to leave, now. In the meantime, Robbie had been given directions to where a few of the returned families were staying. However, we all agreed that it would not be wise to disobey the instruction; we didn't want to jeopardise our work in schools, which a word in the ear of a school principal could easily do. We called the girls to get back into the vehicles and headed off down the hill, taking the ring road out of the area so that the girls could at least see the valley, or what was left of it, for themselves. The kasper followed close behind.

The issue of language had come up a number of times in our team meetings. Beth was taking lessons, Steve was trying to find the time and I seemed to be picking it up as we went along. But I felt strongly that the nature of my work demanded a fluency in Zulu that I did not currently have. I suggested that the best way to learn was to live in the township. However, there was no space with Robbie in his home in Azalea and Themba lived in a room at the back of someone's house in Caluza.

It was agreed we would ask a local family if they would be willing to take me in: Themba would approach the Skhosana family, a local minister and his wife who often took in boarders, and see if I could stay with them for two weeks. They lived up the road from Themba, right on the edge of the border between Edendale and Sweetwaters. Steve had offered me two weeks off work to allow me to immerse myself in the language and I was delighted at the thought of living in the community, not merely sleeping over as I did with the Imbali Support Group. The Skhosanas, while initially surprised at Themba's unusual request, agreed to open their home to me. They had three daughters, one around my age and two younger, so they thought they could both help me with the language during my stay. They also had three sons, an aunt and several other boarders—so it would be cosy.

A week before I was due to move into the township, Msizi came to stay. He was in Durban for two days with work and had come up to 'Maritzburg to spend the weekend with me. It was the first time I had seen him in almost nine months, despite our regular phone calls. Steve and his family were also incredibly fond of Msizi and were very excited that he was visiting. Having to share him with Steve, Beth and the kids meant that we weren't keen to spend the whole weekend visiting friends. We did go to AE to see Fred and a few others, but other than that, stayed at the cottage enjoying each other's company.

It was such a relief to see him again. I was waiting anxiously when he drove through the gate. As he got out of the car and came across the carpark, I held my breath. He took me in his arms and held me and we stayed that way for the longest time, without saying a word. During my first year here, he was my true north, the reference by which I measured all my experiences. Now, living at Phezulu, with him in Grahamstown, I was having a completely different experience working with people he didn't know. He could no longer interpret events for me in the same way. I knew that Robbie had taken over the role of being my sounding board and I trusted his judgment completely, but it was not the same. So I had to get used to the lifestyle of missing him, wishing he was still with me, hoping he was safe. Having him back, even for a few days, meant that the familiar knot in my stomach had the weekend off.

But sitting in the garden at dusk the next day, I realised that another knot was taking its place. I knew that he was holding back on me. We were still in the limbo of living in the moment, not wanting to let go but not seeing a way forward. Secretly I thought if I hung in long enough the environment would change, allowing us to find a way through; I didn't want to force the issue. But it was something else. In the end, I could only assume that it was shyness at not having seen me for so long. He was planning to come back for a week over Easter for a proper holiday, so I let it slide.

My time with Pete and Anne was at an end, with Anne heading back to Sydney and Pete travelling on to Scotland. Anne left first, catching a plane from the local Oribi airport to Johannesburg. Pete had decided on a different mode of transport, taking a long distance kombi to Jo'burg instead. There were greyhound buses that ran between the two cities but the taxis were much cheaper and therefore preferred by most black travellers. As I said my sad goodbyes to Pete at the taxi rank downtown, surrounded by hundreds of black commuters, we hardly noticed the stares that had become the bread and butter of his time in South Africa.

I watched the taxi pull off with Pete's head towering above the others. They were all squashed together like teenagers at a rock concert and I wondered whether he would regret his decision to have one last adventure before he finally left the country. As it turned out, what should have been a six-hour journey became a nine-hour one as the taxi driver took a few detours along the way, getting himself horribly lost.

Pete, in his usual good-natured way unperturbed by neither the delay nor the route choice that took him through unknown townships late at night, finally arrived at Jo'burg station at around one in the morning. He phoned a friend who had agreed to give him a bed for the night, convincing him, despite the hour, to drive downtown and fetch him from the station. Pete waited for an hour, wondering what had happened to his friend who lived only ten minutes away. He looked around the station at the many other travellers who had clearly not found accommodation for the night and were now camped on the ground asleep. Pete also saw a white policeman approach two black policemen who had been patrolling the area. The white policeman then approached Pete and asked to know his business in the train station. When Pete told him, he explained that his friend would most likely be waiting in the 'European' area of the station and proceeded to lead him through to a cleaner, brighter, well-serviced area where no one was sleeping on the ground. Pete very quickly found his friend who, though frustrated with the late night inconvenience and worried about Pete's whereabouts, took him home to a soft, clean bed for what was left of the night.

Seeing Anne and Pete go left a particularly Australian hole in my day-to-day life as I no longer had anyone with whom to share the wonder of the experiences in Africa. I missed the lightness with which Pete held his life and the balance that Anne brought to mine.

However, within a few days my own new adventure was upon me: the big day of my move to the township had arrived. The house was much larger than most—like Mdu's family home, it was a manse of sorts. This house was currently home to seventeen people, including me, though the number seemed to fluctuate. I was to share a room with the three Skhosana daughters, sleeping in one of the two bunk beds that were squashed into the room. The two older sons shared a room out the back and a number of other boarders occupied rooms in the row of five. The youngest son slept inside, apparently not yet old enough to graduate to the freedom of the outside rooms. There were also a few boys who lived with the family; I assumed they were casualties of the unrest that forced many teenagers to find other places to stay once their homes proved too dangerous. Finally, Mama Skhosana's sister, Auntie Ni, also lived there and helped to run this large household.

Baba Skhosana ran a tight patriarchal ship. Men and women had different roles and young men were allowed far greater freedom than the young women in the house; in his mind, I was to be no exception. While I am no fan of patriarchy, for once I was being treated the same—my white skin bought me no particular favours in his eyes and, strangely, I liked it.

Nonsi, the eldest daughter, was exquisitely beautiful, softly spoken and endlessly kind. Sibongile, the middle daughter, while not as beautiful as Nonsi, had a presence and a power that drew attention to her—not that she cared what other people, including her father, thought of her. The youngest daughter, Thembi, was twelve and still in school.

Regardless of our age or disposition, because we were female our day began early. We got up at dawn and heated the water for Baba Skhosana's bath. While the house had running water, which was a rare treat, only cold water ran from its taps. We would fill large pots and place them on the electric stove. After Baba Skhosana, there was a hierarchy for hot water that finished with us, young women who did not work or contribute financially to the household. Mama Skhosana would remove the water from the stove when it was ready and take it through to the bathroom where she filled the bottom of the bath. Being the head of the household, Baba had the privilege of two pots of water to everyone else's one.

Once his water had been boiled and fresh pots set to heat, we began making breakfast for those who were leaving for work or school. We would use a pot of hot water to make porridge, one of us holding the pot while the other stirred with something that felt like an oar. Plastic plates were then laid out on the kitchen table and great dollops of porridge spooned into each one, to be topped with sugar or maple syrup. It required considerable mathematical prowess to ensure that the number of bowls matched the number of diners each morning. When everything was ready Mama Skhosana announced breakfast and the household gathered in the kitchen, each person swooping on a plate. We four did not eat, but managed the logistics of the event. While the rest of the household ate—some sitting, some standing, Baba Skhosana always at the head of the table—we made sandwiches for school lunches.

By seven o'clock, the house had cleared. Setting off in his car—another rare commodity in the township—Baba Skhosana would drop the children to school before he went on his morning pastoral visits in the community. If there were any young men left at home by this time, they became suddenly invisible as the daily housework began. We dusted, scrubbed, polished, tidied, washed dishes, made beds and washed clothes. At about 10.30 we would make brunch for ourselves which usually consisted of porridge, toast and eggs. Mama Skhosana, Nonsi, Sibongile and I would then sit and chat, relaxing at the table and enjoying the rare quiet of the house. After brunch, we'd clean the kitchen quickly and then put the water on for our own baths.

Finally, once we were clean and dressed, the afternoons were our own. Nonsi and Sibongile were often keen to go to town or to a friend's house. One of Nonsi's closest friends, Zodwa, lived a few doors down in one of the outrooms next to Themba's. Zodwa was voluptuous and outspoken with an extraordinary curiosity about life that made me irresistible to her. We spent many hours discussing how things are done in African culture as compared to Australia and other countries around the world. She was the first black woman to speak to me openly about sexual norms and practices in the township. Newly married, she told me of the difference between single and married sexual politics, what the expectations were and how young women felt about it. This line of discussion led to many conversations between Nonsi, Zodwa and myself about identity, self worth, body image and meaning for women in Africa. Sometimes we were still deep in discussion by the time Themba came home from Sizwe and he would be drawn into these exchanges, judiciously adding the views of the African male. We all knew, however, that Themba was a rare man as he didn't agree with the township practice of single men having many girlfriends at one time and all the lying and manipulating that went with it. He was waiting for someone special, and we knew it.

But in my first few days in the township, these conversations were still ahead of me: I was just being introduced to Zodwa and her husband. We spent a few afternoons with her sitting on the stoep outside her room that week, but more often we all went into 'Maritzburg together to wander around the shops and see who we might bump into.

Getting to town was a whole new experience for me and one that I particularly enjoyed. From our house, which was on a road that cut across the bottom of the valley at the foot of Sweetwaters, we walked down the hill past Zodwa's and on to the shop which was about halfway to the main Sweetwaters road. The shop was set slightly back from the road, allowing trucks and kombis to enter and turn on the dirt circle out front. A few tall gum trees were dotted around the shop, giving it the only real shade on the street. The shop itself was quite large for a corner store, made of concrete blocks plastered and painted a pastel yellow and topped off with a corrugated iron roof. It sold all sorts of food stuffs, usually in small amounts, as township homes rarely had refrigerators or sufficient space to store large volumes of food. They did a roaring trade in sweets, chips and soft drinks which seemed to be the staple diet of most township children. It always surprised me that with so little money around, it was these things people chose to spend their money on.

The shop was also the local meeting point and taxi rank. As Caluza was located on the edge of Edendale, on the border with Sweetwaters, it was the end of the line for taxis. The kombis that serviced Sweetwaters tended to enter the city by taking the road past Hilton as opposed to driving through Edendale. Sweetwaters was a predominantly Inkatha area, whereas Edendale was predominantly

ANC. While Inkatha and ANC supporters fought it out in Imbali, the rest of Edendale was relatively aligned. So when the taxis arrived at our little shop, it was the last stop before turning and heading back to 'Maritzburg. As a result, taxis would wait at the shop for as many passengers as possible to fill the seats before making the return journey. In the peak hour, the turnaround was quick but at lunchtime we had to wait until the driver was ready to move. These kombis were the only form of public transport available to the majority of residents. A few homeland buses operated by the Kwazulu government ran through the valley on Edendale road, headed for the western escarpment and the valleys beyond, but they rarely stopped in Edendale valley as they carried passengers from the Inkatha-aligned areas to the west. So for Edendale residents, it was take a kombi or walk.

Each kombi could fit approximately twelve passengers, plus the driver and a young boy who collected money for the driver or helped to load people into their seats. However, some of the women who rode the taxis were so large that only three could fit along the back seat, compared to the usual four. When you entered the taxi, you made a quick mental note of who was already there and who was queuing behind you to try and pick a seat that would still allow breathing space. The taxi driver, who was paid his wages as a percentage of the takings, was always keen to fit as many people in as possible. Sometimes I imagined I saw a gleam in the driver's eyes as they spotted me, skinny as I am; I'm sure some of them thought they could easily squash me in to get an extra fare.

Once the taxi was full enough, the sliding door would close and the driver would pull out onto the road and drive at full speed towards the city. If the kombi was full, he would stop for nothing—pedestrians, potential customers, other cars, traffic lights. It was always a hair-raising ride. If the driver was particularly reckless, the older women would shout at him and try to shame him into slowing down. Sometimes it worked, mostly it didn't. If the taxi was not full, the driver would be on the lookout for more passengers.

During the quiet shift in the middle of the day, he would slow down next to pedestrians, especially female ones, and haggle prices for a lift or sometimes suggest a get-together after his shift. Generally, he would keep an eye out along the road as commuters indicated their destination intentions with hand signals; a single forefinger raised for town, a hand tilted sideways for a township on the other side of town, a finger pointed down for Imbali etc. These hand signals could be made from any location near or far and the taxi driver would screech to a halt to do a pick-up.

A friend once told me she treats taxis like wild buffalos—the most dangerous animal in the African bush—and avoids them on the assumption that they are dangerous and erratic. It would be impossible to estimate the number of deaths caused by taxis in Africa, but they are a major cause of the massive road death tolls in the continent. When you jump into a taxi, you do so with a leap of faith that the death toll will not include you. Then you busy yourself in conversation with fellow travellers so as to block out the many near accidents the driver causes on his way to town. It was these conversations that made riding the taxis so enjoyable for me. Given my tendency to strike up a conversation with anyone I meet, I fitted in extremely well in the commuter culture. It was also a great place to practise my Zulu. People generally wanted to know how on earth I happened to be in the township, why I didn't have a car like every other white person in the country and why I wasn't afraid to ride the taxis. Once these initial questions were out of the way, they wanted to know where I was living, where my family was and how they felt about what I was doing. After my first few trips to town, all of Caluza seemed to have caught up on the answers to these questions, so new ones were then posed: did I like living with black people, was I not afraid of being in the township, how did I learn to speak Zulu?

My language skills were a fascination for everyone. Very few white South Africans learn to speak African languages so when a white person does, everyone wants to hear them speak. As I had learnt my Zulu from interactions with Zulu speakers and not from a series of tapes, my intonation and vocabulary were very colloquial, which people found particularly amusing. In fact, I was a source of evening entertainment in the Skhosana household, with the family wanting to know what phrases I had picked up each day.

Whatever Nonsi, Sibongile and I got up to during the day, we needed to be home before dark. Sibongile took pleasure in telling me that it was a rule for the girls only, to keep us from sneaking off with boys. Boys, she argued, could do whatever they wanted with other people's daughters—her brothers could come home any time they pleased. Aside from this purity curfew, I knew that Mama Skhosana needed us home to help cook for the seventeen people who would be wanting their supper. Baba Skhosana wanted dinner on the table at 7 pm promptly. He and the other adults would be served their supper on the dining room table in the lounge room, with the rest of us eating in the kitchen. As with breakfast, seventeen plates would be laid out on the kitchen table: crockery for the adults and plastic for the kids—which included me as an unmarried woman. Nonsi and I would then dish the appropriate portions of food onto each plate: more meat for Baba Skhosana and any male diners and larger portions in general for adults. Supper usually consisted of chicken, rice or pap with vegetables. From time to time, we would dish red meat but this was more expensive than chicken and while the household was comparatively well off, we had many dependants who were unable to contribute financially to the running of the household.

Each night after supper, Baba Skhosana would host family prayers. These could take anywhere from thirty minutes up to an hour and a half if he thought we needed extra moral correction. He would lead out with a prayer then encourage each of us to pray simultaneously. I soon worked out the longer and louder one prayed, the more approving looks were received from Baba. After prayers, he would read a bible passage and talk to us about the principles contained therein, switching back and forth from English to Zulu. Despite my own church background, I found these evening sessions a test of endurance. I was also careful not to catch Sibongile's eye as she tried to make Nonsi and I laugh. One night she succeeded, with disastrous consequences: an extended sermon on respect for parents. When Baba pronounced the evening prayers finished there was always a collective sigh and a rush for the nearest exit. The boys would disappear outside, whether to their rooms or to the street, and we three girls would retire to our room or sometimes to chat with Auntie Ni who, despite being reliant on Baba Skhosana's goodwill, was more than willing to laugh with us about the entire family's lack of enthusiasm for religious instruction.

One night, Mama Skhosana asked if I would cook one of my favourite Australian meals for the family to try. I tried to explain that Australia doesn't really have its own style of cooking, but that our favourite meals are usually drawn from one of the many communities that make up the eclectic culture of Australia. I told her that I was a big fan of pasta, an Italian specialty that was popular all around the world. She agreed she would like to try pasta and so the next afternoon, I was sent to town with Nonsi—Sibongile being grounded for some infringement or other—to buy whatever I needed to feed the household. I decided to try a carbonara with bacon, mushrooms, herbs and cream. Mushrooms were not part of the staple diet in the township but I thought I could slip them through in the general mix of things. I also bought garlic bread and parmesan cheese, two more new entrants into the household pantry.

Nonsi and I set to it, chasing the rest of the household out of the kitchen so we would have space to work. Mama Skhosana, however, refused to take a night off, as she wanted to learn how to make something new. With her peering over my shoulder, we boiled the pasta, made the sauce and heated the garlic bread. Mama Skhosana was surprised to see the dry stalks of pasta become the soft strands that were dished onto the plates. The household waited in nervous anticipation. I was to be allowed a seat at the table tonight, given I was the guest chef, so plates were dished and brought through to the lounge. I watched Baba Skhosana as he took his first taste, trying to look enthusiastic as he felt my eyes on him. Both he and

Mama Skhosana seemed to enjoy the meal, though it was only Mama Skhosana who asked for a second helping. When I went back into the kitchen to refill her plate, I saw that my efforts had not met with a positive response from the kids' table which had half-finished plates scattered along its length. Determined not to be offended, I dished an extra helping for my biggest fan and returned to the dining table. In truth, I had no experience cooking for this many people, so the pasta was overdone and the sauce lacked flavour.

At the end of my first week in the township, I was feeling very much at home and enjoying the family with all its idiosyncrasies. I delighted in the constant company of young women my own age and felt that I was beginning to make friends with some of the neighbours as well.

That same day, Sunday 25 March 1990, the leader of the Inkatha Freedom Party, Chief Buthelezi, held a rally similar to the one Mandela had held exactly one month earlier. Inkatha supporters were bussed in from all over the province to participate but there were still only 10,000 people present to hear Buthelezi speak, in contrast to the massive crowds four weeks before. The fire of discontent that had been smouldering in the region, fanned by Buthelezi's rage at the lack of support for his rally, now burst into flames and rushed towards us all.

It was reported that a number of rally buses returning to the Inkatha area on the western escarpment behind Edendale valley were stoned as they passed down Edendale Road. Knowing of the rally, Edendale community leaders had requested that police re-route the buses so as not to inflame the situation but this had not happened. Large numbers of young people who had allegedly been chased off the escarpment by Inkatha for refusing to join were now living in Edendale and it was thought to be these youths who had stoned the buses. Some of the other buses from the rally were seen stopping at Edendale hospital, allowing a group to disembark.

There had also been rumours of an Inkatha march through Edendale after the rally. While this did not eventuate, people at the soccer stadium next to the hospital were reportedly attacked and there was a clash between police and local Edendale youth on Edendale Road.

All this happened on the Sunday evening while we were at church a few kilometres away. Later that night, rumours of unrest reached Caluza, but such rumours were frequent and we thought nothing of them. We learnt later that three people had been killed after attacks from the bus occupants, allegedly those who had disembarked at the hospital.

The following day, Monday 26 March, things were quiet again and we went about our daily routine of heating water, making breakfast and cleaning. After lunch, we went down to Zodwa's for the afternoon. The usual evening prayers were said and we went to bed.

On the Tuesday morning, after our chores were done, I sat down to write a letter to an old school friend, Grace, who was also one of my sponsors. After describing the rhythms of my new life, I went on to write:

> *This may sound a little bizarre, but at the moment, the lower part of my area here in Caluza is under attack. All the kids were sent home from school, as it's just next to the fighting. We are safe here, so don't worry. But we hear the occasional gunshot and can see the crowds. Well, that's life here at the moment. Nothing has changed yet.*

Other residents who were closer to the attack got a clearer picture of the magnitude of what was happening. Years later, in 1996, Mrs Mkhize of Caluza made the following statement to the Truth and Reconciliation Commission:

> *We saw big lorries, twenty-nine of them—I counted—they were the big Kwazulu government ones with the number plates. These lorries had many people on board. As we were listening we could hear them singing songs as though they were chanting*

Christian songs. That led us to be confused as to what was happening. As the lorries approached it got us in a panic state. Suddenly we saw children running, coming in our direction and shouting 'Inkatha, Inkatha'. We went to the other road, running, trying to meet the children from school. They told us that the principal released them because it was not safe, saying they should go back home. I went home to phone the Natal Witness newspaper to report the matter. I went back down towards the school where the road crosses Caluza towards Sweetwaters and there I found the youth of Caluza being pushed back by the police. I met the journalist and said, 'I am the one who called you'. He was in such a state, panicking and tense. There were police talking to him and telling him that as he was there, they cannot protect him, he should leave. I spoke to the police and asked them why they don't speak to Inkatha, as they were the ones who were coming to us. I was told to go back home. I had my baby on my back and now I was scared so I went back home. The youth were angry as there was a rumour now that Inkatha wanted to sweep Caluza and kill every resident so that the land will return to the chief.

That was the beginning. We were fighting against people who were fully armed. Inkatha had rifles, R1s and R5s and major ammunition. Most of the youth were injured and taken to Edendale Hospital but were told, 'You are from Caluza and are obviously UDF (ANC)', and they were not helped after that.

Reports were later compiled by monitoring organisations, describing what happened that day. The reports, including this one from the University of Natal, were presented to the Truth and Reconciliation Commission.

Tuesday the 27th of March, from early in the morning there were attacks on Caluza, which if people can see on the map is on the north side of Edendale. It abuts onto the Sweetwaters area of

Vulindlela. Combatants totalled about 2500 to 3000. The attacks were co-coordinated. Groups of about 300-odd would peel off to move to the left or right. In Caluza, a number of people were shot. 130 gunshot cases were reported at Edendale Hospital alone. Houses were burnt, looting took place. Police vehicles were present but police seemed unable to halt this massive movement of forces several thousand strong. At Caluza, armed warriors filed past police to move on to attack other areas. By contrast the defensive actions by residents were dispersed by the police. A number of claims were made that police were handing ammunition over to the Inkatha forces. Later in the day some of these forces withdrew, camping in the Mphumuza area of the northern flank of Edendale in Chief Zondi's homestead.

We could see Mphumuza from the Skhosanas' front stoep. It is also the area where we had been building the community creche in the dialogue and development programs. By late afternoon that Tuesday, we knew things were bad. We also knew that we were cut off. The only road out, where the morning's attacks had first taken place, was below us. Inkatha *impis* or armies were camped up the valley across from us. They were on the road by the water tower above us and behind us—houses were burning all around. I stood on the front stoep next to Baba Skhosana, ears and eyes straining into the growing darkness, and wondered whether we would live through this.

None of us slept that night. We could hear gunshots echoing through the valley. As usual, we women had cooked for the household. But few people had eaten. Each of us had an ear tuned, listening for noises outside. We knew that the young men of Caluza were on the streets in an effort to protect their families. All the young men from our household were also somewhere in the darkness. They had been organised into groups of five or ten youths and each group had a whistle which was to be used in the event of an attack. Each family gathered whatever they had—garden tools, spears, machetes—and handed them to the marshals to be distributed. I knew there were also a few guns, some homemade, some not, but I don't know where they had come from. One of the boarders, Bonani, came back to the house to see if we had any food to spare. Nonsi and I went with him to feed the group that were camped a few hundred metres up from our house. As scared as I was, it gave me something to do, which was better than sitting and waiting for an attack. Sometime after two o'clock, Baba Skhosana made us all go to bed. Nonsi and I went to our room but lay fully clothed on top of our beds, shoes still on, ready to run if we needed to. We talked until dawn, too afraid to close our eyes.

Wednesday, 28 March. People in many parts of the western escarpment were attempting to live outside of political allegiances, hoping that it would be safer to be non-partisan. This did not save them from the attacks that rained down on the area. An Inkatha *impi* some 12,000 strong attacked families on the escarpment who would not align. Convoys of lorries dropped the Inkatha men off at various locations along the main road. One hundred and twenty homes were burnt, eleven men and women were killed. The police were reportedly present but did not intervene.

The university's report to the Truth and Reconciliation Commission said:

> *Back in Edendale, in the Umphumuza/Caluza sector, there were various forays by Inkatha forces. Police were shot at by defenders on a number of occasions, and they in turn opened fire on defenders and a number of people were killed.*

By dawn, I needed to get out. Hiding inside the house, listening in the dark for sounds of gunfire or footsteps, I felt like a trapped animal. Despite Mama Skhosana's concerns, I went onto the street to see what was happening. The group of young men defending above the house had grown with the inclusion of people like myself, people who had emerged from their homes to see if the danger had passed. But the mood on the street told me that it had not. I could still see the *impi* further up the valley.

I returned to the house to see about breakfast. The previous evening Mama Skhosana had sent one of the boys to the shop down the road to buy whatever staples he could. We agreed that sandwiches would be the easiest to distribute to the young men for their breakfast and set to making as many as we could. I returned to the street with three loaves worth of peanut butter sandwiches and handed them out. I had no appetite myself and only returned to the house when all the sandwiches were gone.

We were encouraged to do some housework rather than sitting and staring out the windows but after half an hour, I felt trapped again. I slipped out, having Nonsi cover for me and went down the street to a neighbour's house. The husband was principal of a school further along Edendale valley and his young children spent quite a bit of time over at our house. But today he and his family were waiting at home, like everyone else. I was offered tea. African hospitality still existed, even under these circumstances. I settled for water. We discussed what the principal had seen yesterday on his way back from school, mulled over what rumours they had heard and began guessing how far away the gunfire had been last night. After a time, we went outside to see where the *impi* was and found many people on the street, all gazing up the valley with the same intent. Whether the *impi* had gone inside the chief's *kraal* or homestead, or had dispersed, we could not tell. There was much speculation in the crowd. Suddenly, we heard gunshots close by, coming from the north. The whole street was on its knees instantaneously, waiting for the next round of fire. From listening during the night, I was beginning to learn the difference between the sounds of manufactured and homemade weapons, the latter sounding more tinny and echoey, as if the bullet took longer to reach you. This gunfire sounded homemade. '*Qasha*', the young men called out, confirming my thoughts. With the homemade guns, a second round of fire was less likely so people generally got to their feet a little more quickly. Taking my lead from those around me, I stood up and made my way back home.

In the afternoon we prepared more food to take to the young men, some of whom had come inside to take a nap in preparation for the long night ahead. After distributing the food, I sat down among the group of defenders. Mama Skhosana only agreed to me going outside again if I covered up my hair and skin so they would not draw attention to me. I was wearing jeans and a long-sleeved shirt plus a balaclava that I had rolled up into more of a cap, with my hair tucked underneath. There was much conversation as to what was going to happen next. Most people were convinced that more attacks would come in the darkness. We could hear gunfire in the distance but couldn't see anyone on the road above the house. This road ran up to a large water tower, then turned up the valley and looped back down to Sweetwaters Road on a dirt track that ran parallel to our street. The dirt track was about five or six hundred metres away from where we sat, a deep *donga* or gully separating the two roads.

It was hard to tell how long I sat there, keeping watch on the valley above and the street below. I was losing all sense of time and had not eaten or slept for over twenty-four hours. We all heard it at the same time and searched to see where the rumbling noise was coming from. We knew it was a heavy vehicle and listened as it strained its way up the hill. Next, I saw an armoured police vehicle emerge from the trees at the bottom of the dirt road across the way. It was a yellow truck with round windows along its side, making it look a little like a yellow submarine. Behind it were two yellow police vans. Halfway up the hill, the truck stopped and a crowd of men gathered around it. I was struggling to understand what was going on, until I realised with a shock what I was seeing: the police were unloading arms and distributing them to the Inkatha men who had come down from the chief's *kraal*. My body felt drained of all its heat and my throat closed up, making it hard to breathe. The police were giving these men arms with which to kill us and we had nothing beyond a few garden shovels to protect ourselves. I sat there, numb, watching the police close up the truck and pull off slowly up the hill. I suddenly realised, as did the rest of the defence group, that the only way the truck and vans could now leave was to loop around past the water tower and down our street. Everyone was on their feet, ready to fight or run. Then I heard the voices of some of the marshals saying, '*Hlala pansi*. Sit down, get out of the way and just let them pass. We are sitting here peacefully, just let them pass without trouble, *hlala pansi*'. I pulled the balaclava down over my face, tucked my hands under my knees and kept my head down.

The police came closer and closer, seeming to crawl like turtles towards us, slowly but steadily. '*Hlala pansi. Hlala pansi*', the marshals cooed, mantra-like. They were almost upon us now and I had long since stopped breathing. About thirty metres away, they opened fire. The marshals could not hold us then. We all fled in different directions, some up the street, some down, some into the *donga*, anywhere to get out of the line of fire. In an effort to hide myself I had been sitting tucked in behind a group of young men. When they turned and ran, I sat frozen for a moment and a few of the them fell onto me, the weight of their bodies pushing me into the barbed wire fence behind us, digging the metal barbs into my back. I scrambled up, feeling no pain as yet, and pushed with the rest, trying to break through the fence. I remember the flesh on my legs tearing through my jeans as I pulled myself through. While I was still bent over trying desperately to free my shirt from the fence, Bonani, one of the young men from the Skhosanas', grabbed me and said, 'Take this'. From under his shirt he handed me a gun: 'If they catch me with it, I'm dead'. Without thinking, I shoved it down the front of my jeans and ran towards the house, bent double to stay out of the way of the bullets. I ran down through the bush, reaching the house from behind. There was screaming coming from around the front. I ran through the house, hiding the gun in my room before running out through the front door. There on the driveway was Mama Skhosana's youngest child, ten-year-old Bonginkosi, covered in blood. He too had snuck out of the house to see what was happening.

When the police opened fire up the street, he stood frozen to the spot. As they sped down the road firing into the crowd, he was hit in the chest. Now he lay in his mother's arms amidst the screaming. What I didn't know as I ran over was that the police had used birdshot, not bullets. The blood on Bonginkosi's chest was from the multiple flesh wounds where the birdshot had cut into his body. He was lucky. Baba Skhosana lifted his son into his arms and carried him back into the house where Nonsi and I tended to him.

After cleaning myself up and tending to my own wounds, allowing the shock of the shooting to subside a little, I went to find Bonani and Jabulani, the Skhosanas' eldest son. When I confronted them about the gun they admitted they had had it with them since yesterday. I knew that Baba Skhosana would be furious if he found out it was in the house. I was also angry that Bonani had put me in this situation and told him so. His reasoning was that as a white person, I would have been treated differently if found with the gun but given where I was when I had it, I doubted that. I told them where the gun was hidden and said that if it wasn't gone by supper time, I would tell Baba Skhosana what had happened. The gun was gone within the hour.

After we had prepared supper for the household and the young men on watch, the phone rang. Up until this point, I had completely forgotten we had one as, for cost-saving reasons, it was set up to allow only incoming calls. It was the BBC. The situation was getting the attention of the international media, with many foreign journalists starting to arrive to cover the story. The BBC were looking for someone to interview in the township and, somehow hearing that I was there, they wanted to speak to me. I was concerned about the security police tracking the media, and given I was trying to keep out of sight, I wasn't keen to do it. They assured me they would use a false first name only. They also argued that giving people an understanding that this was not simply 'black on black violence' would help move public opinion. Looking back, I realise they were just keen for a hot story and were unlikely to have thought through the consequences for me. On my part, I was under such stress that my ability to make sound judgments was fading. I agreed.

The journalist phoned back a few minutes later for a live interview from London. They asked me what I had seen and I told them the events of the day, implicating the police in the violence. They asked me how people were feeling. 'Scared', I said, 'too scared to sleep, too scared to eat.' They asked me how many people had been killed but I did not know. They asked me why I was still there and I told them we were trapped. After a few more questions, they thanked me and were gone. They got their story and I had something else to worry about. Fear of the consequences of that interview stayed with me for a long time.

After the interview, I was agitated and needed to get outside. We had heard the rumours about Edendale hospital not treating people from the ANC affiliated areas, so instead of just taking food around to the defence groups, I decided to talk to them about basic first aid. That night, the Skhosanas' eldest son Jabulani and I went from group to group all over the area, talking to people. We heard what was happening in other areas. Imbali was suffering, as were other areas to the west of us, areas where we had run many leadership and dialogue programs. There was word of bodies floating in the nearby Umsunduzi River. Families on the escarpment were also suffering and fleeing down into Edendale. I heard another rumour that made me regret the interview even more. The police had been told that there was a white man in the township gun running for the ANC and they were searching for him. In reality, they were searching for me.

Thursday, 29 March. At dawn, we returned to the house, news of the police search finally driving me indoors. We had heard more shooting all through the night, whistles being blown across the valley calling for reinforcements as the warriors attacked. I went and lay down for a while in an effort to get some sleep, exhaustion finally taking over from fear, forcing me to close my eyes. I woke intermittently as gunshots continued to crack through the air all morning.

Just as I was drifting back to sleep, somewhere around lunchtime, I heard a sound that had me out of bed and back on my feet in an instant. Whistles were blowing on the corner just above the house. We all ran to the windows and saw our defence group retreating down the street. As they reached our driveway, I saw bullets bouncing off the ground at their feet, flinging dirt up into the air. When I went to the front door, there was Baba Skhosana, pressed up against the wall just outside. I watched him as he shot quick glances up the street in an effort to discern how many warriors were bearing down on us. By this time, the houses above us were abandoned, some of our neighbours having taken refuge with us, some further down the street. I watched him as he stood there with a brick in his hand, the only weapon he had to defend us all.

In that moment, I saw him in a different light, not as the master of the house wanting things just so, but as a man who was terribly afraid but was still standing between us and our attackers, ready to die to defend us all. So I went and stood behind him and together we watched the *impi* drive our defenders further down the street.

Then the battle was at our gate. Our attackers were screaming. Bullets were skipping off the driveway just in front of our feet. A few of our defenders were crouched by the gate, trying to avoid the path of the bullets. One of these young men saw us there and turned to run towards us. As he did so, he was cut down. Without thinking, I tried to run out to him but Baba Skhosana grabbed my arm. Above the noise of the guns and the screaming from the young man's friends he kept shouting, 'He's dead, he's dead'. 'No, let me go', I pleaded as I struggled with him. I saw that the young man had been hit in the right shoulder and was lying still a few metres away, but I could not believe he was dead. Soon, though, I saw there was no way to get to him without getting shot myself. Baba Skhosana let go of me and picked up the brick he had dropped, his head turned again towards the bushes above the gate. We both knew the attackers were right there and in a few moments they would see us. As the impact of this sank in I was jolted from my thoughts by the sounds of other whistles, this time coming up the hill. Our defences had regrouped and were now fighting their way back up the road to protect us.

I had no idea how many Inkatha warriors there were on the road above us: I had seen hundreds the day before. As the whistles got closer, I realised that our men must now outnumber them, for they seemed to be pulling back. Soon a group of young men flooded into the yard, Jabulani and Bonani among them. The rest continued to push up the hill. Baba Skhosana and I rushed forward to look for any signs of life in the young man who lay in a heap on the driveway. But we were too late. I sat in the dirt next to his body and wept, all the fear and disbelief of the last few days pouring out of me now. Jabulani was beside me, trying to convince me to come back inside, but I couldn't move. I was completely undone. After a while, he and Bonani dragged me to my feet, saying we weren't safe and the *impi* could be back any minute. They took me inside and then disappeared back up the street, Baba Skhosana shouting after them to be careful.

Up until that moment, I had thought myself a pacifist. But I knew that if I had had a gun to hand, I would have used it against those men. I suspected Baba Skhosana would have done the same and so I took him aside and told him about the gun that Jabulani and Bonani had hidden. After a long silence, he told me that he would keep it in the house in case Inkatha returned.

The report to the Truth and Reconciliation Commission said: 'Again further skirmishes occurred in Caluza, Simero and Ashdown. Police were active, searching and disarming youths going to defend their borders'.

Had the police disarmed our defences, I have no doubt we would have been killed that day.

The report went on to say:

The police were active in Edendale, where they stopped a march by 500 unarmed women protesting against police partisanship and inaction against the attackers. The women were told to disperse, or force, including tear gas and birdshot, would be used. Eleven women were arrested.

In the evening, there was almost continuous shooting in Imbali and a number of houses came under attack from Inkatha groups who roamed around the township on foot and in vehicles. Calls to the Riot Unit to respond to pleas for help were not acted upon. Three members of the Imbali Support Group who were staying in a house saw their vehicle shot up by a group, which included two white men, and it was later petrol bombed.

Repeated attempts to get the SADF (the South African Defence Force) to deploy were frustrated by the police. A ten platoon convoy waited fruitlessly outside Huletts Aluminium for the police to call them in at the height of the Imbali shooting. When calls requesting SADF back up were made, they were told by the police that the army was just off duty and tired. Eventually, apparently at SADF insistence, as they were being deluged by calls for help, they were told to meet the SAP (South African Police) at Huletts Aluminium at ten to seven in the evening. Ten platoons were there at the height of the shooting, fruitlessly awaiting the police. The police never came and they returned to their base and played volleyball. A number of African callers to the emergency services 10111 claim that they were told to ring F. W. de Klerk or Mandela.

After the danger of the attack on our street had passed, the young men returned and removed the body. There were rumours that the morgue at Edendale hospital was full with the bodies of the dead. I stayed inside, not able to face keeping watch. For the most part, I sat on the lounge, lost in my thoughts, as the afternoon drained away. Shortly after dark, Robbie walked through the front door. He had come with the Sizwe kombi and had apparently been trying to get through ever since he had escaped Imbali the morning before. The concern on his face brought fresh tears to my sore eyes. He'd come to get me out. I sat and listened to those words, but knew that I could not leave while the family stayed. Baba Skhosana was afraid that his home would be burnt like all the others if left unprotected, so he was determined to stay. I knew that after the events of the day, he was questioning his decision. After a short argument, Robbie agreed to help me get the children out.

I gathered together the younger Skhosana children and those others who had taken refuge with us. I then went to the neighbours and counted up how many more needed to be moved. We realised it would take two trips. I was certain Monica would help to house one load of children and thought of ETHOS for the second load. I knew it was still dangerous for me to be seen, so I put on dark clothes and the balaclava and blackened my face with shoe polish. Robbie and I put all the children from the Skhosanas' into the kombi, in just the clothes they wore, and drove as quickly as we could along Edendale Road to town. We could hear gunfire as we went but none sounded close by. We sped past Huletts Aluminium in the industrial area that lay between the township and the city, but saw no one; unbeknown to us, the army convoy had just left.

When we pulled up outside Monica's house I let Robbie go in first and talk to her, thinking my appearance might give her heart failure. I was sitting at the driver's wheel, my balaclava pulled up into a cap, my face blackened, with a carload of terrified black children in the middle of a white suburb, when a police van pulled up behind me. My heart was in my mouth and I thought I could taste blood. The van's engine was still running and its headlights were shining into my rear-view mirror when its driver's door opened. The officer emerged and walked slowly over to my window, shining a torch into the kombi onto the terrified faces of the children inside. To my surprise, he simply asked me if I was alright. I told him that I was fine, just waiting for a friend inside. He nodded at me, returned to his van and drove off. To this day, I don't know what he saw when he looked in at me, why he didn't question me or detain me—but I felt that for a second time that day, I had pulled back from the edge.

Monica agreed to take the children and find places for them to stay for a few days, so we left them with her and drove back to the township for a second load. We went house to house up and down our street and collected another kombi full of neighbourhood children, happy to be getting away from the fighting but afraid of leaving their parents behind. We told each parent that their children would be safe at the university until all this was over and then drove back into town, finally pulling up in the driveway of ETHOS. I jumped out of the kombi and ran up the front stairs of the grand old house. Teboho answered the door. He was one of the people selected to receive a scholarship and was now part of ETHOS as a student, rather than as an organiser with Moss. I hadn't seen him since Mandela's rally in Durban over a month before. Teboho seemed peculiarly unsurprised to see me standing there in all my battle finery. I briefed him on the situation and he was sure they could find enough mattresses to house the children there. A few calls were made and within forty minutes, the garage resembled a large bunkhouse. Now that the children were settled, Robbie dropped me off in Caluza before driving back to Phezulu to spend the night. We agreed that if he could get through again in the morning, he would fetch me for a meeting at the town hall where the church and community organisations were planning to discuss what needed to be done.

Saturday, 31 March. The university's monitoring report read:

> *Another attack on Mpophomeni. At Vulindlela a meeting was held at Chief Ngcobo's place. A fair amount of hysteria in the community, as it suddenly dawned on them that they were now cut off from food resources in Pietermaritzburg. An eminent person's group visited Edendale and Vulindlela during the day. They met a heavily armed group of men near Taylor's Halt. They blamed the stoning of the buses by youths for the current strife and said that Inkatha people were only defending themselves.*

In Imbali, sporadic shooting continued. A number of people were killed and wounded and homes burnt. Virtually every street in Imbali was barricaded with burning tyres, cars and rubble. There were many eye witness accounts of Inkatha vehicles, including a six-tonne truck manned by about fifteen people with rifles and shotguns, driving through the area firing at random at residents. There were also reports of police providing weapons and ammunition to Inkatha.

Thankfully, we had a quiet night in Caluza that extended into the morning. Robbie arrived and shared breakfast with us before we headed back into town, taking Jabulani with us to bear witness to the events in Caluza over the past few days. When we arrived at the town hall, it was packed. Monica was there, as well as Steve and Themba, Mdu and a number of the staff from the Council of Churches, the team from PACSA and a number of principals from the local schools that we worked with. Teboho and the ETHOS staff were sitting a few rows in front of us. I began to wonder about people I couldn't see; Sipho and his family, Skhumbuzo and Zonke, Thami, many of the youth leaders we knew from areas that had been badly affected. Had they made it or were they lost? If they were alive, were their homes still standing?

As head of the Centre for African Renewal, David stood up and spoke on behalf of the church. It was estimated that some 20,000 refugees were now in the city, he said, each one having lost everything. Up to one hundred people had been killed and no one could guess at the number of wounded. Neither the government nor the local municipality was willing to help with the refugees, who were for the most part ANC affiliated, for fear of being seen as partisan. Deputy Minister Tertius Delport was quoted as saying that not a cent would be spent in the region until the violence ended. David called for all community organisations to work together to respond to the crisis and committed, with the rest of the eminent persons' group, to raise the issue at a national level. David then invited eye witnesses to stand and speak to the assembly about what they had lived through in what was soon to be known as the Seven Day War.

The monitoring report read:

> *The area was not declared a disaster area. The army was called in eventually to stabilise the situation, which it did after a fashion, and the death toll dropped to a regular thirty-five or so a month in the Midlands for the rest of the year.*

13
APRIL 1990
GUESTS OF HONOUR

A MONTH LATER IN MY NEWSLETTER HOME, I WROTE:

At present, it is estimated that over 160 people have been killed and some 55,000 displaced in the greater Pietermaritzburg area. The Midlands Crisis Relief Committee have been stretched beyond their capabilities to provide food, clothing, shelter, missing persons information, legal advice, help with funeral expenses and the identification of bodies.

The reality of war is horrific and a list of statistics cannot describe the effects on the lives of individual families.

The effects of the war have been far reaching. Schools are yet to fully reopen, with many teachers and pupils fearing for their safety. It is very possible that none of the black schools will reopen this year. There are now eighteen displacee centres across the city functioning on an official capacity and countless others functioning unofficially. The majority of these people have no homes to return to. There is an immense housing crisis in the townships, so finding accommodation will be almost impossible.

> *For me personally, it has also been a difficult time. A friend was murdered while patrolling his area one evening. He was only eighteen years old. One of the men who was defending our street was shot dead before my eyes as he fled the gunfire. Several friends had their homes attacked and destroyed.*
>
> *These and other events have caused nightmares, fatigue and a period of deep grief and frustration. Even writing this letter has been difficult because of the memories and feelings it has brought up. I have experienced fear, anger, powerlessness, and the weariness of many sleepless anxious nights. It is not an experience I wish to repeat, though for many it's a way of life.*

I have no memory of what happened in the weeks that followed the war, no recollection of the depth of emotion that the newsletter described. It is as if a heavy curtain has been drawn across my mind, not erasing the aftermath but locking it away in a place I cannot access. However, the retelling of the events of the war all these years later has left me shaken, with a patch of shingles re-emerging on my body as if the memories are still housed within the tissue itself.

What I am sure of is that I understood then that death attends life as the seasons sit adjacent to each other, spring not possible without winter. It wasn't that I believed I couldn't be killed, invincible in my twenties; it was that I knew I could be, as many others had been, and yet the world still turned. This knowing has stayed with me ever since.

Two weeks after the war ended, Msizi came to visit as promised, staying with me for a week up at the cottage. In my journal I wrote that our time together, as always, cemented our depth of feeling for each other, though I found it increasingly difficult to describe the nature of our relationship. We simply loved each other and that was all I knew for sure. Everything else was like mercury in my hand. However, even the detail of that week together is beyond the reach of my memory and I can only be sure that it happened from the journal entry itself.

The moment when the curtains open and my memory returns is my parents' arrival a few days after Easter. They were to stay with me for a month before going on to London to see my brother, Jon. It was a visit much anticipated by all of us, and for me, a relief to spend time with the two people who most represented stability and security in this place that was anything but stable. Mama Jenny had kindly offered to stay in one of the bunkhouses so that our family could share a home for a while.

In the true style of Africa, my parents had their own adventures on their way to be with me. They flew into Harare, intending to visit Hwange Game Reserve and Victoria Falls before flying on to Johannesburg. They spent their first night in a hotel in downtown Harare and, as the hotel had no airport shuttle, were advised to catch the bus back to the airport in the morning. After a walk in the nearby park and a hearty hotel breakfast, they joined the end of the bus queue, discussing whether or not the bus would be on time. Immediately, the women in front of them turned and tried to usher them to the head of the queue, supported by the rest of the commuters who, for whatever reason, felt that they should be the first to board the bus. Mum and Dad were very embarrassed by this favoured treatment and declined their offer, saying they were more than happy to wait their turn. But the dozen commuters would not be deterred and, when the bus arrived a few minutes later, moved to the side and shuffled my parents and their luggage on board. My parents' only assumption was that their skin colour was already buying them preferential treatment, something they were not comfortable with but would have to get used to.

Upon arrival at the airport, Mum and Dad were told that their flight to Hwange was delayed indefinitely. President Mugabe had taken the plane the night before, flying out of Harare on government business and they were unsure when he would return. Apparently the President did not use a private jet for his travels for fear it would be shot down. His strategy was to commandeer an Air Zimbabwe plane whenever he needed to travel, making his movements indistinguishable from those of ordinary commuters. Unfortunately, this strategy virtually crippled the domestic travel industry as well as making his movements all the more visible to anyone who chose to watch.

My parents, like all the other travellers, made themselves at home at the airport and attempted to adjust to the pace and unpredictability of life in Africa. After a mere three-hour delay, they were boarding the plane. However, just as the doors were to close, the pilot made an announcement indicating that the plane was overloaded by one passenger and he would not take off until one person disembarked. An awkward silence followed. The plane, given its destination, was mostly full of foreign tourists who were unwilling to take pot luck with the President's next out-of-town meeting. Mum had been chatting to members of a tour group of Australian farmers who were here to explore trade opportunities with Zimbabwean farmers. She noticed none of them were interested in abandoning their seat either. After fifteen minutes or so, a courier approached the flight attendant and agreed that he would leave the plane if the pilot gave his personal guarantee that a satchel of documents would be delivered to a government department in Victoria Falls that same day. As the man left the plane, my parents had their doubts that the promise would be kept.

Mum and Dad made the short flight to Hwange where, the night before, a large male lion had settled itself for the evening in the middle of the runway. All attempts to move the animal failed; before finally running off into the bush the lion stood its ground and attempted to attack a plane as it landed. My parents' landing, however, offered no such welcome and they were soon settled into their game lodge, from where they spent three days exploring the game reserve, experiencing the miracle of the African bush. When they had their photos developed in 'Maritzburg, they realised that the lack of a zoom lens had left them with three reels of mostly unidentifiable black dots standing under thorn trees.

After Hwange, my parents took a tour bus through to Victoria Falls which at the time was a small town a few kilometres away from its watery namesake. The bus deposited its passengers on the main road where a cluster of hotel shuttles were waiting. As Mum and Dad disembarked, there appeared to be a commotion a few metres away. They could see a white middle-aged man, presumably another tourist, his face shredded and bloodied. As they stood watching, the man was helped away to find medical attention. Apparently he had just been mauled by a lion that had found its way through the fence surrounding the bus stop. My parents were quickly bundled into an awaiting hotel shuttle bus.

The next day they returned to the bus stop on their way to the Falls, and heard other tourists discussing a large dent in the fence. My parents questioned the tour guide on her thoughts about the lion attack but she told them that nothing of the sort had happened. Mum assured her they had seen the victim of the attack on this very spot, but the guide continued to deny that anything like that was possible. 'Bad for business', my father whispered to my mother as they moved off in the direction of the Falls.

Two days later, my parents made their way to the small airport just outside Victoria Falls, where they were once again told that the President was afoot and had commandeered their plane. This time, however, due to the lateness of the hour, all the passengers were taken to the Victoria Falls Hotel for the night. They were each given a meal before the men were led off in one direction and the women in another to bed down for the night. The women were taken to a small conference room where mattresses, pillows and blankets were waiting. However, it soon became clear that there was not enough of everything to go around and so the women would have to share. They were also shown the bathrooms they could use: two showers and two toilets for approximately fifty women. My mother is the most patient of women yet even she was harbouring ill will towards the President by this stage.

After a restless night, the women were ushered into the foyer to take the bus back to the airport. My mother found my father amongst the crowd of men waiting there and was told of the excess bedding that the men had found in their spacious ballroom, some sleeping atop a pile of five mattresses to save the effort of unpacking them. It was a quiet ride to the airport.

My parents' connecting flights to Johannesburg were uneventful, but the delay in Victoria Falls meant they arrived two days later than planned. As they made their way through customs, a humourless official queried the authenticity of my father's camera. Dad made a move to demonstrate its functionality, but his hand was batted away, the official seemingly interpreting his actions as a threat. Welcome to South Africa.

Meanwhile, I'd been pacing the floor for the past two days since hearing of their delay, so it was a joyous reunion when they finally turned their hire car into the gravel driveway. We spent the evening sharing tales of their adventures in Zimbabwe and I marvelled at their ability to graciously adapt to whatever was thrown their way. I knew Mum, in particular, was keen to catch up on my news as I had kept them largely in the dark about recent events, thinking it better to tell them in context. But it was getting late so we decided to call it a night and go to bed.

The next few days flew by. I was back at work and, given the displacee crisis, we were run off our feet. Mum and Dad quickly joined the rhythm of our little community, offering to take on some of the daily chores and joining us for our team lunch on the stoep. One of their favourite chores was to fetch the milk which we collected in two five-litre containers from the dairy across the road. Phezulu was located in an area where 2.2 hectare properties were common although some, such as the dairy, were much larger. If Beth went to fetch the milk, she often drove but if Mum and Dad fetched it, they went on foot. They soon learnt that white people in South Africa rarely walk. Local residents would stop and ask them if they were alright. Black people, who did walk everywhere, would stare curiously at them as they passed by. However, as soon as they began using the Zulu greetings I had taught them—Mum having more success than Dad—their fellow pedestrians ceased staring and were all smiles and conversation. To get to the dairy, it was quickest to go via the old gate, which took them in the opposite direction to the cottage entrance, buckets in hand. Two of the three streets that bordered Phezulu were lined with tall pine trees that stood like sentinels along her boundaries. The trees also filtered the hot African sun, making my parents' journey a pleasant one. After turning off the main street some 500 metres beyond our gate, they walked down the long driveway towards the dairy. While it was very different from the dairy my parents had owned for twelve years in the wheat belt of central New South Wales—that was all flat grassland and scrub as opposed to the lush pasture and forest they were now walking through—the sounds and smells of the cattle were the same. They were both instantly taken back twenty years to the clanking milking machines and the swaying gait of the Friesian cattle as they wandered up to the shed for their morning milking. While they waited for the black farmhand to fill their containers, the white farmer, delighted to meet fellow cattle lovers, chatted about South African breeds and yields and the challenge of running a small dairy against the larger conglomerates in Natal.

Mum and Dad also took it upon themselves to collect the post each afternoon at the small local post office which was two kilometres down the road in the opposite direction from the dairy. The road sloped down into the valley, pine trees giving way to the hedges and iron gates of the old established homes that dotted the landscape. The tiny modest post office and its adjacent grocery store stood alone like two Shetland ponies in a stable of thoroughbreds. Given that the post office was a government building, it was also staffed by another rarity, an Afrikaans-speaking official in an almost exclusively English-speaking town. By law, schools were required to teach both English and Afrikaans, so the postmaster made the assumption that all custom could be handled in his mother tongue. When Mum and Dad arrived at the post office and sought to strike up a conversation, they discovered that it was not a political statement the postmaster was making but rather, his English was so poor that he struggled to make himself understood. However, they managed to muddle through; Mum and Dad eventually left the post office with Sizwe's mail in hand. They then made their way back up the valley towards Phezulu, stopping to explore a few intriguing country lanes along the way. (This was an annoying habit my father had developed during my childhood. When on holidays, he would follow his nose, taking interesting side routes on our way to our final destination. Despite being driven to distraction by this habit, Jon and I learnt that if we complained, Dad would take a few extra detours just to teach us patience.)

On their first trip to the Phezulu post office, Dad's exploring got them completely lost. They stood looking up and down the road for a familiar landmark and were just about to pronounce themselves in need of help, when Mum looked behind her and discovered they were standing with their backs to the Sizwe gate. The thought occurred to Mum that if they needed to ask for help, it could only have been from the black passers-by as the white residents were firmly locked away behind gates and fences.

For my parents' first weekend, I had arranged for us to stay with the Skhosanas, allowing Mum and Dad an experience of township life. Whatever happened in the weeks between the war ending and my parents arriving, the township now felt completely different. While the army, still on patrol in their large armoured vehicles, were a constant reminder of the conflict, the mood in the township had quickly returned to its relaxed, friendly pace. We planned to spend Saturday in Caluza and then attend the funeral of a cousin of Mama Skhosana's on Sunday.

As we turned into the driveway of the house Mama Skhosana was there to greet us, her husband still busy with pastoral visits. Nonsi, Sibongile and Thembi were also at home and helped Mum and Dad with their small overnight bag, taking it to Auntie Ni's room where they would be spending the night. I planned to bunk in with the girls as usual. After introductions, Mama Skhosana went to the kitchen to put on tea while Nonsi and Sibongile continued with the lunch preparations.

We gave Mama Skhosana a gift to thank her for her hospitality. I knew she very much wanted a hose and watched with delight as she clucked over the simple present. She told us she was going to store it in her bedroom so no one else could use it and in that way, keep it safe. She also told us Baba Skhosana had recently bought a lawnmower, much to her exasperation. She was still washing clothes by hand—an enormous chore in such a large household—yet her dear husband had only thought to buy something the boys could use as they mowed the tiny 10 square metre patch of stubborn grass that grew in front of the house. She joked that with the hose she could make sure the grass grew, giving the boys something to do with their new toy.

I knew my parents' visit was a big deal for the family. It was one thing to have me stay with them but it was another altogether for my parents to spend the weekend. What seemed to us such an ordinary occurrence was extraordinary by South African standards. You might occasionally find a young white community worker in the black townships but this lifestyle choice was rarely something the parents supported, let alone became part of. For many, the decision to work with the black community had cost them their relationship with their families; most white South Africa parents felt betrayed by their child choosing a black world view and cut them off to express their displeasure. I was touched that my parents had not thought twice about coming to stay despite the many stories that exist about the dangers of the townships. While Caluza had been extremely dangerous a few weeks before, now it was simply a place where ordinary people lived.

After a leisurely tea in the lounge room, discussing family and my parents' experiences in Zimbabwe, Dad retired to the front stoep leaving Mum and Mama Skhosana still chatting while I went through to the kitchen to see if I could help with lunch. Dad made himself comfortable on a crate and sat enjoying the view up the valley, back towards Phezulu. Across the road, the principal's six-year-old daughter spotted him sitting there and decided to come over to investigate. As a frequent visitor to the Skhosana household, she no longer found the sight of a visiting white person odd and confidently approached Dad to ask him who he was. They introduced themselves and then Phumzile asked Dad if she could sing him a song. My father, enchanted, agreed. Dad did not generally have a way with children, being a little gruff without meaning to be. In fact, he had been known to make children cry just by staring at them the wrong way, much to his own distress. But as he aged, he softened a little. Phumzile's confidence had allowed her to slip under his defences and he sat mesmerised as this little girl sang and swayed, moving through her school and church repertoire of English songs as she sought to entertain him.

So engrossed was he that he didn't look up until the army truck was almost upon them. The armoured vehicle holding a dozen young white soldiers, M5 rifles poised, pulled to a halt by the front gate, blocking the driveway. As the soldiers climbed down a young lieutenant, baffled by my father's presence, approached and demanded to know how he had got there. I emerged from the house just in time to hear Dad reply through gritted teeth, 'By hire car'. Trying to calm him with a warning look, I explained that we were simply visiting the minister and his family for lunch. But the officer was unimpressed: he had come to search the house for guns, he told us. Out of the corner of my eye, I saw my father's shoulders tense moments before he started berating our unwelcome visitors for disturbing the family. Half a dozen soldiers entered the house, guns at the ready, and chased all its occupants out onto the stoep. I stood nervously waiting, hoping that Jabulani and Bonani had long since removed the gun they had given to Baba Skhosana a few weeks earlier.

After twenty minutes, Mama Skhosana had had enough. She stormed back into the house and gave the lieutenant a dressing down: 'This is quite enough. I have international visitors in my home for lunch and before the food is completely ruined I want you out'. I was as astonished as the lieutenant. Mama Skhosana, though certainly a strong woman, had always patiently served her husband and her family without protest. Clearly a line had been crossed. I suspect the lieutenant was already satisfied there were no guns to be found, but in any case Mama Skhosana's bold words brought proceedings to an abrupt end. The soldiers left without a word of apology. Quickly, I stepped in front of my father to ensure he made no parting comment that might reverse their departure and watched with relief as the vehicle turned and slowly made its way back down the hill.

Lunch was served in a flurry of excitement as the girls teased their mother for chasing the army away. However, their visit precipitated a discussion of the recent Seven Day War, something I had yet to explain to my parents in any detail. Too late, I heard Mama Skhosana say, 'You must be very proud of Sandy. She was very brave'. What followed was a blow by blow description of the conflict with each family member adding their own slightly exaggerated account of my activities. I don't know why I had always sanitised the information I gave my parents about my life in those first years in South Africa. I told myself I was trying to protect them from worry, but perhaps it was me I was trying to protect. As I watched their faces that day, I wasn't sure pride was one of the emotions written there. But I was to see over the ensuing weeks, as my parents experienced some of the inequities of apartheid, that they would have done the same.

After lunch I took Mum and Dad for a walk around the neighbourhood, bumping into Themba and Zodwa, popping into the shops, all with Phumzile in tow. If Mum and Dad thought walking through the streets of Hilton had attracted some attention, it was nothing compared to the show-stopper this afternoon stroll had become. By now, my Zulu was progressing well. One of the delights of understanding a language that people don't expect you to speak, is eavesdropping on conversations you are never meant to hear. As we passed each group on the street, exchanging polite Zulu greetings, they would walk off expressing astonishment and speculating as to the reason for our presence in the township. Their theories varied but it was always the fact that we were on foot that was most puzzling.

When we returned to the house, Baba Skhosana was home and horrified to hear that his guests had been subjected to a search by an army patrol. Tea was once more served in the lounge so that stories of my parents' travels, family history and life in Australia could be told, filling Baba Skhosana in on what he had missed.

Mum commented to me later that the tone in the house changed dramatically when Baba Skhosana was around, everyone seeming to withdraw from the common areas of the house, virtually leaving him to hold court. I explained that while African culture was still heavily patriarchal the running of South African households varied considerably. Respect for the patriarch was certainly more prevalent in rural areas than in urban ones but the earning capacity of the man was also a major factor. In this household, Baba Skhosana was a strong provider and so was accorded respect and deference. However, I had observed in other households where the men were unemployed that a powerful matriarchy prevailed. The next morning, Mum noticed another distinguishing feature of Baba Skhosana's presence in the house—he was the only one who had the knack of flushing the toilet. The cistern was particularly temperamental, giving the family another reason to be glad of Baba's return home each evening.

After breakfast we set off early for the funeral which was to be held down the south coast. Because it was a family member, Mama Skhosana had been there earlier in the week to take food and cash to help with the hosting of the funeral. We drove in two cars, taking the freeway down to Durban and then heading south for another hour, turning inland at Umkomaas towards Umgababa. We drove up into the green, treeless windswept hills until we came upon a cluster of houses that marked the area where Mama Skhosana had grown up. I spotted the large white marquee that signals the open community feast of both weddings and funerals and wondered how this event would differ from the many urban funerals I had attended.

After greeting the elders of Mama Skhosana's family, who sat in the shelter of the house, we made our way to the marquee where speeches and prayers had been flowing since dawn. Despite my parents' protests we were ushered up to the front of the gathering where the coffin stood on an undertaker's trolley, tilting slightly on the uneven ground. As we sat, the minister stood. From a temporary lectern set up next to the coffin, he launched into a typically exuberant African sermon. After thirty minutes of this Mum, not having sat through an African sermon before, leant across and asked whether perhaps he was inciting the people to violence. I assured her that his enthusiasm was only for the Lord and that he was inspiring us to join God's army, not a Zulu *impi*.

During this hour-long sermon (the longer the sermon, the more respected the deceased was) the marquee was full of other activity. Guests came and went, children ran through the open sides of the tent and two men returned to the coffin at regular intervals, appearing to measure the coffin against a stick one man was holding. When Dad couldn't contain his curiosity any longer, he followed the men out of the tent as they made their way to the graveside. He returned to his seat and whispered that these men were gravediggers and were using the stick to measure their progress on the depth of the grave. Finally, just before the minister finished his speech, a dog wandered through the open tent flap near the coffin and proceeded to lift its leg on the undertaker's trolley, with my parents and I seeming to be the only people who found this odd.

From the marquee we moved to the graveside where the gravediggers stood proudly beside their handiwork. The coffin was lowered in and a few more words said before it was covered over. I could only assume that Mama Skhosana's cousin was old and therefore his death not unexpected, as the whole event had the festivity of a church picnic.

From the graveside, Mama Skhosana took us to a house further up the hill. As we made the climb, I was taken aback by the beauty of the area. Despite the howling wind and the harsh light, the view back towards the coast was breathtaking. At the top of the hill was a larger house that, to my mother's delight, boasted a pit toilet. Mama

Skhosana told us we would be having our meal here to avoid the long queues back at the marquee. We were treated to a fabulous lunch along with stories of the family's history in the area and their great pride at Mama Skhosana marrying a minister and giving him a large, healthy family. My mother was asked how many children she had. 'Two—a boy and a girl', she replied proudly, only to receive commiserations from the women present. 'She was sick', I whispered in Zulu. 'Ah', they nodded sagely. It was a question and response Mum quickly became used to during her month-long stay.

I returned to work the next day, with Mum and Dad slipping back into their Phezulu routine. Where I could, I took them with me when Robbie and I visited a school or a youth group, giving them a better feel for what I was doing.

On the Wednesday of that week, we were sitting around the lunch table when a call came through from Mdu. His boss, Victor Afrikander, who was the head of the Pietermaritzburg Council of Churches and a local Imbali minister, had been shot in the head while sitting at the traffic lights. He had been taking his granddaughter to preschool when the assailants pulled up alongside his car and put a bullet through the window. Victor was dead and his granddaughter in a serious condition in hospital, the bullet having gone through her grandfather and lodged in her body. The assassination had taken place downtown and its audacity was shocking. Mdu told me he was now afraid for his life and would be going underground for a while.

I took Mum and Dad to the commemorative ceremony where thousands of people turned out to honour Victor's memory. Sitting at the front of the enormous hall was his granddaughter, her tiny bandaged head bowed in grief. It is an image that has stayed with us to this day.

On one of my days off, my parents and I went to visit a friend, Bongani, whom I knew through the youth leadership programs we ran. He was keen to meet my parents so I promised we would drop in when we got a chance. As there was no phone in the tiny shack he shared with his grandmother visits were always hit and miss. When we arrived at his home on the edge of Imbali, Bongani was not there but his grandmother was delighted to welcome us regardless. The house was made of corrugated iron and consisted of three rooms: a lounge, a kitchen and a bedroom. Bongani's grandmother offered us a seat in the tiny lounge while she went into the kitchen to boil water on the small paraffin stove. While waiting for the water to boil, she went to wake Bongani's nine-month-old son who was asleep on the bed. Mum was given the baby to hold and he stared up into her face with round, surprised eyes. Over tea, the grandmother told us that she was constantly afraid, living in Imbali. She pointed to the wall around the front door and there, unnoticed until now, were twenty or thirty bullet holes. She told us she had decided to take the baby and return to the rural area where she was born. She believed that if they stayed, her grandson and great grandson would not survive. Bongani was refusing to leave but agreed, for the safety of his son, that she should go.

The following day, we invited Nonsi to go down to the Durban beachfront with us, inadvertently providing my parents with yet another experience of what it meant to be a black South African. We arrived in Durban mid morning with enough time before lunch to wander along the boardwalk and browse though the craft markets that lined the walkway like clusters of colourful annuals.

The boardwalk stretches along the coast from Pirates Beach in the north to Addington Beach in the south, a distance of about 4 kilometres. As an Australian used to uninhabited coastline fringed by long, sweeping beaches, the Durban beachfront always made me laugh. The four kilometres of coast were divided into nine or ten separate beaches, some by a pier and others by distinguishing north from south. What really tickled my funny bone is that surf reports were given for each tiny beach; while my friends assured me that the surf was actually different beach by beach, it always struck me as overkill.

On top of that, the beachfront was anything but uninhabited. Half the human race seemed to descend on Durban each weekend, some taking to the surf, some happy to play or lie on the sand and a great many just taking a stroll along the concrete boardwalk. Neither Nonsi nor my parents were dressed for the beach itself—Nonsi had never swum in the sea—so we fell into the latter category and were simply 'strollers'. We took our time chatting to the women who made and sold African crafts as they sat with their legs stretched before them, industriously producing the next item for sale. We found a shell-covered jewellery box that we knew Mama Skhosana would like and tucked that away to surprise her with on our return.

Along the street next to the boardwalk, Zulu men dressed in flamboyant traditional outfits offered rickshaw rides to tourists. They reminded me of peacocks, their headdresses spraying out like feathers, competing for attention with the next colourful male. One young man came up to Nonsi and told her in Zulu that if she could ditch the old people, he would give her and me a ride for free. He got an evil stare from Nonsi who had a boyfriend and did not take kindly to being propositioned, while I burst into laughter at his bold offer. Realising he was not going to make any headway, he disappeared back into the crowded street.

By now we were hungry and spotted a hotel across the road with an open air cafe that spilled out onto the street. After almost ten minutes of waiting to be seated, chatting happily amongst ourselves, we realised it wasn't the fullness of the tables that was causing the delay but rather the attitude of diners and staff to Nonsi's presence. Nonsi stood there, looking like an entrant in a Miss World competition as always, yet the white patrons looked at her as though they saw a bag lady waiting to collect leftovers from their plates. Irate, my father ushered us back onto the street, loudly berating the narrow-mindedness of people who couldn't see past the colour of a person's skin. While I supported his sentiment, I was afraid the volume of his tirade was going to land us in trouble with some of the burly men seated nearby, so I grabbed his hand and pulled him across the street and out of earshot. Dad adored Nonsi and to have her treated like this when he believed things were changing in South Africa was a slap in the face. Nonsi, on the other hand, had appeared nervous as we approached the cafe. I should have foreseen the problem too, but thought she was hesitant because she had never eaten at a restaurant before. Wandering along the beach with my parents had allowed me to momentarily forget where I was.

We decided to go down to the wading pools where there were a number of fast food shops, finally deciding on some fish and chips. I tried to lure Nonsi onto the stepping stones that crossed the shallow pool, wanting to recreate the lightness of our earlier mood. She stepped out bravely, taking my hand as we slowly crossed from one concrete cylinder to the next. But we were all now aware of the disapproving stares of those around us and found a place to sit on the grass that was a little less under the public eye. From there, we began some people-watching of our own. We saw a large group of black primary school children—clearly seeing the ocean for the first time—being herded along by two harassed looking teachers. After about an hour, we decided it was time to head home, Dad still angry about the irrational racism towards Nonsi and perhaps a little frustrated that he could not make it right for her.

On Mum and Dad's last weekend with me we had a very different experience. We had decided to go and visit Fred who was now working for World Vision in a remote rural area of Kwazulu just outside Tugela Ferry. Setting out early in the morning, we drove out through Greytown and past what served as a border between South Africa and one of its homelands. Kwazulu, like a few other homelands, did not have a single border that delineated it from South Africa. Rather, it was composed of a multitude of areas: you were never sure when you were in and when you were out. For the most part, though, the Zulu homeland consisted of areas that white farmers didn't want—although it was still situated in a part of the world that was so exquisite it made you gasp.

Arriving at the border that morning, we pulled up outside a small building inside which sat two bored Kwazulu officials. Fred had phoned late the night before, apologising profusely that he had forgotten to get the local chief's permission and warning that this might create problems at the border post. I asked Mum and Dad to stay in the car and, feeling that the best form of defence was attack, walked through the door with a very formal Zulu greeting, asking after the health of many of their relatives, before going on to explain why we wanted entry. I hoped that my Zulu abilities might distract them from their usual business of saying no, allowing us to proceed to Tugela Ferry. While I knew I did not speak the 'deep Zulu' of rural areas, I hoped my urban slang would still prove entertaining. I was soon back in the car, permission in hand.

Not far from the border was a small town made up only of a few shops and houses lining the street. Displayed along the fences in front of each building were bolts of material flapping in the wind—purple, turquoise, burnt orange, gold—giving the impression that this town was simply a gust of colour blowing across the tar.

Twenty minutes later the road had turned to dirt and we began our ascent to the top of an escarpment. As we crested the final ridge, the valley opened out beneath us. On a lush flood plain cut open millions of years ago by the Tugela River we could just make out the small plots of patchwork crops being grown close to the river. The road dropped down into the valley and split into the two on the far side of the river, one road running to the east and the other to the west. Fred had told us that he lived near the fork but we would find him about two kilometres along the western road at the workshop. Either way, I knew we could find him by simply stopping and asking for the '*mlungu*', as he was certainly the only white man living in this part of Kwazulu. We followed his directions until we spotted a small building made of concrete blocks set just back from the road. It stood in stark contrast to the traditional round mud brick rondavels with their thatched roofs and parked outside was Fred's trademark red four wheel drive bakkie.

We pulled up just as Fred emerged through the front door, waving and calling out a Zulu greeting in his thick Cockney accent. He was followed by two middle-aged women, both in traditional Zulu attire. One of the delights of visiting rural areas was to meet people who are less influenced by American advertising. While Coca Cola billboards could regularly be seen outside a rural corner store, people were less likely to own a television set or dress like US rap stars. These women were wearing the thick Zulu leather skirts trimmed with hand-beaded edging, large red dish-like headdresses and thick beaded anklets decorating their bare feet. Their faces were smeared with white clay which acts as both sunscreen and face mask. The only glimpse of a western influence was the T-shirts they wore, one advertising Omo washing powder and the other a Durban football club.

Fred gave me a big hug followed by warm handshakes to each of my parents. His co-workers were introduced: Mama Mkhize and Mama Dlamini. The three of them were employed by World Vision to set up employment-generating enterprises in Tugela Ferry, Fred being the primary contact; he had employed the women as local fieldworkers when he arrived. They had two projects under way: one was a wire fencing business that employed three local women and the other a mud brick business that employed another four. Both projects were relatively new but Fred and the women were proud of their early successes.

Beth, Steve's wife, had been to visit Fred about a month before and had given us photos to take to the two women. She was a keen photographer and had shot a few reels while she was here. Through Fred, the women explained that they had never seen photos of themselves. In fact, they had never even seen themselves in a mirror and were very keen to have a few of the photos to keep. They were thrilled when we told them we had a gift from Beth and quickly opened the envelope, poring over the images it contained. It was one of the more bizarre situations I had witnessed since coming to Africa. These women had no idea what they looked like and therefore each had to be convinced by the other that the person in the photo was in fact her.

Fred took us to see the wire-making project first, leaving Mama Dlamini and Mama Mkhize to finish the work they were doing at the new community creche. Its concrete structure was the first thing Fred had created when he arrived and it would soon be finished. We left the hire car where it was and jumped into Fred's truck to drive a little further along the valley, Fred firing off questions about all our friends in 'Maritzburg. Before long, we pulled up beside a mud brick building where some women were sitting outside in the shade waiting for us to arrive. News of visitors travels fast in a remote community and my parents' new car had clearly given us away.

After greetings all round we went inside and saw what looked like a large loom, but instead of cloth this loom produced wire fencing. One woman showed us how she hooked the wire across the various pegs from one side of the loom to the other. Where pieces of wire touch they are then twisted into the recognisable shape of mesh fencing. Fred explained that this project was quite successful as it did not introduce a new product to the local market but simply gave people the means to produce it for themselves. The loom was also easy to maintain, entailing little reliance on others for success. Fred's job, once the women had been trained, was to help set up processes that allowed the fencing to be sold.

Many development projects were now targeting women as they proved to be the most reliable workers and always ploughed profits back into their children's education, nutrition and health care. Men seemed to find other more pressing uses for the money they earned, some of which left them in no condition to work the next day. The only catch was that the men didn't like being cut out of the manufacturing and were therefore reluctant to buy the project's products. Because this was a rural area, the women had less purchasing power than women in the city—so there was a fine line Fred had to tread.

After visiting the fencing project, we went on to the mud brick project where another group of local women were hard at work setting another row of mud bricks. To one side were the stacks of dry bricks, hard and ready for sale. Then there were rows and rows of bricks in various stages of drying, some turned out this morning, others from yesterday. The women told us how happy they were that

Fred had come to work with them as they now had both an income and a purpose. It was also clear they had other intentions for Fred, hoping to set up a match between him and one of their daughters. But Fred, who was shy in matters of the heart and had a long-term girlfriend, was quick to change the subject.

We left the project site and drove back to Fred's rondavel for lunch. His home reminded me of Dr Who's tardis, being bigger on the inside than it appeared from the outside. It was also surprisingly cool despite temperatures reaching the mid to high thirties outside. Inside, Fred had built a low wall that arched around one side of the room, dividing the kitchen from the rest of the living area. On the larger side of the division was a bed, a bookshelf full to overflowing with an eclectic mix of reading material and a spacious area that acted as the living room, containing a lounge suite, a coffee table and a large dog bed.

Fred's huge dog, Mandy, had come with Fred from 'Maritzburg—the only constant between his two worlds. She went everywhere with him, diving into the back of the truck in one easy leap. She was a pavement special, as Fred described her, but had grown to the size of a Baskerville hound in the three years since he'd had her. She served as companion and guard dog. While the locals owned dogs, they were usually small scrappy things that never grew beyond your knee, whether due to breed or malnutrition I was not sure. So Mandy stood out as an ogre, keeping both Fred's truck and his home free from theft.

While he made our sandwiches Fred told us how much he was enjoying his life here. He was now functionally fluent in Zulu, albeit with a Cockney twang, and had found the community incredibly welcoming. Mama Mkhize and Mama Dlamini in particular had quickly connected him up with all the key families in the area, including the chief's. He loved the work as it was so easy to see the impact of what he was doing. I was always a fan of Fred's, given his warmth and easy generosity, but my respect for him deepened as I saw what he was doing here. I knew, despite all he said, that there would be moments of loneliness that must have made him question his choice—yet he had stayed.

After lunch we went for a walk to see some of the local farmers and their produce. While we stood looking out over the bend of the river and the lush harvest that skirted its edges three of Fred's female neighbours approached, hoping for an introduction to the visitors. Fred obliged and explained, as was custom, the relationships between us all. After this initial exchange, the women were keen to know more about Mum and Dad. They too asked how many children my mother had, showing the appropriate sorrow at her small, tenuous brood.

Dad, spurred on by the success of Beth's photos earlier in the day, offered to show these women photos of my brother. The women quickly accepted, as I translated his offer. But their delight turned to horror as my father proceeded to undo his belt and loosen his trousers to access the hidden pouch around his waist. Having no idea what this white man was doing, but not liking the look of it, they began to scream and cover their faces with their shirts. I jumped to reassure them that my father was only wishing to show them the photos and nothing else while Dad quickly pulled out the plastic photo holder before turning and making himself decent again. By this time, Fred was almost paralytic with laughter, red-faced as he struggled to take a breath. Once I had the photos in my hand I convinced the women to remove their shirts from their faces. I promised that Dad, now fully clothed and presentable, would not shame them further. They seemed to enjoy looking at the photos but kept a wary eye on my father while they did so.

As we continued our stroll along the road, the sound of bells and singing wafted past. Up ahead, having just turned the corner, was a group of some twenty girls in full, bare-breasted Zulu regalia. They wore the attire of young maidens: short leather skirts, long loops of beads over their bare chests, and thick anklets and bracelets covering every limb. We realised that the tinkling sound was coming from the shuffling movement the girls made with their ankles and feet, some of which were strapped with bells and others with soft drink tops, all of which shook and rattled as they pounded their feet in time against the earth. We asked Fred what the occasion was and he guessed that it was part of a wedding celebration taking place further up the valley that weekend. We stood and watched as they snaked their way past us, vibrant with colour and song, waving and smiling at their exotic audience on the roadside.

The day before my parents were to leave, Robbie was working with Themba on a tin craft workshop as he had yet to bend the tin to his will. While he was busy cutting a piece of tin to size, the cutters slipped, sending a small shard of tin into Robbie's eye. Themba ran for Steve and together they took him to a hospital in the city to get the injury seen to. Mum and Dad had been collecting the post when this happened, so only heard of the incident when they returned. I agreed to take them to see Robbie the next morning, as they didn't want to go without saying goodbye and we had dinner plans that night. They were very fond of Robbie and had particularly enjoyed the meal we shared with him and his sister Happy at their home in Azalea township.

But this night, we were having our last supper at a Greek restaurant in town. Mdu, who had been in hiding for a few weeks, was very keen to meet my parents before they left and decided to risk meeting us in a public place. We drove to the restaurant and were shown through to our table. Mdu had asked me to book a table in the back so that he could keep an eye on the front door. While this might have seemed like cloak and dagger material to my parents when they first arrived, they now knew that it was simply a necessary precaution. We sat at the table and waited for about twenty minutes, at which point I suggested we order, thinking perhaps that it had been too hard for Mdu to get to us. Just after we had placed our orders, however, he appeared through the door to the bathrooms, telling us he had jumped over the back fence and entered the restaurant from the rear. I laughed at him at the time, but in a few years his best friend would be gunned down as he left a city restaurant by the front door; I was wrong to make light of his situation. After the drama of Mdu's entry, we settled down to a marvellous meal. Mdu was his usual charming self, taking great delight in telling my parents about a few of my adventures that I had forgotten to divulge. They were impressed by his articulate intelligence and insight into the many topics that he and my father discussed. They commented on the way home that the country would be poorer if men like Mdu were lost.

The next morning, we set out early to visit Robbie in hospital. At the Med-citi Clinic we were told that Robbie was no longer there: he had been taken to casualty but after seeing the doctor, and without Steve's knowledge, he had been transferred to Edendale Hospital. My parents by now understood the unspoken implication—the Clinic was for white patients; black patients belonged at Edendale Hospital in the township. My father, though clearly angry, was no longer surprised by this kind of discrimination. When we finally found Robbie, it was almost eleven o'clock. He had a large white patch on his eye and was clearly pleased to see us. Robbie told me later that his treatment in the hospital dramatically improved after our visit, his status having been raised by the attention of three foreign visitors.

Saying goodbye to my parents again was hard. I had become used to sharing my life with them, having someone with whom to discuss my marvel, distress or anger as the events of each day unfolded. Over the course of the month, I had taken my parents to a wedding and two funerals, a youth rally and a jazz club. We had visited friends both black and white. They had been to a rural area, stayed in a township, been tourists and volunteered their time fetching milk, bread and post. Dad had even done some landscaping around the cottage in his spare time. They had been asked to confront discrimination, violence and despair and yet through it all they had displayed a graciousness and curiosity in each situation that made me proud to be their daughter.

I doubt whether many people in their mid fifties would have handled themselves so well. Mum and Dad's exposure to the world had been largely through printed word at that stage. After leaving the dairy farm to return to Sydney for Jon's and my schooling, they had bought a small library in Chatswood that they turned into a highly successful bookstore. Mum read everything and was the kind of person who would be able to locate a book based on a whiff of a clue: 'I think it has some red on the cover and the author's name begins with a T'. Dad, on the other hand, read only non-fiction which gave him the ability to have an in-depth conversation on any political or economic topic imaginable. Though neither had finished school, both had educated themselves beyond what any Masters degree would have had to offer.

Having them share the fabric of my life in South Africa so fully was a gift that ultimately allowed me to stay. It would have been so easy for them to take fright at the dangers my life presented but they chose not to, instead leaving me to do what they knew I felt I must.

14
May 1990
Goodbye and Hello

'Hello? It's me.'

'Hello me. Did you forget to tell me something?'

'No. I have to talk to you.'

'About what?'

'About coming down to Grahamstown.'

'I can't wait.'

'I don't think you should come.'

'Why?'

'Because we have to stop.'

'What do you mean?'

'It's too painful, Sandy. I can't do it anymore. We have to stop this.'

'Don't give up on us. I love you.'

'That's the problem. I love you and I can't ignore the reality anymore. It's too hurtful to be with you, knowing that it has to end.'

'We can have a future if we want it badly enough.'

'I can't do it. I won't survive if I'm cut off from my community.'

'I don't want to be without you. I'll live with whatever that means.'

'Sandy, I can't.'

'What are you saying?'

'I don't want that life for either of us.'

'Are you saying it's not worth it?'

'I couldn't bear to always be different, always apart, simply because of the colour of my wife's skin. I can't live that life.'

'I can.'

'I don't want you to. In the end, it will be too hard and it will fall apart with us hating each other.'

'It won't. I believe it's possible. I can't accept that apartheid is right.'

'I'm not saying that.'

'That's what it means.'

'I just can't. I will always love you, but I can't.'

'So you'll marry a black woman instead, just because it will be easier?'

'Sandy.'

'Even the thought of it ...'

'Stop.'

'Msizi, don't give up.'

'Stop.'

'Don't give up.'

'You have to let it go.'

'I don't know how when I still love you.'

'I will stop calling.'

'I couldn't bear that.'

'I'm sorry. I'm so sorry.'

And so it ended, after more than two years of Msizi turning my world, grounding my experiences, giving me courage. I knew I was asking a lot of him, but I had always hoped that the strength of our connection would see us through. And it did—just not in the way I had imagined at the time. We have always stayed in touch, not so close as to resurrect anything between us but close enough to remain friends.

At that time, though, I saw only a future without him. I had a depth of connection with him that was almost unreasonable. My brother could not see what we had in common that kept us together but our bond was like an underground spring that sustained us both. The thought of being without that, particularly after the trauma of the Seven Day War, blew through me like a gale rattling an abandoned house. I was bereft and without direction and a depression began to creep over me that turned my limbs to stone.

But life went on in the days that followed and so I allowed the work to fill my waking hours. Robbie, of course, was my confidant during our many hours in the bakkie, driving from one part of the township to another. He wisely offered little advice, but rather listened as my thoughts turned round and round in search of possibilities that always ended in a stalemate. In the evenings when I was alone at the cottage—Mama Jenny usually in bed before 9.00—I set aside my mental fight with Msizi's decision, leaving my heart the opportunity to miss him. Even though we had spent the vast majority of our relationship apart, the knowledge that he was no longer accessible to me—despite still caring for me—festered like an open wound.

A week before things ended with Msizi, Matt and Bee had returned to 'Maritzburg and were staying with us at Phezulu for a couple of weeks. Matt was now working for an Australian aid agency and was visiting to approve our proposal for funding. He, Bee and Steve were also working on a book for use with church youth groups, based on case studies of some of the young people we worked with. Given that Matt and Bee were visiting, it was harder to pull away and be on my own; this probably saved me from turning too far inwards and letting the emotional heaviness take me over. Despite myself, I enjoyed Matt and Bee's stay at Phezulu. Bee, who was now a journalist back in Sydney, had retained the same quirky sense of humour that couldn't help but break the darkness of any mood. And Matt's 'cup half full' philosophy of life was as infectious as always. They laboured away on their writing during the day but joined in as many community activities as they could, including team lunches, weekend programs and home group.

Home group was a weekly get-together of a number of friends who, like myself, were struggling to find a way to hold onto their faith while still working within the harsh realities of the South African experience. We had been meeting for well over a year now and the group included Steve and Beth, myself, Jacques and Margie from ETHOS, Brian and Anthea who had been at the Centre with us (with Anthea now working at the local newspaper), Fred when he was in town, his girlfriend Heather and any other ring-ins who were visiting. Robbie joined us from time to time as did Mdu and Themba. Even Sipho was a regular while he lived with us. Mum and Dad had also been a part of it during their stay, despite being agnostic themselves. Of late, Jacques and Margie often brought Teboho with them, particularly as he didn't go back to Jo'burg for the mid-semester break, so I was getting to know him a bit better as well. We took turns to meet in each other's homes, sometimes sharing a meal, sometimes just dessert and coffee. Home group was a haven where we all laid down the troubles of the day and helped each other find sufficient meaning to keep moving forward. It also cemented many of these friendships so that they would last for many years to come.

When it was time for Matt and Bee to leave, I decided to catch a lift with them to Jo'burg and spend my long weekend with Barry and Rags at their new home on the edge of the sprawling Thembisa township. Through their friendship with Jacques and Margie, they knew Msizi and so were happy to provide my means of escape for what would otherwise have been a very lonely break back at Phezulu. They showed me around the township where they were now doing very similar work to Sizwe's but focusing primarily on dialogue between black and white churches in Jo'burg. In fact, Barry was facilitating an overnight visit by a white church group that weekend. They were staying in the homes of members of the black church, a first for everyone involved, with Barry running a workshop on Saturday on the Church's role in apartheid. The visit finished with the white group joining their black hosts for church on Sunday morning followed by a lunch. Normally, this would have been an exciting program to be part of.

But I needed a break from my day-to-day routine so Rags and I took the chance to sit back and relax, catching up on all the news from Sizwe and the recent events in my personal life. I vividly remember sitting in Rags' kitchen over breakfast on Sunday morning telling her that, at twenty-four, I now had no hope for a long-term relationship. It brings a smile to my face as I write, but at the time, I was despondent. My life was predominantly in the black community and yet, if Msizi was to be believed, there would be no hope of a life partner there. However, the choice to work in townships had effectively alienated me from the majority of the white community. On top of that, my South African experiences were so far removed from the lives of an average Australian that I didn't see how I could find one who would identify with how I now saw the world. Rags, good friend that she was, sensed my despair and chose not to jolly me out of my somewhat melodramatic conclusion. Instead, she listened and understood.

I returned to 'Maritzburg somewhat refreshed and decided it was time to move back in with the Skhosanas, if they would have me. I reasoned that if I was committed to being in the township I should be there fully. I had also enjoyed the strong sense of community I experienced in Caluza, even during the war. After a discussion with Baba Skhosana it was agreed that I would move back in, though this time he would let me have an outside room, given that I was a working woman and needed to come and go. We agreed on a monthly contribution to the household for food and rent and then I went off to buy myself a bed and a cupboard.

Because the cottage was furnished and my monthly stipend small, I actually owned very little—just my clothes, my cat and a small stereo. I agreed to leave the stereo with Mama Jenny as she enjoyed the music and in return, she agreed to look after my cat. I didn't think Sombu would do too well in the township where pets are simply functional and frequently end up under the wheel of a car. On top of that, the Skhosanas had just got themselves a dog, a friendly little 'pavement special' as Fred called dogs of dubious heritage, whom the kids instantly named Freedom. The irony was that Freedom was tied up on a chain in the yard twenty-four hours a day. He fell over himself with delight when anyone bent down to give him a pat. So while Mama Jenny adopted Sombu for a while, I promised myself I would keep an eye out for Freedom.

I settled back in quickly, with Robbie fetching Themba and I at the bottom of the street each morning on his way up Sweetwaters Road. It would have taken hours of connecting taxis for Robbie to get home each night under his own steam, so Steve had long since agreed that Robbie would drop Themba in Caluza and then drive on through Imbali to Azalea, keeping the bakkie with him overnight and returning via the same route in the morning. Robbie and I were soon run off our feet with a series of dialogue programs and leadership training.

On my weekend off, I had been invited to a farewell party that Sipho and his family were throwing for one of the volunteers in the Imbali Support Group. This volunteer was returning to the United States and many people from across Imbali wished to send him on his way with their thanks and best wishes. We had a great night, Sipho's parents in particular seeming to enjoy hosting their friends in their home during these happier times, in stark contrast to when we stayed over as part of the Support Group work. Sipho's father was a taller version of Sipho himself, clearly a larrikin in his younger days but now an affectionate father and husband. Sipho's mother was stout of body and heart and was the source of courage for each one of her children. As a family they had suffered a great deal and I watched with delight, seeing them together again under the same roof.

I was stunned therefore when, two days later, the news came through that Sipho's father had been gunned down on his way to work. The gunmen, though identified by witnesses, were never tried for his murder. The family had been regularly harassed and attacked by some of the more notorious members of Inkatha, partly for Sipho's involvement with the UDF and partly for his father's. We all assumed this was all part of making the family pay for their choices as well as deterring others from following their example.

So I stood with the family that weekend as we buried Sipho's father, still yet to become accustomed to the loss of those who had become so dear to me. Some of the women beside us began to sing a haunting lament, '*Senzeni na, senzeni na?*' What have we done, what have we done, we black people, to deserve this? Their singing swept around us all as tears fell onto the dirt at our feet. I could not imagine how Sipho's mother bore the burden of more grief in her life. I was glad for her rock-like faith in God but wondered if one day it would break from the constant testing. I suspect that Sipho's heart was broken as it was not long afterwards that Monica began to look into the possibilities of him studying in Canada.

After I'd been living in the township for a few weeks Steve raised the issue of my language studies which had largely been interrupted by the war. He told me that there was to be a two-week intensive language lab at the University of Natal and asked if I was interested in attending. I was impressed by Steve's commitment to the development of the team. He regularly provided opportunities for us to improve our effectiveness and I was keen to one day become fluent in Zulu—so I jumped at the offer and enrolled.

For those two weeks, instead of going to work with Robbie and Themba each morning, I jumped a taxi into town, then caught another to the university ten minutes drive from the city centre. I knew a few people on campus, mostly lecturers and a few who worked for organisations affiliated with the university. Brian, who with his wife Anthea was a regular at home group, lectured in the Science Department. I also knew Fiona and her husband Rod. Fiona worked in the newly established Centre for Academic Development and Rod ran an environmental consultancy.

Sizwe had quite a strong relationship with the Department of Organisational and Family Psychology which, given the nature of our work, was often involved in the rehabilitation of some of the young people under our care. One of their psychologists by the name of Vernon had also been running stress management workshops with the team each month since the beginning of the year, again something that Steve had put in place to support both the development and the mental health of the team.

But my closest connections were with ETHOS. I had become very close to Margie since she and Jacques moved to 'Maritzburg and, through her, had come to know many of the students: Alice, Teboho, Pat, Nimrod and others. Hearing that I was going to be on campus every day, Margie invited me to join them for the daily community lunch they had at the ETHOS residence. So this became my habit and it led to the forming of a number of relationships—one in particular—that would be very influential in my life.

Of all the ETHOS students, I had spent the most time with Teboho up until that point. What I didn't know then was that Teboho had been smitten with me ever since I turned up at ETHOS late one night a few months before, face blackened, asking for help with a kombi full of children who needed somewhere safe to stay. He apparently told Pat, his closest friend at the residence, 'Now there's a woman after my own heart'. It seems the real reason he had started attending home group was that it was his only opportunity to get to know me better. So when Teboho heard that I would be on campus for two weeks and—thanks to Margie who was a hopeless matchmaker—that I was no longer spoken for, Teboho was determined to make the most of the time. In the first few days on campus, I did notice how attentive he was—but I also knew that Teboho was a complete extrovert, constantly surrounding himself with friends, so I thought nothing of it. I was also still licking my wounds from my breakup with Msizi and a new romance was not on my mind.

I was enjoying the language study, understanding for the first time why I said some of the things I had learnt to say by rote. My strategy up until that time was to copy what was said by others in particular situations without understanding the component parts of the phrase that was being used. I simply knew when the phrase was appropriate. Over time, I was able to piece together the meaning of parts of phrases from other words I was learning but it was not until the language lab that I understood the grammar. I found the classroom environment a little artificial compared to what I was used to but I tried not to let that dampen my enthusiasm for learning. What's interesting is that my overly rational, analytical approach to all elements of my life, including matters of the heart, did not apply to how I learnt a language. My language acquisition was a far more intuitive process. Given my success in ultimately learning a number of African languages, there was clearly a lesson for me there.

One night when I was back at home in Caluza, the phone rang as we were all sitting in the lounge watching a local African drama. Baba Skhosana picked it up, as he always did when he was home, so that he could monitor calls. If he was not around it was usually Sibongile who ran for the phone, convinced it would be for her which it usually was. Her friends seemed to have a knack for knowing when her father was not at home. This night, the phone call was for me. In disapproving tones, Baba Skhosana told me that there was a young man wanting to speak to me. I caught Nonsi's eye as I took the receiver, clearly understanding that this was not a good thing. In black culture, young women do not admit to having boyfriends. It is considered disrespectful to bring a young man to the house unless you have been promised to him in marriage. I pulled a face back at Nonsi, the meaning of which was 'he's not my boyfriend'. Regardless of this fact, under the watchful eye of Baba Skhosana I kept the conversation very short, telling Teboho that I would speak to him on campus. When I got off the phone, Baba Skhosana raised an eyebrow at me as I attempted to assure him that it was just someone from class asking for some help with an assignment. However, Nonsi took my hint as I left the lounge room and headed for the bedroom, following behind me in hot pursuit.

'You've got to be more careful', Nonsi told me. 'Baba will be watching you like a hawk now.' Nonsi had been seeing someone for well over a year without the family knowing. She often used Themba or Zodwa as a go-between, giving her both a venue for meetings and a conduit for messages. Themba was considered to be one of the household at the Skhosanas' and could come and go at will in the evenings without raising suspicion. He often brought messages for Nonsi when he came. But Nonsi was over-estimating the situation with me. I was hiding no one. She quickly pointed out that Teboho may be hoping for something different. 'Why else would he go to all the trouble of getting this number when he could just find you tomorrow?' she asked. I realised she had a point—I just hadn't been looking.

Though Baba Skhosana's rules may have seemed draconian to many, I had learnt that in African culture a woman is a child in the eyes of her family until she marries. She then moves from the care and responsibility of her father to that of her husband. So despite Nonsi and I being in our twenties, this mindset had Baba treating us like wayward teenagers. I took it lightly as I knew I could move away if it really became a problem, but I knew that other young women had no such choice. I also knew that Baba Skhosana's intention was to protect us and the image of him holding a brick in his hand, ready to defend his family with his life, tempered my feminist views on the subject. I was also touched that he treated me with the same concern as he did his daughters.

Despite all this, I was yet to be convinced that you waited until an engagement period to find out more about a man so the next day over lunch, I considered Teboho in a different light. His extroverted personality made you feel as if the sun was shining on your face whenever he was near. Yet he also appeared to be a sensitive person who cared deeply about the needs of others. After many days of looking after the children I had brought him that night during the war, he also ensured that the large garage and its side rooms were made available to the housekeeper at ETHOS, Mama Florence. She lived up on the escarpment above Edendale valley where she and her family had lost their home in the violence; it had been looted and burnt down one night as they fled into the valley. Her family were now living on the property at Teboho's request while new accommodation could be found. I also noticed that he did not change his behaviour around white people as many black people did, becoming more withdrawn and less likely to say what they were really thinking. He seemed to stand up for what he believed in regardless of the power or influence of those he addressed. The final thing that was abundantly clear to me was that Teboho was constantly surrounded by women. Perhaps he was like many other township men who felt no pang of guilt pursuing and confessing their love to multiple women at the same time.

I went home that night and discussed this with Nonsi. Her thoughts on the matter were, 'As long as a man marries you, it doesn't matter if he has many girlfriends along the way'. I wondered if African women had become so tolerant by necessity. I hadn't heard that Nonsi's boyfriend was a 'player' and I hoped for her sake he was not. I was also aware that many African men did nothing to curb their passion for many women once they married and I didn't know if this was something I could cope with. I remember my horror when the husband of a black South African friend I had known in Canada asked me out of the blue if I wanted to sleep with him. I replied that he was married to my friend and I had a boyfriend, but clearly these were not obstacles in his mind. When I spoke to Msizi about it, he had simply laughed at my naivety.

The following day was my last on campus and classes were finishing at lunchtime, as it was also the last day of term before the July break. Teboho found me in the morning and asked me if I wanted to come with him to Durban that afternoon. He had to go to the offices of an organisation he was doing some work for and wanted some company on the journey. This time I was not so naive as to misunderstand the purpose of the trip and so I agreed; I was keen to clarify what was going on between us, if anything.

We met back at ETHOS at lunchtime and after grabbing some *padkos*, some food for the road, we set off on the hour-long drive down to the coast. Teboho spent the first thirty minutes telling me about one or two women who were often at the lunch table and how he had had the opportunity to have a bit of fun with them. I felt the embarrassment start to rise red in my neck as I listened to him, thinking how foolish I had been to misunderstand his intentions towards me. Just when I was about to stop him from going any further, he told me that he had not pursued anything with them because he believed that if you were with someone, you had to consider them someone that you could potentially marry—otherwise you were simply abusing the situation. My throat, which had been constricted with embarrassment, now relaxed and opened up again, allowing the air to fill my chest. Just as we were nearing the city, Teboho finally got to his point.

'I would like you to consider a relationship with me. I knew you were the woman for me when I saw your bravery during the Seven Day War. On top of the other things that attract me, you are also courageous in the face of the violence that black people face every day. So I am proposing a serious relationship, not a quick fling. But before you decide, I want to talk to my family and friends back in Mohlakeng to see if this is something they would support. Last night, we spent a couple of hours debating the idea amongst the ETHOS guys and they finally agreed that they would be open to it.'

I sat listening to his proposition, thinking it was the most unusual one I had ever heard. What put my nose out of joint was that he had sat debating the possibility of our relationship with his friends at ETHOS before even raising the idea with me! He must have been incredibly confident that I would say yes. But I saw from the look on his face that his intentions had been honourable, if a little eccentric. He knew of the reasons for my split with Msizi and wanted to raise the issues first before risking a repetition of the hurt I had suffered there. So I agreed that I would think about his proposal over the holidays and we would discuss it when he returned.

The remainder of the trip to Durban passed quickly and in no time we were back at ETHOS. Teboho was leaving the next morning to go back to Jo'burg for three weeks. So he invited me to come in for a bit before he dropped me back in the township. We went to the room that he shared with Pat and as he stole a kiss, I struggled to reconcile feelings of betraying Msizi and hope for a new start.

Over the three weeks that Teboho was gone, I spent quite a bit of my spare time with Margie, the one who knew him best, trying to understand more about who he was and whether pursuing this relationship was the right thing to do. Of all the students, Teboho was Margie's favourite. She thought he was one of a kind: funny, principled, considerate and intelligent. She confessed to having been promoting my attributes to Teboho for a number of months now as she had paired us off in her mind at the beginning of the year. Margie was married to a very special man and enjoyed a close, tender relationship with him. She was now pregnant with their first child. I think she wanted for me that happiness she had in her own marriage and saw something in Teboho that convinced her it was possible. So we sat and chatted and knitted, a surprisingly tame pastime for me but one which, thanks to Margie, I found both soothing and contemplative. Margie was knitting for her baby and so I knitted a jersey which I had decided I would give to Teboho if the answer was yes on both our parts. If the answer was no, I had a large, warm jersey to see me through the remainder of the winter.

During those weeks, I was fortunate enough to attend the National Conference of the Anglican Student Federation that was being hosted at the seminary on the outskirts of Imbali. The keynote speaker and honorary president was Desmond Tutu. On the day he spent with us he was not dressed as an archbishop—in fact he looked rather like a member of the French underground. He wore a black beret and a black jacket with a mandarin collar which he accessorised with his trademark impish grin. He spoke passionately about the situation facing many young Christians in South Africa at that time. In responding to the political discrimination by the State, many young people were being alienated by their churches as radicals who had lost their faith. He knew that we struggled, as he did, to find a way to marry faith with suffering; a life in the church with a life in the struggle. He suggested that we had two options—leave the church or liberate it. Neutrality was a luxury. Unless we act against racism, we become racist; unless we act against sexism, we become sexist—so great are the forces of conformity in South Africa.

I felt enormously grateful to be living in a place that gave me the opportunity to meet and listen to people like Desmond Tutu. He and many others like him seemed to have been refined by the fire of their own suffering, allowing them to become people who held their line and encouraged others to do the same. I found South Africa was the kind of place that asked me every day: 'Who are you really and what do you stand for?' While this daily challenge was exhausting, it helped to clarify the essence of what was important in life. Money, careers, status and material possessions could not easily stand up to the daily test of 'What do you stand for?' leaving only human dignity, equality and peace in their place. However, my challenge since then has always been to come to my own conclusions about what is important in life without judging those who choose differently. Choosing the 'high ground' can take you precariously close to arrogance and if it does, you come tumbling down and are forced to begin again.

Teboho arrived back at ETHOS on the Sunday before classes began. I had heard nothing from him during those three weeks and had no idea how things had gone for him. He simply phoned me from Harrismith, the halfway house between Jo'burg and 'Maritzburg, and asked me to meet him in a few hours at ETHOS. I was waiting there when he arrived. I watched him as he exuberantly stepped out of the car and caught sight of me on the stairs to the house. 'Hello, my sweetheart', he yelled from the driveway, bag in hand, as he sprang towards the house.

A few minutes later we were sitting in the lounge which was uncharacteristically empty with few students yet back from holidays. He took me by the hand and told me in detail how his consultations had gone. He spoke to Moss and Khumo first. I had met Moss at the beginning of the year at the ETHOS opening and Khumo was his wife who ran the Women's Desk at the South African Council of Churches' head office. Khumo, being no wallflower, was the toughest critic. She told Teboho outright that mixed marriages in South Africa are too hard on everyone concerned, with neither partner able to find acceptance. Teboho had been friends with Khumo for many years. In fact, he was the go-between in the courting of Khumo and Moss when their relationship was still a secret. Khumo loved Teboho and wanted the best for him. His previous relationship had left its scars on him and she hoped that he would find comfort in a new relationship after almost five years alone. But she felt this choice seemed to be asking for trouble. They spoke about it many times over that three-week period and then she stood back, having said her piece. He knew she would support him whichever decision he made, and she did.

Moss was more circumspect, as was his way. Being a minister and peacemaker, he was able to see both sides of the argument, but having the added advantage of having met me, he decided to support his friend's wishes. Teboho also spent many hours debating with his male peers, a number of whom he had lived with for many years. Eventually, the inner circle felt that it wasn't a bad thing, depending on my ability to assimilate. They also told him that they never expected him to make a predictable choice in anything he did, as he had always marched to the beat of his own drum. However, he also told me that there were a few who challenged him in private about being a sell-out to the struggle if he chose to be with a white woman. Taking this on board he went, last of all, to his family. As I sat listening to this long tale of consultation, it was like watching a roulette wheel spin, waiting for the ball to fall. I had learnt by now that African storytelling is a time-honoured art, one not to be rushed—but I could have done with an executive summary at this point.

He spoke to his older brother, the teacher, who had no issue. He spoke to his younger brother whom he had sent to a multicultural high school in Mafikeng. He, too, saw no problem with the idea. He spoke to the brother born after him who, like Teboho, had the mould broken when he was born—and he loved the idea. (In years to come, Doki would break a number of conventions of his own to be with the woman he loved.) He then spoke to his mother who just shook her head and laughed. 'Just like you', she said. 'We never know what to expect.' Last of all, he asked his father's second wife, to whom he was close, and to his surprise, she said, 'Over my dead body'. Given the family had been supportive up until this point, he was a little taken aback. He pushed to further understand Ma Ellen's thinking.

She had explained: 'When two people marry it is not just the two who become one, it is also their families who do so. If you are asking me to consider joining with a racist white family, after everything we have suffered under apartheid, I can never agree'.

Seeing the problem immediately, he pointed out, 'But Ma Ellen, she is not a South African, she is an Australian'.

'Oh', she said, 'that's completely different. Then you will have no problems with me, Ntebu.'

And with a flourish, the story finished. He looked up at me, eyes wide with expectation, waiting for my response.

'So what are you saying?' I asked, needing a little more clarification.

'I'm saying that if you'll have me, we have the support of my family and community. The few whose support we do not have do not matter.'

I took a breath. I knew that Teboho made me feel good. He was someone who inspired possibilities. But I also knew that I did not feel the same way as I had felt about Msizi: the passion, the connection was not as deep. Yet I remember thinking to myself that I should take a risk and see. In hindsight, I believe I said 'yes' because he was willing to believe in the same thing that I did: that colour, class, gender or religion should not be what determined who could be together as neighbours, friends or lovers. And in all honesty, I said yes because he was willing to take a chance on me, because he thought I was worth it where in my mind at that time, Msizi had not. And so our relationship began, its unorthodox start simply a sign of things to come. Soon Teboho was seen sporting his new grey and white fair isle jersey, bragging to all who would listen about the creative talents of his girlfriend.

In the weeks that followed, the big excitement was that Mandela was coming to 'Maritzburg and was planning a rally in Edendale to celebrate Women's Day. The stadium, which is probably an overstated description of the playing field and a few rickety stands that surrounded it, was a thirty-minute walk from the Skhosanas' and many people in our area were planning to walk down there together. No doubt, the singing would start along the way, adding further electricity to an already excited township.

When the day arrived, the household was up early. It was a Sunday; we had to go to church in the morning before the rally in the afternoon. Everyone was also keen to be done with any chores and errands that might otherwise delay them when we returned from church. Church in the township was a time-consuming affair. I often felt as though the longer it went, the more the old people enjoyed it. The same couldn't be said for the young, particularly those who had a rally to get to. This day, the singing went on for what felt like an eternity, followed by one of the longer sermons Baba Skhosana had ever given. I thought for a minute I caught a twinkle in his eye as if he sought to teach his children a lesson in patience, seemingly a pastime for fathers the world over. Given that we were part of the minister's family, we were obliged to stay and socialise with the congregants, chatting about the health of various family members and recent events in the neighbourhood.

I knew from other rallies I had attended that there would be plenty of older women who would be coming along, but a number of these church ladies prided themselves on their ability to steer clear of politics, seemingly believing the doctrine that many white churches espoused. These churches argued that it was against the teachings of the bible to undermine the government as it was God's appointed instrument of law and order. Therefore, the most godly course of action was to stay well out of anything political and simply pray. Those church women who choose to attend the rally would argue that it is not in God's will for people to support unjust laws; rather, it was their duty to work for justice in an unjust society.

In fact, women had always played an integral role in the struggle against apartheid. Women, both black and white, had led the way in the protests to ban the carrying of passes. Under the apartheid laws black people were required to carry a pass that stated where they worked, their place of origin, tax payments and any encounters with the police. They could not leave a rural area for an urban one without having a pass and upon arrival, they had seventy-two hours to organise a work permit allowing them to stay. If they were caught without a pass they were instantly detained. Police carried out daily raids into the townships in an effort to arrest those without passes, with millions falling prey. Though the passes were ultimately done away with, they came to symbolise the worst of the apartheid laws. Women were also a powerful force in the unions, in the ANC and in the churches in bringing about change. But it is most true to say that women held the fabric of the family and community together when the apartheid policies were designed to tear them apart. And it was this total contribution that Mandela was going to be recognising at the Women's Day rally.

Finally, church was over and we headed back to the house for lunch. Though my household workload was reduced under the new living arrangements, it hardly seemed fair to watch Nonsi and Sibongile cooking and cleaning without pitching in. So together we made quick work of what needed to be done, including serving up a hot Sunday lunch.

After our meal, I ducked out and went down to the store where there was a public telephone. As part of Baba Skhosana's anti-boyfriend regime, he had the only key to the telephone and would lock it when he was out; and there was no point trying to make a private phone call when he was home. At the store, I made a quick call to Teboho who could not come to the rally because he had a major assignment due the following day. He was now regretting his procrastination but was trying hard not to show it. After I hung up, I waited for Nonsi and Themba on the street. Soon enough, half the Skhosana household was walking down the road with Themba and Zodwa in tow.

We joined up with many others who had gathered at the store and made our way down to Sweetwaters Road. Instead of turning left to go up to Phezulu, we made a right turn and headed towards Edendale Road. From this slightly elevated position we could see thousands of people already en route to the stadium. It looked as if the usually busy Edendale Road had become a walkway, with a lane on each side of the road now devoted to pedestrians. At the intersection with Edendale Road, we again turned right, away from town and Edendale Hospital and towards the far end of the valley and the escarpment above. In just under a kilometre, with the crowds now walking six and seven abreast, we turned right towards the stadium. The singing and chanting had started on Edendale Road, a favourite being, 'Strike the woman, you strike the rock'.

The crowd flowed into the stadium like a river. I knew Steve and Beth were there somewhere but there was no way to spot them. Jacques and Margie were also coming with a few of the ETHOS students and Anthea was covering the event for the local newspaper. I did spot some familiar white faces from the Imbali Support Group and Legal Aid. The crowd that day was not only more mixed and, obviously, more female than at the Durban rally; the average age was also a lot older. This gave the rally a more mature yet no less exuberant flavour and tone.

We had passed clusters of police vans on the way to the stadium and now there was a substantial police presence at the gate, but their mood seemed less confrontational in comparison to other township events. As the only white person in my group entering on foot, I drew some unwanted attention but tried to ignore the disapproving stares of the police as I passed through the gate. The ANC marshals directed us onto the field, having filled up the stands with the early arrivals. Fortunately, we were given a spot not too far from the stage and quickly made ourselves comfortable on the ground. In Africa, women sit very comfortably for long periods of time with their legs stretched out before them. I was yet to learn this skill, or perhaps I simply lacked a shapely behind that made it possible, so I sat cross-legged on the grass. Whenever I did so, a few comments were inevitably thrown my way. Some found it unladylike while others wondered at my flexibility. What I lacked in the size of my behind, I made up for in length of leg.

Amidst the good-natured teasing, of which Zodwa was the queen, the crowd continued to swell. And so too did the singing. A number of groups came into the stadium marching under banners—'Imbali Youth Organisation', 'ANC Women's League', 'Smero Youth Organisation'—each group sporting their own T-shirts, singing their own songs. As always, the rally was a South African version of a Mardi Gras: all that was missing were the floats.

Before long, the stadium was full to overflowing. We turned our attention to the stage as the chairs that had been placed there began to fill. Skhumbuzo and Thami had each taken a seat, next to Harry Gwala, the ANC leader of the Midlands area. The local chairperson of the ANC Women's League was also there. J. J., the lawyer to whom Mdu and I had submitted statements on the funerals, was seated next to her. There were a few others I did not know and there was still no sign of the great man himself.

A few minutes later, Thami was standing, warming up the crowd though they needed no encouragement. He instigated the call and reply that was characteristic of all political rallies. '*Amandla*' reverberated across the stadium. '*Awethu*' came the reply. 'Power—is ours' the mantra said, reminding the participants of their power in numbers and the righteousness of their cause. A song broke out spontaneously which served as the crowd calling for Mandela to take the stage: 'Nelson Mandela, Nelson Mandela, *agekho fana nawe*', there is no one like you. As they sang, tens of thousands leapt to their feet and began to dance. There was a particular movement that went with this song and we all knew it and danced it as one. The ground trembled as thousands hopped from one foot to the other in time with the song.

And so Madiba took the stage once more. This time I was close enough to see his expressions. He spoke eloquently about the role of women in the struggle, honouring each contribution, large and small. He spoke of the work of the ANC Women's League, the Federation of South African Women, the Black Sash (an organisation of white women who worked tirelessly for change despite ridicule in their own community). He spoke of our mothers who gave us love and courage, who fed us, clothed us and gave us someone to want to come home to. Mandela had a way of bringing down divisions between people by going to great efforts to point out the value in each person, each community. And though my own efforts to bring about change were small indeed when compared to the sacrifices others had made, that day I felt honoured too.

After many more speeches and choirs had rounded out the day the crowd, elated yet well satisfied, made its way back out onto Edendale Road, spreading like a smouldering lava flow over the area as the music and dancing continued. Those of us who lived in Caluza peeled off at Sweetwaters Road and began to shuffle our way up the hill, to renewed singing of 'Nelson Mandela, *agekho fana nawe*'.

About halfway up the street, we hit a police road block. The police vans lined the road and a row of policemen standing two deep forced the crowd to filter through them like a funnel. I was all too aware that I was once more the only white person in the group; the others had arrived by car and left the same way. As I neared the police, I was grabbed and pulled off to one side. I suddenly regretted wearing my new Sizwe T-shirt to the rally; I didn't wish to give the police any additional information. While the rest of the crowd filed past, many continuing to sing in protest at the intrusion, I stood surrounded by police, terrified about what might happen next. The circle of men parted and an officer took me by the arm and dragged me to the back of the police van. I assumed he meant to throw me in the vehicle which would mean detention and deportation. I was in South Africa on a work permit and though my nationality would probably keep me safe from torture, I would lose my permit and the right to ever return.

As I stood by the van the officer, still holding my upper arm, leant into my face and said, 'We know all about you. We've been watching you for a while now'.

The thought flashed through my mind that this must be what they say to everyone, wanting to give the impression of being an omnipresent, omniscient power over people, to intimidate people into self-censorship.

He continued in his thick Afrikaans accent, 'We know what you are doing there at Sizwe, driving around in your little red bakkie and we know about the Imbali Support Group too'.

I stood with my shoulders squared, trying to appear unmoved by his intimidation—but I was beginning to flounder. How much was bluff and how much did they really know?

'We are keeping a file on you, you know. If I ever find you at a rally like this again, dancing along the street like a slut, I'll have you in prison and out of this country so fast. You are a shame to the white race. Now get out of here, but you remember that I'll be watching you.'

And with that, he flung me back into the crowd. I was deeply shaken, wanting only to be out of their sight. I went quickly up the road and turned left into our street but at the last minute, thinking I shouldn't go back to the house just yet, turned off down a side lane until I found a quiet corner where I could sit on the grass. From this position, I could see back over the valley to the road block and the main road beyond. Thoughts whirled around my head like a cyclone as I ran through all the possible scenarios. I did not see how I could do my work without being in the township, without bumping up against the police. And deportation would put an end to my relationship with Teboho before it even began.

Eventually I became too choked up to think, and the tears began to flow. I sat curled up into a little ball, making myself small so that the danger would pass me by. I don't know how long I sat like this but when it was starting to get dark, the Skhosanas' eldest, Jabulani, appeared next to me. Having heard from Nonsi and Themba what had happened Mama Skhosana has sent him to come and find me. As I told him what the officer had said to me, he sat listening without saying a word. But soon the fear had closed my throat again and I began to sob. He put an arm around me and said, 'You have to live your own life. If this is where you want to be, then be here. But you cannot live in fear'.

Then we sat together for a time in the gathering darkness and listened to the sounds of the township night before turning for home.

15
LIFELINES

TEBOHO CAME FROM A LARGE, WARM AND INCLUSIVE FAMILY BUT IT TOOK ME A LONG TIME TO UNDERSTAND ITS COMPLEXITY. MUCH OF HIS UNIQUENESS SEEMS TO HAVE SPRUNG FROM THE EXTRAORDINARY UPBRINGING HE HAD AND I WAS ALWAYS EAGER TO KNOW MORE. I THINK, IN MANY WAYS, IT WAS HIS REMARKABLE LIFE STORY THAT I FOUND AS MAGNETIC AS THE MAN.

Teboho was born in Mohlakeng township in 1963, the third son of Phuti and Manana. At the time of his birth, Phuti had three other children with Manana and two with his second wife Ma Ellen, with a third on the way. Ma Ellen also had a child from a previous relationship. The whole family lived in a tiny four-roomed house with concrete block walls and an asbestos roof, no running water and no electricity. While bigamous relationships were less and less common by this time, it was extremely rare that the wives shared the same home. But the family could not afford to run two households, despite both wives taking on domestic work when they could find it. Surprisingly, there was an abundance of laughter in this unusual home. All three adults were determined to create a family where all were welcome and no distinctions were made between their children in terms of parentage. All were loved. All were wanted. Teboho's name in Sesotho means 'a gift from God'.

A year after Teboho's birth Phuti was killed, leaving his son with no memories, only stories of the enigmatic man he was. After a time, it became clear that the women could not support the family alone, so Ma Ellen agreed to marry one of her many suitors and took three of her children with her to Rustenburg, two hours to the northwest. She left her youngest daughter with Manana, as Silwane and Teboho had been raised like twins and would not be separated. Manana stayed on in Mohlakeng but was also under pressure to remarry.

Teboho remembers very little of the time before his mother's second marriage. His stepfather Bophundlovu worked as a first aid worker at a mine outside Krugersdorp on the far west reaches of Johannesburg. It was only fifteen minutes from the township of Mohlakeng where Manana had lived with Phuti and Ma Ellen. They moved into the mine's family accommodation which consisted of a long row of small rooms, two per family, with one acting as a bedroom and the other as a kitchen. Bophundlovu was afforded more privileges than the other black mine workers as his role was considered to be semi-skilled; hence his access to family accommodation as opposed to the hostel accommodation most black miners used.

Bophundlovu was not overly interested in Phuti's children and Teboho had to ensure that he was never a nuisance to the old man. From the age of six he ran errands for both parents, helped to cook and clean and with his sister, Ma Ellen's daughter Silwane, stayed away as much as possible. The two were always together, of a similar age and size and therefore assumed to be twins. When asked their names on the mine, they told everyone it was 'Jelly and Custard'. And so Teboho's life seemed to have improved for a time, with enough money for food and school and his 'twin sister' for company as they roamed the mine. Yet Bophundlovu's sternness could often suck the laughter out of their home—or at least it did when he returned from work.

However, Bophundlovu's demeanour changed with the birth of his first son. To everyone's surprise, including his own, he adored

Doki and soon his world revolved around him. Perhaps he was the son he never thought he would have, perhaps it was that Doki was the mirror image of him. Whatever the reason, he was a doting father.

A few years later, Teboho's mother gave birth to her last-born, Willie, the apple of her eye, who slept in bed tucked under his mother's arm each night. By then, Mama and Bophundlovu had four children—Teboho, Silwane, Doki and Willie—living with them in the mine accommodation. Teboho's three eldest siblings had all moved on. Caleb, the eldest son, had found teaching work back in Mohlakeng; Tshidi, Teboho's eldest sister, had married Reggie and moved to Itsoseng in the west; and Ephraim now lived with Ma Ellen in Rustenburg.

Under apartheid laws, black adults were not permitted to live in South Africa if they were not working and actively contributing to the economy. They were only permitted to live in 'homelands'—small pockets of land located in remote areas of the country that were considered to be separate and sovereign nations in which black people could pursue their own 'separate development'. There was one homeland designated for each tribal or language group. Some homelands were located in a single block; others were scattered like confetti on a map. For the most part, they were also situated on land of little commercial value with poor soil quality or in dry arid areas—so the chances of separate development were slim at best.

When Bophundlovu retired he was no longer allowed to live on the mine nor, for that matter, in South Africa. The family was relocated to the homeland of Bophuthatswana, of which Itsoseng was a part, where Tshidi and Reggie lived with their baby son. They put a small amount of money down to purchase the tin shack next to Tshidi and Reggie's. However, the homeland of Bophuthatswana was a Tswana homeland and Mama and Bophundlovu were Sesotho speaking. As a result of this administrative error, neither Bophundlovu nor Manana was allowed to work in Bophuthatswana.

Mama found work back in South Africa, which was only a short distance away. She worked as a labourer on a nearby farm, walking the seven kilometres to work and back six days a week as the taxi fare would have cost more than her total wages. To support the family, Bophundlovu began roasting nuts in an old drum at the side of the house and selling them in the neighbourhood; when the officials found out they shut him down, as he lacked the proper work permits. So it was that the family survived on Mama's small income for a number of years. Caleb sent money when he could from his teaching job in Mohlakeng. However, he had also married and had a child of his own.

With the move to Itsoseng, Teboho's life was at a crossroads. He could choose to stay with his family but the high school opportunities in Itsoseng were virtually non-existent. The second and more difficult choice was to stay behind. He was twelve years old. He chose to stay. So as Manana and Bophundlovu shuffled the other children into the kombi that would take them to their new home, Teboho, small bag in hand, stepped into another kombi bound for Mohlakeng.

It broke Mama's heart that Teboho left her care so young, even though he was to live with Caleb. In an annual gesture of love, she gave him the equivalent of her monthly salary at the beginning of each year to help him buy school books. His family's poverty and his mother's sacrifices gave Teboho an entrepreneurial drive beyond his years. Every afternoon after school he would sell sweets on the streets of the township. Without ever eating a sweet himself, from his afternoon rounds he was able to raise enough money to purchase a simple camera. With this camera, a rare commodity in the township, he got into the more lucrative business of photography, taking photos on the streets and selling them individually once the film was developed. Through these two businesses he was able to support himself all the way through high school, as well as helping with Doki and Willie's education back in Itsoseng.

There was another driver for Teboho's financial independence: Caleb's wife was not willing to have another dependant drain his modest teacher's salary so she forbade Teboho eating with them or sleeping in their home. This was an incredible hardness of heart, so rare in the African communities that Teboho kept the situation from his mother who simply assumed her daughter-in-law would be taking care of her young son. Caleb, torn between pleasing his wife and caring for his brother, came up with an arrangement: Caleb would leave the door unlocked so that after his wife went to bed Teboho could enter the house, eat the leftovers Caleb had hidden for him and sleep on a bed of dirty clothes under the kitchen table. Teboho would be gone by dawn, making sure to leave no trace of his visit. Some days, weary of the deception, Teboho would simply choose to buy food for himself and sleep in the bush on the eastern edge of the township, near the high school.

Teboho's life continued in this way for a number of years. Not surprisingly he was struggling at school, having no time, place or energy to do homework. He also had a slight reading disability that went undiagnosed because he had developed a strategy of memorising all the work on the board in order to answer his teacher's questions and pass exams.

Towards the end of Teboho's high school years, Caleb's marriage began to break down. Caleb had been warned by a neighbour that his wife was trying to bewitch him. There were also questions as to his wife's fidelity. Caleb's concerns of foul play escalated when he found a small parcel wrapped in animal skin hidden in his cupboard amongst his clothes. He took the parcel to a *sangoma*, or witch doctor, who examined it and then asked him to look into a bowl of liquid: it would act as a window and show him who had hidden the *muti*, or charm, in his house and why. As Caleb stared into the bowl, he saw an image of his wife opening his cupboard as he slept and hiding the *muti* inside. The *sangoma* explained that the wife was trying to bewitch him so as to control the money he earnt. As a teacher, he was more highly paid than the vast majority of his community and lived in a four-room brick house on a paved street, as opposed to the tin shacks that many in Mohlakeng were forced to call home.

On the strength of this information and worn down by years of her harsh attitudes towards his family, Caleb asked his wife to leave.

She informed him that she was pregnant again, yet Caleb doubted that this child was his and insisted that she go. The two other children, Nooi and Dosi, remained behind with Caleb as he was keen to keep a strong relationship with them as well as caring for them financially. Teboho moved in shortly thereafter, finally recreating the close-knit family unit they had known years before.

Teboho's time on the streets had given him a strong empathy for those without homes or simply doing it tough. Soon Caleb's house became a way station for young boys who needed a place to call home for a time. Both Caleb and Teboho were community activists by this time, with affiliation to teachers' unions, community leadership structures, the ANC youth league and their local church group. There was a catch phrase at the time, 'the personal is the political', and for the two brothers it was their daily experience. There was no need to campaign, no university politics through which to recruit. The daily experience of black people was enough to push even the most docile into some form of protest or activism. For Teboho, whose life had been so punishing, to whom so much damage had been done, activism was the only response.

After Teboho finished high school, Caleb bought a larger home in another part of the township and left the four-roomed house to Teboho and his 'lost boys'. It was the first home Teboho had ever had and he would always love his brother for his generosity. By this time, Teboho had found work in a factory that made sanitary ware—bathtubs, toilets, basins. He had always wanted to go to university but neither his finances nor the apartheid policies were opening doors at that time.

While Teboho was working in the factory he was able to support the family, both biological and adopted. He purchased furniture and clothes, paid for books and transport, sent money to Mama for school fees for Doki and Willie. In fact, through Teboho's support, Willie was able to go to the International School in Mafikeng, which was one of the first integrated schools serving not only black and white South

African children but also the children of those who had come to work in Mafikeng from other countries. The apartheid government had put lucrative tax breaks in place for homeland industry in order to attract both foreign investors and foreign skills into the country. As a result the private schools there were afforded privileges that were yet to be granted in South Africa itself.

This was a time in Teboho's life when he felt he was able to make a contribution to the lives of others—and it felt good. His philanthropy eventually extended to the workplace and he began to organise a union there to better represent the rights of the workers whom he believed were being abused because of their low education levels. Not long after the union was established and came to the attention of management, he lost his job.

At about the same time, Teboho was dealt another blow that would wound him for a very long time. He missed a payment on the house and as he was trying to make alternative arrangements with the council, explaining that he had just lost his job, they informed him that they had sold the house to recoup the money. It was very close to Christmas by this time and on Christmas Eve, he and his friends were evicted. In many ways, he has never recovered from this event. A darkness descends each Christmas Eve that he still finds hard to shake. To add salt to the wound, it appeared that the people who bought the house paid next to nothing for it: they were family of the councillor who had made the decision to repossess. Many years later, Teboho took me to that house to show me where we should have lived.

So in 1986, Teboho moved back in with his brother and began to look for work. The next job he found was to change the course of his life.

A good friend, Khumo, put him in touch with the organisation she had been working for. It was called SUCA (Student Union for Christian Action) and worked on university campuses to organise the churchgoing students to take action against the political situation in the country. It combined a number of the things Teboho was passionate about so when Khumo was looking to replace herself as she moved on in the organisation, he was the perfect choice.

The job at SUCA opened up many avenues for Teboho. He travelled all over the country, often with Khumo, and met like-minded people, black and white, with whom he was able to build long-term friendships. Not only was it an avenue for his political commitments, it reignited his interest in tertiary study. At the time, the historically white universities were starting to loosen their entry requirements and opportunities were being snapped up by bright, ambitious young black people.

Khumo's husband, Moss, worked for an organisation called Concerned Evangelicals (CE). It had similar goals to SUCA's but worked among all the evangelical churches, not limiting itself to the student population. One of the programs that it established was the Evangelical Theological House of Studies (ETHOS). Historically, pastor training for evangelical churches was done in small theological colleges that lacked the rigour and stretch of a large tertiary institution. As a result, it was felt that evangelical pastors were not adequately equipped to serve the needs of their communities. ETHOS was established in partnership with the University of Natal in Pietermaritzburg to provide future pastors with high quality education.

Through SUCA, Teboho was involved in establishing ETHOS and went on to become, at Moss's insistence, included in the first intake of students. He and I first met at the opening of ETHOS on campus in January 1990. I had no idea that he would return a few weeks later to begin his studies.

Over time, Teboho told me of his history. I admired so many things about him and his experiences. He learnt the importance of family through the love of his mother and siblings. He learnt discipline, entrepreneurship and empathy through his years on the streets. He demonstrated generosity, courage and perseverance. Above all, he retained a sense of humour and perspective that saw him through tremendous difficulties. But underneath all these strengths, I also saw a simmering rage about the injustices he and his family had suffered. It was a rage that was impossible to express in full without destroying everything around him, so the rage, when it did surface, often found expression in depression and inertia. At some level, he knew that to survive he had to keep the monster at bay and keep moving forward, creating a future that would be different from his painful past.

I think Teboho is very like his father: a man who marched to the beat of his own drum. So it may have been that my soul recognised a kindred spirit in Teboho, someone who was always uniquely himself. Neither he nor I wished to be like everybody else, but rather to live our lives feeling free to take risks, try new things and take a course of action because it was, ultimately, the right thing to do.

16

August 1990
A New Roommate

SEVERAL PRIVATE SCHOOLS IN SOUTH AFRICA HAD EXPERIMENTED WITH RACIAL INTEGRATION FOR THE PAST FEW YEARS. THE NUMBERS OF BLACK STUDENTS WERE SMALL, AND THEY OFTEN FELT VULNERABLE AND EXPOSED. ALL THE SAME, IT WAS A BRAVE IDEOLOGICAL MOVE. RACIAL INTEGRATION WAS NOW SOMETHING THAT WAS ON THE CARDS FOR ALL SCHOOLS IN THE COMING YEARS AND THEREFORE A TOPIC OF DISCUSSION AT SIZWE.

While our work could serve to lay the foundations for integration among students, we were very aware that the teachers, who would be most influential in leading or blocking the success of multiracial schooling, were not yet part of our programs. And so we began to discuss ways to leverage our strong relationships with local schools to include a teachers' program. After much thought, we decided that a teachers' exchange would be the most effective way of giving teachers a glimpse into the lives of their peers and, hopefully, shifting their thinking. The logical conclusion of multiracial schools was not only a mixed student body but also a racially mixed faculty, something that would ultimately prove far more unacceptable to white parents than even the thought of a sixteen-year-old black boy sitting next to their daughter. Black teachers also worried that they would be unable to instil any kind of discipline in a classroom where the only relationship white students had had with black adults was one of servant and master.

It was into this cauldron of emotion that we launched a new program. To our surprise, and to the credit of the schools in 'Maritzburg, many principals and teachers signed up for the program, wanting to be on the front foot with integration before it became law. Neither we nor the schools had any idea what the outcomes might be as we began to book program dates for the end of that year and into the following.

About that same time we had a few more Australian volunteers coming to work at Sizwe, all of whom had been part of my church in Australia. Phil and Kathy, a married couple, were coming to stay for a month on their way back from a year in the States. Natalie, a very close friend of mine, was coming to stay for two months and had agreed to stay in the township with me; Kathy and Phil were using my old room in the cottage.

I was loving living in the township and was now feeling very much at home. Nevertheless, the idea of sharing the experience with Nat had me on the edge of my seat in the weeks before her arrival. I was looking forward to sharing the life I had created for myself with someone who had known me for years. I was also aware that she might calibrate this experience for me as I had rapidly become acclimatised to township living and was now taking much of it for granted.

Nat told her parents that she would be visiting me as part of a year travelling and working overseas. While she told them of her plans to do volunteer work with us for two months, she neglected to tell them that this would involve living in a black township. She feared, as I had, that imagining your child living in a township was much worse than the reality of it; best tell them about it after the fact.

Nat—easygoing, intelligent and respectful of others—is the kind of person who is loved by everyone. In fact, my parents had long since selected her as the person they most wished my brother would marry. Sadly, my brother did not bow to family pressure on this one. The Skhosanas fell in love with Nat immediately and were more than happy to have her share their home. She stayed in the outside room with me since, despite their open arms, there was as usual precious little space inside. So Nat and I had what felt to me like a two-month slumber party. For Nat, however, things took a little getting used to.

I had long since stopped noticing the stares I received when I was out and about in the township. On our first visit to the shop down the street, Nat stood by the door watching as all other business came to a standstill while I picked out the items we needed for supper and went up to the small grille window to pay. I must admit that two white women shopping in the township was a rare occurrence, but two tall blonde women made the contrast even more apparent.

I had also learnt to ignore the stares of young men who seemed ever confident in their ability to win the hearts of young township women, despite constant refusals. It was accepted practice for these young women to send their potential suitors packing, regardless of their interest in them. In African culture, it is not becoming for a woman to appear too enthusiastic: it is a man's job to chase, a woman's to deny for as long as possible. So when young men began approaching Nat with promises of undying love, she politely told them she was just visiting and while she was very flattered by their compelling offer, she wasn't in a position to marry them at this time. I had got to the stage of telling them to get lost with the same dismissiveness as my township peers, no longer concerned that they might be hurt by such directness. Nat's longwinded and kind response gave them hope that she was indeed impressed by their proposal and it was only a matter of time and due process before they would have her.

Nat had to learn the hard way, as had I, about the longsuffering determination of young African men in the pursuit of a trophy girlfriend. She spent weeks hiding from the young men who would loiter outside the house, out of view of Baba Skhosana, or follow us to the taxi rank, all in the hopes of convincing Nat to be their girlfriend.

Nat was also horrified that despite all this effort, her young suitors would almost definitely be pursuing three or four other young women with the same dogged enthusiasm. By the end of the two months, Nat could turn on a young man as he tenderly uttered 'I love you' and dispatch him with razor-sharp words.

She also discovered that I had become an agony aunt and women's health consultant in the township—I can only assume that the colour of my skin provided me with the mantle of 'she who knows'. I was consulted on issues as diverse as stretch marks, skin irritations, boy problems and career advice. But when one young woman asked me how to tighten her vagina after her second child was born, I was at a loss. She continued to press me for help, afraid that her boyfriend would leave her for a younger woman who was 'tight'. I timidly suggested pelvic floor exercises to this virtual stranger and made a hasty escape.

After this experience, Nat and I went to consult our own oracle—Zodwa. She was a woman of the world and not afraid to talk about it. She explained about the sexual politics of the township in some detail, describing how sex was a currency among young people, to be bartered and exchanged. A young man, once the magic words 'I love you' were offered up and, in time, accepted, expected sex to be immediately forthcoming. Sex would involve quick penetrative intercourse in some dark corner near the young woman's house—black teenagers lacking the automotive venue many of their white counterparts possessed. Should the young woman refuse, it was over. She also knew that he was seeing many other young women who would be more than willing to meet his demands.

I sometimes wondered whether township violence, which seemed to cost many young men their lives, simply meant that there were fewer young men around, leading to this kind of behaviour—that was certainly what they told me in their own defence. 'We are nation building', they would say, if challenged. 'There are not enough men around so we are willing to sacrifice ourselves for the good of women everywhere. Each one has a right to a man, after all.'

I asked Zodwa about women's sexual pleasure and orgasms, but she stared blankly back at me. Not high on the agenda, I surmised. She went on to tell me, to my horror, than many men liked their women to be dry as it increased the friction and therefore their pleasure. She described a herb that could be used to promote dryness. However, I suspect that a lack of attention to a woman's pleasure and the speed at which these interchanges occurred would be enough to sort that out.

While the township was relatively quiet, allowing plenty of time for many of the in-depth conversations we had been having, there was still an army presence that I preferred to avoid. In Nat's first week of living in the township she lay awake one night unable to get to sleep. I was out for the count in the bed across from her. Lying there in the dark, she thought she heard a distant rumbling. As she strained to hear, her body tense with worry, she suddenly knew what it was: the sound of a truck in low gear. The noise continued for what seemed like hours, coming ever louder and closer. Nat was convinced it was the army which, having heard we were here, were coming for us. Soon the noise was loud enough to wake me. As I opened my eyes I saw Nat sitting upright in bed, eyes wide, looking towards the window. She saw me move and raised her eyebrows questioningly, but neither of us spoke: we were both holding our breath as the rumbling climaxed. The truck must have now been directly outside. We heard it change down a gear and continue its strenuous journey up the hill and around, seeming to retrace the route taken by the police vans during the Seven Day War.

As the sound passed, I started to giggle, which was followed closely by Nat aiming her pillow at my head. The look of crushed relief on Nat's face, lit by the outside light that shone through the curtains, sent me into waves of laughter. My concern had lasted only a few moments, whereas she had virtually given herself a stomach ulcer with the worry of what might happen to us. But soon we were both laughing as Nat recounted the thoughts that had run through her head.

A few days later, we were rushing to get ready for work, having agreed to meet Robbie down at the shop five minutes earlier. Nat grabbed her knapsack and ran out of the room while I stopped to lock the door. When I turned around to follow her she was standing frozen at the corner of the house, looking up the driveway. She waved one hand for me to stay where I was.

'What is it?' I hissed.

'It's the army', she replied out of the corner of her mouth.

'Well, get back!'

'I can't. They've seen me. They're in the driveway.'

I stood there for a moment, weighing up options but clearly there were none. So I came around the corner and walked up to the soldiers gathered by the gate. I tried to walk straight past them with simply a greeting. Nat, taking my lead, tried to do the same. But it was no good. The soldiers were clearly astonished to see two young white women emerging from the back of the house and moved quickly to block our path. The officer in charge leapt down the stairs from the front door where he had been standing, firing questions as he ran. I calmly told him that we worked with a community organisation and were simply staying overnight with friends. I added that we were now late for work and had to go. But he was having none of it and wanted our names and the name of our organisation. I felt Nat stiffen behind me. My brain started whirring—is it better to give false names or tell the truth? I was all too aware that Nat was here on a tourist visa; there would be problems for her and for Sizwe if they did check up on us. In the end, there was nothing for it but to tell the truth. I tried to push away the feeling of a chastened schoolgirl as I stood in front of the officer, watching him note down our names. Before letting us go he warned us that he didn't want to see us here again.

As Nat and I walked down the road towards the shop I could see Robbie standing next to the little red bakkie. I knew Nat was scared but I was more angry than anything, angry at the invasion of our privacy. Seeing the look on Nat's face, I assured her the army guys were regularly rotated and that, if we bumped into an army patrol again, it would probably not be the same officer. In fact, we had been lucky it was not the police whose territories are more constant and who tend to hold grudges. I gave her a questioning smile which she bravely tried to return. We filled Robbie in on our way up Sweetwaters Road and he roared with laughter at the thought of us both standing frozen in the driveway. I also found it funny in the retelling, though it took Nat a good week before she could look back on it and laugh.

Nat, Phil and Kathy were involved in all aspects of our life and work at Sizwe, including home group. Someone new, with whom I would form a strong friendship, had also recently joined home group and I watched as he expressed more than a passing interest in Nat. Justin, who was a friend of Jacques and Margie's from Grahamstown where he had studied at Rhodes University, was now on campus in 'Maritzburg. He became a regular at the ETHOS lunches as well as joining us for home group. Justin's father was a wealthy mine executive but Justin wanted a different life for himself; he wanted to make a different kind of contribution and was also interested in the work of Sizwe, ETHOS and other community based organisations.

Up until this point, the time that Teboho and I had spent together as a couple was very much out of the public eye. We often met up at ETHOS on weekends, saw each other at home group, or went to social events with the community development workers or activists in 'Maritzburg. What we rarely did was to go out for dinner or a movie, go to the park or have lunch at a cafe in town. I had learnt from being out in white society with my black friends that even a platonic relationship was not well tolerated, let alone a love affair. With just the two of us, I felt exposed and a target for verbal or physical abuse. Having Nat with us, and later Justin, gave me a sense of normality as our foursome was less visible and therefore less vulnerable. During the months that Nat spent with us, our relationship became less cautious and less guarded. Yet I was never to feel completely relaxed in public, always keeping one eye open for trouble. Even with all the changes that were to occur in South Africa, I retained this habit.

Friends of Kathy and Phil had a penthouse apartment on one of the beaches in the north of Durban and we were all invited down to make use of it for the weekend. So we borrowed the kombi one Friday afternoon and made the hour's drive down to Durban, arriving at Umhlanga Beach at sunset. In 1990, Umhlanga was yet to become the holiday resort it is today and was still more like a suburb of Durban. We pulled up in front of the apartment, excited to see that it was directly overlooking the beach. Our excitement turned to awe as we entered the apartment: it was two storeys high with a sweeping staircase inside and full-length glass windows that made the most of the jaw-dropping view. The owners were overseas, so it would just be Phil, Kathy, Nat, Teboho and I for the weekend.

Being in the company of three other Australians at the beach, it was easy to forget where we were. But that bubble was burst when we were walking back towards the beach after having lunch at a local cafe. We passed a mother who was walking down to the shops with her young son who could not have been more than six years old. Teboho, Nat and I were walking three abreast, with Teboho walking closest to the kerb. As Teboho stepped aside to let the mother and son pass the small boy, his face screwed up with venom, looked up at him and said, 'What are *you* doing here?' We three were so taken aback by the boy's comment that we stared blankly back, making no reply. His mother seemed to support his opinion but rather than engage with us, simply pulled her son by the arm to get him away from such an unpleasant sight. We stood there and watched as the pair stormed off down the street. Teboho and I set off walking again but Nat was so shocked by the exchange that she stood rooted to the ground, mouth open.

'What was that?' she asked of Teboho and me.

'It was a reflection of the beliefs of the parents, not the child', Teboho replied.

'But how could such a small child be so full of hate?'

'They are surrounded by it from the day they are born.'

The following week we were preparing to run our first teachers' exchange program. Our friends at Smero High School had volunteered to host the white teachers and send a few of their own teachers into town. I have to admit this brought a smile to my face as Smero was arguably the poorest township school we dealt with, being simply a horseshoe of classrooms standing in the dust of a vacant patch of land. Maritzburg College, the white school that put its hand up to pilot the program, was the wealthiest state school in the district. Its facilities were so outstanding that it was often mistaken for a private school.

I was to accompany the College teachers to Smero and Robbie would take the Smero teachers to town. For our pilot, we had arranged to exchange five teachers from each school on the Thursday and Friday, followed on the Saturday by a workshop to discuss what they had learnt. The team was both excited and nervous as the day approached, knowing that this program would be either groundbreaking or a complete disaster.

Robbie and I went to Edendale first and waited at the central meeting point we had agreed with the Smero teachers the day before. They arrived one by one, looking particularly well dressed and buttoned up, ready for the day ahead. The kombi was soon full of nervous chatter as we drove through to town. Maritzburg College did in fact have one or two black students by this time but the only black adults on the property were groundskeepers and cleaners. We arrived just as the school bell rang. The Smero teachers stepped out of the kombi as hundreds of white teenage boys filed past on their way to assembly. Many eyed them with curiosity, having been told about the innovative program, and others simply stared, eyes hooded and reserved. My heart lurched in sympathy as I watched the teachers disappear into the bowels of the school.

I was led through to the staffroom where the College teachers were waiting. In sharp contrast, these teachers were relaxed and jovial. I did wonder how much of it was a cover as I suspected that many would not ever have had cause or opportunity to visit a township. I could only imagine the stories their friends and families must have told them in the lead-up to this day. Yet I knew each one had volunteered, wanting to be part of a different future. Robbie and I had briefed them a few days before but I ran through some of the main points again as we drove back to Edendale. Smero is located at the far end of the valley, accessible only by rough and twisted dirt roads once we'd left the tar of Edendale Road behind. The kombi became quiet as we neared the school, the teachers taking in the poverty of the area. The homes were made of the same kind of wattle and daub we had used to make the Sweetwaters creche. Few had electricity or running water. Animals and small children looked up as the kombi crawled past, surprised to see the white faces peering back. We pulled into the school grounds in silence.

Mr Khuzwayo, the school principal, was there to greet us. Despite the poor school facilities, Smero was blessed with the most talented principal in the township. He was well educated, intelligent and highly committed to his craft. During his time as headmaster, he had turned the school from a poor performer among its township peers to achieving the top results in Edendale, even beginning to compete with those of some of the schools in town. The College teachers were quick to see that he was a man with a mission, with his firm handshake and engaging stare. He led them around the school and briefed them on what they were trying to achieve here. What they saw was a school where all the students were in class, all the teachers actively teaching and, in the absence of the exchange teachers, some students were studying under the supervision of prefects. While this may have seemed an ordinary scene in any school in town, it was a rare sight in the township. Given the conditions and the difficulties with securing resources, many teachers and principals had simply given up. In many township schools students and teachers arrived and left when they wished, their presence in class only a pretence at learning since they knew that sitting for exams in competition with white students in town would surely lead to failure.

Mr Khuzwayo and I had slotted the College teachers into the Smero timetable a week before and now students were waiting to take them to class. They were shown through to classrooms that housed more than twice the number of students they were used to, some sitting two to a desk. The only teaching resource was chalk, which was not left at the blackboard but guarded by a student who handed it to the teachers when it was needed. The school had no electricity and therefore no photocopier, computer, printer nor even a telephone. Mr Khuzwayo made all his calls to the Department from home.

At break, I gathered with all the teachers in the staffroom which was merely an empty classroom at the end of the horseshoe of rooms. There, Mr Khuzwayo introduced the visitors and opened the floor as they passed their regards from their colleagues at Maritzburg College and thanked the school for hosting them for the two days. Smero had prepared a welcome morning tea to allow the teachers to mix. Water was boiled for tea on a small paraffin burner and cakes and biscuits had been baked and brought from home. I noticed that the College teachers had shed the air of confidence they had worn like coats that morning, their eyes now wide with each new reminder of the difference between this school and theirs, only fifteen minutes away.

After a few more classes, it was time for lunch. The Smero teachers took their new colleagues to the gate where four local women sold food to students and teachers alike each day. They explained that you could buy the fruits and sweets displayed or have a hot meal that was cooking on the pots behind them. The local favourites were pap and curried meat. I imagined I saw each one of the visiting teachers make a mental note to bring a packed lunch the following day.

After three more lessons, school was finished for the day. The teachers had taught a variety of subjects from maths and science, to English and Latin. The Latin teacher, Tansey, was later to become a friend. She never forgot the irony of that first day of attempting to teach Latin in a township school. That evening she decided to take a different tack and threw Latin out the window in favour of English the following day.

On the way home the kombi was abuzz with observations, most regarding the respect they had for the teachers who taught there day after day. The College teachers discussed what a different proposition it was to teach forty or fifty kids without a single teaching aid including, in many cases, a textbook. But to their credit, all of them were committed to returning the following morning, having first raided their own classrooms for supplies. I later heard that the school had decided to set up a partnership arrangement with Smero to support them with learning materials on a more regular basis.

Robbie and I had a chance to catch up and compare notes at the end of the day. The Smero teachers were as awestruck as those from College, but for completely different reasons. They were amazed at the endless facilities and the quality of teaching resources. They seemed almost to salivate when discussing what they could do if they had these tools at their disposal. The teachers also commented on how oblivious the students appeared to be to the opportunities the school provided, while their own students were exuberant when they had a textbook they didn't have to share. Robbie had also seen the nervousness of the morning dissipate over the course of the day, as the teachers were well received by students and faculty alike. I remember the triumph I felt when I heard that one student had commented that he wouldn't mind having a black teacher after all.

At the end of the three days, we felt that the program had been worthwhile, giving all the teachers a new perspective on the education system, helping them to think through what integration might mean and how they could be better prepared. The unintended consequence, and one we were never able to get around, was that once the black teachers had seen what it would be like to teach in a town school they made every effort over the next few years to leave the township education system behind.

I had similar concerns about all our dialogue programs. Were they of more benefit to the white participants than to the black? Did the black participants spend most of their time educating their new white friends about what South Africa was really like for the majority of her people? Sometimes I was afraid that all we were doing was fuelling the desire of black people to escape, to leave behind any reminder of the hardships of their childhood. My own experience of the township was that it provided me with a far richer experience of community living than my childhood had permitted. I felt that if living standards could be raised, the townships could become a vibrant alternative to suburbia. For many, however, the townships were to be left behind with as much speed as their salary would allow.

Ironically, I too was soon to leave the township behind for a time. Justin was looking to get a small house in the inner city, an area of 'Maritzburg that was referred to as 'grey'—neither black nor white, but a place where all races lived in defiance of the Group Areas Act that prohibited such integration. As the year drew to a close—my third in this gypsy lifestyle—the idea of throwing down some roots was appealing. I also knew that in order to grow my relationship with Teboho I needed the space that Baba Skhosana would not allow. So, despite being very happy living in Caluza, I felt it was time to build a household of my own where I would be an adult member and not a child.

Justin soon found a place that was perfect, a white cottage in a quiet side street with matching cottages repeating down its length. The house was two rooms wide, with the front stoep nudging the pavement while the rest of the house fell in behind like a bridal train. We had a small, untidy garden that ran down one side and round the back of the house. Despite its external appearance, the house boasted four bedrooms and a small study at the back. Before we had even moved in, Teboho had compiled a list of potential boarders, black students who typically found it impossible to rent a room in town. Justin and I liked the idea—it would be our domestic community service—and so it was agreed that when the university opened, so would our home in Oxford Street. As it turned out, one of our new housemates would be Teboho's youngest brother, Willie. He had done extremely well in his matriculation exams at the school Teboho sent him to in Mafikeng and had won a scholarship to study science at the University of Natal. Willie would have some groundbreaking of his own to do in this bastion of white, male academia.

Nat was with me for the house hunting process, but left before we moved in. Her departure was the hardest I had faced. I had many friends who had become part of our community, part of my South African experience. But my relationship with Nat was the deepest and when she left I was reminded of what it cost me to live in South Africa. Friendships with people who have known you from your childhood and teen years are irreplaceable; they are a haven of forgiveness and acceptance forged by the perspective of time. They have a flavour that friendships you make as an adult can never replicate.

When Nat left, I knew I was forgoing this depth of knowing and being known. There is a photo of Teboho and me on the steps of ETHOS just after having said goodbye to Nat. My face is tear-stained and drawn, as if after an illness. I tried to throw it away, not wishing to be reminded, but Teboho wouldn't let me, insisting my face was full of love.

17

DECEMBER 1990
A TOWNSHIP CHRISTMAS

I WAS AWASH WITH MIXED EMOTIONS THAT DECEMBER—EXCITED TO BE MOVING INTO OXFORD STREET, SAD TO BE LEAVING THE SKHOSANAS, HOMESICK FOR MY FAMILY AS CHRISTMAS APPROACHED, AND NERVOUS AT THE THOUGHT OF MEETING TEBOHO'S FRIENDS AND FAMILY. I HAD AGREED TO SPEND THE HOLIDAYS WITH HIM IN MOHLAKENG.

Justin had moved into Oxford Street ahead of me and was working on a few renovations with Fred who was back in town on holidays. Justin was also busy decorating the house and getting the garden under control. By the time I moved in, it already felt like home. In fact, it was hard to leave Oxford Street a few weeks later when Sizwe closed for the year and I headed off to Jo'burg to be with Teboho. He had gone ahead of me at the end of November once his exams were over. It was agreed that I would catch the Greyhound bus and be met by Moss, who worked in the city. When I arrived, Moss was waiting with his small son, Boggie.

Moss, as I later learnt was his habit, was running late. We were not heading straight back to Mohlakeng, the township where both he and Teboho lived, but were going first to the Institute of Contextual Theology's Christmas party at the Carlton Hotel where his wife Khumo would be waiting. We were due there in half an hour but still had to drop Boggie to his aunt's home in Soweto before returning to the city. This entire arrangement was news to me but I resisted the urge to say that I felt tired and underdressed.

Surprises like this were part of the landscape; by the end of my four weeks I would become accustomed to continuous delays and changes in plans. It would be tempting to call this 'African time' but it was something else altogether. This was about being a resourceful person in a resource-poor community. Moss, Khumo, Teboho and other well-known figures in the township were constantly called upon to attend this meeting or that, resolve a conflict, help this family, give that one a lift somewhere—the list was endless. As for me, I was committed to going with the flow, even on my first night in the city. So I buckled up and prepared for a whirlwind drive in peak hour Friday night traffic to Soweto and back. I then smiled my way through a few hours of a Christmas party where the distinguished Father Albert Nolan and the who's who of Johannesburg's Church activists were on the dance floor.

I spent the night with Moss and Khumo as their house was large enough to offer me a spare bedroom. The household consisted of Moss, Khumo, Boggie and Moss's father, Papi, who was to become one of my greatest fans. The next morning over breakfast, Teboho blew in and swept me off my feet. While I felt very comfortable with Moss and Khumo, it was still a relief to see his smiling face. He was staying with his eldest brother Caleb for the duration of the holidays, in a house on the other side of the township. He had come to pick me up to go to his sister's wedding in Itsoseng, where a branch of the family now lived. We would be going up with the church youth as they had planned a retreat in Kopela, an hour's drive past Itsoseng, for a few days after the wedding. I said a hasty farewell to Moss and Khumo, who would be joining us later, and rushed out the door, bag in hand.

Outside, the kombi was half full with young people from the local Ebenezer church where Moss was the minister. I had heard about many of them from stories Teboho told me and it was nice to put faces to names: Kgotla, Dumi, Ri, Dennis, Phillip and Nooi, Teboho's eldest niece. We spent the next hour driving from house to house filling the kombi to capacity before setting out for our destination.

Itsoseng was a two-and-a-half-hour drive towards Botswana so we had plenty of time to get to know each other. We were also driving through the rural heartland of the Afrikaaners so we had no plans to stop. Teboho was driving, with Dennis and me on the seat next to him. Dennis was a young law student: intelligent, articulate and observant—a great travel companion. He too had lived with Teboho for a time while Teboho helped him get started with his university career. Over the weeks this became a familiar story. It seemed that most of the people I met had in some way or other been helped by Teboho through a difficult time, to raise money for their studies, find a place to live or simply to imagine a different future. I was deeply moved by the quiet contribution he had made in the lives of people in his community, and loved him more for it.

When we arrived at Itsoseng, Teboho's mother's house was surrounded by a crowd of some three or four hundred people. Mama lived in a four-roomed tin shack just around the corner from where the wedding reception was being held. It was actually China, Ma Ellen's youngest daughter, who was getting married but in the tradition of their extended and interchangeable family, the wedding was being hosted at Mama's house. We parked the kombi near the hall and made our way slowly through the crowd, greeting relatives and neighbours as each pressed in to see if the rumours were true. Finally we found ourselves inside Mama's house.

'She will love you because she knows I do', Teboho whispered in my ear as we walked through the door.

He then began to call loudly: '*Mama wa ka, o kae? Moratuwa' ka u teng*', Mama where are you? My beloved is here. Sesotho was about as different as you could get from the Zulu language but I understood the gist of what he said.

Out from one of the rooms emerged a woman weary from days of non-stop wedding preparations but with love etched across her face.

She beamed at her son and reached up to embrace him. As she did so, he picked her up off her feet and, despite her protests, swung her around in the air. As he placed her down again, she peered around him to look at me, the warmth she felt for her son immediately radiating in my direction. Teboho spun around and made his introductions. Mama sighed and said, 'Ah, so it is true! With Teboho you never know. You are welcome'.

I was to learn more about this remarkable woman in the months and years to come and for me she represents all the graciousness of Africa. Mama was born in 1937 and grew up in the Free State. The Orange Free State, as it was then called, was famous for a particular and obtuse apartheid law—no Indian person was allowed to set foot on its soil. Therefore, if anyone from the Indian community wished to pass through the Free State (which is in the centre of the country and forms a key route between Johannesburg in the north and Cape Town in the south) that person would have to drive straight through without stopping for food, petrol or even a bathroom break. Such was the conservative nature of the province.

Mama, who was born into the Southern Sotho tribe, one of the nine African tribes of South Africa, lived with her family until the age of eight or nine when she and her older sister were taken to work on a farm a few hours away. I'm unsure of what 'taken' really means when Mama tells her story. I don't know if the white farmer wanted to 'take' them so that they could work in return for food. Perhaps it was 'taken' in the slavery sense. Mama doesn't really remember, just that she didn't want to go and that there were many members of the family she never saw again.

Being the younger of the two sisters, Mama was set to work not in the fields but in the house, taking care of the cooking and cleaning. She remembers the hours as long with little or no time off, week after week, month after month. She lived in servants quarters little better than a shed, behind the farmhouse. It was a very sad and lonely time for the first few years with no contact with her family at home.

It became a little easier for her when she was about eleven or twelve. A new baby was born, giving her someone to love and to hold. Mama tells me that she held that little blonde baby girl in her arms and prayed to God that he would give her a baby just like this one. At the time, she was too young to realise the biological impossibility of the request, but she believed that God would answer her prayers. It was not until she met me that she felt God had finally heard her. She says that I will always have a special place in her heart as I am the child she prayed for all those years ago.

Farm life was hard and monotonous for Mama and the divide between black and white was brutal. She tells a story from when she was a teenager: she picked up the farmer's favourite cup out of the garbage—he had chipped it and thrown it away. As she had no cup of her own, she rescued it and used it for herself. A few days later, he caught her drinking tea out of it and chased her with a gun, screaming that she had drunk out of the same cup as him. She managed to evade him but was left in no doubt as to how things were.

Not long after this incident, Mama decided to run away from the farm and move back closer to where she was born. It was then that she met and fell in love with Phuti, Teboho's father. He was a flamboyant character, charming, intelligent, articulate and a dreamer. Phuti was a young minister in the Zionist church; as a popular orator with a flair for the dramatic he was well suited to the role. He also supported his essentially voluntary position with a little diamond smuggling on the side. There were harsh penalties for those who were caught but Phuti was able to trade undetected for years.

Mama, still not much more than a teenager, adored him and soon they were married. Caleb and then Tshidi were born soon after. However, around this time, Mama became aware that Phuti also had a relationship with another woman—a woman who, ironically, was a childhood friend of hers. She recalls carrying Ellen on her back when she was a toddler as their families had been neighbours and friends. While the affair with Ellen broke Mama's heart, especially when she learnt that there was a child, she went to Phuti with a suggestion. As they had no money and could not afford for Phuti to be supporting a second household, she suggested that Phuti take Ellen as his second wife and she come to live with them in their small shack. Mama describes this as the hardest moment of her life. Despite the affair, she still loved him and having to share him, even with a dear friend, was a daily devastation.

When I asked Mama how this arrangement worked, given they initially lived in a four-room shack with four children and three adults, she just laughed and said they did what they had to do to get by—but it was difficult. As hard as it must have been, she still had her beloved Phuti. But when Phuti was killed several years later, it felt like the final blow for Mama. He had simply stepped off a kerb without looking, probably calling out to a friend in greeting, when a passing bus ran him down.

She grieved for a long time. The two women stayed together for as long as they could, struggling to support their now nine children. However, Ellen eventually moved away to Rustenburg some two hours to the northwest and married there. Mama remained in Mohlakeng until Phuti's family came to visit. They told her that, as is tradition, she must now remarry and a husband would be chosen for her from one of the men in the family. In African culture, the children belong to the man and his family and if Mama married again, the children would pass on to another man. As this was an unacceptable situation, Mama was pressured to marry back into the same family. She resisted this pressure for as long as she could, but ultimately her concern for the children's welfare wore her down. Bophundlovu, Phuti's first cousin, was fifteen years Mama's senior, in his mid-forties. He was an unusually tall and very sober man. He had a short fuse and was quite particular about how he wanted things to be done. He had not married until now for that reason. While it was an arranged marriage and Mama did not love him, she tried to make the best of their life together.

When Bophundlovu reached retirement age and Mama once again became the primary breadwinner the only work available to her was labouring. Mama was paid the equivalent of four Australian dollars a month to walk behind the combine harvester with a handful of other women, picking up any useful remnants of the crop that the huge machine left behind. While money was always scarce and the life in Itsoseng dry and barren, Mama enjoyed being with her children and grandchildren, as she and her husband lived in the shack next to Tshidi's. Tshidi went on to have seven children, six of whom survived. A two-year-old daughter was allegedly lost to witchcraft, a cruel but common occurrence in Africa.

After Bophundlovu's death, Mama continued to live in Itsoseng, raising Doki and Willie and lending a hand with Tshidi's children. Tshidi and Reggie's two-room tin shack was like a sauna in the hot summer months and a fridge in winter. Itsoseng suffered from extreme temperatures, being located in a semidesert area of the North West Province. Mama's house was slightly larger than Tshidi's, with two bedrooms, a lounge room and a kitchen. Both homes were made of tin, walls and roofs alike, with no insulation and no electricity, running water or sanitation inside. Water was fetched from a tap in the dusty yard and the toilet was a pit latrine dug out the back. There were one or two trees in each yard that the family gathered under in the summer heat. Mama attempted to grow a small vegetable garden with corn (known locally as mealies), spinach and tomatoes. As Tshidi's family grew, the older children moved across to Mama's house where there was more room.

Mama eventually left her farm labouring job when she found domestic work in Itsoseng. Her black employer worked in a government department in the homeland structure and wanted someone to clean house and look after her two small children. Mama worked for her six days a week, up to twelve hours a day, until her retirement. Thankfully, her employer treated her with respect and would often help out with clothes and food for the children still in Mama's care. Mama also had the house to continue to pay off, in small monthly instalments. Around the time Mama became a domestic worker again, Reggie had an accident at work, losing his sight in one eye. He never received compensation nor was he able to keep his job. This left Mama as the sole breadwinner for both families. So life continued as it always had, with lots of love and little else.

This was where Mama was when we first met. What surprised me was her continued graciousness despite the hardship in her life. She still believes in a loving God who blesses her life with many gifts and so she holds her life, and its many griefs, lightly and has no bitterness for anyone, black or white. She and women like her, as they say in Africa, hold up the sky.

After spending a few minutes with Mama, we were ushered out of the house as the church ceremony was about to start. As was often the way, only the closest friends and family attended the wedding ceremony while the rest of the community joined in for the reception afterwards.

At large events such as these, I sometimes felt as though I was underwater, with the conversations happening above my head in a distorted-sounding language I could not follow. Events swirled around me but I often felt cushioned and removed, unable to connect. This day, thanks to Teboho, I felt neither cut off nor the centre of attention but, rather, part of the family. I later learnt that Teboho had taken great care to set this up for me, speaking to the family about how they might treat me, not singling me out but welcoming me into their midst. Given my experience with the Skhosanas, I wondered how this was possible. I also wondered whether he was disrespecting his mother by bringing home someone to whom he was not yet engaged. Mama later explained that the family knew Teboho marched to the beat of his own drum and they had learnt to expect the unexpected. It had been five years of silence, then one day he came home and said, 'I've found the woman I wish to marry and she's white'.

China's wedding was a wonderful event, warm and relaxed despite the large numbers. There had been the usual wardrobe changes, from the white wedding dress and suits to the traditional African attire for the dancing and celebration. China, her husband

Dan and their large wedding party, to my surprise, had more than one change of traditional clothes and I later learnt that China had made them all from rich, colourful material bought from a Ghanaian trader who passed through the area a few times a year.

This wedding also gave me the opportunity to meet China's mother, Ma Ellen, for the first time. Mother and daughter shared a calm and inclusive way about them that made old friends out of strangers. Ma Ellen was taller and broader than Mama and under her gentle demeanour, I thought I caught of glimpse of steel. While Mama had survived through her acceptance of whatever life presented, Ma Ellen, Teboho confirmed, had an underlying determination that allowed her to cut through adversity. Side by side, they presented an interesting contrast and a formidable team—Mama like the willow that bends in the wind and Ma Ellen like the immovable mountain.

All Teboho's sisters were variations on the theme of their mothers, though it was Tshidi, Silwane and China that I would get to know better than the others. Teboho's brothers were all different characters with only a few physical characteristics to bind them together. Doki reminded me the most of Teboho—a maverick like his brother, flamboyant and verbose. Caleb, or Cali as everyone called him, appeared slightly harassed as firstborn and responsible siblings often do. Having said that, it was clear Cali was a generous man who welcomed the opportunity to celebrate with his family, laying aside the burdens of providing for them for a time. Philemon, Ma Ellen and Phuti's eldest son, displayed his mother's calmness rather than his father's theatrics. Ephraim was painfully quiet and, though I felt he was happy to meet me, hardly said a word over the two days we were there. And lastly Willie—who would soon become my housemate and my dear friend—Willie reminded me, at nineteen, of a puppy who is soon to be full grown: long-legged, curious, intelligent and wonderful company, though slightly clumsy and likely to trip over himself at the most embarrassing moments. For all these reasons he was to become my favourite and in his mother's eyes and mine, could do no wrong.

We set out late Sunday afternoon for Kopela with the Church Youth Group. I didn't ask where they had all slept overnight; no doubt they had simply been absorbed into the modest homes of friends and neighbours as all the visitors had. Moss and Khumo thought it was not appropriate for me to stay with the family: allowing Teboho to live by his own rules was one thing but in some areas at least, protocol should be followed. So they had arranged for me to stay with them at Khumo's brother's house in nearby Mafikeng. Khumo's brother Sam was already one of the few successful black businessmen in the country and would go on to be a major economic force. His home in Mafikeng was beautiful, even boasting an in-ground swimming pool, perfect for defeating the summer heat. It was in many ways a strange experience for me as it was the first time I had stayed in the home of a wealthy black family in South Africa. My township experiences in 'Maritzburg did not reflect the breadth of financial means in the black community across the country, even at that time.

I had been to many youth camps in my teenage years, more than I could count, and I'm not sure what I was expecting of the African equivalent—but I hadn't been expecting this. We arrived at sunset in a small, remote village, the sky glowing pink and purple against the red earth. There were only a few dozen modest homes scattered in amongst the acacia trees. We parked the kombi on the edge of the village and began to walk towards the houses. The sounds of the bush were broken only by a mother calling her child inside to eat. Suddenly, a noise cut through the air, its relative proximity making me jump. 'A jackal', said Teboho. 'But it won't come any closer.' As the adrenalin subsided, I couldn't help but be overcome by the beauty and tranquillity of the place. I was struck by the thought that Africa is still a wilderness. Despite the 'speediness' of the global economy and cosmopolitan lifestyles, a village like this still exists where time is marked simply by the taking of each breath.

As we walked towards the west side of the village, I realised that our retreat would not be like any other I had been on. There was no conference centre, no cabins, no tents. I asked Teboho what the arrangements were and he told me we would be staying with Dumi's uncle who lived alone in a house on the edge of the village. Our retreat was to be like any other African holiday—spent in the home of relatives.

Dumi's uncle was delighted to have us stay, saying it gave his house some life again. We had arrived with boxes of food so as not to be a burden, including some treats that weren't available in the small village store. After a hearty meal and lively conversation, most of which was beyond my reach, moves were made to bed down for the night. Dumi's uncle's home was like many of the township homes I had stayed in before, consisting of four small rooms: two bedrooms, a lounge and a kitchen. There were twelve of us, including the old man. It soon became apparent what the arrangements would be. Dumi's uncle would sleep in his own bed, the girls in the remaining bedroom and the boys in the lounge.

I was never sure whether Teboho had failed to mention the details of our retreat for fear I wouldn't come or whether he genuinely forgot—but I suspect it was a sin of omission. I, like the other girls I would be sharing the floor space with, began unpacking every piece of clothing I had brought with me, making a mattress on which we would all sleep. The room was so small that we would need to spoon on the floor in order just to fit. I made a token effort of brushing my teeth, then lay down in the tiny space saved for me between Dumi and Nooi. They had been considerate enough to save me a spot in the middle, so that I would not freeze on the edge. While I appreciated the kind thought, I found being wedged in between two peacefully sleeping bodies as I struggled to ignore the lump in my ribcage and the cold concrete floor an additional challenge. I longed to roll over to give my bony hip a reprieve, but knew that doing so would wake the whole ensemble, so I counted the hours until dawn.

The following day the rest of the group, refreshed from a sound night's sleep away from the sounds of the city, were ready to take part in sessions. Exhausted, I slunk off to the kombi to sleep. The second night was a repeat of the first. As a result I have very little memory of the daytime activity of the retreat, but can still taste my frustration at trying in vain to fall asleep on the floor. When we left Kopela, I was unwashed, sleep deprived and cranky. The kombi broke down on the way back to Itsoseng, finally arriving after three hours of travel with only two gears in working order: second and reverse. I was no advertisement for a prospective wife, aid worker or even multiculturalism by the time we pulled up in front of Mama's house. There were no hysterics as I was mostly silent and withdrawn, but the message to Teboho was clear—I was completely over this adventure.

We finally made it back to Mohlakeng where I, somewhat ashamedly, kissed the ground in gratitude for a bed to myself and running water. For the next five days, life was a little more normal with trips to the movies, visiting friends and a bit of Christmas shopping. It was a relaxing hiatus for Teboho and I as we had rarely had the freedom and space to spend chunks of uninterrupted time together. I also wanted to make the most of the opportunity of getting to know him in context: where he grew up, who his friends were, the school he went to. I noticed the bush out behind Cali's house where I assumed he had spent many nights 'sleeping rough' as a boy.

Soon Christmas was upon us. We were to go to friends of Moss and Khumo's on Christmas Day, stay the night with them and then leave in the morning for Namibia, Teboho's friend having invited us to join him on a holiday there. Twenty-two years of Christmas mornings in Australia had conditioned me for gathering under the Christmas tree in my pyjamas while gifts were given out to each member of the family to be opened in anxious anticipation.

It didn't even occur to me to check if this was a tradition followed here, though I should have twigged when Khumo said they didn't have a Christmas tree as it's just a symbol of the materialism of the west. I had bought Moss and Khumo a huge indoor pot plant and carefully arranged my presents for the family around it. I then loitered around in my pyjamas for a few hours, waiting for the gift giving to begin. Before I knew it, everyone was dressed and ready to walk out the door. When Khumo asked what on earth I was still doing in pyjamas at eleven o'clock, I described the scene I had been waiting for. She almost fell over in sympathetic laughter, apologising for not clarifying while explaining that wasn't the way Christmas was done in the township. Then she offered to pack up the gifts and take them with us while hurrying me towards the bedroom to change. To this day, Khumo can be reduced to breathless tears of laughter at the mention of that first Christmas morning.

Mohlakeng is located on the far western reaches of the sprawling metropolis of Johannesburg and we were having Christmas lunch on the far east, so it took us almost two hours to get there. Khumo's friends were part of the growing black middle class and though they still lived in a township at that time, it was purpose built for the aspirational.

Pinky is not an uncommon name for a black woman but when she introduced her husband as Winky, I found it hard to keep a straight face. Like Sam, Khumo's brother, they now formed part of the black business elite—but I couldn't help thinking it must have been that bit harder for them than most, if my reaction to their names was typical of the white business people they met.

After introductions, we were ushered through to the lounge. The house already seemed full of visitors yet it did not appear that lunch was imminent. Just as we made ourselves comfortable, Moss announced he had to go back to Soweto to see Caesar, Khumo's other brother, before he flew out to London the next day. I couldn't believe Moss was intending to drive an hour and a half back in the direction from which we had just come—but I was even more astonished when he asked Teboho to go with him. Seeing the look on my face, they promised they would be back in time for lunch. Khumo assured me there was plenty of time and off they dashed. Once again I had to readjust and go with the flow.

I spent the next few hours struggling to keep up with the conversation which oscillated between Tswana and English. I was also aware that, unlike my friends in 'Maritzburg, the people I was now mixing with were not fazed by my skin colour, making no compensation, offering no special treatment. In fact, they got on with their conversations almost as though I wasn't there, expecting me to fit in as best I could.

I admit this was its own kind of culture shock. I didn't speak the language, I didn't know the people, I didn't really know what to expect. There was a strong self-assurance amongst some of Teboho's friends that I had not experienced before in the black community. Here, there was no room for paternalistic charity, nothing they needed from me but my friendship if I chose to give it. I suspect that these relationships kept me from falling into a dependency mindset that can plague aid and development work. They kept me from overestimating my own abilities and contribution, keeping me a little more grounded.

I spent a few hours in the kitchen making myself useful with lunch preparation before Moss and Teboho returned and we sat down to a wonderful Christmas lunch which lasted well into the early evening. We finally rolled away from the table and collapsed onto the couch in time to catch the Christmas screening of *Gone with the Wind*. Sitting there, I was struck by the incongruities of my township Christmas.

Once the movie finished, Pinky began allocating rooms for the many visitors to use for the night. It quickly became apparent that Teboho and I were the only people there who weren't a married couple and although we were well in our mid to late twenties, this was still a Christian household: there was no question of us sharing a room. I wasn't fazed by this as we had never spent the night together, given our living arrangements for the six months we had been dating. But Khumo and Pinky took the opportunity to tease us about being the only ones who would not be celebrating Christmas that night.

The next morning, before Teboho's friend Joe arrived to collect us for our trip to Namibia, I took Teboho outside and had a belated gift giving ceremony out of the boot of Moss and Khumo's car. Joe arrived shortly after, having already fetched the rest of the gang for our

Namibian trip in his kombi. Joe and Teboho had become good friends when Teboho worked at SUCA. Joe had just completed his commerce degree and was now working in a corporate job in Pretoria. We said our goodbyes to Moss and Khumo and thanked Pinky and Winky for their hospitality before jumping into the kombi and onto the freeway for the long drive to Windhoek, some twenty hours away.

Once more, the kombi was full of friends, though this time it was only six others besides Teboho and myself, making the journey a little more comfortable. They all knew each other from SUCA and so were studying at various universities across the country. While I was once again the only white passenger there was a mix of language groups in the kombi; English, as a common denominator, made a more regular appearance.

It was somewhat frustrating to me that just as my Zulu was becoming comfortably conversational, I was switching to languages that were at the other end of the African linguistic spectrum. Both Sesotho and Setswana, the more common languages of the northern part of the country, as well as Lesotho and Botswana, had a completely different rhythm. Zulu has a regular beat to it, with every syllable being pronounced. Sesotho and Setswana have a lilting tone that tumbles like water over a rocky creek bed, more complex and irregular than the drum beat of Zulu. While I had enjoyed learning Zulu, there was something exquisite about listening to the music of Sesotho being spoken, spurring my desire to begin again.

After travelling all day and well into the night, we arrived at the little desert town of Springbok which marked an end to our easterly trek and the beginning of the drive due north to Windhoek. We pulled up at a petrol station and all piled out of the car to stretch our legs. As Teboho and I walked towards the kerb of the empty street, I asked him if we were stopping here for the night. I was exhausted and my body ached for a comfortable bed. He laughed, as did Joe who was nearby, and I suddenly realised my first world assumption: I was on holiday with a bunch of black university students; a motel room was beyond the scope of the budget. While my mind understood this, my body screamed out in protest as I dropped into the gutter and cried. My own lack of stoicism during these holidays was embarrassing—which made me cry even more. The image of that dark empty street, the solitary lights of the petrol station, the feel of the cold concrete beneath me is still burnt into my mind, so sharp were my feelings of helplessness and disappointment.

While I had hoped to hide my minor breakdown from the rest of my travelling companions, of course everyone knew by the time I came back to the kombi. They were each full of understanding—naturally, they said, I was not used to being poor as all white people stayed in hotels on their holidays and flew to their destination, not being subjected to twenty hours in the back of a kombi. While my own childhood holidays had been car trips and simple motels, they assumed that the wealth of white people was uniform and considerable. Teboho just gathered my head into his lap, making me as comfortable as he could so that I could sleep. We were soon on our way again, driving into the utter darkness of the desert night.

We arrived in Windhoek just after dawn. We were staying with another friend who had been part of SUCA and was now a member of the newly formed independent Namibian parliament. Dani was one of the few white people who had been a member of either organisation. Despite his white Afrikaaner heritage, Dani was a simple African man. He was still living in a modest four-roomed cottage in the suburbs of Windhoek. As we pulled into the driveway, I realised that while this would be a different experience to Kopela, the sleeping arrangements would be similar. We spent the next week with nine of us camping on the floor of Dani's house. Fortunately, mattresses made a huge difference to my enjoyment of our stay. We spent New Year's Eve celebrating in the township, discussing the future of Namibia and dancing until dawn. We spent a day at Swakopmund, enjoying the beach will all shades of local beachgoers. Dani also arranged for us to have dinner at the Cuban embassy. Much to the surprise of my friends, I was more impressed by the ambassador's expansive book collection that covered all the walls of the large study than I was by the opportunity of talking to notorious Cubans—I am, at heart, the daughter of booksellers.

After a fabulous week, we made the long drive home. This time I was mentally prepared for driving through. When we stopped for petrol just inside the South African border, only Teboho and I were awake. Dawn was still four or five hours away. We were both feeling fine, enjoying the opportunity to talk about the experiences of the last three weeks without other people listening in. Teboho drove and I was his navigator. While I could read a map, I could not read Afrikaans and my inability to distinguish between two similar sounding towns took us on a four-hour detour to the south, almost halfway to Cape Town. Teboho and I fell about laughing when we realised, glad that the others were still asleep.

As dawn broke over the desert, with just the two of us to see it, I felt so fortunate to be with him, having adventures that would otherwise have escaped me and being able to enjoy them in the warmth of his effervescent love.

18

January 1991
The View from Oxford Street

AFTER LIVING LIKE A GYPSY FOR A MONTH, I WAS THRILLED TO COME BACK TO A HOME THAT WAS MY OWN. I STARTED BACK AT SIZWE THE DAY AFTER OUR RETURN BUT EACH EVENING HAD THE DEEP JOY OF NESTING, HANGING A PAINTING HERE, PLACING A PHOTO FRAME THERE, UNPACKING BOOKS AND MEMORIES. AS NEITHER JUSTIN NOR I OWNED A TV, THE EVENINGS WERE ALSO OPPORTUNITIES TO TALK AND READ, FURTHER DEEPENING MY SENSE OF HOME. BY THE TIME OUR NEW HOUSEMATES ARRIVED FOR FIRST SEMESTER, JUSTIN AND I HAD THE HOUSE JUST THE WAY WE WANTED IT AND I HAD MY SWEET LITTLE CAT SOMBU BACK.

The relative solitude each night also gave me the opportunity to reflect on the events of the recent weeks. Teboho and I had taken some time out in the days before I left to talk about our future. To mark the seriousness of the proceedings, we had constructed a list—a long one—with every possible issue that needed to be aired and discussed in the consideration of a mixed marriage in apartheid South Africa. Teboho knew I still bore the scars of Msizi's decision to separate after seeing only unhappiness down that road.

What I had observed in my weeks in Jo'burg was a city that managed to accommodate a broad range of world views—the arch conservative Afrikaaners holding onto the past, the corporate liberals who saw the writing on the wall, the black middle class driving upwards, the urban poor and the migrant workforce struggling to survive—each sector carving out its own part of Jo'burg in which to live and build community. It also offered a large city's anonymity, allowing many to live as they wished outside the descriptors of race and class. Teboho and I discussed a future that might find a home there as part of the community of Mohlakeng, buffered by the bigger city. The western suburbs of Jo'burg, known as the West Rand, were home to the radically conservative Afrikaaners. Yet the area was dominated by the large townships of Soweto and Kagiso which were melting pots of language and culture, occasionally clashing but for the most part creating open-mindedness.

Aside from our environment, we also discussed our attitudes to the day-to-day stuff of marriage: work, money, children, parenting, family, domestic roles and responsibilities, church and community service. As much as these issues can be discussed in abstract, we appeared to share the deep values that create a framework on which a family could be built. At the end of our two-day round table discussions, we emerged with a sense of optimism that we could find a way.

In the late evenings, lying in my bed in Oxford Street in the largest bedroom I've had before or since, I enjoyed the thought that I might well have found someone with whom I could do the work I loved in a country that I wanted to call home. When I left Australia to come and work at Sizwe, I knew I was making at least a five-year commitment but hoped I would be able to find a place in the community in which to live more permanently. The past three years had given me a sense of purpose and meaning that I had never imagined possible when growing up in Australia. In hindsight, I also see that those were the years when I was satisfied with today. I have always been someone who lives with one foot in the future but at that time, the present was more than enough.

At Sizwe, the working year started with its usual bang. Almost immediately, we were running programs two weekends out of three. The teacher exchange programs were gaining a reputation and we were now running one a month. One white teacher wrote in his evaluation form: 'It was the first real opportunity we have ever had of encountering the practicalities of Black Education, and we have been moved, impressed, stunned, saddened and excited by turns'.

We had also begun to develop a relationship with an orphanage in Edendale township called Thembalihle, beautiful hope. As our work at the creche in Sweetwaters was now complete, we had approached the principal at Thembalihle about sending groups of students to work with them as part of the development and dialogue program. The orphanage had never received this kind of support and they were thrilled at the opportunity. So we painted, repaired beds, made curtains, fixed toys and, most enjoyably, played with the children. Their ages ranged from newborn to teenagers, many orphaned by the violence in the Natal Midlands and many more by AIDS, though no one would speak about it. A number of the school students were so moved by their visit to Thembalihle that they returned with toys and books purchased by funds raised at their own schools.

I was also becoming increasingly attached to the orphanage and its children. I once brought a visiting Australian film crew to visit as part of a piece they were doing on the Seven Day War and its aftermath. As always, when the children saw me they came rushing towards me like a tidal wave, all smiling eyes and outstretched arms yelling 'Mama Sandy'. The journalist asked if the kids could do it again so as to catch it on film for their piece!

I was excited to see all the connections that had been made between schools and communities during the last two years of our work in 'Maritzburg. Many of these relationships now had a life of their own: student exchanges, joint cultural events, principal visits, swapping of resources were all being organised, and one school in the township received a gift of many thousands of dollars. In the context of the division that had once existed, these events were like a small revolution, one I was proud to be part of.

We once again had a number of volunteers coming to work with us this year, the first arriving in January. Her name was Fiona and she planned to work with us for three months. Fiona was mixed race, half English and half Indian, causing much curiosity in our work. I also spent many hours listening to stories about her childhood, my own interest piqued by the thought of perhaps having mixed race children of my own one day. Fiona and I became fast friends, being the only females of the same age at Sizwe, and before long she was staying with us at Oxford Street most weekends.

There were also a number of other friends in the neighbourhood around which an inner city community feel was being built. Home Group's Brian and Anthea and their baby Gemma lived in the next street in a similar sized cottage to ours, where we often shared meals or simply a quiet afternoon in the garden. In March, after having finished his two-year contract with World Vision, Fred moved back to 'Maritzburg and bought a place nearby. Tansey, the Latin teacher from Maritzburg College, was also only three streets away. As well, there were a few friends I knew through my connections with the university, one of whom lived in our street. I loved this fluid, inviting inner city life that was lived on the streets or in the homes of neighbours. Justin, Fiona and I would often sit on the wall of our front stoep with our legs dangling over the edge as if we were fishing rather than relaxing at home. From this vantage point we would chat for hours, greeting neighbours who passed by and always paused to say hello.

There was also regular traffic between Oxford Street and ETHOS. Teboho came not only to visit me but also to spend time with Willie. They had not lived in the same town since Willie was a young child. Justin and I were often at ETHOS catching up with Jacques and Margie and the other students we were close to. Jacques and Margie were now parents, Margie having given birth to a gorgeous, plump-cheeked baby girl called Stephanie who was the sweetheart of ETHOS. Jacques and Margie's parents took some time getting used to the idea of their first grandchild being babysat by black university students, but they did eventually adjust. Stephanie seemed to love Teboho the best as he made her laugh, speaking to her in imaginary languages that only they understood. Mama Florence, the housekeeper, was also seen whisking Stephanie up onto her back, tucking her into place with a blanket or towel, where she slept happily as had many African babies before her. Alice also provided a ready pair of hands, missing her own child as she did.

Alice, the only female student at ETHOS, was also a regular at Oxford Street. Not only were she and I good friends, but Justin had taken her son under his wing. Alice was one of those rare people who are completely who they are—no camouflage or deceit. As with so many of my black friends, her life up until this point had been very difficult. After falling pregnant with Stanley when she was just a child herself she was forced to raise him alone, pushing her own education into the background in an effort to earn enough money to keep them both alive. And, as for so many, it was the church that saved her. She was a member of Ebenezer in Soweto, where Khumo's brother was the minister. This was the sister church to Teboho's church in Mohlakeng and it was through this connection that she had applied to be part of ETHOS.

One weekend I had a long conversation with Fiona about her parents' marriage. As she was getting serious with an Englishman, Iain, the same mixed marriage issues were looming for her. She described the hardships that had resulted in her parents' eventual separation. Since she identified with both lines of her parentage she felt it was vital that Iain understood this. As it was, Iain was white but had been born in India and spent his early childhood there. He had lived between England and India ever since. Fiona felt this would give their relationship a much better chance of survival, seeding the idea in my mind that if Teboho and I did marry, we should also plan to spend some time in Australia.

As the months in Oxford Street passed, I felt something in myself restored. Teboho believed I was more self-confident, settled and independent since the move. I suspect the state of shock I was in from the violence of the previous year was passing, as Oxford Street restored a sense of security. Regardless of the reasons, I was clearly thriving.

In April, Fiona returned home and I experienced the same sense of loss as I had with the departure of Nat, Pete and Anne. My life had evolved into a rhythm of constant companionship followed by absence and loss. But as with all cycles, this sadness passed and new volunteers arrived, once more from England. Fortunately, Peter and Heidi were planning to stay longer than a few months. Peter was a newly ordained Anglican minister and had negotiated a year's secondment to the diocese in 'Maritzburg. He also had a classics degree from Oxford University which secured him a teaching role. In order to acclimatise to the issues in South Africa, Peter and Heidi had asked to spend their first two months working as volunteers at Sizwe. Heidi was the daughter of an English minister who, in a strange coincidence, had met Steve through his first parish role. Because Heidi had taken Peter's name when they married, this connection was only realised later.

When Peter and Heidi arrived, Heidi was already several months pregnant with their first child. It had been agreed they could use the cottage as Fiona had, and others before her. However, after two weeks, Steve told them he would be needing the cottage and asked them to look for accommodation in town. We were happy to offer them space in Oxford Street for a week or two while they looked around, and they quickly found a place to rent around the corner: the crisis was resolved. With Robbie driving to work via Oxford Street, their transport to Sizwe was not an issue either.

Within a few weeks, Heidi found volunteer work with Margie who was now running an organisation called Thandanani, meaning 'love each other'. Thandanani provided further training and resources for the creches that littered the townships. Many teachers in these township facilities were untrained or lacked the resources to allow the creche to offer anything more than babysitting. Thandanani understood the value of investing in preschool education and its team worked hard to equip the teachers with improved skills. The organisation went on to work with the many thousands of AIDS orphans in the province.

As a preschool teacher, Heidi's skills were put to better use at Thandanani than at Sizwe so it was Peter who remained as a volunteer with us. However, over lunch at Oxford Street one day, Heidi mentioned that she never felt welcome at Sizwe and was happy to find another organisation to work with. As she was the first to express such a sentiment I put it down to a personality clash between her and Steve because both of them are strong-willed and forthright.

In May, though it had been on the cards for some time, Teboho proposed. He took me to the same Greek restaurant where I had eaten with my parents when they met Mdu the year before. This time, we both entered through the front door. After a delicious meal, he took my hand in his and said, 'Any last words as a Blackburn?' before slipping a ring on my finger. I was delighted, although I must confess the question did make me pause, sharply aware that one phase of my life was ending and another beginning. For a moment I held on to all that being a Blackburn meant: my family, my history, my life in Australia, my identity. But the moment passed as Teboho laughed and kissed me, despite the undisguised stares of our white fellow diners.

There was instant celebration at ETHOS when we arrived home from the restaurant with Margie particularly thrilled, taking credit for having set up such a fine match. Alice burst into ululation—*he le le, he le le*—as she danced in circles around us. She and Pat began to sing a much loved wedding song, '*Makoti ke di nako*', New bride, now is the time. Willie and Justin were equally exuberant when we told them the news. Still in high spirits, we phoned Mum and Dad. I can't imagine what it feels like to get a call from your daughter saying she is marrying a man from Africa whom you have met only once in a sea of faces at a picnic. But as always, seemingly unsurprised by my choices in life, they were happy for us and we celebrated together over the phone. The celebrations continued at Sizwe on Monday morning.

Two weeks later, Teboho went to France. The trip had been organised by the French Protestant Council of Churches, taking Moss, Teboho and Nimrod (another ETHOS student) to Paris, Lille and Strasbourg for three weeks. They spoke at various church meetings and conferences, stayed with Christian communities and held discussions with organisations who had an interest in what was happening in South Africa. It was the first time Teboho had ever left the region.

Almost two weeks into the trip I received a long awaited postcard:

Hello Darling,

Our arrival went well and safe. I still can't believe that I'm here. I think I'm now beginning to understand where the concept of fun comes from. There are moments when I miss you dearly. In a place like this, I think it is only healthy to travel with the one you love. We arrived on a long weekend and that's why this is posted so late. I LOVE YOU—I know that! The cost of living is too high here. Say hi to all there.

With love,

Teboho

I received another postcard from Fiona a few days later. It showed a black and white photo of a bride walking along a country road, suitcase in hand. On the road walking next to her is a cow. Fiona wrote: 'Thought this could be you walking to the wedding with the meat'.

While Teboho was overseas, I made some time to take Heidi to Thembalihle as she had heard from Peter that it was one of the organisations we were working with. Heidi's parents had fostered children as long as Heidi could remember. She also had two adopted siblings from Vietnam who were now in their late teens. While I had seen the pragmatic side of Heidi that allowed her to run a busy preschool with an efficiency that would put the military to shame, what I saw when she entered Thembalihle was the response of someone who had been born to love the unwanted. We spent hours there together, taking time with each child we met, Heidi asking questions about their circumstances and hoping for an eventual adoption. While many children in African communities are informally adopted by their extended families and communities in the event of the death of their parents, formal adoption rates are extremely low if not non-existent. So Heidi was told that these children would most likely spend the rest of their childhood here at Thembalihle.

During the course of the afternoon, we met one little girl whom I had not seen before. Her name was Ayanda, which means 'we are increased'. The details of her arrival at Thembalihle were sketchy, the staff simply thinking that her parents were dead. They were not even sure how old she was. Ayanda did not play with the other children; she simply sat. We did not see her stand or even crawl for the hour or so we played with her. She simply took one look at Heidi and held her arms out.

Two days later we were back, this time with Peter. Heidi hadn't slept and most likely neither had Peter, both of them finding it unbearable that Ayanda was wasting away in the orphanage. Heidi had convinced Peter, despite her own pregnancy, to investigate whether they could foster and then adopt Ayanda. Given Heidi's childhood experiences, this had been something they discussed when they were first married. While they hadn't anticipated it would happen so quickly, meeting Ayanda added a sense of urgency to their plans.

I had a quiet word to the principal who was delighted, but sceptical that something could be organised quickly—Heidi didn't want Ayanda to spend another night in the orphanage. While Peter and Heidi spent the next hour in discussions with the principal, I went off to find Ayanda. She was sitting exactly where we had found her two days before. I wondered, given she never complained and was therefore less trouble than the other children, if she was plonked down there in the mornings, fed and then placed in bed at night. The image of her was in sharp contrast to the colour and movement of the other children, noisy and never still. While I initially thought Heidi was acting too fast, I saw then that if this child was to be drawn out at all, it would need to be soon.

Somehow, it was four of us, not three, who came home that day as Ayanda found her place in her new family. We also discovered, after a number of visits to doctors, that Ayanda was actually two years old and chronically under-developed for her age. Since Peter and Heidi lived around the corner, I spent a great deal of time with Ayanda; I felt like something of a step-parent to her myself, having been there from the beginning. As Heidi's belly grew and Ayanda could no longer fit on her lap, it was into my lap that she crawled for consolation. When Heidi eventually gave birth, a long and horrendous experience, Ayanda needed extra attention which she got from a number of residents at Oxford Street.

Peter and Heidi did eventually adopt Ayanda, having to live in South Africa for four years and become South African residents to do so. By that time they had two sons, first Daniel and later Joel; when they finally returned to England, they were a family of five.

Teboho returned from France after three weeks that felt to me like three months. I managed to whisk him away from his homecoming celebrations at ETHOS for a quiet dinner at Oxford Street. Over the meal, he regaled us with stories of his adventures in France, making the most of all the cultural faux pas and linguistic confusion. As he already spoke ten of the eleven South African languages fluently, and had once lived in Venda for three months just to learn the eleventh, he had picked up French easily, returning with many colourful phrases.

With our bellies aching from a big meal and much laughter, we retired to my room to spend some much awaited time alone together. As he held me in his arms, I remember feeling like a sponge, wanting to soak him into muscle and bone so as not to be without the essence of him again. I had missed his optimism, his laughter, his shoulder and the sunshine of his love.

So I entered the second half of the year enjoying my new home and the growing community in which it was located, with both work and home groups providing stretch and purpose. Teboho and I were busy planning two weddings: one in early January in Sydney and the second in early February in Mohlakeng. All was well in my world as I celebrated my twenty-sixth birthday and I was very, very happy.

Do we tempt the gods when our worlds are awash with joy? Perhaps. Suffice to say that Heidi's disquiet, long forgotten by the rest of us, would trigger a chain of events that was to tear the fabric of my world apart.

19

October 1991
And Then It All Falls Apart

TEBOHO CAME TO OXFORD STREET ONE DAY WITH SOME UNEXPECTED NEWS. ETHOS WAS A PROGRAM THAT WAS OPEN TO SINGLE STUDENTS ONLY AS THE HOUSE COULD NOT ACCOMMODATE COUPLES OR FAMILIES. OUR IMPENDING MARRIAGE HAD BEEN TAKEN TO THE BOARD TO DETERMINE WHETHER THIS WOULD LOCK HIM OUT OF THE PROGRAM AND THE SCHOLARSHIP THAT WENT WITH IT. THE GOOD NEWS WAS THAT THE BOARD WAS WILLING TO LET TEBOHO STAY ON AT ETHOS ON CONDITION THAT WE DIDN'T LIVE AT OXFORD STREET AS WE HAD PLANNED, BUT AGREED TO LIVE IN COMMUNITY AT ETHOS.

With his scholarship intact, Teboho was elated but I was forlorn at the thought of leaving my beloved new home. Teboho tried to console me with assurances that we would be given the largest room in the old house, with lovely wooden floors and views over the garden and towards the hills that surrounded the city. Yet I was angry with the ultimatum—take the offer or leave the program. The Board argued that living in community was a crucial part of the training and one they would not compromise on. I felt like a teenager who had been grounded, not a grown woman who was about to marry and make her own home with her new husband. I sulked and raged in turn for weeks until I finally gave in, knowing the decision was out of my control. ETHOS would not bend and if Teboho left, there was no money for him to finish the last two years of his studies.

I wrote to a friend back in Australia, struggling to find the middle ground: 'Living with single students won't be easy but we'll try and make the best of it. At least it will be a stimulating environment as the community is constantly trying to stretch and apply its faith'.

Despite having many friends at ETHOS and loving the time I spent there, I knew from Jacques and Margie that living there as a married couple would be a challenge. They had bought a house down the street after Stephanie was born, as it had proven too hard to have both family and community in the same house. I was also aware that it wasn't an ideal way to begin our marriage but Teboho was confident we could make it work and I trusted him. He had a gift for carving out space in our busy lives so that it felt as though only the two of us existed, a space where I felt cherished and connected. I believed he could find a way to make it work for us at ETHOS.

Shortly after Teboho's news, Robbie came to Oxford Street with news of his own. Mr Khuzwayo, the principal of my favourite school, Smero, had been promoted to District Inspector, effective immediately. I suppose it was to be expected. Such talent doesn't go unnoticed and swiftly gets siphoned off, promoted up. Yet the school, its teachers, students and parents mourned Mr Khuzwayo's leaving as if it was a death in the family. In a way it was. The school would never be the same again, such was the effect of his gifted leadership. There was even some graffiti on one classroom wall that said, 'We love our headmaster more than education'. As his promotion was effective immediately, the school was in disarray.

The worst of it was that it was only two months before the matriculation exams for the senior students and they were now without an English teacher as well as a principal. In desperation, they had sent Robbie to call me. While I had no formal teaching qualifications, only a Bachelor of Science degree, the staff reasoned that I was the only English-speaking person who had a relationship with the school; that put me at the top of their list. Steve and I immediately agreed that Sizwe would free me up to teach at Smero for three weeks until a replacement could be found. So for the rest of September, I was to teach three double periods of Senior English each day, as Mr Khuzwayo had done every day of his time there. How he had time to run such an amazing school on top of this class load, I do not know.

The school had twelve hundred students, fifteen classrooms, twenty-two teachers and me. A quick calculation revealed that I could be teaching up to eighty students at a time. I was terrified and excited in equal parts. I also knew how important this was to the matriculating students, with exams bearing down on them. Standing at the front of the room that first morning, I felt nervousness place a hand around my throat and squeeze. Those three weeks were a whirlwind of eager faces, crowded classrooms, late night preparation and marking. I saw how far behind many of the students were and realised there would be no chance they would pass their final exams. And yet I also saw a great many students who had been given such a gift by their years at this extraordinary school that they believed anything was possible.

Despite my involvement in the teacher exchanges and my many years of running youth programs, I found facing a classroom of seventy, three times a day, gave me a new appreciation for teachers and what they do. More than once, I arrived ready with a lesson prepared for 10A only to be met by the smiling faces of 10B who had done that same work that morning and were now looking forward to what came next. It taught me how to think on my feet and never lose my confidence, knowing that teenagers could smell fear from forty metres. I also learnt how to teach in a large classroom with only my voice and a piece of chalk as my tools.

It was both a fabulous and sobering experience. I was constantly comparing it to my own high school experience at North Sydney Girls High, a selective government school where no effort was spared to push and challenge the students. At the time, I didn't think of us as a well-resourced school, squashed as we were into a small block on the edge of the city with no space to move, but I knew we had extraordinary teachers who got to know what we were capable of and set the bar just out of our reach to stretch us. Smero shared that same spirit of believing in its students and wanting them to succeed. But the comparison ended there, as that was all they had to offer. And yet—it was amazing what could be done with school spirit and a blackboard.

When I went back to work at Sizwe, I was completely spent. Thankfully, I had two weeks before the next dialogue program in the middle of October, which would be followed by another teacher exchange. In the converted office that I shared with Lee and Robbie, something felt a bit different. Lee, who was always a quiet person, seemed even more reserved yet also a little agitated. I asked Robbie about it but as Lee had not volunteered any information, we decided to let her talk when she was ready.

On the weekend, I popped in to see Heidi, Peter and Ayanda and their new baby Joel. Heidi's mum had recently visited to meet the baby and Heidi told me about a strange conversation they had during her stay. The gist of it was that Heidi's father's encounters with Steve in England had not always been harmonious and that perhaps this accounted for the absence of Steve and Beth's renowned hospitality.

I spent the rest of the weekend trying to make sense of what Heidi had told me. I had nothing but respect for Steve and had been in some pretty tight situations with him where he had always acted with courage and honour. He was one of the few people who had shown me how to live in a society that constantly asks individuals to state what they stand for. He never shied away from the complexities of South Africa, the moral dilemmas that faced us because we knew those on all sides of the conflict did things that were indefensible. He met it face-on and still found a way to do what was right. So it wasn't just his actions I admired but his intellectual rigour when he posed the questions that most people were afraid to ask.

I also knew that Steve had been brought up in a series of foster homes, his mother dead and his father unable to cope with the tribe of young sons. I understood that growing up poor and unwanted leaves people with a lifetime of baggage and it takes someone extraordinary to set it down and move on. And while I believed Steve to be extraordinary, to the extent that I had more or less put him on a pedestal, the conversation with Heidi left me feeling unsettled.

The following week was a blur of preparations for the program weekends that followed, yet Lee still seemed distracted and withdrawn. By Friday, I could no longer wait and in my usual forward style, asked her what was going on. With some encouragement, she told Robbie and me that she was concerned something was not quite right with the Trust. She refused to say anything more as she wanted to be completely sure of her facts before she discussed her concerns with Steve. I said nothing, but my small seed of uncertainty began to take root.

After a weekend of preparation, Lee went to Steve. I watched her walk up the driveway towards the house and Steve's office. I listened to the gravel crunch beneath her feet.

Robbie and I waited as the minutes ticked by, sitting in silence, pretending to work. After an hour, I could no longer stand the heaviness and I told Robbie about my conversation with Heidi. I couldn't tell if the knot in my stomach was anger or fear. I watched Robbie's face as he tossed the information around in his mind. He felt the same way as I did about Steve. Some of the political prisoners he was with in detention had teased him for going to work in an organisation run by a white priest, claiming it would be liberal and ineffectual. He had stood his ground then and since, defending Sizwe in general and Steve in particular. I watched the emotions flicker across his boyish face, disbelief changing to confusion.

And we waited. It was almost another hour before I heard the crunching of the gravel announcing someone's approach. But it wasn't Lee, it was Steve. He sat down and told us that he had some difficult news to share. He said he had been concerned for some time that Lee, who had worked with him for so many years, was no longer happy; that they had talked at length but were unable to resolve their differences and that, sadly, Lee was leaving. I had an unwelcome vision of Lee in his office, sitting with her face in her hands. I didn't know what to think and was close to tears. Robbie was silent, his face masked so that it could not be read.

Steve left and went back up to the house. After a few minutes we heard footsteps again. Lee walked straight past the office, got into her car and drove off. Moments later, Mama Jenny's voice rang out, calling us all for lunch up on the stoep. 'I can't eat right now', I said to Robbie. 'Let's go and find Themba.' Themba was running a tin craft workshop in Edendale and would be unaware of the events of the last few hours. So we grabbed the bakkie keys and left without a word to anyone.

As we drove down Sweetwaters Road, I found it hard to think straight. I wanted to believe the best of people—I had chosen to live that way. I had been with both Steve and Lee since the beginning and could not imagine my life in South Africa without either of them. Part of me didn't want to address the situation at all because I knew that with this splitting of the original team things would not be the same, no matter what happened from here. As we reached the bottom of the hill and arrived in Caluza, the almost hypnotic tempo of the township reached me, calm, soothing and regular like a heartbeat.

After finding Themba and leaving him as shocked and confused as we were, we drove into town and went looking for Lee. Her car was parked outside her house. She opened the door, seeming unsurprised to see us. We sat in her small living room and she told us what had transpired with Steve. She said that when she presented him with her concerns, he simply turned to her and suggested it might be best if she packed her belongings and left. They argued briefly, but Lee was prepared for this: she had been mulling things over and making notes for weeks now and had kept them with her in a file at home. Lee talked us through the details, but I could no longer hear her. I felt as if I might throw up. I felt as though all my efforts, all my hard work had been built on shaky foundations; that my world had splintered into a thousand pieces and I was watching it all blow away.

Lee told us she was going to go to the Trustees to discuss the situation. Robbie and I thought we should talk to Mdu as he was on our management committee and connected to many of the Trustees. We agreed that we needed to move quickly. As we made plans, the part of each of us who had been through so many crises—the Table Mountain refugee camp, the Seven Day War—clicked into place and we were resolute about what needed to be done.

We found Mdu at his office just as he was about to leave for the day. We described the chain of events in detail. Mdu was silent for a time and then simply said, 'OK'. I watched the burden of disappointment climb onto his shoulders, causing them to droop a little. Like Robbie, he had gone out on a limb with his political associates when he joined the management team of Sizwe. We agreed to talk some more over the course of the week.

As we left the Council of Churches, I could hold it in no more and asked Robbie to take me to ETHOS. We made the short drive to the University where Robbie dropped me off in the driveway. I watched him leave and then turned towards the house. I climbed slowly up the stairs to the open door, my body like lead, making each step an effort. From the stairs, I heard Teboho's laughter echoing through the house and it spilled outside like a flock of parrots taking flight. My tears were close to the surface now. I followed the sound of laughter to the hallway and up to the first floor where I found Teboho and Alice recounting the events of the day in his room. I ran across the room, heaving great sobs of despair, and he stood to catch me in his arms.

After a time, the three of us sat on his bed and the chain of events came tumbling out through my tears. I found it hard to express the depths of disappointment and despair I felt at that point—morally, personally, spiritually. My faith in the organisation was deeply shaken. I had thrown my whole being into our work and I was not sure who I could be in this country without it.

'You will be my wife', Teboho assured me, 'and you will be with me. I need you. My family needs you and my community needs you.'

Robbie and I went to see Steve on the Wednesday after spending Tuesday working in the township, keeping ourselves a safe distance from Phezulu. We had decided to resign. With unresolved doubt in our minds, we could no longer be part of Sizwe. I was leaving for our wedding in Australia in four weeks. Robbie was confident he could find something else. We both felt guilty for letting down the groups that were coming that weekend and the next, expecting Robbie and I to run programs for them. Perhaps Themba would take over and see that it didn't fall apart. Although he understood our decisions, Themba was not in a position to consider resigning as he was financially responsible not only for himself but also for his family back in Stanger. He would have to weather the storm for now.

I hadn't eaten or slept properly for a few days and was a shaking mess by the time we entered Steve's office to tender our resignations. In truth, I knew it would end our relationship and, despite all the unresolved questions, I dreaded the moment. There was no righteous anger in me then, only fear and loss. Once it was done, a steel shutter came down and Steve and I never spoke a word to each other again.

20
DECEMBER 1991
DANCING IN THE AISLES

BEFORE WE LEFT FOR THE WEDDING IN SYDNEY, CALEB, TEBOHO'S OLDER BROTHER, THREW A FAREWELL PARTY FOR US. THE EXTENDED FAMILY ARRIVED FROM ITSOSENG AND RUSTENBURG. MOSS AND KHUMO, MEMBERS OF THE YOUTH GROUP AND MANY OF THE NEIGHBOURS CRAMMED THEMSELVES INTO CALEB'S MODEST HOUSE TO WISH US WELL. MOSS AND KHUMO SPOKE ON BEHALF OF THE CHURCH, TEASING TEBOHO ABOUT MEETING MY PARENTS FOR THE FIRST TIME ON THE EVE OF OUR WEDDING, CLEARLY CONFIDENT THERE WOULD BE NO LAST-MINUTE CHANGE OF MIND ON MY FATHER'S PART.

Caleb spoke on behalf of the family, expressing his regret that Teboho should be making this journey alone as it is tradition for the uncles to go ahead of the young man to ask permission and negotiate a bride price or *lobola*. *Lobola* is the price in cattle that the bride's family ask in compensation for losing a daughter. In modern society, *lobola* increases with the education levels of the bride. Caleb joked that perhaps it was a good thing there was no *lobola* in my case, as a university degree would put me out of the family's reach. What I didn't know was that Teboho had five cows in his luggage to give my father: one wooden, one ceramic, one metal, one plastic and one stuffed toy cow.

After Caleb finished, Mama told everyone how happy she was that Teboho was finally marrying; she had been worried about him never finding a wife, crazy and outspoken as he was. She gave me my new family name, a tradition denoting the passage from girl to woman, from family to family when a woman joins her new home. She announced that my name from now onwards would be *Malerato*, meaning 'mother of love', for she felt that I must really love Teboho to leave everything and settle here with him. I was close to tears as she had given me a beautiful and powerful name. It was an indication of her love for me and I knew it.

Teboho encouraged me to respond on behalf of the two of us and I did so in Zulu, knowing that it would please the family. I thanked them for welcoming me into their family and their community and promised them I would be a good wife and daughter, a good *makoti*, at which they all laughed. A *makoti* is a new bride who enters her husband's family and, as the least powerful adult member, is required to be a type of servant until one of the other brothers marries and replaces her with a new *makoti*, allowing her to move up the social ladder. In some families, the *makoti* can become a kind of Cinderella, but I suspected that Mama would not make me play that role, gentle hearted and fair spirited as she was. So we all laughed at the thought as Caleb offered a toast to the bride- and groom-to-be and wished us every happiness in our journey.

We were flying out the next afternoon and Caleb had hired a few taxis to take everyone to the airport to see us off. It was not lost on me that I was standing in Jan Smuts Airport, a single white woman among twenty or thirty black people, saying heartfelt goodbyes. It must have been an odd sight for white South African travellers.

Teboho stood at the front of the church in Sydney wearing the smile of a man whose dreams have just come true. The emotional storms of the past five weeks were put behind us for the moment and the long awaited day of our marriage had arrived. Whispers and giggles rippled through the packed church as Teboho began to dance to the music in his head. The Australians gathered there had no idea that spontaneous dancing is commonplace in Africa. With a nod from Terry, the minister, Teboho turned and lit the candle that held a silent vigil on the cloth-covered table next to the pulpit. Then the sedate, respectable old church in the heart of leafy Wahroonga, one of Sydney's upper class suburbs, began to throb with an African rhythm. The Zulu wedding song spilling out of its doors had passers-by stopping to speculate about what was going on at St Andrew's that day.

The congregation turned as the wedding party burst into the church, each pair dancing down the aisle in time to the wedding song, two steps forward, one step back, hips and arms counting time as they swayed backwards and forwards. After a frantic week of practising on the paving surrounding my parents' pool, my old friends Nick and Grace, my brother Jon and my dear friend Nat danced down the aisle while the congregation's clapping urged them on. They all wore traditional African outfits, though Nat and Grace dressed more adventurously than Jon and Nick. Grace and Nat wore printed African dresses, tall-shouldered and slim-waisted, with matching pill box hats they had substituted for the headcloths I brought with me from Africa. Jon and Nick wore suit trousers with white African shirts over the top, subtly embroidered around the neck.

The words of the song compel the bride to come forward and marry her groom while her mother cooks the celebration feast. With my hand on Dad's arm, I danced towards my own groom, letting the music and the joy in the faces of my family and friends carry me down the aisle. I saw Phil and Kathy, Pete, Anne, Matt and Liz, Charlie—and through them, all the faces of our friends back in 'Maritzburg shimmered as if to wish us well.

I wore a white dress made in the style of an African traditional outfit, high shoulders with the sleeves tapering at the elbows, a scooped neckline edged with blue embroidery and beading, a sash around the narrow waist and a long straight skirt falling to the floor. The long veil sat over the blue and white flowers that formed a ring around my head. As I reached the stairs leading up to the altar, I thought the blue and white of Teboho's traditional attire merged in with the colours of the stained glass window behind him as if he wore a multi-coloured cloak and crown. For a moment we locked eyes, and what passed between us were all the difficulties we had overcome to arrive at this moment, all those who would have stood in our way. Yet here we were surrounded by the delight of those who loved us as they anticipated the vows we were about to make. I felt the tears escape for a moment and seeing this, Teboho reached for my hand, bowed his head to my father in recognition and drew me forward to stand next to him.

Terry asked, 'Who brings this woman to be married to this man?' and my mother stood up next to my father as they said, 'We do'. I handed my flowers to Nat and looked up at Terry. I had known him for almost ten years. I joined the church when I was sixteen, though it was some distance from my home. St Andrew's had a large youth group and not enough young women to take on the leadership responsibilities. So I was 'headhunted' from a church half an hour away to join the leadership team. It was here at St Andrew's that I had learnt about youth work, leadership and community. It was here I made my mistakes, was coached and mentored. It was this church that had supported me to work in Africa and Terry had been a driving force in all of this. In Terry's smile I saw all this history folded into the words he now spoke as he guided us towards the future.

Teboho and I turned to one another and made promises of care, love and loyalty. We exchanged rings that, once blessed, would represent the eternal element of this new relationship, and of love itself. After a kiss that sealed the vows, Teboho once more began to dance, round and round in a joyous circle as the congregation cheered and applauded. After a few words, songs and readings from friends, the wedding party made its way back down the aisle, dancing to a second wedding song, this time with friends and family joining in. We spilled out into the garden and onto the street, with Teboho and I waiting to thank each guest as they emerged dancing from the church.

The celebrations continued afterwards in the church hall. We had decided on a simple reception so that, in true African style, all those who wished to come could come. There was no formal sit-down meal, just more music, and lots of food made by the church's women's group as their wedding present to us, and served to our guests by members of the youth group. We ate, we drank, we laughed, we danced and we wished each other great happiness. For years afterwards, friends would tell me that this was the most joyful wedding they had ever been to and one that the sleepy suburb of Wahroonga would not soon forget.

Despite the happiness of our wedding, a poisonous undercurrent flowed beneath the surface, one that had followed me from South Africa. In the weeks before we left for Sydney, things had deteriorated and my reputation was under a cloud. The story around 'Maritzburg was that I had pocketed some of the Sizwe funds raised in Australia and bought myself a personal computer. The irony is, I did get a computer during my earlier visit to Sydney—but it was generously given to me by someone at my church to assist with fundraising. The kernel of truth in the lie had people wondering.

Yet despite the attacks on my integrity, I felt somehow protected through my relationship with Teboho. I imagined that marrying him put my own priorities and allegiances beyond doubt. The turn of events at Sizwe would bring into question the commitment of each of us and I felt that, for me to continue my work in South Africa, credibility in the black community was critical. I was already seeing that it was the white community who were torn over whom to believe—Robbie, Lee and I, or Steve—whereas the local black youth leadership came down in support of our version of events.

I heard that Steve was planning a fundraising trip to Australia, yet was struggling to convince any black person attached to Sizwe to accompany him. Robbie and I worked hard to ensure that any youth leaders he might approach were aware of our resignations. Steve then let it be known that he would be approaching all Sizwe's contacts in Sydney, including my church network and all the volunteers who had worked with us over the past two years.

Although I had not told anyone what was happening while I was still in South Africa, once I was back in Sydney I made it a priority. Before the wedding and honeymoon, I took the time to speak to everyone I thought Steve would visit during his fundraising trip. Each one was shocked and saddened, but deeply sympathetic to the situation that I and the rest of the team were now in. It was particularly hard to tell Terry that things had fallen apart in the way they had, as the church had put so much effort into supporting me at Sizwe.

The only person I could not speak to in time was my old friend Matt. He was still working for an aid agency and only arrived back in town the day of the wedding. I decided to send him a fax outlining all that had happened, in case Steve tried to contact him before we spoke. Given the long-term relationship Matt had with Steve, he was shaken by the contents of the fax and felt it only fair that Steve be given an opportunity to respond. With this in mind, and unbeknown to me, he sent Steve a copy of my fax. As a result, the breach between Steve and myself widened further—with disastrous results.

Had I had more perspective when this was happening, I would have contacted a lawyer and been more careful in my actions. But I had spent the last four years working in an environment that did not trust the legal system. The anti-apartheid movement worked through mobilising people around injustices and building powerful networks to drive change. This was all I knew. Steve, on the other hand, had approached his lawyer and was preparing to engage in a different kind of battle, one that I was ill prepared to fight.

After the wedding in Sydney, we had two honeymoons planned: one just for us, and one with friends so that we could say our goodbyes. Anne's parents had a holiday house at Leura in the Blue Mountains, about one and a half hours drive west from Sydney. They had offered it to us for the week after the wedding and we jumped at the opportunity.

From that week there is one distressing memory, inexplicably nestled among the happy memories that spill like favourite holiday photos across a table. On the second afternoon, after lunch at the village, I went off to take a nap. As I lay on the bed, not yet asleep, it seemed as if the earth fell away beneath me, leaving me stranded on the bed miles above the ground—which had turned to desert rock. My terrible fear of heights had me clinging to the bed for fear of falling, yet the overwhelming emotion was one of being utterly alone. It was as if there was no one left alive below: the earth was barren and I was now alone. I lay on the bed and sobbed. Teboho came in but I could not explain what had happened and would not be comforted. He tried to rock me like a child, telling me it was just a bad dream. I covered my head and continued to cry until I did finally fall asleep, fearing this was more premonition than dream.

I have thought of this many times since and wondered about the irony of such a vision on a honeymoon. It took a day or two to shake the feeling that I was now on my own, without support from anyone. While Teboho struggled to understand, I allowed the experience to break the emotional intimacy we had shared up until this point. He was not a huge believer in shamans and communication with the ancestors but he did not underestimate the power of visions and dreams. So he waited until it seemed to have drained out of my consciousness. I suspect, though, that it seeped deep into my subconscious only to resurface many years later.

Our second honeymoon was by the sea. We had booked a beach house at Avoca, an hour and a half's drive to the north of Sydney. Jon had gone back to work, but we invited friends to come and stay for as long as they could during the week that we would be there. Nat, Pete and another friend, Dion, stayed the whole week, with others coming and going as their commitments would allow. It was a week rich with friendships celebrated through shared meals, laughter and long languid days on the beach. I remember it as one of my happiest holidays.

While Teboho enjoyed our time at Leura despite the combination of my strange behaviour and our being without any other friends for the week, his gregarious nature meant that the second honeymoon was also a highlight of the trip for him. On the whole, he was deeply moved by the hospitality of my family and friends who took him to heart as if they had known him for years.

Soon it was time to leave and there was yet another tearful farewell at the airport. We had spent almost eight weeks with my family, during which time they had got to know Teboho well. Apparently my father had taken him aside the night before we left and made Teboho promise to take good care of me. Though we were sad to go and had no plans as to when we would return, our heads were already turned towards the upcoming celebrations in South Africa. We would be arriving the day before the wedding and there was much to do. After long, lingering hugs, we boarded the plane and sped back to South Africa to begin our married life there together.

Back at Jan Smuts airport we were greeted by family and friends who had once again organised kombis to the airport. This time we were a married couple, though the family would refuse to recognise our union until it was made official on African soil in less than two days time. There were more hugs and kisses and more stares from the astonished white travellers looking on.

With one day left before the African wedding, Caleb's home was like a beehive, each member of the family seeming to know what to do without being told. Not long after we arrived, a bakkie pulled up in front of the house. Amazingly, in the cab at the back was a large bull, struggling to be free. While I was still standing by the front door, mouth agape at the sight, Khumo and my new sisters-in-law came rushing over to say that it was not right for the bride to see the bull slaughtered and it was time for us to go. I was torn between relief and curiosity but had no say in the matter as they whisked me off to Khumo's house where there was a reprieve from the frenetic activity, and Khumo and I had a chance to catch up.

Khumo was to be my matron of honour and it was her job to organise the wedding party the following day. I was yet to discover the level of complexity that would be required, but Teboho had explained it was important to have your closest friends in these types of roles rather than as best man or bridesmaids. Our bridal party consisted of Joe's girlfriend Sara, whom I had got to know during our trip to Namibia the year before, Dumi, whose uncle we visited in Kopela with the youth group, Daddy, an old friend of Teboho's who had recently returned from the ANC school in Tanzania and my dear friend and housemate Justin, because I insisted. Moss, Joe and Beans, also fresh from Tanzania, were charged with overseeing the activity at the wedding ceremony and the reception. The family would take care of lunch which was to be held at Caleb's house before the reception in the evening.

No sooner had Khumo and I got comfortable than Teboho's sisters Silwane (alias Custard) and China arrived for the final fittings with the bridesmaids. As a wedding gift, China had made the outfits for both the Australian and the South African weddings. As she unpacked, she revealed a special surprise of new outfits for Teboho and me. We had not planned to change between the wedding and the reception as most African couples do, in order to keep things simple. But China wanted us to do things properly and now presented me with a beautiful dress, resplendent in red and gold. While I was trying it on, I heard Sara and Dumi arrive and soon the house was full of women in various states of undress and others cooing over the beautiful outfits. I stood there for a moment and thought about how wonderful it was to feel welcomed into a community in this way, to become part of another family.

African community living is open hearted, full of customs, yet none of it is forced or rigid. Mama had told me that *lobola* is more than a payment for the bride. Gifts of an equal value are given to the groom's family and to the couple themselves. These gifts serve to bind two families together, which is what a marriage really is. Because of this, Mama was saddened by the fact that, though we were getting married, she was yet to meet my parents. It would take some years for this final piece to fall into place for her, but when they did eventually meet, the fondness and mutual respect that grew was worth the wait.

After the dresses had been checked and final adjustments made, Silwane and China felt it was safe for us all to go back to Caleb's. It would be dark soon and time for the visiting family and guests to be fed. Seeing how many mouths there were to feed, Teboho and I slipped away to where we had planned to spend the night. We had been offered a bed by another friend of Teboho's by the name of Lekgoa, which means 'white person'. While Lekgoa was certainly not white, he was quite fair skinned for an African man. Lekgoa and his wife were putting us up in their home in the nearby township of Kagiso. Mohlakeng now resembled Bethlehem on the night Jesus was born.

The next morning after a hearty breakfast, we packed up our wedding outfits and made the drive back towards Mohlakeng.

You are invited to celebrate the marriage of

Teboho and Sandy

At East Extension, Mohlakeng

Randfontein, West Rand

At 12 pm, February 1st, 1992

And afterwards, the reception at 3 pm

At Ramosa Hall

In the inclusiveness that characterised Teboho's family, the invitation to the South Africa wedding came from all branches of the extended family—Teboho's father's side, Mama's second husband and Ma Ellen's. Given my previous experience with township weddings, I knew better than to ask why the venue for the church had not been included, the real celebration only starting with the food at Caleb's house.

Teboho dropped me off at Khumo's house so that I could change. Given the noise emanating from inside, I suspected I was not the first in the bridal party to arrive. The numbers of the household had swollen considerably since the day before with Khumo's sisters and their children having arrived from Soweto. As I entered the house I heard the familiar voices of Jacques and Margie. Running towards the kitchen, I suddenly realised who they were talking to—it was Elaine, my friend from Canada and her husband Anthony. They had decided that my wedding was a good enough reason for a trip to Africa. Grabbing each other, we jumped up and down in delight. I was deeply touched that she had come so far to see me. Jacques and Margie had driven up from 'Maritzburg the day before, collecting Elaine and Anthony along the way. With Justin in the bridal party, and his parents and sister also joining us, bringing with them Matt's father Graham who was in South Africa making a documentary, there would be a number of white faces in the township this day.

Ironically, Graham was the only person to take part in both weddings; he was introduced as my 'uncle' and asked to speak on behalf of the Australian family. He agreed to the twist in our relationship with a twinkle in his eye, knowing that being introduced as my ex-boyfriend's father would be awkward.

After tea and coffee and a plateful of biscuits, we got down to the business of getting ready. Khumo was wearing a loose fitting white kaftan with gold embroidery, well suited to the fuller figured, happily married woman. Khumo's sisters explained that my body size post the wedding would be a direct indicator to all those around me of the happiness of my marriage; should I fail to fill out, not only would my husband find me bony and unattractive but questions would be asked about his success as a husband and provider. Given my family's genetic predisposition to leanness, this didn't bode well for Teboho.

We were all dressed and ready to head off to the church when the phone rang. We were forty-five minutes late already, but I seemed to be the only one who was concerned. Caleb was phoning to tell us that Khumo's brother Caesar, who was to be the minister at the church ceremony, had not yet arrived. Khumo told Caleb we would wait half an hour and then come across. We arrived at the church an hour later, with me more than a little agitated. Apparently guests at the church had been kept entertained by the youth group who were happy to sing for their supper. Once we stepped out of the car, the excitement of hundreds of people milling outside was infectious and I quickly forgot the delays. Caesar had just arrived, almost two hours late. We later discovered that his car had broken down and he was forced to hitchhike all the way from Soweto.

News of our arrival quickly spread and the road became choked with neighbours wanting to see this strange thing—a white woman marrying a black man in a township. Khumo was forced to walk in front of us and clear a path to the church doors. Despite the interest, the church itself was only half full, most people content to wait outside for the ceremony to finish. As we entered, the congregation rose to its feet and, despite its relatively small numbers, the song they sang seemed to shake the foundations. We danced down the aisle—with no rehearsal being required this time—as the guests clapped and swayed in time to the music. I noticed the delighted yet slightly bemused faces of our white guests who were not quite able to find the beat.

Soon Teboho and I were standing together before the altar, Caesar looking remarkably composed. As we were technically already married, he changed the order of service slightly to bless the union before giving a short sermon on the importance of marriage. What followed was a waterfall of singing that carried us down the aisle and out onto the street. With Khumo in the lead, the dancing snaked its way down the street, seemingly with half of Mohlakeng joining in. The numbers had increased while we were inside the church, with well over five hundred people now cramming the streets. Once we had danced our way about a hundred metres down the road, Khumo turned us and we began to make our way back up, with the large crowd providing song after song in celebration.

After almost an hour of dancing, we were shepherded back into the cars: it was time to join the feast. I had been surprised that so few of the family were at the church service and asked Teboho about it in the car. He explained that the real party was happening at Caleb's house and everyone would have been needed there, even Mama. As we rounded the corner into Caleb's street, I suddenly understood what he meant: the entire street was packed to capacity. There must have been close to six hundred people who had long since begun without us. As the cars could proceed no further, we parked them on the corner. Eager face after eager face turned towards us and the high-pitched ululation rang out: '*He le le, he le le*'. Once more the singing began, deep baritones rumbling and the harmonies ringing in my ears. '*Makoti ke dinako. A jiga jiga. Makoti wa kgana na*', Makoti, now is the time. You won't refuse? I took that as a rhetorical question.

At the head of the wedding party, Khumo had been replaced by two of the neighbours, each carrying a broom, one with a white cloth attached to the end. Before I could ask Teboho what these were for, their use became apparent. The neighbour holding the cloth raised it in the air like a flag to mark our passage and the other used hers to strike at the legs of the revellers so as to make a space for us to pass. Even being struck in the leg did not deter our guests from their singing and dancing. With the relentlessness of a lava flow, we finally reached Caleb's house. I saw Mama waving from the side of the house, still holding a large wooden spoon in one hand and cloth in the other. While Jacques and Margie, Elaine and Anthony had joined the dancing, I spotted Justin's parents in front of the house, looking overwhelmed yet intrigued. I turned back to catch Justin's eye but he had also spotted them and was waving his greeting, knowing that a shout would be useless.

As we passed Caleb's house, our two broom-wielding friends turned the parade and swung it back on itself. From under my veil I tried to ask Teboho if we were going to enter the marquee that had been erected on the small patch of lawn, but he just winked and pulled me around with him. We seemed to be heading back the way we had come. We passed a row of porta-loos, half a dozen small boys balancing on the electricity meter to get a better look and the occasional face of someone I recognised. Soon we were being ushered back into the cars and whisked away.

'Where are we going now? I thought it was time to eat.'

'It is, *MoRatua*, my love, but first we have to change. That was just a sneak preview.'

Twenty minutes later, Teboho and I emerged from Moss and Khumo's in our red and gold outfits, feeling like African royalty, and were then driven with the rest of the bridal party back to Caleb's house for the real celebrations to begin.

After dancing our way back down to the marquee, we and the rest of the bridal party were seated at the head table. At the next table were all the guests of honour: Justin's parents, Elaine and Anthony, Graham, Jacques and Margie and Cliff and Eileen, an American couple who worked with Caesar at the church in Soweto. There were also seats for Caesar, Moss and Khumo, but they were nowhere in sight.

I later discovered that Caesar and Moss were dealing with a photographer. It was only after the bridal party had arrived at Caleb's house that Caesar realised the man snapping hundreds of photos was not the family photographer but a journalist from the *Sunday Times*. The family photographer had phoned the night before to explain that, due to a death in his family, he would not be able to come. However, this message was not relayed to anyone at the church so no one knew to question the man at the time. It was only Caesar's exposure to the media that prevented the entire event being open to the press. Moss and Caesar chased the photographer off with threats of legal action against the newspaper, causing them to arrive a little late at the table. Given that it was now almost three o'clock, well past the midday lunch promised on the invitation, I couldn't imagine anyone was particularly concerned about their late arrival. Perhaps this is another reason wedding invitations are not used at African weddings.

Outside the marquee, I saw long queues of guests crisscrossing the road as they waited patiently for plates of food. The most important criteria for a happy guest appeared to be the presence of meat and the weight of the plate. No one cared for elegant table settings, floral arrangements or even where they sat, for most stood and ate in circles of friends on the street. The elderly were supplied with chairs, having plates brought to them by young children, and sat happily sunning themselves while catching up on news of old friends and family.

Teboho and I and our seated guests were fed first, with Teboho being brought a plate that contained a single massive vertebra from the bull that had been slaughtered the day before. Elaine leant across and asked me if that was an important wedding tradition.

'No', I replied, sorry to disappoint. 'Teboho adores meat off the bone and his brothers are having a joke with him.'

It was two hours before I saw Mama who finally emerged from the kitchen, having left her daughters to finish the dishing. Amazingly, people were still queuing to be fed. She carried a plate of food but seemed reluctant to sit. Teboho insisted that he would go and work in the kitchen himself if she did not. She shrieked at the thought and promptly sat, knowing Teboho would follow through if she hesitated.

I asked Mama how on earth they had catered for so many. She told me that they had been cooking for a week; they had expected a large crowd because everyone knew about the wedding and wanted to see it for themselves. I mentioned that she must be relieved it was over. She turned to me and laughed, saying she was expecting many more people at the reception tonight so there was still plenty to do. My eyes widened at the thought.

A few hours later, we were ready to enter the reception hall. We had changed back into our original wedding outfits and were waiting in the car for our cue. I had noticed at the church that Daddy was the only one not wearing his matching attire; this was my first chance to ask him what had happened. He told me he had left it at the house he was staying at in Soweto and only realised his mistake when it was time to change for the church. With no time to go back and fetch it, Teboho and Beans had done a mad rush around Mohlakeng to find someone who had a blue traditional shirt. Grey was all that could be found so they had made do. I laughed at the irony of it, imagining what a drama this would have been at an Australian wedding where everything is generally planned to the last detail. Such things didn't matter here. In fact, I'd noticed that few people had dressed up for the wedding at all. What was important was the fact that people came, not how they were dressed. By those standards, Teboho and I were blessed. These thoughts lingered in my head as the doors were thrown open and the dancing began once more.

The large hall was packed with guests in row after row of plastic seats. We made our way down the left hand aisle and up onto the stage where a long table waited. It was draped in a long white cloth, with blue and white flowers dotted along its length. Between the flowers were bowls of sweets and plates of wedding biscuits. Behind the table was a large homemade sign that read: 'Congratulations Teboho and Sandy'. The hall itself was decorated in white and blue streamers and balloons, with the colourful clothes of the guests resembling shimmering bouquets of flowers. Everyone was on their feet and danced where they stood, causing the hall to shudder with each footfall. Each time I thought we would sit, someone else leapt up onto the stage and led another chorus of singing and dancing. Finally, Moss, as the MC for the evening, called the hall to order and asked everyone to take their seats. Members of the youth group appeared from the kitchen behind the stage and passed plates of sweets and chips down each row for the guests to snack on. It was time for the speeches.

There had been no speeches over lunch, so Moss invited a number of special guests to the stage: Caleb, who would speak for the family; Pat, who would speak for ETHOS; Matt's father, Graham, for my family; Joe for Teboho; and lastly, Margie for me. Moss was also acting as translator, switching languages between English and Tswana as required. Between speeches, there seemed to be compulsory singing so we all leapt to our feet and obliged. By the fourth speech, I must admit my energy was flagging and I was longing to kick off my shoes and relax. When it was Margie's turn to speak, she recounted the story of how Teboho had won my heart, which seemed to be the burning question in the room. Teboho had often been asked by black men, 'But what did you say?', as if some magic combination of words had been able to convince me. To the delight of our guests, Margie finished the story with the knitting of the jersey as my 'Yes' to his proposal, firmly establishing that jersey's place in the Mohlakeng hall of fame.

Lastly, Teboho spoke on behalf of us both, thanking our guests for coming from as far as Australia and France; the family, the neighbours and the church for hosting the wedding and providing all the wonderful food, and finally me, for agreeing to be his wife, making him the luckiest man in South Africa. At this, everyone was on their feet, cheering and stomping, the singing bursting out afresh.

The next morning, after catching a few hours sleep at Lekgoa's house in Kagiso, we were driving out of the township on our way back to Mohlakeng. We stopped at the major traffic lights next to Leratong Hospital; as at traffic lights the world over, young boys stood selling the Sunday morning papers. One boy, approaching Teboho at the driver's window in an attempt to get an extra five rand for bread with the sale, peered inside the car and spotted me. A white woman leaving a township on a Sunday morning would be enough to draw a second look, but we soon realised that it was the newspaper he was staring at. 'It's you!' he stammered in amazement.

There on the front page of the *Sunday Times* was a full-page spread on our wedding the day before. The headline read, 'Here comes the bride—and she's white'. The young boy began to shout to the other paper sellers as the lights changed and we pulled away. I looked aghast at the colour photo of us dancing in the street outside the church. 'What does it say?' Teboho asked urgently. I read the article aloud as he drove. He listened in stony silence as it described every aspect of the wedding, as well as all our personal details. We turned to each other with the same conclusion dawning in our minds. It was time to go home. Though it was 1992, we were still in the far West Rand of Johannesburg, the place many of the South African equivalent of the Ku Klux Klan call home. If they were disgusted by what they read—and they would be—they now had enough information to find us. A cold chill ran through me as I felt the vulnerability of our position.

We drove quickly to Mohlakeng to say our goodbyes and then straight on to Natal, stopping only once to get petrol along the way. Even there, people were pointing and staring, copies of the *Sunday Times* scattered next to the cashier's desk. Only when we pulled up outside ETHOS did I feel safe. Home at last.

For years afterwards, people would introduce themselves by saying, 'You remember me, I was at your wedding'. I would smile as graciously as I could and reply 'of course'. There were estimates that as many as three thousand people had celebrated with us that day. But the most memorable of those encounters was when an old man approached me, toothlessly smiling and nodding. Without a word, he asked me to wait while he fished inside his pocket for his wallet. I waited with patient curiosity as out of his wallet he produced an old newspaper cutting, worn with many years of handling. He carefully opened it up and held it next to his face, saying, 'I too was there that day. I came from very far to see such an amazing thing. I never thought I would see this in my lifetime. Thank you'.

21

February 1992
Annus Horribilis

1992 WAS THE QUEEN OF ENGLAND'S *ANNUS HORRIBILIS*. IT WAS ALSO MINE. I HAD HOPED THAT I COULD LEAVE BEHIND THE DISAPPOINTMENTS OF SIZWE AND START AFRESH. BUT NOT ONLY DID THEY FOLLOW ME LIKE A STRAY DOG, OTHER HEARTBREAKS AND BETRAYALS WERE TO LITTER MY PATH. YET I WAS UNAWARE OF ALL THIS AS I UNPACKED MY FEW BELONGINGS IN THE ROOM TEBOHO AND I WERE TO SHARE AT ETHOS. HAD I KNOWN, I WOULD SURELY HAVE TAKEN MY BAGS AND LEFT. AS IT WAS, I MISSED COMING HOME TO OXFORD STREET. IN AN ATTEMPT TO SHAKE OFF THIS FEELING, I TOLD MYSELF HOW SPACIOUS THE ROOM WAS, WHAT BEAUTIFUL GARDEN VIEWS IT HAD AND HOW THE SHARED BATHROOM WAS CONVENIENTLY LOCATED NEXT DOOR. WE ALSO HAD THE GRAND OLD HOUSE TO OURSELVES FOR A FEW MORE DAYS AND I WAS DETERMINED TO ENJOY IT. AS NO ONE KNEW WE WERE BACK AND MANY OF OUR FRIENDS WERE STILL IN JO'BURG, WE KEPT TO OURSELVES, PRETENDING WE WERE ON YET ANOTHER HONEYMOON.

Our peaceful start to the year was broken a week later as one by one, all the students returned. Like a hen rearranging her chicks, the old house fluffed its wings and settled down once more. With the house full again, we let go the notion of privacy and embraced the thriving atmosphere of community living. We were also told the news that ETHOS was to have a new principal at Easter. Tony and Jacques, when they accepted their roles at ETHOS, knew that their leadership as white South Africans would be temporary and that a black South African would be needed to lead a theological program for black students. So Danny and his family would be joining us as soon as he finished his studies in Europe in six weeks time. With this decision came an unexpected windfall for us: ETHOS had purchased the house next door for Danny and it came with a small cottage at the back; this was offered to us as an alternative to a room in the house. I was delighted with the shift as it meant, after Easter, we would have our own kitchenette, lounge area and bathroom.

With the university opening and classes commencing, it was clear that it was time for me to start looking for work. One of the smarter things I had done before we left for the weddings was to enrol in a Graduate Diploma of Adult Education that the University of Natal ran from its Durban campus. I was keen to do further study in the area I was now working in, and I also knew it would be the perfect place to build a broader network to help me find a job.

There were four of us doing the course who lived in 'Maritzburg, so it was agreed we would drive down together. Lungisani worked at the Centre for Adult Education on the 'Maritzburg campus, Dudu worked for the Natal Parks Board as an education officer and William had established an environmental education program at Umgeni Water. There were another twenty-two people in our class from Durban who worked in a variety of adult literacy programs, creating a rich forest of experience which, for four hours each week, we meandered through. One woman was the great niece of Gandhi himself, and proud to uphold his traditions in service of the Indian community in Durban. Another, Shelley, who was to become a close friend of mine, went on to be nominated for South African Woman of the Year for her work in creating engaging reading material for the black community. Tuesday nights were the highlight of my week, creating a space where I felt stretched and stimulated, a place where I could leave behind the vacuum that existed in the rest of my life.

While Jacques was still involved in ETHOS, Margie was now dividing her time between motherhood and working at Thandanani. This left a gap in the workings of ETHOS that I was asked to fill in the interim. I was delighted to be of use so I became responsible for the shopping and cooking at ETHOS, with Mama Florence taking care of the cleaning and laundry. I jumped at the role with vigour and though by no means a talented chef, I attempted to provide the best meals I could with the budget we had. After a flush of enthusiasm, I began to notice that whatever I cooked, the students drowned it in tomato sauce and mayonnaise, to my mind obliterating the taste of the lovingly prepared meal. Teboho assured me that the meals were tasty and needed no augmentation, so after two weeks of biting my tongue I finally hid the condiments, much to the displeasure of those around the table. After the stand-up argument that ensued between Teboho and the other students, I knew my time in the role would be short-lived.

A month after our return, I received a lawyer's letter outlining Steve's intention to sue me for defamation. He had the fax forwarded to him by Matt as evidence. It had never occurred to me that he would go to the courts and I was totally unprepared. As we had no real income, I went to the local Legal Aid office. After a week of nervous waiting, they told me that as the fax had been written and sent in Australia, it was highly unlikely the courts would entertain me being sued in South Africa. It was not the financial threat of being sued that kept me awake night after night—I had almost nothing to my name, in any case—but the feeling of being exposed and vulnerable. The news that the legal case was most likely impotent relieved my anxiety, but the feelings of vulnerability remained. The following week, I began to pursue permanent residency.

Soon, the rumours about Sizwe escalated. The development community was divided down the middle as to what had really happened. Jacques and Margie, torn by conflicting loyalties, slowly drifted away from me. This was a blow, given my intimate friendship with Margie in particular, as well as my love and respect for Jacques and his role at ETHOS. At the time, I could not see that I was placing my friends in an impossible situation—making them choose. Of course, everyone in our home group was affected: Brian and Anthea, Fred, Justin, as well as colleagues at PACSA, the Centre and even ETHOS. While a number of friends listened to me, many simply chose to distance themselves. When news came through that the garage at Phezulu had been petrol bombed, the tension became unbearable. The police believed that the petrol bomb had been thrown from the road and someone apparently reported hearing a motor bike engine just prior to the explosion. It was noted that I had owned a motor bike in the past. My sense of vulnerability increased.

As much as I tried to immerse myself in my studies, the pressure created by the petrol bombing was unbearable. The police investigation had gone nowhere, and I didn't know what to believe. I just knew that the whole thing had gotten out of hand. How had it come to this?

In the world around me, other changes were unfolding. The ruling National Party, under the leadership of F. W. de Klerk, had begun negotiations with Mandela and the ANC. To allow the country to transition to a democratically elected government, a new constitution would be needed. De Klerk took the step of asking white South Africans to come to the polls alone one last time. He asked them for their support in continuing with the negotiations and to the surprise of us all, they answered with a resounding yes.

Yet the optimism that sprang from the results of this referendum was momentarily suspended with the announcement that Mandela was separating from his wife of many decades. Not only had Winnie been apart from her husband for almost thirty years during his long imprisonment, she herself had been banned and exiled to a small town in the Free State under house arrest. Yet her own political leadership became increasingly controversial. She was widely quoted as saying 'with our boxes of matches and our necklaces we shall liberate this country'. The year before Mandela's announcement, she had been convicted of being an accessory to the murder of a fourteen-year-old activist, killed at the hands of one of her infamous bodyguards. They were already estranged, but Mandela could no longer align himself with the actions she had taken in his absence and so the end of the marriage was announced. Though no one was surprised, we all knew it was the end of an era: a love story without a happy ending. The image of Mandela's release from prison, as he and his wife held their hands high, flashed through my mind. Clearly, the image could not capture the complexity of all that lay beneath.

With Easter came the new principal of ETHOS, Danny, with his wife and their two children. All the students were excited about the family's arrival and helped them settle in as quickly as possible. Danny's wife Agnes was heavily pregnant with their third child and the move took a toll on her. Alice and I, in particular, tried to help her wherever we could, cooking, cleaning and unpacking.

Danny was eager to get his teeth into the new role and quickly began working long hours, meeting with the students and staff, holding discussions with the university faculty and, once mid-term break had ended, lecturing and tutoring. All the ETHOS students and black students on campus warmed to him immediately, his style reminding some of the activist Steve Biko whose last years were captured in the movie *Cry Freedom*. Danny encouraged black students to work hard, raise the bar, expect more from themselves and others. His persona seemed to instantaneously increase the profile of ETHOS on campus and we could almost hear the Board congratulating themselves on a fine appointment, all the way from Jo'burg.

However, it wasn't long before the shadow of Danny's style began to bear down on me. His powerful influence with students was built on increasing the confidence of black people in their own abilities, despite the damage done by apartheid, combined with an undercurrent of mistrusting the intentions of all whites. Tony and Jacques were initially the focus of this mistrust, to such an extent that they were forced to justify their presence at ETHOS. But before long, it was Teboho and I who bore the brunt of his position. We had attended the weekly community meetings since the beginning of the year, but these had now turned from casual get-togethers to a witch hunt. What began as an occasional taunt that Teboho had made compromises became a weekly community attack, condemning him for becoming biased and weak in his thinking. He had broad shoulders wrought by years of hardship, but hearing these words from the mouths of friends wounded his spirit. The only person in the community to stay true to our friendship was our beloved Alice. Teboho did his best to protect me from the tirades but they were impossible to ignore, living as we did.

Just after Easter, I had started doing some voluntary work at the local community centre. They held regular coaching sessions for high school students taking their final exams. Similar classes were held at various locations across the province, coordinated out of an office in Durban. The organisation was sponsored by the Urban Foundation and when they heard that someone with my qualifications was volunteering, they suggested to the young director, Andile, that I might be of assistance in establishing the fledgling organisation. After some discussion, it was agreed that I would travel to the Durban office three days a week and on the remaining two, coach students at Thembalethu Community Centre as I was currently doing.

I was excited to be back in a community organisation and threw myself into the job. The project had been started when its director, only three years out of school himself, began a study group in his township in an effort to help fellow students pass their exams. He called on teachers, education department officials, lecturers, anyone to help teach additional lessons. The numbers of students coming to the study groups grew as the students' performances improved. After graduation, Andile approached the Urban Foundation for funding to duplicate the idea elsewhere and the project was born. They also began to target kids who had dropped out of school and wanted to sit for final exams but could not find a place back in the overcrowded township schools. By the time I joined the organisation, there were approximately 2000 students meeting each day to receive coaching in venues across the province.

My first month as part of the project team was exciting as I got my head around its scope and flavour. But I soon saw that most of the money entering the organisation was staying in the Durban office and not finding its way to the satellite classrooms. After my experiences at Sizwe, my antennae for any kind of possible irregularity were up. In this case, though, I saw a young man who had been successful too quickly and lacked the maturity to handle the responsibility for the benefit of others. With a rapid inflow of funds, he was soon employing close friends as project workers and fitting out the office and their employment packages as if they were successful young professionals, rather than a new community project. With the necessary governance of an experienced board not yet in place, good intentions became entitlement. After two months, I saw I would be unable to turn things around. So I informed the Urban Foundation of my concerns and resigned, unemployed once more.

My disastrous attempts at finding work further undermined my confidence in my own judgments as well as my sense of stability. The hostility at ETHOS, the difficulties at Sizwe and the conflict among our friends had the effect of reducing the amount of time I spent out of the house. I wanted to hide myself away as the levels of conflict at every turn scared me, particularly in my vulnerable state. As I had no avenue for venting my anger at those involved, I turned my anger inwards.

I had always been slim and would not eat in times of stress, causing noticeable weight loss within a few days. While I wouldn't describe myself as anorexic, my weight never endangering my health as I was always realistic about my body image, I understood the pleasure of feeling in control of my body when I couldn't be in control of my world. Angry with myself, I began denying myself food. I took the nagging feeling in my stomach as a reminder of my stupidity and naivety. Strangely, the more I punished myself, the more resilient

I felt, the discipline of withholding food seemingly cementing my resolve and restoring a level of confidence. I stayed in this angry state for months, medicating my sense of helplessness by denying myself food for days at a time until I felt a bit more in control, then returning to normal eating patterns. While no dramatic or permanent weight loss gave anyone a clue of the spiral I had fallen into, it began to drift me towards a kind of depression.

In the July holidays we took the opportunity to go to Itsoseng to escape for a week. We stayed with Mama, Tshidi, Reggie and the kids, allowing ourselves to heal a little in the warmth of their welcome. It was as if we had forgotten what it was like to feel at home. Mama's small house was always full of visiting family who had come to welcome me as the new *makoti*. Being constantly followed around by a group of neighbourhood children so that I risked the pit toilet only at night, and sleeping in the freezing cold tin shed that was the family home, were small prices to pay for feeling loved.

Tshidi had also had a new baby since we last saw her—her sixth, a little girl whom they had named Mamello, which in English means perseverance. I had always taken delight in the naming of African children. No name was random, each had significance. If a child followed one who died, as Mamello had, they were sometimes named after unpleasant things in an effort to trick the ancestors that this was not in fact a baby at all and the child would not be taken. Other children were named after the aspirations their parents had for them, such as Chemist and Doctor. The first time I met someone by the name of Chemist, I had to have this explained to me. There is a famous South African soccer player by the name of Doctor Khumalo. I wonder if his parents supported his ultimate choice of career.

At the end of our week in Itsoseng, we reluctantly got in the car to drive back down to Natal but, thankfully, did not return immediately to ETHOS. Tony and his family had invited us to join them at their beach house on the south coast for a few days so we took a welcome detour for some more family time. Tony and Felicity had four girls who were a testimony to their wonderful parenting and we soaked up their hospitality, growing a relationship that would prove increasingly important back at ETHOS in the months to come.

Too soon, term started once more and we were back at ETHOS. To our surprise, one of the male students arrived with his wife in tow. We were shocked: the rules of the scholarship were clear, as we had found out the year before. Not only had this man failed to inform the selection committee of his marital status, he had not asked permission for them to live in the house as a married couple, as we had been forced to do. Trevor explained that his wife had been ill and he did not want to leave her in the village without any medical care. Danny, instead of taking the issue to the Board as had been the case with us, simply asked Alice if she would move from her room to make space for the couple. Not long after, it became known that Elsie, Trevor's wife, was not sick but pregnant and would be giving birth at the end of the year. Danny's wife Agnes seemed delighted at the thought of another new baby and quickly took Elsie under her wing. There was no discussion of what the implications might be but I saw the writing on the wall.

I had long stopped going to the main house, tired of being ignored, blamed or criticised. However, my difficulty was that the only way out of ETHOS was either past the main house or up the driveway and past Danny's house, either way risking a run-in with someone. While I didn't exactly feel relaxed in the cottage, knowing it was still ETHOS property, staying indoors simply meant I didn't have to see anyone, didn't have to fight. It became so bad in my mind that now I was only leaving the cottage to go to class. Despite visits from Heidi, Justin, Willie and others, I felt my perspective disappearing.

I vividly remember sitting in the bedroom one day, staring out the window towards Danny's house. It was a sunny spring morning and the room seemed to throb with light. Though the cottage was small, this day it felt cavernous and empty. I had nowhere I needed to be and lost track of time as I sat on the bed. The lawn, yet to return to its green summer glory, was in need of rain. The backyard was empty save for a single large tree, the branches of which seemed to flee its trunk in search of light.

As I looked towards Danny's house, I felt my anger against him swell. I doubted that he had any sense of the pain he was creating for Teboho and I, the damage he had done to what had been a diverse and thriving community. I felt that I could have coped with the loss of Sizwe and my resulting unemployment, but to feel under constant attack in our own home made our lives unbearable. I began to fantasise about ways to let Danny feel the severity of the situation, to make him see it. I then imagined that if I climbed the tree in the backyard and threw myself out of it, Danny would be forced to pay attention, literally be forced to clean up his own backyard. I felt it would surely make him see, repay him for all his harshness and put an end to my pain. I sat there and considered this for some time, before I heard the words echoing in my own head and wept to realise how low I had sunk. Teboho returned from class and found me sobbing on the bed. I told him what had happened and I think I scared him as much as I had scared myself.

A few days later it was my twenty-seventh birthday. Teboho was in class all day and I was alone at the cottage. Knowing my fragile state, he sent a different friend from campus to drop in on me every hour on the hour, each one bearing a small gift to cheer my day: flowers first, then a card, a chocolate; another came with lunch, then later a cake and finally Teboho came home early to surprise me and cooked a special dinner for two. I think he saved me that day.

In an effort to claw my way back, I decided to speak to a few members of the ETHOS Board about our experiences there. While I didn't receive a positive reception, the process allowed me to feel less of a victim. I also got back into my adult education networks. Lungisani, my classmate and fellow commuter who worked at the Centre for Adult Education, helped to hook me up with what was happening locally. I felt a bit sheepish about going back to Thembalethu after leaving the coaching project but went anyway as there were a dozen organisations working out of the community centre. I also threw myself into my studies, determined to do well at the end of year exams. It took a few months, but by the end of term I felt more myself. I was yet to find work but managed to finish top of my class and later received the Dean's Award for Academic Merit, a timely boost to my wobbly confidence.

Our political destiny as a nation was also progressing, even if it was two steps forward, one step back. Mandela and de Klerk announced an interim government, known as the Government of National Unity, to transition the country towards a democratic election. However, Inkatha broke the three way negotiations in protest, perhaps thinking that the National Party should have handed power over to them, as their black allies of many years. Violence broke out between the ANC and Inkatha in the township of Boipatong just south of Jo'burg, as Inkatha hostel dwellers attacked township residents, leaving forty-six people dead. A protest march of 50,000 people in the Cape, led by Cyril Ramaphosa, the Secretary General of the ANC, to call for an end to the rule of a corrupt homeland leader ended in tragedy. The crowd was fired on by troops, leaving twenty-four dead and 150 injured. Images of Ramaphosa and other senior ANC officials running for cover flooded the pages of papers across the country. We were all shocked that these things could still happen in 1992, knowing we were so close to a breakthrough—but clearly it was too early to take that for granted.

For me personally, there was one more card to be dealt before my *annus horribilis* was over. With Elsie nearing the end of her pregnancy, Agnes was concerned that it was not healthy for her to be walking up the stairs to her room, believing that such exertion could harm both mother and baby. So she suggested that Teboho and I be asked to move, making way for Trevor and Elsie to use the cottage. They had recently revealed that not only had they failed to disclose the marriage when the scholarship was awarded, but they also had a three-year-old son whom they would like to bring to live at ETHOS with them and the new baby. This sealed our fate and we were asked to leave. I should have been delighted with this news; it was just that we had nowhere to go and they wanted us out immediately.

It was then that Tony and Felicity offered us the cottage in their garden. Their tenants had given notice and they could let us have the cottage through until the end of Teboho's degree in a year's time. Given that Tony was on staff, this arrangement was acceptable to everyone and didn't jeopardise Teboho's scholarship, as long as he continued to participate in all community activities.

So as the year ended, it heralded a fresh start to 1993. Things at Sizwe were yet to be resolved but I heard that the matter was going before the Trustees. Living in Tony and Felicity's garden cottage meant I need have no contact with ETHOS. All that remained was to find meaningful work.

But that would have to wait until after Christmas. As we drove up to Jo'burg, Teboho and I were grateful that we had made it through the year very much together. We had become each other's soft place to land, bound closer by the difficulties that assailed us throughout the year. Though it wasn't an ideal first year of marriage, we felt stronger having survived it together.

22

January 1993
Starting Over

THE FRESH START I HAD HOPED FOR IN 1992 ARRIVED A YEAR LATE. WE RETURNED FROM HOLIDAYS JUST BEFORE THE START OF TERM AND MOVED INTO TONY AND FELICITY'S GARDEN COTTAGE, WHICH NESTLED BEHIND THEIR CARPORT AND WAS SLIGHTLY LARGER THAN THE ONE AT ETHOS. WHERE THE OLD COTTAGE HAD BEEN SOUTH FACING, THIS ONE WAS NORTH FACING. WHERE THAT ONE LOOKED OUT ONTO AN EMPTY YARD, THIS ONE LOOKED OUT ONTO A LUSH TROPICAL GARDEN THAT INCLUDED A GRASSY AREA WITH OUTDOOR FURNITURE, PERFECT FOR A QUIET LUNCH.

Tony and Felicity, perhaps out of compassion for the year we'd had, virtually adopted us into their family. The girls, particularly the youngest two, found Teboho to be a constant source of entertainment, always laughing and joking. Tony, despite being a respected university professor, was also a child of the African bush. He had been born near Victoria Falls in Zambia and grown up wild and barefoot. Nothing made him happier than camping in the bush, away from the bustle of the city. Though 'Maritzburg hardly qualified as a cosmopolitan hub, it was more city than Tony needed. He regularly disappeared for weeks at a time over university breaks, returning to the sanctuary of the bush. His older girls, twins, shared his affinity: one ultimately became an environmentalist for the national parks and the other an advocate for permaculture. The rest of the family, while enjoying camping, were a little less passionate about weeks on end without showers and flushing toilets.

Felicity was a librarian and though not a big city person either, I think she enjoyed the hospitality that a quiet suburban life allowed her to create. Their home always had space for a few more, whether it was students Tony had brought home or friends of the girls, so there was usually an extra plate or two at the dinner table. With this way of life echoing that of an extended African family, Teboho and I felt at home and small green shoots of happiness began to break through.

As our home environment improved, so did my quest for work. I had a meeting with a woman called Fiona, who worked on campus in a unit called the Centre for University Education Development. I knew of Fiona by reputation: a bold woman in the world, dedicated, intelligent and active in the development community. Fiona was also heavily involved in local women's programs, working hard to give aspiring black women opportunity and profile.

Some found Fiona intimidating; I found her inspirational. Fiona was almost twenty years my senior, married with two teenage daughters and had a long history in the field of education. In conjunction with her role at CUED, she worked for the South African Association for Academic Development, an organisation that sought to transform tertiary education to include students of all racial backgrounds. SAAAD's members were all university lecturers working for units similar to Fiona's. Their passion was to see the curriculum expand to recognise that South African universities and technicons were based in Africa, not Europe, and needed to offer degrees and diplomas that would prepare students to find solutions to African problems in a global economy. My focus up until this point had been on my local community and the impact of provincial and national politics on its people—but this would soon expand.

Meeting Fiona changed many things for me. By offering me a job supporting her work with SAAAD, she gave me a fresh start as well as opening my eyes to a broader professional area on which I could focus my efforts. She also became a mentor and a friend. Her deeply ingrained integrity and honour allowed me to trust again and provided me with a role model for engaging with large organisations without losing your soul. While I saw what it cost her to hold the line, I understood it was the only way to be. My work with Fiona was only part-time and much of it administrative, but she gave me a psychological and intellectual home that drew me out of the shell I had closed over myself the year before. And with the boost in my confidence, it wasn't long before I picked up a second job.

It was through Lungisani, my car pool buddy, that I was approached to develop a workbook for adult literacy classes on democracy and voter education, a project jointly sponsored by Thembalethu and one of its tenants, the Centre for Legal Education. The government had just announced plans for the first democratic elections to be held the following year. This was cause for great celebration but also the signal for massive amounts of preparatory work to be done. The workbook I was commissioned to produce had a simple English page of explanation with translation of key words into Zulu, followed by an illustrated worksheet to be photocopied and used in class. I loved the challenge of organising the content, hand drawing all the illustrations and then working on the light box at the Centre for Adult Education to pull it all together, just as the team there did for the weekly newspaper supplement.

Before I knew it, life was full again. I spent mornings at CUED with Fiona, afternoons working at home or on campus and Tuesday night at class in Durban. Teboho and I also felt less besieged and so our home and marriage ceased to be a fortress. While the year before had brought us close in mutual protection, now we had a playfulness in our relationship that had been missing for some time. Teboho was also in a better space himself. Another black minister by the name of Luke and his wife Rebecca had joined the ETHOS team, allowing

Jacques to move on. I don't know whether Luke tempered Danny or whether he simply decided that the constant conflict wasn't worth it, but the politics at ETHOS also settled down and calm returned to the old house once more.

Teboho also found a part-time job, managing a cafe on campus. Not only was he the first black manager of the cafe, but its first ever black employee. While it took many weeks for the white students to warm to the idea of a black boss, his likeable personality soon won them over. The cafe also started to make a profit as Teboho's natural entrepreneurial skills came to the fore. I was so proud of him for making it work during his busy honours year when he also served on various university committees.

On the back of this success, Teboho took on a second part-time job. Tony owned a small flat-bed truck and between them they agreed that they could run a weekend removalist business on the side. Tony liked the idea of physical labour to balance out the heady pursuits of his week as a professor. He also liked the expression on people's faces when they realised he held a doctorate but was still happy lifting fridges onto the back of a truck. Each Saturday morning, Tony, Teboho and one of the other students from ETHOS would head off to their job as removalists. Not only did Tony delight in the juxtaposition of his two professions, but it was a running joke between them that Teboho would call him '*baas*', a phrase equivalent to 'master', when they were out on the job. At some point, Tony would let slip that his workers were not illiterate casual workers he picked up from the township that morning, as his clients might have assumed, but his honours students at the university. The quizzical faces of their customers as they drove away had them laughing all the way home. I had a suspicion Tony would have done this work for free as his contribution to screwing with the stereotypes in the minds of white South Africa. Tony was a man before his time, suited more to the country's democratic future than its colonial past. It was a good thing too, with us living in his backyard.

On 10 April 1993, the peace was shattered. Suddenly, the whole country teetered on the brink of civil war.

Chris Hani, the wildly popular Secretary General of the small but powerful South African Communist Party—second only to Mandela in the hearts of black South Africans—was gunned down in the driveway of his suburban home in Johannesburg. He was living in a previously white neighbourhood in a modest area of Boksburg in the city's east. That morning, he was getting into his car to drive his teenage daughter to school when a white man walked up his driveway calling his name. He stepped back out of his car and was shot in the head, dying instantly. The white man, a Polish immigrant by the name of Janusz Walus, ran back to his car and drove away, but not before Hani's white neighbour took down the number plate details and phoned the police. Walus was captured almost immediately, and the gun he had used was found to belong to a senior conservative party official, Clive Derby-Lewis. Both men were later tried and convicted of the murder. To my horror, Derby-Lewis's journalist wife Gaye, an Australian woman, was accused of compiling a hit list, complete with names and addresses, that her husband had used as part of a plan to assassinate a number of key figures. On the list were Chris Hani, Joe Slovo and Nelson Mandela. Walus and Derby-Lewis were sentenced to life in prison for Hani's murder, but Gaye Derby-Lewis was acquitted, much to the disbelief of the majority. For a long time, I was not proud to say I was Australian.

The news of Hani's assassination spread through the country like an earthquake: Hani, Mandela's successor; Hani, the trade unionist; Hani, the soldier, leader of Umkontho we Sizwe, the military wing of the ANC; Hani, the man who thinks for himself; Hani, our hope—gone. The white community, while not knowing who this man was, felt the reverberations and began to prepare themselves; gun sales went through the roof in the week leading up to his funeral. Mandela spoke to the nation, as if already the president he was soon to become, and appealed for calm. The two negotiation teams sprang into action and ultimately announced a date for the election, 27 April 1994, in an effort to demonstrate progress towards the goal of democracy.

On the eve of Hani's funeral, an all-night vigil was held at the large FNB stadium just outside Soweto in Johannesburg. As the vigil drew to a close, the anger of the crowd spilt over into the streets and some of the youth began attacking cars and burning houses near the stadium. Two people died in this violence as the riot police moved in. One of the two to die when his house was torched was a member of the AWB, a right wing Afrikaaner group led by Eugene Terreblanche. On hearing of this death, the AWB activated its East Rand commando unit based in Boksburg where the funeral was to be held the following day. In the weeks that followed, Terreblanche spoke at an AWB rally, saying that if he thought Hani's murder could incite a state of war, he would have shot him himself. The speech was captured by a news crew and charges of incitement to violence were quickly laid against Terreblanche.

Teboho and I, along with millions of others around the country, joined the funeral day marches that happened in every city in South Africa. One hundred and fifty thousand people attended his Johannesburg funeral alone. In Boksburg, where Hani was to be buried, heavily armed AWB men were standing guard over the white residential properties lining the route to the funeral. Police were forced to keep the AWB contingent apart from the mourners who commandeered buses, taxis and any vehicles they could find in their attempts to travel from the stadium to the burial site. In 'Maritzburg, what began as a peaceful protest march turned to violence when some of the youth ransacked shops and cars in the city centre. This scenario was repeated in every major city in the country as Hani's body was laid to rest in Els Park cemetery. None of us knew if this was the beginning of the end.

Thanks to Mandela's calm hand, things stayed quiet for a time, but there were two retaliation attacks by APLA in the months that followed. The Azanian People's Liberation Army, APLA, a militant left wing black organisation, opened fire on a white church congregation in Cape Town, killing eleven and wounding fifty. They followed this with an attack on a white bar in Heidelburg, just south of Johannesburg, killing four and injuring many more. Despite moving towards our first democratic election, the impact of all the violence and the killing was stifling, as if we may yet all drown in blood.

Back in 'Maritzburg, we were fast approaching the July holidays as our lives moved relentlessly forward despite the turmoil. Teboho and I were both busy with mid-year exams and looking forward to a well-earned break. We were planning a trip to Mama's house in Itsoseng. I could only take three days off now that I was working, but Teboho had a three-week break ahead. We had found a nice rhythm in our weekly routine. I had done more around the house in our first year of marriage, virtually to give me something to do, but now that we were both busy Teboho had stepped up to share all the daily chores. He proved to be a good cook and made sure the house was clean and tidy.

There is a stereotype about the poor: that poverty and filth go hand in hand. This was rarely my experience. While public spaces were often littered with paper and plastics, private homes were always kept spotless. This was certainly the case in Teboho's family. Mama and Ma Ellen had taken the slightly unusual path of requiring daughters *and* sons to clean and cook, not just the daughters, as was the case in many other households. But either way, homes were swept, mopped and dusted daily. In our home, we didn't quite have time for a daily clean, but Teboho liked to leave the house tidy. We didn't have a washing machine, but would take turns going to the laundromat. When we married, I knew Teboho wasn't a typical traditional African man, but I was delighted that he followed his words with actions. Our marriage felt like a partnership, a well-matched team.

Our busy days contrasted with quiet nights. After cooking supper together, there was plenty of time to catch up on the events of the day—we did not have a TV to distract us from spending time together. We also talked about what we wanted the future to look like. Prior to getting married, we had agreed that after Teboho finished his honours degree we would go to Sydney and both do Masters degrees, his in sociology and mine in adult education. We had applied to Macquarie University and would soon book tickets to fly over for Christmas.

Teboho was as excited as I was about the next chapter of our lives together. I was grateful he had made friends with Nat, Pete and others so that settling in wouldn't be too difficult. Our plan was to go for two years: I was keen for Teboho to have an experience of living in a country where race didn't dictate his every move. As much as we both loved South Africa, the constant tension of it could wear you down. After our stint in Australia, we were planning to return to live in Mohlakeng where the tables would turn and I could be happy that I had developed friendships with Khumo, Moss and many others to help me find my way.

As we sat cuddled on the couch after supper, we imagined how it would be to live back in Mohlakeng. Teboho still yearned for the house his brother had given him but since it currently belonged to someone else we resolved to build on the other side of the township where Caleb now lived. I was looking forward to the end of our gypsy lifestyle and the opportunity to throw down some roots in the community.

Although I loved 'Maritzburg and would have happily stayed on there, Teboho didn't feel as much at home as I did. The only place Sesotho was spoken was on campus, by students from the north. I was surprised that even with the little Sesotho I spoke, I could impress all my friends in Edendale; so insulated were the Zulu-speaking communities of Natal that they could do no more than greet in other African languages. Outside of the Cape, where people spoke mainly Xhosa (a language similar to Zulu but littered with the clicking noises made famous through the movie, *The Gods Must be Crazy*), and Natal itself, my black friends routinely spoke five to ten different languages, sometimes in the same sentence. They would speak their mother tongue plus English, Afrikaans and three or four of the other African languages of the region.

For Teboho, English was the fifth language he learnt as he was growing up. While I was fast becoming multilingual myself, I was amazed at this latent talent my African friends took for granted. It also spoke to me of a far more diverse and cosmopolitan way of life in Johannesburg and Pretoria than I was yet to experience in 'Maritzburg. Despite loving my adopted home of the last four years, Jo'burg felt like an adventure. Teboho and I had also agreed that because I was already away from family, being back in Mohlakeng would at least allow one side of the family to be close by. It all seemed reasonable and sensible.

As we sat curled up on the couch like two contented cats, we spoke about getting some land in amongst the gums trees that bordered Caleb's house and provided a deep screen to the open veld and the busy road that lay beyond. We imagined building a little house there and starting a family—Mama was already quietly pressing for an heir. We imagined more of the happiness we were now at leisure to feel.

While we were always happy to visit Mama during the holidays, this trip we were also on a mission. Compared to the year before, we now had numerous sources of income, more than we needed to feed and house ourselves in 'Maritzburg. We had been talking for some time about the need for Mama to retire as her long days and irregular time off as a domestic worker were straining her health and energy. While she preferred keeping busy to sitting idly at home, it was the need to meet monthly home mortgage payments that kept her at work. We had found out through Tshidi that there were only a few thousand rand left to pay—the humble tin dwelling had not been expensive in the first place—but the debt meant that Mama would need to keep working for years yet as she only earned a few hundred rand a month and had Tshidi's kids to feed. Teboho and I agreed that with the money we had saved in the last six months, we would pay off the house for Mama and suggest she retire. This was our mission when we made the eight-hour drive to Itsoseng in the July holidays.

We arrived on a crisp winter's day and drove into the empty yard, wondering where the family was. Just then, a little face peered around the corner of the house and began shouting, '*Lekgoa, Lekgoa*', white person. She took a few cautious paces forward, but scuttled out of sight once we opened the car doors. It was a long time since we had seen Mello, Tshidi's youngest, and she seemed to have found both her legs and her voice in the past eight months. She was now two and I was curious to see how her personality had developed.

As we approached the house Tshidi and Silwane appeared from around the same corner, wiping their wet hands and forearms on their skirts. Mello walked in Tshidi's shadow, one hand clutching her mother's skirt and the other waving wildly in the air as she commented on our every move. She only stopped talking when we hugged and greeted each other, her mouth slightly agape as she finally saw me from close up. As I scanned her little face, I suspected her experience of the white phone technicians and electricians who drove through Itsoseng from time to time did not include watching them hug and kiss her mother.

We all went inside the house and, though my Sesotho was still rudimentary, I heard Mello telling her mother, 'Look, Tshidi, they are coming inside'. As it turned out, she gave up-to-date coverage for Tshidi on our every waking hour for the next few days, quickly earning the nickname of CNN.

Teboho and I took our overnight bags through to Mama's room and I quickly closed the door behind me.

'Why did no one tell me Tshidi was pregnant?' I hissed. Tshidi looked as if she was about to give birth and when we hugged in greeting, I tried not to let my astonishment show.

'Because I didn't know until just now', Teboho replied calmly.

Amazed, I asked, 'Why would no one tell us?'

'Oh, we don't talk about it until the baby is born, just in case you bring bad luck to the baby.'

I pulled a face at him as he tried to push past me and open the door.

'You know I don't believe in such things', he said, correctly interpreting my expression, 'but the family does, so I go with the flow.' And with that he rejoined his sisters in the kitchen, asking them for news that didn't relate to babies.

After we'd had something to eat and drink, we decided to drive to the other side of Itsoseng where Mama worked and bring her home, saving her the long walk back. Mello was desperately curious about the car so Teboho asked if she'd like to come for a drive. Being an Australian brought up on seatbelts and age appropriate child constraints, I hesitated. I realised my fetish for road safety was a frequent cause of mirth among my black friends, so I held my tongue as she joyously climbed in the back, her initial wariness of me momentarily put aside. During the short drive, she and Teboho chatted merrily, uncle to niece, with Teboho asking her about her favourite food, the names of her friends and the activities of her day. When we arrived at Mama's work, Mello appeared to be in no rush to leave the car but began crawling between the two front seats with her eye on the steering wheel. We left her there and went to knock on the kitchen door. As Mama opened the door, her curiosity turned to delight. Teboho swept her into his arms and swung her round with a kiss on the cheek before setting her down next to me. Mama, being only slightly shorter than my own mother, also fitted neatly into my shoulder for a hug.

'*Malerato*! When did you arrive? Did you travel well?'

I assured her we had arrived only recently and safely. While this was a common question to ask a guest, for us there was an element of serious enquiry. To get to Itsoseng, we were forced to travel through some of the most conservative parts of the country, including Ventersdorp, home to Eugene Terreblanche, the AWB leader. The month before, he and his followers had stormed the World Trade Centre in Johannesburg in an effort to stop the multi-party negotiations under way there. The following year, they would invade the homeland where Mama lived, Bophuthatswana, in an effort to uphold the reign of its allegedly corrupt homeland leader,

Lucas Mangope. Images of his men being killed by the army in a stakeout at Mafikeng airport would be broadcast all over the world. Most chillingly, he would soon be sentenced to six years in prison for the assault of a black petrol station attendant, as well as the attempted murder of his own black farm worker. While the first of these men recovered, the second was left severely brain damaged from head injuries he sustained after being dragged behind a bakkie. There was every reason to be nervous as we passed through Ventersdorp, where Terreblanche was a hero. I thought it best to recline my seat and lie back out of sight, hoping we would not have to stop at a traffic light. I did not know what the AWB would do to a mixed couple in Ventersdorp and I had no desire to find out. Mama's question was not to find out whether we had enjoyed the scenery during our long drive north but rather, whether we had encountered any problems along the way. Thankfully, we had not.

Mama's employer assured her she was happy to cook dinner for her family this night, allowing Mama to go home early and be there with us for our family dinner. We stopped off at one of the supermarkets in Itsoseng, though the prices were hugely inflated compared to those in town. Silwane was also visiting which meant there were three extra adults to feed, and we didn't want to place a burden on Mama during our stay. We also made sure the family ate well, stocking up on meat and fresh vegetables to complement the mealie meal, rice and beans that were the local staple. Both Mama and Tshidi kept a vegetable garden alive in the harsh, dry climate but neither garden yielded enough to feed the family, the soil being so poor.

As we sat around the kitchen table that night, warmed by many bodies cramped into the small space, I felt very much at home. Though a great deal of the conversation floated past me, in this cosy room lit by paraffin lamps and candles I felt safe and protected against the cold night. As the younger children were put to bed by their older siblings, the room gradually dimmed: one by one, the candles were moved away to serve as night lights for the children who slept two or three to a single bed. Mama had given us her room and she planned to put a few of the older children on the floor when she was ready to sleep. Tshidi and her husband would sleep with Mello next door, though I knew Mello was soon to be replaced by the new baby and would then move into a corner of a bed at Mama's house.

We waited until everyone else had gone to bed before telling Mama about our plans to pay off the house. She was overcome, hugging and kissing us both in gratitude, her relief palpable. We agreed we would go to the council offices in the morning and sort out the paperwork, transferring the house into her name. After this, I excused myself, knowing that she and Teboho would wish to talk late into the night as was their habit, catching up on all the details of their months apart. Teboho was the first in his family to go to university, and would be the first to graduate. His life was so foreign to Mama's and she sought to understand how he now lived, often shaking her head in amazement about how things had changed from when she was a child. Teboho was also hungry for family news, feeling a little disconnected living so far away. As I drifted off to sleep, I could hear the soft murmur of their voices in the room next door, soothing as a lullaby.

We all woke with the dawn, the house being small and the walls offering no soundproofing. I heard Tshidi's eldest daughter, Nthabiseng, go out and collect water from the tap before putting it on the small paraffin stove to boil. I had no desire to get out of bed, as the tin walls seemed to be radiating the chill of the early morning air. So I snuggled back under the covers and spooned Teboho for some extra warmth. I had not heard him come to bed but suspected he had not slept more than a few hours. He has that rare gift of getting by without much sleep and I knew he would soon bound out of bed appearing refreshed.

As I lay behind him, my arm slung over his thigh, I listened to the sounds inside and outside the house. Living next to campus in 'Maritzburg was in many ways akin to living in a suburb anywhere. Yet when we were here, I felt myself to be in the middle of Africa. Without me in the room, there was no English spoken, only Sesotho and Setswana. The familiar smell of paraffin and porridge filled the air. Few cars passed on the dusty road outside but I could hear the footsteps of our neighbours, their early morning conversations, a greeting called out to a neighbour as they threw a basinful of water onto the ground outside the kitchen door. There was no morning peak hour traffic, no rush to an all-important, all-consuming corporate job. Instead, the bird sounds reminded me of my first morning in Africa, the doves cooing as if to greet the morning sun.

Once more I felt the privilege of my life with Teboho. Marrying him had opened a door that allowed me to be part of African family life, not simply to observe it from the outside. In return for the family's open-heartedness, I sought to embrace the culture as fully as I could. I had taken the family name despite never wanting to relinquish my own; I did not want the family to feel hurt or to think that I was ashamed of having an African surname. I was busy learning a second African language, Sesotho, though it was completely different to the Zulu that now rolled fluently off my tongue. I tried to fit in and do what was expected of any family member, at least as much as the family would let me. I did not want to be thought of as a typical white woman, someone who was generally described as 'having no hands'—afraid of hard work or afraid of embracing an African way of life. I was also happy to help the family financially, as we were about to do today; sharing what little we had seemed the only fair thing to do when confronted with the poverty of their lives. The family never asked for or expected our help even though, as a white person, I was likely to have more than they did. We were just doing what every African family did: those who had work supported those who did not, as best they could.

With these thoughts in my mind, I reluctantly pulled the blankets back and eased my toes to the floor. The cold took my breath away and I quickly threw on more layers of clothing before brushing my hair and venturing into the kitchen, quietly closing the door behind me. Five eager faces turned towards me. During our shopping expedition the day before we had bought breakfast cereal as a special treat for Tshidi's kids but she had declared the cereal could only be dished by me, to make sure no one took too much. After polite greetings and enquiries as to how I had slept, I went to the small wooden cupboard and produced the much awaited box of cereal. Six bowls were already waiting on the table next to a carton of long-life milk. I would have far preferred normal milk but without a fridge it would soon sour, even in the dead of winter. I poured a bowl of cereal for each child and one for me before we all huddled around the coal stove that Nthabiseng had long since lit to warm the kitchen. Each one sat in silence for the first minute as they tasted the cereal, weighing up the flavours and textures, then they all spoke at once like chattering parrots as they explained what they each liked about the cereal and how it compared to porridge. Mama and her daughters laughed and, despite encouragement from the children, said they preferred porridge on a cold morning. I knew they would not dream of robbing the children of the pleasure of cereal for the next few days and so contented themselves with porridge as always.

Joseph was Tshidi's eldest child, born when she was still a teenager on the mine in Krugersdorp. Teboho had helped him get a student loan to study in 'Maritzburg and he was back home for the holidays after his first term studying agriculture. It was easy to see how much his siblings looked up to Joseph, hanging on his every word, wanting to know what went on at university. In many ways, he had become the man of the house. Reggie's disability and his subsequent struggle to feed his family seemed to cause him to disappear into the background. Joseph, as the eldest son and now a university student, appeared to be stepping into the breach.

We spent the next few days sorting out payment for the house, doing the chores that required a car and taking the family to visit friends and family in some of the more far-flung parts of the area. Above all, we were enjoying being with family. Tshidi's children were a pleasure, all as sweet as honey. Though I generally found black children to be very well behaved, particularly the ones brought up outside the larger cities, Tshidi's children displayed a good-heartedness and gentleness that stood out. All except for Mello. Even at two, she was her own person, bold and brave and vocal about what was on her mind. While she continued to make regular reports on our movements, she had also warmed to the idea of me and began to follow me around, firing off questions as we went. I didn't understand much of what she asked, but was happy to let her investigate my toiletry bag, my clothes, the feel of my skin and hair. As I sat outside in the morning sun on our last day, helping with the washing of clothes, she kept us all entertained with her stories of the visit so far, recounting again and again her trips in the car.

On the morning of the fifth day, it was time to leave. As always, I had loved our stay with Mama and the family. But the highlight of this trip for me, beyond the look on Mama's face when we gave her the news about the house, was Mello. Teboho had seen this and was equally enchanted with his little niece. As we said our goodbyes, Joseph was struggling to extract Mello from the driver's seat. He eventually succeeded and brought her over to me for a kiss goodbye. As he did so, Teboho turned to Tshidi, and teasingly said, 'Oh come on, Ousi Matshidiso, you have so many beautiful children, can't you spare us just one? *Just one*. Let Mello come home with us.'

Reggie, who had come across from his house to say goodbye, leapt in saying, 'No, not Mello. She is my sunshine', clutching his chest as he did so.

We all laughed, but I was taken aback by Reggie's strength of feeling: this was the most I had heard him say.

'Poor us', Teboho replied. 'Let's only hope we have children as beautiful as yours. You will have to tell us how you did it, Ousi, what you ate, how 'Buti Reggie kissed you.' Mama, who was standing close by, let Teboho know he wasn't too old for her to swat him over the ears.

And with that, we were on our way back to 'Maritzburg for our last term before we both graduated.

23

August 1993
Mamello

LIFE WAS BUSY ONCE WE WERE BACK. THE ANNUAL SAAAD CONFERENCE WAS ONLY A FEW MONTHS AWAY AND WE WERE HOSTING IT IN NATAL. FIONA AND I HAD ONLY WEEKS BEFORE THE CALL FOR PAPERS CLOSED AND WE WANTED TO MAKE SURE WE HAD THE HIGHEST CALIBRE WE COULD POSSIBLY GET. THEN THERE WERE ALL THE LOGISTICAL ARRANGEMENTS WHICH WERE LARGELY MY DOMAIN. I HAD ALSO BEEN WORKING ON A PAPER OF MY OWN FOR A MATERIALS DEVELOPMENT CONFERENCE IN SEPTEMBER.

As part of my graduate diploma, I was required to undertake a research project and, given the nature of my work on voter education, I had chosen visual literacy as my topic. This was a study of what people understood in the images they saw. Through the research I had learnt that some of the drawing conventions commonplace in the western world, such as shading and cross-hatching, made a person look ill through black eyes. Instead of concentrating on what the person was doing in the drawing, people were asking what had made the person sick, thinking that was the moral of the story. The results of my research, along with those of a woman by the name of Anne who worked at the Centre for Adult Education, had been accepted as a conference paper. It was a huge deal to me—the first time I had presented at a conference; and it made me feel I was becoming a professional in a field of study.

Teboho was also knee deep in assignments at the end of the first week back. The cafe had reopened and the removalist work had been busy right through the holidays. Despite being flat out during the week, we had plenty of time on weekends to catch up with friends and family: Willie, Justin, Peter and Heidi, Brian and Anthea, Robbie, Themba, Nonsi and Fred. Life was full and I loved it that way.

A few weeks into term, a letter arrived from Joseph in Itsoseng—he was yet to return to campus as he still had to complete a field research project. We rarely received letters from the family, who mostly preferred the phone to writing. Dropping our things, we sat on the couch and Teboho read it out loud, with me trying in vain to peer over his shoulder.

> *Dear Rangwane and Rakgadi* [uncle and aunt], *How are you? I hope you travelled safely back to 'Maritzburg. We are all well this side. The new baby, Mojalefa, is well and has a big voice.*

'I still can't believe she was so close to giving birth and we didn't know. By the way, what does the name "Mojalefa" mean?'

'It means Tshidi is done having babies.'

'How can you tell?'

'The name means "the one who inherits" which is always the last born. You know how Moss and Khumo now live with his father? Well, that's because, as the last born, Moss inherits the parents' house, but also the care of his parents, in their case, Papi.'

'I see. So Mojalefa will be expected to do the same.'

'Tshidi and Reggie will expect him to.'

'Hmmm. Go on.'

Everyone sends their love, especially Mama who is still smiling about the house.

'It felt so great to be able to do that for her.'

I am writing to you to tell you that we had a family meeting after you left, to talk about your request.

'What request?'

'I don't know. Let's see.'

We think that Mello coming to live with you would be the best thing for her as it would give her an opportunity to go to a good school and to travel overseas.

'What are they talking about?'

'I don't know.'

'That was a joke, what you said when we were leaving. They knew it was a joke, didn't they?'

'It seems like they took it seriously.'

Please consider it and let us know. Ousi Matshisidso knows that you will say yes, Auntie. She saw how much you loved Mello.

'What does he mean, "Tshidi knows we'll say yes"? What are they talking about? Why would Tshidi want to give away her own child?'

'She's not giving her away. We're family. If we raised her, it's the same as if she and Reggie did.'

'How can you be so calm about this? This is crazy.'

'It happens all the time in African culture. It's not a big thing. The brother who is doing well is often asked to take a child from a sibling so they can send them to a good school. Or sometimes they give you a child to raise if you can't have children of your own.'

'But we've only been married eighteen months. They can't be thinking that! I just can't believe it.'

'*Moratua*, my love, it happens all the time in African culture. Try not to judge.'

'Well, it doesn't happen all the time with me. How could Tshidi let her go? You saw how Reggie was. Why would he agree?'

'Because he loves her and wants what's best for her.'

'But it's not just about who has the most money to care for a child.'

'You don't understand. With them or with us, it's the same. We are the same family. They would not give us Mojalefa, as the last born, and Teboho at six is too old, so Mello is a good choice. And they saw how much you love her.'

'She's adorable, but that's not the issue.'

'There is no issue for me, so why don't you take some time to think about it? Then decide and we will phone and tell them.'

I was in a state of shock. Despite Teboho's explanations, I couldn't understand why Tshidi would give Mello up. She was such a special little girl, such a standout, and clearly very attached to Tshidi. How could she even consider it? I could never give up a child. I knew that they didn't have much money, but how much was not enough before you made an offer like this?

I didn't sleep much that night, tossing and turning with indecision. Teboho, on the other hand, slept soundly. Despite my initial shock, I realised that if I said no I would still see her each holidays, knowing it was I who had sentenced her to a life of poverty in the dustbowl of Itsoseng. How I could look her in the eye as she grew up, knowing I could have changed that for her?

The next morning, despite mountains of conference work to do, Fiona and I spent time discussing what had happened. After a fitful night, I felt it might be too difficult to say no and was leaning towards taking her whereas Fiona, in her usual wisdom, was pushing me to consider the longer-term implications. One of our white colleagues at CUED was married to a black South African. They had two small boys of their own and had also, a few years before, taken on his niece so that she could go to high school in 'Maritzburg. In the rural area where her side of the family lived, there was no such option. Her friend had agreed and had struggled ever since with making it work. While I heard what Fiona was saying, I also knew that Teboho was nothing like this woman's husband, who left his wife to take care of everything while he went off with friends, doing as he pleased.

Without my knowing, Teboho spoke to Moss and Khumo, seeking wise council of his own. Khumo, just as when he had asked her opinion about a mixed marriage, was very against the idea of our taking Tshidi's child. She argued that it never worked well, with the child ultimately becoming a kind of Cinderella to the family, never able to feel truly part of it. For reasons of his own, Teboho never shared this conversation with me; Khumo told me about it many years later.

After days of wrestling with the idea on my own, I finally sat Teboho down and told him what my decision was. At the time, I was so consumed by the pressure of making a decision that I did not realise I was making it alone. Instead of working through it with me—as a couple—Teboho had left it to me to decide. He most likely felt he was doing the right thing by letting me have the final say but I felt pressured to do what was culturally acceptable. I felt alone in the decision and, much later, betrayed by his lack of protection from the weight of its impact. It was a decision to be made together, in the best interests of our marriage and Mello's wellbeing, both sides in balance. As it was, I felt cornered into saying yes although I could not admit that to myself for a long time. We sat down together and I told him I would agree to taking her, on one condition: I wanted us to adopt her legally. I knew of circumstances where children were sent to town to go to school, then sent back to their original family after a change in circumstances. I felt that if we took Mello, we took her for good. Though adoption was rare in the black community, Teboho agreed it would be a good idea. In the end, it was the guilt of knowing I would have denied her a better life that made me agree to the arrangement. But once I had agreed, a seed of delight germinated within me at the thought of raising that adorable little girl as my own.

Teboho phoned Tshidi and Mama the next night to tell them the news. Tshidi said she was never in any doubt that I would say yes. It was arranged that we would drive up to Mohlakeng in four weeks time and Tshidi would meet us there, bringing Mello with her. There was a lot to do in those four weeks: set up the small study as a bedroom, enrol her in preschool for the mornings when I would be at work, buy her new clothes and shoes. We would also have to delay our travel plans for Australia, allowing enough time to process the adoption and get a passport and visa for her. Then there was the most important thing on the list—telling my parents.

I recalled the phone conversation I had with my parents a few years before.

'Hi, Mum. Hi, Dad. Guess what? I'm getting married. Yes, you'll meet him when we come over for the wedding at Christmas.'

It was like deja vu.

'Hi, Mum. Hi, Dad. Guess what? You're going to be grandparents! Tshidi and Reggie have asked us to take their two-year-old daughter and raise her. So we'll be bringing her with us when we come over, though it will mean we won't be there for Christmas.'

My longsuffering parents who, many years ago, had learnt how to mask their surprise at the choices I made, congratulated us and wished us well. They listened intently as I described Mello and the chain of events that had led us here. I promised to phone them in a few weeks when Mello arrived.

Before I knew it, we were pulling up outside Caleb's house to meet Tshidi and Mello. Tshidi had told us on the phone that Mello was excited at the news she was going to live with us. In the kombi on the way to Jo'burg, she had told any fellow traveller who would listen that she was going to be driving in a car with her aunt and uncle. I wondered whether, without her keen interest in cars, she would have refused to come with us.

As we walked up the short path to the kitchen door, I stopped for a moment and took a breath, nervous as a teenager on a first date. The day before I had gone through all the clothes I'd bought for her, imagining her in each little outfit. I held up a pair of tiny bottle-green suede sandals and felt a rush of anticipation and longing. I was about to become a mother to a beautiful little girl. Now, standing outside the house, I wondered if it would be what I had fantasised about for the last few weeks. Did she really understand what was happening and would she agree if she did, bonded to Tshidi as she so clearly was? I heard the sounds of greetings—Teboho had gone ahead of me—and knew I could delay no longer.

I walked through the kitchen door to find Tshidi leaning against the sink chatting to Teboho. Ousi, Caleb's second wife, was sitting at the dining room table with a cup of tea in front of her.

'*Dumelang*', Hello everyone. '*Le kae?*' How are you all? '*Ri teng*', We are well.

'*O Tsamaya hantle?*' Did you travel well? Ousi asked. '*O lapile? O batla tea?*' Are you hungry? Would you like some tea?

With the greetings over, I asked the question I most wanted an answer to: '*Mello o kae?*' Where is Mello?

'*Oa tsamaya le Katie*', Tshidi replied, tilting her head down the street in the direction of the small store that one of the neighbours ran from their garage. As it sold sweets and drinks and was closer than the main supermarket many blocks away, this was a convenient meeting point for all the kids in the street. Mello had gone off with her older cousin Katie, Ousi's last born. Katie was five years older than Mello and would no doubt have her well in hand.

We were all sitting around the table catching up on family news when the sound of two little voices wafted past the window.

'*Mphe, Katie, ke batla sweetie*', came the smaller of the two voices, begging for a sweet.

'*E e Mello, o tlo hlatsa*', replied the voice of wisdom, describing the unpleasant consequences too many sweets can have on a child.

'*Mphe*', replied the defiant little voice of my daughter, confident she would not throw up.

They rounded the kitchen door locked in mortal combat over the bag of sweets, then stopped in their tracks, catching sight of the four grownups staring at them.

'*Ke a ho bolelle Mello*', said Katie at last, sensing she had the moral high ground by the look in Tshidi's eye. I told you, Mello.

'Mamello', Teboho cried, reaching her in two steps and lifting her into the air. She giggled uncontrollably as he tickled her with one hand and held her aloft with the other.

'*Dumela*', Auntie, said Katie beaming, as she approached me for a cuddle. Of all of Caleb and Ousi's children, Katie and I were the closest. She was a beautiful, affectionate child who had never been reserved with me, allowing us to form a bond early on. I pulled her up onto my knee for a hug though she barely fitted anymore. As I did, Teboho brought Mello over, whispering something in her ear. She leant down towards me and said, 'How are you?' in three careful words, as if they were drops of water from a leaky tap.

Everyone burst into laughter. Tshidi told us that Joseph had taught Mello to say this, her first English sentence, in preparation for this moment. Mello was beaming as Teboho congratulated her on her fine English. Delighted as I was by her efforts and the impish little smile that went with them, I glimpsed the enormity of what I was doing—she didn't speak any English and I had so little Sesotho. How would we communicate, how would we form a bond? But the moment passed quickly as Teboho placed Mello on my other knee and the three of us sat snuggled up together, Mello still wanting to discuss the future of the sweets.

We all stayed overnight at Caleb's house, enjoying a large family meal that evening as everyone eventually returned home after visiting friends and neighbours. As always it was a tight fit: Caleb and Ousi, their five children, Tshidi, Mello, Teboho and I, all in their three-bedroom home. Spare mattresses—always at the ready in extended family living—were pulled into the lounge room for the kids to sleep on. Mello spent one last night sleeping next to her mother before the whole world changed.

Straight after breakfast the next morning, we set out on the long drive south. Mello, not understanding that she was doing anything more than taking another holiday with relatives, gleefully climbed into the back seat. This time I was prepared. There was a child seat bolted into the back, which she hopped into without a moment's hesitation. I leant into the car after her and struggled, like any new parent, to unlock the secrets of the buckle while Mello wriggled and kept leaning across me to wave goodbye to Tshidi and her cousins. After a few fumbling minutes, the buckle finally clicked into place. Teboho and I kissed each one goodbye and got into the car ourselves.

Although I said nothing, I wondered why there was no greater exchange between Tshidi and Mello than if she was coming to stay at our place overnight. Perhaps Teboho was right: Tshidi understood Mello to be staying within the family, so there was no need for a tearful goodbye; or perhaps she was simply happy that Mello was getting a chance at a better life. I did not know, but I found it foreign and could not understand. As I was thinking these thoughts, Teboho pulled the car away from the kerb, put his hand on the horn, we waved our goodbyes out the open window and we were gone.

On the first half of the trip back home, Mello gave us her usual CNN commentary on what she saw through the car window while Teboho provided me with the translation. As always, we stopped at Harrismith, our halfway point in the journey, to fill up with petrol and get something to eat. I took Mello into the Wimpy (this is the real name of a large fast food chain in South Africa that always made me laugh, though no one else shared the joke—in Australia 'wimpy' is slang for something small, useless and often cowardly). I saw from the look on Mello's face that the Wimpy was a new experience. Ordering her a small milkshake and chips, I was aware of the eyes of the other patrons on us—a white woman with a black child was still a rarity. Once our order was ready, I took Mello outside to sit at a table and eat. Not long after, Teboho joined us, further increasing the number of eyes that watched this odd family setting.

It was sometimes hard to know how to interpret staring in these situations. When we were in Randfontein, the small town of which Mohlakeng is a satellite, it is safe to say that those who stared at us were disgusted at what they saw since the whole area is Afrikaans speaking and deeply conservative.

In situations like this one, it was impossible to guess what people were thinking: some may be despising what they saw, believing it heralded a future they could never accept, while others stared because it was different and they were curious. Feeling the burning stares of those around me this day, from people of all races, I reminded myself that I too stared when I saw a mixed couple or a black child with a white family, simply observing another version of my own choices. I tried to make a conscious effort to stop myself interpreting the actions of others as a judgment or a threat. But I could feel a different response welling up inside me now—not fear, not frustration, but a fierce protectiveness of Mello. I knew at that point that I would be a lioness when it came to defending this little girl, should it ever come to that. In contrast, I watched Teboho shrug it off. 'Let them look', he said loudly enough to snap the nearby starers out of their trance, as he continued playing with Mello, making her giggle so much she could hardly eat her food.

Soon we were back in the car and on our way once more. This was my favourite part of the trip. As we crossed the border between the two provinces and entered Natal the road arched around and dropped down off the escarpment into the green valley below. The sheer beauty of it made me smile. But as the scenery changed from the harsh, flat highveld of the Transvaal to the green forests of Natal, Mello's mood also changed. A stream of words no longer fell out of her mouth; instead, she sat quietly looking out the window. After a time, I realised she was crying. A rapid volley of thoughts fired through my head—was she missing Tshidi? Had she realised she wasn't going home? Was she sick of the car? Was she car sick? When the crying didn't stop and she wasn't answering Teboho's gentle enquiries as to what was wrong, he pulled the car over onto the side of the road. I got out and rushed to take Mello out of her car seat. She climbed into my arms and continued to cry. I stood rocking her by the car for what seemed like hours, casting anxious looks at Teboho as she wept. Eventually he suggested that I put her back in the car and sit with her while he drove. We pulled back onto the road, with tears still streaming down her little heart-shaped face. I sat helplessly next to her, my own state of mind being slowly shredded. After a long time, she stopped crying and fell asleep, exhausted. Since the crying started she had not spoken a word; we never knew the exact cause of her tears, though she certainly had reason.

We pulled into the carport in front of the cottage around mid-afternoon, Mello still asleep in the back of the car. Teboho took our things inside while I gently woke her, telling her we had arrived: '*Ri fihlilie Mello*'. My Sesotho consisted of travelling phrases, of comings and goings: we're here, hello, how are you, where is, we're going, goodbye, thank you; as well as the basic needs of food and drink. Mello's Sesotho vocabulary far outstripped my own and I once more wondered how we would learn to communicate. As she woke, her eyes sprang wide open and she looked around, but I could see that she was yet to take in her new surroundings; her wide-eyed look was simply surprise at having been asleep. I was to learn that she often woke this way and she took some time before she was fully alert. She is not much of a morning person, even to this day.

As I watched her that afternoon, she turned to face me, finally focusing on my enquiring smile and asking a question I couldn't understand. I extracted her from the car seat and carried her inside as she continued to question me in Sesotho and I chatted to her in English, each of us ignorant of what the other had said. Once inside, I handed her over to Teboho in case one of those questions was 'Where's the toilet?' or something equally pressing. He assured me she was just curious about where we were, but thought a toilet stop was a good idea. As I carried her through to the bathroom, I remembered the pit toilet she was used to. Caleb's house had indoor plumbing, and Mello was fascinated to explore all the bathroom components: toilet, taps, basin, bath. As I listened to the tinkling into the toilet she gave me the first of many Sesotho lessons: '*Ke a tshiba*', she explained. 'Good girl', I replied. I showed her how to wash her hands with soap and made a mental note to buy one of those little stands that allow children to step up and reach the taps. I also realised I needed four arms to hold her up, turn on the tap and soap her hands, all without dropping her.

Back in the kitchen, Teboho had been making some sandwiches for us. He gave her a peanut butter one on a plastic plate and took her to sit on the carpet and eat it. Once we were all fed, I took Mello through to her room and showed her the clothes we had bought for her, along with a few toys and books. Finding children's books in African languages was almost impossible at that time, so these were in English. She began to ask questions again, ones that I didn't understand, so I called for a translation. Teboho popped his head around the corner and, smiling down at his new daughter, said, 'She wants to know if these things are hers to keep'. I nodded that they were, with Teboho assuring her in Sesotho that this was true and she beamed back at the both of us: '*Ke a leboha, Rangwane*', thank you, Uncle.

We had spoken about what she might call us. Given that she, like all of Tshidi's children, called her parents by their first names and her grandmother 'Mama', the names 'Papa' for Teboho and 'Mummy' for me were still available. Teboho explained to Mello what she might want to call us. As she tried 'Mummy' on for size in her squeaky little voice, I felt my chest tighten in response.

We were playing with the toys when I heard Tony's diesel four wheel drive pull into the carport, noisy old beast that it was. Felicity and the two younger girls, Kate and Emma, popped in to meet the newest member of the family. Felicity and I watched the girls play with Mello outside on the grass as I recounted our journey. We stood and marvelled at how much had changed in her life this weekend, yet she appeared to be untouched. I was anticipating huge changes for all of us but as I watched her, my heart ached with delight. I also noticed for the first time, such was the studious nature of my mother's gaze now, just how alike she and Teboho were. They shared similar eyes and identical eyebrows with a characteristic large gap in between them that centred both their faces on the bridge of the nose. There were no photos of Teboho as a child yet I felt I was now looking at a good likeness. After Felicity and the girls went home, it was time for supper. We popped Mello up on the counter and she watched with her usual curiosity as we chopped up all the ingredients for the stew. Mello carefully named each one she recognised, firing off questions about those she did not. Once the stew was on the stove, it was time for a bath.

'*U hlo hlapa, Mello*', Teboho explained.

'*Hlapa*', I mimicked clumsily, as the sound rolled around my mouth, similar to Zulu but not the same.

'*Hlapa*—to wash', Teboho explained.

Up until this point, Mello had only washed in a plastic basin, as I had been taught to do in my first year in South Africa. With a small child, it is easy for them to squat inside the basin while the parent or sibling soaps up the child and scrubs them clean. As I filled the bath, Mello ran in and out of the bathroom asking Teboho about what was going on. When the bottom of the bath was covered, I called Mello in and explained to her in English what I wanted her to do. Soon she was in the bath playing with the bath toys Felicity had given us, holding up each one, talking to it before letting it fall with a splash back into the water. I sat on the edge of the bath watching the pantomime unfold. Teboho would pop his head in from time to time, asking her if she was ready to get out. '*O feditse*?' he would ask. '*E e*', No she would reply each time.

After forty-five minutes—her skin was wrinkled like an old woman's—I lifted her out of the bath, amid much protestation. But I soon had her wrapped in a towel and was rubbing her dry, giggles emerging from somewhere inside. I stood her in front of me, the towel around her shoulders, and gave her another rub, explaining this was how her Grandpa used to dry me off when I was her age and had just come out of the swimming pool. I remembered that it made me feel safe, wrapped up and warm in my father's care.

Once she was clean and dry and in her pyjamas—the first she had ever owned—the three of us sat down in the lounge to eat. Teboho once more dished her food into a plastic bowl and put it on the carpet for her. This time he lay down a towel to protect the carpet from any spillages. As we neared the end of the fine stew, without a word, father and daughter both dropped their forks and picked up the bones that lay scattered about the dish. They began to chew the bones to get at the meat that had been impossible to remove with a fork. Teboho glanced at me and smiled: 'See, she is from the tribe of lions, like me. She is the perfect daughter'. He returned to his eating, Mello now standing chewing at his knee as he pointed out a piece of meat she had missed.

After supper, I helped Mello brush her teeth, a job normally done by her sister Nthabiseng with a cup of water that she had collected from the tap outside. I had to show Mello that she could spit into the basin and I would rinse it away with water from the tap. Job complete, she went to say goodnight to 'Papa'. '*Robhala hanle*', Sleep well, Teboho told her as he wrapped her in his arms and planted a kiss on her round cheek.

I took her through to her room and tucked her into bed on the mattress we had bought for her. I gave her a kiss and whispered good night, then I sat next to her for a while, waiting for her to go to sleep. When I thought she had drifted off, I went back through to the kitchen where Teboho was clearing up. 'Good as gold', I replied to the lift in his eyebrows. A few minutes later, however, we heard the padding of little feet and Mello emerged squinting into the light. '*Ha ke robali*', I can't sleep, she told us. I took her back through to the bedroom but she was reluctant.

'Do you think she wants to sleep with us?' I asked. 'Isn't that what she's used to?'

'I don't want her to sleep in bed with us though.'

'What about if I bring her mattress through onto the floor next to the bed?'

'That's fine', he replied, soapy hands still in the sink.

So I brought the small mattress through and put it next to my side of the bed. Our room was not large, and Mello's mattress fitted snugly against the wall. I put her into bed once more and lay on the edge of mine, letting my arm drape over the side to pat her body. After a time, she fell asleep but I stayed on in case she woke again. Eventually I fell asleep myself, my hand still on her shoulder.

24

September 1993
Red Tape

In the weeks that followed, we settled into a new routine as a family of three. My work on the voter education materials was complete and soon to be published which left me with the afternoons free to spend time with Mello. My first priority was to teach her English and for me to improve my Sesotho. Both improved exponentially, me out of necessity and Mello out of curiosity. She absorbed the language like a sponge, wanting to explore everything in this wonderful new world. At the end of her first week, we phoned my parents to let them hear her voice. She managed a very beautiful 'How are you?' and 'I'm fine', though I don't imagine she knew who she was talking to or how important these two people would become.

We had enrolled Mello in the same preschool as Peter and Heidi's daughter, Ayanda, and they became fast friends. There was another little black girl, Ningi, at the preschool who was the foster child of the white mayor and his family. There were only a handful of black children at the creche, so the three of them often played together, though Ningi lacked the confidence of Mello and Ayanda and was often left behind. With the scrapping of the Group Areas Act that had previously made it illegal for black people to live in the white suburbs, the schools in town were gradually becoming more integrated—but it was a slow process.

Mello also become best mates with Brian and Anthea's daughter Gemma, who was a year older than her. We spent many a lazy Sunday afternoon at their house around the corner from my old home in Oxford Street, watching the girls play together in the garden.

I was surprised at how quickly my depth of feeling for Mello developed. I was loving being a mother. For me, motherhood was a powerful, palpable state, as though it were an entity with a life of its own. Mello too seemed to form a deep attachment, though whether it was out of need or simply the joy of undivided attention, I do not know. Teboho, though sensing the closeness, did not allow it to exclude him and he was a doting and playful father.

With my ever-increasing love for Mello came a growing concern that I wasn't doing the best job I could as a parent. I often turned to Fiona, my mentor, for advice. Despite her initial words of caution, once the decision was made she was generous with her time and wisdom as always. Fiona saw that my feelings towards Mello could easily become a need to compensate for the hardships she had endured in her short life, combined with the massive change of coming to live with us. She advised a firmer hand than I was currently providing, lest Mello become spoilt and precocious. As always, Fiona's advice was insightful; she was able to express the hard, but necessary, truth.

Gradually I found my way into parenthood, one step at a time. I had to learn to balance my work, marriage and studies with taking care of Mello, easing her transition into her new life yet maintaining a life of my own.

At the end of November, we were due to go back to Itsoseng to the local magistrate's office for the adoption hearing. As the date approached, I became increasingly nervous. I felt that Mello had now settled in and we had formed a family life together. I was afraid that problems with the adoption might derail this and began having nightmares that the magistrate had ruled against the adoption and sent Mello back to live with Tshidi.

In the two weeks before we left, the rush of final exams for both Teboho and I kept my mind busy, distracting me from what was to come. Our plan was to make a quick trip in and out rather than the usual family visit, so as to cause as little disruption as possible to Mello's routine. Before I knew it, the time for the hearing was upon us.

We stopped overnight with Moss and Khumo in Mohlakeng on our way through to Itsoseng. First thing the following morning we were at the hospital to collect documentary evidence confirming that Mello had been born there. Without it, the adoption could not proceed.

We were shown into the matron's office, a large, airy room with windows on both sides that let in the morning light. The office contained a single desk, three chairs, two filing cabinets and a side table that hosted a kettle and a tea cup. The walls were bare save for a few posters of black mothers and babies that promoted breast feeding and immunisation. We sat and waited for what seemed like an hour, but was probably only ten minutes. All the while, I clutched Mello on my lap for safe keeping.

The matron, when she arrived, was a warm and outgoing woman who was happy to chat with us. In order to provide the necessary documentation, she needed to be clear about the details of Mello's situation. Coming from Itsoseng herself, she knew Mama and had heard that Teboho was married to a white woman, but the grapevine hadn't yielded the current developments with Mello. The matron listened intently as Teboho explained that Mello had come to live with us, and that we planned to travel to Australia to study. He also explained that we needed to adopt her and get her a passport so that she would be able to travel with us.

I felt the sweat prickling between my breasts and at my temples. There seemed to be so many hurdles to jump before I could be sure Mello would be able to stay with us. Only a few months before, I had everything I wanted in the world and was happy. But since the day we collected Mello from Tshidi in Mohlakeng, there was something I wanted more than anything, something that a woman like the one sitting in front of us could withhold, sending my dream crashing down. And yet there was nothing I could do to influence the decision. I knew if I tried to pressure the outcome, a bureaucrat could simply do the opposite of what I wanted. It was so hard not to use the skills that had always got me where I wanted to be, so hard to simply let events run their course in their own time. The process was taking all the restraint I had. Teboho, more accustomed to being at the mercy of a bureaucratic machine, seemed calm and patient by comparison.

I suddenly realised I had been holding my breath as Teboho spoke, so afraid was I of the matron raising an unforeseen objection. She asked a few more questions that in my panicked state I could not decipher. Then she stood and walked across to the filing cabinets and began to rifle through their contents until she found the file containing a record of Mello's birth. It took only a few minutes for her to sign the documents the courts required and provide us with a copy. As we left her office, my legs seemed barely able to carry me, such was my relief. We were one step closer to Mello being ours.

The appointment with the magistrate was set for two o'clock, so we drove to Mama's house for lunch. I felt conspicuous as I stepped out of the car in Mama's yard. I was wearing the only suit I owned, a dark purple skirt and jacket that I had bought when I was in London with Jon. The high-heeled shoes I had on seemed to sink into the dirt as if it were quicksand. Teboho was also dressed for court and looking smart though, as always, he refused to go as far as a tie. We had also decked Mello out in her Sunday best, though as I lifted her out of the car seat, I thought I should change her in case her dress got dirty before we left for court.

At that moment, Tshidi emerged from the house with a baby strapped to her back. Instantly, Mello wriggled free and rushed over, burying her face in Tshidi's skirt. And I realised there was one scenario that was yet to enter my nightmares: the possibility that Mello would not agree to leave Tshidi again. I had been so busy worrying about the layers of red tape we would need to break through to take Mello to Australia that I had forgotten the emotional ties she had with Tshidi.

From that moment on, Mello glued herself to Tshidi's side. The confidence I had slowly built up as Mello's mother over the last few months was trampled underfoot. I felt a kind of rejection reach out and fill my lungs so I couldn't breathe. I was suddenly invisible to Mello whereas the day before I had been the central figure in this little girl's life. As I watched her I realised that she was now viewing her time with us as a holiday from which she had just returned home. I felt a rising panic that she would beg to stay with Tshidi and would refuse to return to 'Maritzburg.

Teboho must have seen the colour drain from my face, as he took me aside to find out what was wrong.

'Have you seen Mello? She's so happy to be back with Tshidi. She won't want to come home with us', I moaned.

'Of course she's happy to see Tshidi. She hasn't been gone that long that she would forget her. What were you expecting, *Moratua*?'

'I don't know. I just didn't expect to feel jealous.'

'Just give her a chance. Mello loves you. When it's time, she'll come back with us. Don't worry.'

I knew he was right. I should have expected it. And Mello needed the time to be with Tshidi again. But at that moment my feelings were more powerful than my rational mind—I felt I had such a lot to lose. So I struggled my way through lunch, the sandwiches sticking in the back of my throat.

Afterwards, Tshidi and Reggie also changed into their finery before the five of us, plus the baby, squeezed into the car and headed towards the magistrate's office. The building was set in a dusty lot next to the police station and like government buildings everywhere, was pale and soulless. After reporting to reception, we were shown into a room that was empty save for the table and chairs. Our footsteps seemed amplified on the linoleum floor as we walked across the room to take our seats and wait. There were two chairs to the left of the desk, two chairs to the right and one larger one behind. So Tshidi and Reggie sat to the left with Mello and Mojalefa and Teboho and I sat to the right, as though we were warring parties in a divorce settlement. Teboho tried to lighten the mood, making a few jokes about the family being in trouble with the law, but the look on Reggie's face made it seem as though that might be true and no one laughed. Tshidi seemed a little more relaxed than her husband but was still visibly uncomfortable.

I kept my eyes to the front as I couldn't look at the picture of the four of them together as a family. Part of me felt jealous and the other part of me guilty at the thought of splitting them up. So I sat staring straight ahead, trying not to lose my nerve, feeling withdrawn from the whole arrangement. I remembered the words Reggie had spoken when Teboho initially joked about them giving Mello to us: 'Not Mello, she is my sunshine'. I remembered the way his normally emotionless face had suddenly contracted as he said it. Yet since our arrival, he had said nothing. I could only imagine that he thought he was giving Mello a better life. I knew this was what Tshidi wanted, as the lightness about her today suggested, yet I couldn't shake the feeling that I was about to cause something to break.

After about fifteen minutes, a black middle-aged woman entered the room and sat in the chair opposite. I was unsure if she was the magistrate, as a black woman magistrate would have been incredibly rare at that time, even in a homeland where all the officials were black. Yet she had an air of confidence about her that suggested she was comfortable with authority. Despite her powerful presence, she exuded a warmth that served to put us all a little more at ease. I also noticed when she walked in that she did not seem surprised by the colour of my skin although it was hardly what anyone would expect in a magistrate's office in Itsoseng. Since I had taken Teboho's name, I was aware that I looked black on paper and it had already caused many raised eyebrows when I was not who people expected. But perhaps this woman, like the matron at the hospital, also knew Mama and knew of a white daughter-in-law.

She introduced herself and let us know that she would be managing the adoption hearing today. We each in turn introduced ourselves and what our interests were in the matter. The conversation was held in Setswana, the official language of the homeland, with a little English thrown in for my benefit. As it was, the Sesotho I was learning was actually a hybrid between Sesotho and Setswana, as was spoken in Jo'burg. Moss and Khumo were Setswana speaking, so their vocabulary leant more towards Setswana, whereas in our family, the leaning was more towards Sesotho. As I sat listening to the conversation about the best interests of this child, I was able to follow the general direction of the discussion.

Once the proceedings began, they were brief and to the point, yet for me they seemed to stretch for hours as the now familiar fear crept out from its hiding place and took me hostage. I felt my heart begin to race and my breathing become a little shallow. Would this woman be the one to break my heart? There was considerable controversy about whether interracial adoptions were in the best interests of a child. Given we were in a remote rural area, opinions were generally less cosmopolitan than in the large cities. Not only could I not control the outcome, I realised I didn't even know enough to guess what the outcome might reasonably be.

To my enormous and instant relief, the court had no objections to the adoption because it was a simple intra-family affair. Documents were sighted, papers were signed and stamped and hands were shaken to congratulate us as the new parents when we rose to leave. For the second time that day I felt a flood of relief as another hurdle was overcome. But was it too soon to let myself believe that Mello could not be taken away? By now I had learnt that South African bureaucracy is a long and winding trail, so I continued to hold myself in reserve.

As we drove back to Mama's, we agreed we would just stay for a cup of tea before heading back to Mohlakeng. I was keen to put this day behind me and get back to our lives in 'Maritzburg. If Tshidi was disappointed that we weren't staying the night, she didn't show it. Had I been more gracious that day, we could have allowed the family more time together. But I didn't see it at the time as I was in pain and wanted it to end. I told myself that it would confuse Mello if we stayed longer, but I suspect the only confusion would have been mine.

Mama had come back from work early to try and catch us before we left. As we drove in, she was standing by the door watching for our arrival. Mama was always good medicine for me. She was calm and open hearted regardless of the situation and, as always, I found her state of mind contagious, calming me as well. We sat in the kitchen drinking tea while Teboho filled her in on how things had gone at the hearing. Mello, now changed out of her dress, was playing outside with her siblings who had just returned from school.

'Will you go to Sydney now?' Mama asked.

'Not yet. There are still some papers we need to get', I replied.

'Really? Still more?' she said, eyebrows raised.

'Many more. We still need to get her a passport and then a visa to go and stay in Australia.'

'Will that take a long time?'

'Still a few more weeks. Perhaps we will leave at the beginning of January', I said, glancing across at Teboho who was now chatting to Reggie. We really didn't know how long it would take. Our deadline was 20 February, so that we could be in Australia to register for our Masters degrees. We were confident it wouldn't take that long and I was holding out a secret hope that we could be there for New Year's Eve which was always a huge celebration on Sydney Harbour.

It was soon time to leave, if we didn't want to be driving in the dark. So we began to say our goodbyes. I was watching Mello out of the corner of my eye as I hugged and kissed each member of the family. Teboho was with her, encouraging her to do the same. She seemed to take the cue and ran towards the car. I held my breath. Would she realise that Tshidi was not coming with us and change her mind, asking to stay? I felt my stomach lurch at the thought of having to drag her away crying. Who would she understand me to be then?

As she reached the car door, she opened it and climbed up into her car seat. Then she turned and began waving goodbye to everyone. Without a word, I fastened her buckle and closed the door behind her. Still she did not protest, just continued to wave and smile. I sat in the front seat next to Teboho and closed the door, time seeming to drag as if attached to a ball and chain. As Teboho hit the horn in farewell, time snapped back into place and we were away. I looked behind me and Mello was her usual self, chatting about what she had done with Nthabiseng and young Teboho while we were inside. As I turned my head to the road Teboho caught my eye and smiled, as if to say that all would be well with the three of us.

Once we arrived back home, I lost no time in moving things forward. With Mello's papers in hand, I approached the Department of Homeland Affairs for a passport the following morning. To my horror, they informed me that she could not be issued with a South African passport as she was a citizen of Bophuthatswana.

'But no one recognises Bophuthatswana as a sovereign state and she won't be able to travel internationally on papers from there', I replied, exasperated, to the clerk in the busy office.

'I can't help you', he commented flatly.

'My husband is a South African citizen. Can she be recognised through him, her adoptive father?' I already knew from the Australian embassy that Mello could be given permanent residency through her relationship with me.

He nodded. 'You will have to register her in South Africa and then apply for the birth certificate before you can apply for the passport. Fill in this form and then queue over there', he said, pushing another pale green form in my direction and pointing to a queue that looked at least two hours long.

As I stood in the queue to register her, completed green form in my hand, my mind sifted through the new information. There was a strong possibility that we were not going to wade through this red tape in time to register for university—but I felt that if I allowed myself to give in to this conclusion, all our plans would fall apart. So I stood in the queue and sought to gather my will behind the belief that it could all be done in time.

While we waited once more, our life continued. There was plenty to do at SAAAD. The conference had been a success and we were now looking to implement some of the initiatives that had been discussed. I had also enrolled Mello in swimming lessons in the afternoons as I was keen to ensure she could swim before I took her to Australia—it is a dangerous place for a child who doesn't know how. Peter and Heidi had enrolled Ayanda in the same class. Peter and I looked a sight, our fair skin stark against our dark-skinned daughters' as we all floated around the pool, blowing bubbles and kicking our feet.

I spent a lot of time with Heidi in those weeks. She was looking to set up her own childcare centre in the New Year, now having three children of her own under five. She was a qualified teacher herself and somewhat frustrated with some of the practices she saw in the local preschools. She felt the children were under-stimulated, with teachers often acting more as babysitters than educators. Going to Peter and Heidi's house was like visiting a preschool, such was Heidi's creativity with her children's development. Our friendship with Brian and Anthea also continued to strengthen through the relationship between our two girls. Though I didn't realise it at the time, I was beginning to lose track of my single friends, as our social lives were often driven by finding a playmate for Mello.

About this time, I heard via the grapevine that Steve had finally reached an out of court settlement with the trustees in regard to Sizwe. As I let the news swim around in my head, I felt no great sense of relief or triumph. All that remained was sadness. I had lost my place in an organisation I was deeply committed to, one that now no longer existed. I had lost my friendship with Steve and his family whom I had loved, who had given me a home and a place in their lives. Even my innate belief in the goodness of people had been damaged and perhaps my faith as well. There was also a hole where intimacy used to be between Teboho and I and Jacques and Margie. Though we were still friends, we never spoke of the rift or the ruling by the trustees that vindicated the team. Time had simply passed and we all moved on.

Each afternoon after work, at the barking of the neighbourhood dogs, Mello and I went out to the letterbox to check for mail. For weeks, there was nothing. Though Mello seemed to enjoy our little ritual, my own anxiety increased with each empty letterbox. Finally, a letter arrived in the middle of December, informing us that Mello was now registered and we could apply for the birth certificate from the Department. That night, in a flood of relief, we discussed how to proceed. We had just over eight weeks before we had to be in Sydney. We would now have to wait four weeks for the birth certificate, given the time lost over the Christmas break, then a further two weeks for the South African passport. The Australian embassy said it would take a week or two to process the visa once they had received our passports, the adoption papers and a copy of my birth certificate. So it was tight, but possible. Early the next morning I was back in the queue at the Department of Home Affairs, intent on making it work.

The family had decided that every second Christmas we should gather together all twelve brothers and sisters, along with their spouses and children, and celebrate the occasion as one large extended family. Everyone wanted the family to stay intact, to know where they had come from, to whom they belonged. This year, it was Philemon's turn to host the get-together. Phili was Ma Ellen's son with Phuti, Teboho's father, and he lived with his young family in a peri-urban township outside Rustenburg. Rustenburg was two hours north west of Johannesburg, quite close to the famous resort of Sun City. Phili had built a large house by township standards, boasting three large bedrooms and a row of outbuildings to the side. Ma Ellen lived with the family inside the house, with both Ephraim and Doki, two of Mama's sons, living in a room out the back. Ma Ellen's eldest daughter also lived nearby with her family, making Phili's house an ideal location to hold the family gathering.

A big family Christmas was perfect for us that year, allowing us to say goodbye without travelling all across the country to do so. Caleb and his family were coming up from Mohlakeng, Tshidi and Reggie from Itsoseng, and China and Silwane and their families would travel in from the neighbouring rural areas they called home. As we drove up to Rustenburg, planning to arrive on Christmas eve, I was plagued by the fear of a repeat of my experience in Itsoseng a few months before. Though Mello and I had continued to cement our relationship, I had no idea how she might react to seeing Tshidi again.

It was dark when we arrived, Mello already fast asleep in her car seat in the back. We bumped up the dusty road towards the house with the sounds of our straining engine echoing off the hill in the still night. The house gave off a warm glow as the paraffin lamps and candles lit the lounge room, calling us in. We parked between the outbuildings and the house in a half-hearted attempt to keep the car hidden from view overnight. On hearing the car pull up, Phuti, Phili's eldest son who was named after his grandfather, led a troupe of smiling children out to the car to greet us. No sooner was the engine off than there were hands at the car door, the girls fighting to be the one to take Mello out of her car seat and carry her inside. We followed with our overnight bags, stepping up onto the stoep and into the lounge that was now filled with family. Boisterous greetings were exchanged with those we had not seen all year. As Mama had decreed two years before, no one used my English name in greeting. 'Malerato, *le kae*', how are you? each one said. I heard there was a two rand penalty for anyone who didn't comply.

As is tradition, we were immediately offered food and drink. Though we had eaten along the way and neither of us was hungry, we both accepted a large plate of rice, coleslaw and stew. As I sat picking at the food, Teboho filled the family in on all our recent developments. They were astonished at all the papers you needed in order to leave the country. As none of them had ever been on an aeroplane, let alone travelled overseas, they assumed that all you needed was a ticket, just as on the bus. Phili asked after our studies, clearly proud of his brother's achievements. We had just received notification that Teboho had passed and now had an honour's degree, the first in the family's history. But it was my results that Teboho wished to speak of.

'I am a lucky man to have married such an intelligent wife. She received top marks again this year, all distinctions, and was offered a scholarship to do her Masters degree in Durban.'

Murmurs of approval passed around the room.

'Imagine how many cows her father would have asked for now?' Teboho added cheekily, though it was common knowledge that I had not cost him a cent.

After I had finished a respectable amount of food, I put my plate down and went to find Mello. She was in one of the bedrooms surrounded by a circle of cousins whom she was entertaining with stories of living in the suburbs. I stood in the darkened doorway for a while to listen. She explained that water came out of taps inside the house whenever she wanted and that she was learning how to swim in a pool in a white person's backyard. As they sat back in silent wonder, I took the opportunity to announce that it was time for Mello to go to bed. I reached over and picked her up, returning with her to the lounge to confirm sleeping arrangements. As I entered the room, Teboho's sister China, seeing Mello on my hip, whispered to me, 'Mello is too big to be carried now. You will spoil her if you continue to pick her up'.

I had noticed how quickly children move from babyhood to independence in African culture. I had seen babies nursed and carried on their mother's backs as if they were an extension of their own bodies. How secure it must feel to be an African baby—never without the touch of another's skin. But I had also seen mothers walking along the roadside with a child as young as two trailing a few metres behind. At some undiscernible moment, the toddler leaves infancy behind and becomes part of a peer group of children, mostly siblings and cousins, who take care of each other with seemingly minimal parental supervision. Perhaps China was right and I was spoiling Mello. The exemplary behaviour of so many African children suggested that their parents were doing something right. But I knew I wasn't ready to pass her into the hands of her cousins just yet.

Catching my eye and correctly reading my needs, Ma Ellen took us through to her room where we would be spending the night. I never knew whether to be honoured or embarrassed when people gave up their rooms for us. I knew that other family members would be sharing beds, even sleeping on the floor, but I also knew that it would be insulting if I turned down the offer of the room. I thanked Ma Ellen and dropped Mello on the bed.

'*Mello, ke nako ho robala*', Mello, it's time for bed. She nodded dutifully. Just as I realised that our bags were still in the lounge, there was a knock at the door and a small voice saying, '*Ragadi*, your bags'. I recognised Phuti's voice and asked him to come in. He shyly dropped the bags inside the door and wished us both a good night's sleep before disappearing back into the dark corridor.

By the light of the paraffin lamp that Ma Ellen had left for us, I changed Mello into her summer pyjamas, aware that she would be the only child in the house in possession of such garments, and tucked her into bed. I lay next to her and sang as I was in the habit of doing, while she concentrated on the business of falling asleep. It wasn't long before I felt her little body go limp beside me. Once I was sure she was asleep, I went in search of water with which to wash my face and brush my teeth before slipping into bed beside my little daughter. I drifted off listening to the sounds of family devotions getting under way, knowing it could well be a few hours before they were done, despite the lateness of the hour.

The next morning, the overflowing household was up with the sun. Teboho had joined us some time during the night but I was too tired to have heard him. It was Christmas morning and, thanks to my previous experience of a township Christmas, I was under no illusions as to what the day might hold. The joy of Christmas was not in the presents under the tree, but rather in the whole family being together. As with many black families, a lot of the adults worked six days a week with only a few weeks off at Christmas, so it was no small thing to have all twelve siblings and all the grandchildren together in one place. It was certainly reason enough to celebrate. I also knew that Mello, like all the other children, would need to be dressed in her Christmas outfit which for most was the only Christmas present they received. Since Mello had been given toys and books a few months before, it was the only present she was to receive this Christmas too. However, in honour of our imminent departure for Australia, we had bought her a traditional African outfit that Teboho's sister China had sourced from the Ghanaian seamstress who sold them locally. China had also made me a traditional outfit, this time in a shirt and trousers, that I planned to wear. But it was just before six and I was keen to wash and eat before either of us got dressed up.

I rolled over to see if Mello was awake. As she often did when the three of us shared a bed, she was fast asleep with her arms and legs splayed out as far as possible, as if she was doing cartwheels in her sleep, leaving very little room for an adult to sleep comfortably either side. Teboho heard me stir and opened one eye.

'Merry Christmas', he whispered, though Mello was a heavy sleeper and unlikely to wake.

'Merry Christmas to you too', I replied with a smile. 'It's our first Christmas as a family.'

'Ah, we were always a family, even with just the two of us, *Moratua*.'

'True, but it always feels more special when there are children about.'

'Will you miss your "white" Christmas?' he asked.

'I was just thinking about that. If I'm not expecting it I won't miss it. But I warn you, I'm going large next year when we're back in Sydney, so watch out, you Grinch.' I had explained the story of the Christmas Grinch to him a couple of years earlier and he laughed at the comparison. I knew it was mainly his own painful memories of being evicted on Christmas eve that made him play down Christmas. I felt that this year would be a good cure for his usual reluctance.

'Mama and Ma Ellen will be happy, having everyone together', I suggested, drawing him into my line of thinking.

'Do you know, I think there are forty-three grandchildren now? I was trying to count last night.'

'You weren't counting during family devotions were you?' I asked, feigning surprise.

'It is a holy practice to consider the number of times God has blessed our family with children', he replied with a smirk.

'Admit it. Two hours of family devotions and prayers tested your stamina', I teased.

'You can talk. I noticed you used Mello to get out of it', he countered.

'I was just doing my duty as a mother.'

'Hmmm', he said as he tickled the arch of my foot with a toe. 'How about your duty as a wife?'

'My duty as a wife will have to wait until we are not sharing a bed with our child and a house with fifty of our closest relatives', I whispered.

'Coward. Parents all over Africa find a way', he laughed.

'Call me what you will. You're out of luck this morning, Romeo.'

And with that, I pulled the sheet back and swung my feet onto the cool concrete floor. I picked up the plastic bowl that I had used to wash my face the night before and went in search of fresh water.

25

DECEMBER 1993
THE TURKEY AND THE WITCH

CHRISTMAS DAY WITH TWO MATRIARCHS, TWELVE SIBLINGS AND THEIR PARTNERS, FORTY-THREE GRANDCHILDREN AND A FEW NEIGHBOURHOOD FRIENDS UNFOLDED GENTLY AFTER WE HAD WASHED AND DRESSED. MELLO WAS LOOKING EDIBLE IN HER ORANGE GHANAIAN OUTFIT, THE SMALL MATCHING HEADCLOTH FRAMING HER CHUBBY FACE. I FELT MY HEART TWIST WITH DELIGHT AS SHE STOOD IN FRONT OF ME, SPINNING AROUND TO SHOW OFF THE FULL EFFECT.

'You look like an African princess, *Mosetsana aka*', my little daughter, volunteered Teboho as he rummaged around in our bags looking for something to wear.

'And me?' I asked, doing a similar spin to show off my blue African attire. Mello giggled and added a few more spins herself before toppling over against the bed.

'You, *Moratua*, are my Queen', he replied with a flourish of his hand.

'Well said', I acknowledged, with a nod of my royal head.

Mello was reluctant to wait for her father to dress as she wanted another audience to show her new outfit to. So we left Teboho to it and went to the kitchen to look for her favourite uncle, Willie. Once found, Willie dutifully appreciated his niece's fine looks and asked if he could take her with him to the shops as Ma Ellen had asked for more mealie meal. I relinquished Mello into his care and went to see if I could help with the cooking.

The kitchen was full of women hard at work, peeling, chopping and grating great mounds of vegetables, and chatting away. China and Silwane soon put me to work peeling large pumpkins that would be made into mash. As it was one of my favourites, I was more than happy with the task. My sisters-in-law all wanted an update on our lives in 'Maritzburg so I described the goings on of the year. They were clearly very proud of their brother and his graduation from university; he was soon to be the only family member to live overseas as well. I was also keen to hear their news of births, deaths and marriages across our large family, so the few hours before lunch passed quickly and pleasantly.

The rest of the day was spent eating, talking and cooking once more. In the afternoon, the adults retired to the shady side of the house while the kids played in the yard. Mello was enjoying being surrounded by so many cousins again. Periodically, I would go and seek her out just to make sure all was well. Invariably she was under the watchful eye of an older female cousin who was as doting as I.

Just on sunset, Mama, Teboho and I were alone for the first time that day. Mama put a proposition to us as we sat there enjoying the evening coolness and the sounds of activity in the valley around us. Before we left for Australia, she wanted us to visit a member of the family I was yet to meet. He was the brother of her second husband, Bophundlovu, who lived with his family some hours to the west.

The discussion was a hesitant one as Bophundlovu's brother's wife was the one accused of poisoning him—and, inadvertently, Mello's older sister—all those years ago. In fact, the family farm that Mama wanted us to visit was given as the reason for Bophundlovu's death. I had been told that Bophundlovu's sister-in-law was a witch and she had poisoned him so that her husband and their sons would inherit the land. With Bophundlovu gone, Doki and Willie's inheritance would have no champion and be lost to them as well. Mama wanted Teboho, Willie and me to go and visit the family, leaving the next day.

I was surprised by her insistence, given the circumstances. I had heard the story about the deaths of Bophundlovu and Mello's older sister many times, but it seemed so surreal that I almost had no emotional response to it. It was like listening to a gruesome bedtime story. I couldn't, or didn't want to, think about Tshidi losing her child who must have been about Mello's age, nor about Mama's loss of a husband. But Mama, for reasons I perhaps will never understand, wanted to keep connected; they were still family.

I was beginning to see that, in the absence of government social security, it was extended family and community that kept people safe and taken care of when need or tragedy occurred. In order to keep the family safety net strong, it had to be tended, regardless. I always enjoyed visiting the extended family, going to parts of the country that white people rarely visited. There was a gracious rhythm about these deep rural areas that challenged the complexity of our lives in the big cities, a rhythm that I respected and enjoyed. And while we would no doubt be warmly greeted by the family if we visited, I was nonetheless very nervous about meeting this woman who was such a large figure in our family's story.

I had grown up with a westerner's storybook impression of witches, but this was real life. When I first moved into the township I was told that a number of witches in Africa worked their mischief within their own families, increasing their personal wealth and power through removing or intimidating those who stood in the way of family assets. I was told that these people also passed their trade on to their children, male and female, so that a family could suffer under the hands of a line of witches over generations. While I knew many women were accused of being witches when illness or misfortune befell a community, and these innocent women were cruelly treated and sometimes killed, I also knew that there were those, male and female, who did not deny who they were and what they did.

The witch in our family was said to be very powerful, able to take many forms—even using zombies to do her work, so the story went. While my rational, western mind was struggling with this, I had learnt to suspend my disbelief and simply listen. I did, however, draw the line at believing she could shrink her body and ride around on a pumpkin in the dead of night.

Both Willie and Doki, who were Bophundlovu's only biological sons, felt bitter about their father's death and often talked about the injustice of what had been done. They told me they believed that, after their father's retirement to Itsoseng, the witch had sent someone to poison him by placing something in his food. This first attempt allegedly resulted in the death of Mello's sister who was just a toddler at the time, living next door to Bophundlovu and Mama and, like all Tshidi's children, often sharing their meals. A month later, Bophundlovu died an identical death, also poisoned. Willie and Doki apparently went to the police about the poisoning but nothing was done.

Teboho, Mello and I, together with Mama and Willie, had travelled for many hours to reach a small rural village in a remote area of South Africa, towards the border with Botswana. The road cut through flat countryside, with small bushes and thorn trees flicking past as we sped along. The heat shimmered off the road in front of us, causing the world to dance and sway. Mama was chatting with her sons about family news in Sesotho, a language I was beginning to understand, although now the heat seemed to be leeching it out of my head. I abandoned the conversation and gave my attention to the landscape, knowing my daughter was fast asleep in the back seat. I loved these trips into the country—it was like taking a deep breath, filling the lungs with life and perspective. The monotony of the scenery and the sounds of Sesotho bubbling around the car had put me into a kind of trance, though after many hot hours, with sweat sticking my shirt to my back, I now longed to arrive.

Just as the sun dropped over the horizon, instantly robbing the air of its heat, we turned off the tar road and set out into the bush along an ambling dirt track that had been worn into the earth until it looked like a trail of gnarled tree roots, making the going slow in our little sedan. As the light faded, so did my sense of direction. In the darkness, without any signposts or street lights, I was amazed that Mama was able to guide us through numerous seemingly identical villages before finally arriving at the village and ultimately the house of her late husband's family.

There was a cluster of houses on the edge of the village and we had pulled up outside one of the larger ones. A hundred metres in front of us was a fence bordering a large field that stretched off in either direction into the darkness. The houses were lit with only candles or paraffin lamps which emitted their gentle light through the small windows. Once we had switched off the car's headlights, the quiet night pressed down on us like a blanket.

As we emerged from the car, dusty and travel weary, the door to the house opened, casting light onto our dirty Toyota Corolla. Several adults appeared, greetings echoed out into the night and introductions were made. These were Teboho's cousins and it was many years since they had seen each other. The family welcomed us warmly and we were quickly ushered inside to be given food and drink after our long journey, as was the tradition of hospitality in Africa.

Prayers and conversation went on late into the night, each person keen to hear news of distant family and life in other parts of the country, which seemed as much a mystery as the bottom of the ocean. After a few hours, the long journey caught up with me and I was suddenly exhausted. I was unsure where we would sleep and whether it was polite to ask for a bed, Mello having long since fallen asleep in my lap. The language floated over me as I struggled to stay awake, wishing to be polite but only catching a few words of each sentence as it passed by. So I smiled and nodded, shifting Mello's head slightly to relieve the ache in my shoulder. A few questions were directed at me in Sesotho, slowly, as if I were myself a child. I reassured my hosts that I was well fed and did not wish for any more tea. Soon I noticed a shift in the tone of the conversation and before long, the men stood. One of them was my husband. I gladly followed him into the dark corridor, only the candle light hinting at the rooms and sleeping bodies they contained. The bedroom we were to occupy hosted a double bed, a simple wooden wardrobe and an old dressing table. I noticed it was twice the size of our bedroom at home.

In the deep rural areas, where land was less of an issue and all that was required to construct a home was enough willing adults to build the mud brick walls and money for a tin roof, the houses were much larger than those I was used to in the black townships of South Africa's cities. This branch of the family appeared to have both men and means. The main house, though smaller than this one, was next door, where the parents of this extended family lived.

We were spending the night in the house of the eldest son, with other siblings' homes scattered nearby. It seemed that the whole family pulled together to work the fields to the south of the homestead. Mama had told me on the journey that the farm was a large one by black South African standards. It was certainly the first such farm I had seen since my arrival in South Africa many years before—the only farms I knew were owned by white South Africans, with black workers living like slaves in rows of tiny houses by the equipment sheds. I was both excited and cautious about our visit. While I was delighted to see a black family prospering, there was a shadow over the source of their prosperity.

Once in our bedroom, I let Mello fall from my arms and onto the bed, sure at this hour that she would not wake. I could feel the film of dust that covered my body and wanted at least to wash my face before I slept, so I asked Teboho for water as he entered the room behind me. As with all the rural households I had visited, there was no running water, only what could be fetched from large plastic containers at the kitchen door. He disappeared into the darkness to arrange it for me. The house was now quiet and I could hear the sounds of people sleeping across the hall. Mello rolled over, splaying her arms and legs and taking up most of the space. I stood in the middle of the room and tried to remember where I had packed my toothbrush and soap.

I was still standing lost in thought when Teboho re-entered the room, making me jump. A smile creased his face as I clutched my chest in mock terror and then nodded my thanks for the water he was carrying. We both washed silently and efficiently before falling at last into bed, our child fast asleep between us.

The household was up early and though the hours of sleep I had snatched were not enough to remove the weariness in my limbs, I rolled over and put my bare feet on the cool concrete floor. Young female voices filled one end of the house, as did the sounds of breakfast. I threw on some clothes that would be considered sufficiently modest for the rural surrounds. Women's roles in rural Africa were quite clear and rarely challenged. As a guest in the family's home, I did not wish to stand out any more than was necessary and so as usual would go along with the family's rhythms during our stay.

I left the room with my little family still sleeping and went through to the kitchen, looking for a familiar face. With a small sense of relief, I found Mama sitting at the kitchen table chatting to three female cousins gathered there: the wife of the house, her eldest daughter and the wife of the brother who lived next door. The room, like all the others, was large, with exposed wooden beams and plastered walls painted a pastel green. Despite its size, the kitchen had very little in it. There was an old wood stove, a metal table and four white plastic chairs, a single metal wall unit and two large blue plastic containers holding the household's supply of water. There was a pantry attached to the kitchen that housed canned food and plastic dishes full of fresh vegetables. Though it was still early, the promise of a blistering day was already pressing down on the tin roof above.

Mama greeted me warmly and asked if I had slept well. The other female relatives then greeted me in turn and asked me about my trip. Greetings completed, I was offered a chair and some food. Porridge is the staple breakfast in South Africa, regardless of one's colour or race. In Australia, it is not, and I was still finding it an acquired taste. Instead I asked for bread, another favourite, usually reserved for lunch. White bread is common in most homes, preferred not for the flavour but because it is slightly more expensive than brown. While many families in South Africa are poor, I was told that buying brown is a sign of having hit rock bottom. As the branch of the family we were visiting was relatively wealthy by local standards, it was white bread and peanut butter that was placed before me, two massive slices that must have taken a third of the loaf to create. I was offered tea with the bread, but took only water with my breakfast, cool and slightly brackish, from the containers by the kitchen door.

Before I had finished eating, Mello appeared in the doorway rubbing her eyes, searching for my face amongst the group of women. Her hair, as every morning, was like an explosion on the top of her head, tight dark frizz pressed up and out in her sleep. As her eyes found mine, she locked onto me like a homing beacon and headed straight for my lap without a word. She climbed up and took the last of the bread, eyeing the unfamiliar women around the kitchen table. She smiled when she saw her grandmother, but continued eating. Mama told me that after breakfast she would take me to meet some more of the family in the neighbouring homes. While I knew it was important for us to meet the family, nothing in my Australian suburban childhood had prepared me for a situation like this and I was not looking forward to visiting the main house. I finished my water and took Mello to wash and change.

As Mama and I walked towards the neighbouring homestead, Teboho having offered to take Mello while Mama and I went visiting, I questioned her about our stay. If this woman had killed Mama's husband, why on earth were we visiting her? Mama shrugged and said that she was still family. I decided it was simply Mama's nature to forgive and get on with her life. She did this regardless of whether it was an entire political system or an individual who had caused her harm. She had shown that time and time again over the course of her life. I did not have her graciousness, nor her courage, so I let her walk into the yard first, thinking I would just follow her lead as I had no idea how to handle the situation.

As we entered the yard, marked by a small plastered mud brick wall that surrounded part of the house, we announced our presence with a greeting, followed by a loud '*Ko ko*', Knock, knock as we ventured through the door. '*Dumelang*', Hello both of you, a voice replied out of the darkness. We crossed the room to see a tiny woman almost hidden inside the deep armchair in which she sat. The two small windows barely lit the room but I was able to see her wizened face; she looked just as one would imagine a storybook witch to look. Her skin was deeply lined and she was painfully thin. While she looked physically frail, her eyes showed a knowingness that pierced through me and I had to look away. Mama had reminded me on the way over that African witches do not cast spells on white people so I should not be afraid. However, her gaze had unsettled me and I was left hoping that our visit would be brief.

Mama began to ask after her health as she approached the armchair where her sister-in-law sat. The old woman rose stiffly, saying that we had found her well, and Mama leant forward to kiss her. She then stepped aside, allowing me to approach and greet. I had no choice but to bend and kiss her myself, feeling a chill as I did. Willie had told me this woman kept her zombie hidden away in the back room during the day. While I remained cynical about the existence of zombies, I did shoot a glance at the closed door behind her. The three of us took our seats and chatted briefly about the journey up from Rustenburg. We were then served tea by a young girl, presumably a grandchild, who had come to wait on us.

Though my language abilities were progressing, on this day feigning ignorance was a blessing. Family or not, the small house felt oddly cold and the whole experience unsettling. The sooner we were outside the better. After half an hour of smiling and pleasantries, we took our leave and began the walk back. Once out of earshot of the house Mama began to giggle. And I knew just what it was about.

'Why did you make me kiss the witch?'

She turned and shrugged saying, as she has said often before and since, 'Ah, what could I do?'

After our visit, I told Mama I would like to see the farm. She suggested I go and find Willie and ask him to take me; she was going to drop in on another nephew who lived in the opposite direction. So we parted ways and I headed back to the house in which we had spent the night. As I rounded the corner, I stopped dead in my tracks. Two black, round bullets masquerading as eyes peered at me with a clear, murderous intent. I inched slowly towards the kitchen door, surprised and annoyed at the sudden threat before me. I was embarrassed by my cowardice yet unsure what damage a turkey the size of a large dog could do to me. Clearly the turkey had no doubts, so I retreated into the cool of the house.

It was the first time I had seen a free range turkey, except on a Christmas plate at my aunt's house in Sydney. Not only was this one big, it also looked mean. As I stood pressed against the wall just inside the kitchen door, contemplating the dispositions of large turkeys, I suddenly realised I wasn't alone. The eldest daughter of the household, Warona, was standing in the doorway to the lounge with her hand over her mouth, trying not to laugh at the ridiculous scene before her. When I started to giggle she let her guard down and was soon bent over double with laughter. I explained to her that I was looking for Willie and had bumped into the turkey. To my surprise, she agreed that the turkey was a bad one and many people were afraid of it. Warona then offered to go and find Willie for me, an offer I quickly accepted.

In about fifteen minutes, Warona reappeared with Willie in tow. As we left the house, I quietly put Willie between myself and the turkey and with an eye on the wicked bird, headed over to the fence where two male cousins about Willie's age were rigging up a homemade cart to two donkeys. Assuming they were about to head off to the fields, Willie asked if we could come along for the ride. Once we were seated, one cousin flicked a small whip over the heads of the donkeys and we were off. We headed up the fence line to a gate, the homemade cart proving a speedier ride than appearances would have suggested. I was enjoying the wind in my face as we sped along, clinging to the back of the bench in front of me, and couldn't suppress a laugh at the sheer unexpected pleasure of it.

Once inside the gate, we trotted along the dirt road that ran between two rows of mealies. The cousins, with a little help from Willie, told me about their work on the farm. They both recognised the opportunity that their family situation presented to them and were working hard to secure the family's future. The mealie field stretched on for a few kilometres, giving the four of us time to chat. The cousins asked after Willie's studies—he had just begun a Bachelor of Science degree at the University of Natal, specialising in botany and agriculture. One cousin mentioned that he himself was planning to go to a technical college the following year to study agriculture.

After circumnavigating the field, we were dropped off at the same gate we had entered through and the cousins left to get on with the work at hand. Willie and I then went walking amongst the various family homes that dotted the area and as we passed each one, he explained their relationship to us. When we greeted an aunt who was washing clothes in a large dish in her yard, she asked how I was enjoying my stay. I told her it was wonderful and Willie then said we would see her that night. At my quizzical look, he explained that the family was having a feast in our honour and would be slaughtering a goat this afternoon. Something to look forward to.

We continued our stroll around the village, now heading back in the direction of the house of our hosts. By this time, our unusual duo had gathered some followers with a few of the local children walking behind us, firing questions at Willie about who I was. When he told them, they laughed, having never heard of such a thing. He assured them that I was in fact married to his brother and we were here visiting family. This piece of information made my presence all the more interesting and they stuck to us like glue after that.

As we came past the witch's house, we saw a horse grazing in the yard. Willie knew of my childhood obsession with horses and asked if I wanted to ride. Despite the intimidating identity of its owner, I jumped at the chance as I hadn't ridden in a few years. He quickly organised a bridle while I spent a little time getting acquainted. Willie gave me a leg up and I walked the white mare around the yard and out the gate. To my surprise, the children started shouting and calling for others to come and see. I asked Willie what all the fuss was about as he walked along beside me and he told me that women don't ride in Africa; that it is considered a man's activity. I gave him a look that said I would get him later and kicked the horse up into a canter. The children screamed with delight and the women from neighbouring houses shouted to one another, passing comments on my seemingly magical abilities.

After an enjoyable but highly public ride, I dismounted, thanked Willie's uncle and his wife who had also come to witness my prowess, and walked back towards the main house with four or five children in tow. Mama came out to meet me, having now returned from her own morning visits, and added her praise to the shouts of the neighbours. When I explained that horse riding was a pastime more common with young women than young men in Australia, she was astonished. She found many things I had to say about Australia astonishing.

Lunch was prepared by the time we returned to the house. Teboho and Mello were there, catching up with various members of the family who had come calling. But Teboho had already heard about my efforts on horseback.

Mama dished up a plate of meat and pap. After four years in Africa, I had tried ever variety of pap there is. Each time I indicated that it wasn't really my favourite food, the woman of the house would assure me it was only because I hadn't tasted her special recipe. Despite hundreds of taste tests, it still tasted like glue to my western and somewhat limited palate. So despite my misgivings, I dished for Mello and myself. With the heat and the heartiness of the meal, I found I had little appetite and gave Mello the larger of the two servings, making sure to include plenty of meaty bones.

After the household—including the children who had followed me home—finished eating, people began to drift off to prepare for the evening's entertainment. I was longing for a nap, given the lack of sleep from the night before. Teboho assured me I wouldn't be expected to do anything for a few hours yet and should feel free to go and sleep. With Warona offering to take care of Mello, I retreated to my room and fell asleep almost instantly.

I was woken just over an hour later by a commotion outside and lay in the bed for a moment, trying to make sense of the words that floated through the window. From the tone alone, I could tell it was a robust debate between a few of the men. Then I heard a word I knew; it was *thipa*, the Setswana word for knife. With that, I was out of bed. I threw on my shoes and headed outside.

There was a group of men, Teboho in their midst, standing around a large male goat that was tied to a rope staked into the ground. Each man seemed to have an opinion on how the goat should be properly slaughtered. Another cousin then appeared around the corner of the house rolling an old tyre in front of him. I had no idea how this connected to the issue of the goat, so I watched to see what he would do. He went to fetch the large knife from his father's hand and set about splitting the tyre into two. Once he was done, two donut shaped tyre halves lay on the ground. A few men grabbed the bleating goat and dragged it over to the tyre. I had no doubt what was about to happen next. However, I was also aware that I was the only woman present. I tried to catch Teboho's eye to check if this was a problem. Seeing my imploring look, he came over and whispered that while this is generally considered to be man's work, I might like to see how it's done. As was often the case, I was excused from a number of traditional gender roles because of the colour of my skin. In this case, I was torn as to whether it was a privilege or not. I didn't want to see this animal die and yet I did want to see how the family treated such a central cultural tradition, so I stayed.

The goat was pushed to the ground, with its neck stretched over the upturned half tyre. As the man of the house drew the knife across its throat, I understood the purpose of the tyre—it caught the blood that gushed from the goat's throat rather than letting it spill over the ground. Next, in a moment that truly turned my stomach, the yard dog snuck over and drank the warm blood that had collected inside the tyre.

While the goat lay bleeding out, a large metal sheet was brought over. The body was thrown on top and the skinning process began. At this point, Mama and a few of the aunties arrived, all carrying plastic basins. Quite a crowd had gathered to watch the festivities, my small fan club of neighbourhood children along with it. Once the skin was off and passed to waiting hands, the belly was slit open and the stomach and intestines removed. These were whisked off in a separate bowl and I was assured that they would make a tasty treat. The thought made my eyes widen and my lips purse in anticipation. The liver, pancreas, gall bladder, lungs and other items commonly referred to in Zulu as *ama-insides* found their way into another waiting dish. Culinary delicacies aside, I was amazed as Mama told me what each and every part of the animal would be used for—nothing was to be wasted. Some parts had symbolic significance and needed to be offered to special individuals, including me in this case. Other parts would be used for religious ceremonies and traditional medicine, and the skin for floor coverings.

Before long the sheet of metal held only a carcass, ready to be thrown on the fire and cooked. One of the women had begun the task of building a fire for this very purpose. However, looking around I doubted that the one goat, as big as it was, would be able to feed all those who had gathered there. I sent up a silent prayer that the evil turkey would be likewise sacrificed to the communal pot. As if summoned, the nasty beast appeared on the edge of the crowd almost as soon as the thought had formed in my mind. Not wishing a repeat of my earlier encounter, I kept close to the middle of the festivities, with one eye on the turkey. I noticed it had one eye on me.

Back in the kitchen the stomach and intestines were roughly cleaned and then steamed in a large pot. Willie told me the dish is tastier if the cleaning of insides is not overly thorough. White people who like a thorough cleaning of their tripe, he explained, lose all the flavour that the contents of the stomach and intestines hold. I struggle to be in the same room in which tripe is being cooked, so I thought I would take Willie's word for it. While the insides were cooking, the liver was being specially pan-fried for me. As the guests of honour, both Teboho and I were to be offered the freshly fried liver. Not a big fan of liver either, I thanked my hosts and offered to share mine with Mama.

A few hours later, as darkness fell, the meat was finally ready. I had been in the kitchen helping to prepare vegetables, pap, sauce and coleslaw. There were also a number of chickens that had their necks wrung and their feathers plucked before being dropped into a large pot. Sadly, the turkey escaped playing a role in tonight's feast, much to my disappointment.

The process for the meal was to take a plate, go to the pit, have some meat cut from the carcass and then return to the dining room table to add all the other items to your plate. The extended family and neighbours moved through in a snaking line some forty or fifty people long. After the main meal was consumed, tinned fruit and custard were placed on the table in large plastic bowls and the queuing process was repeated once more. According to the cousins, our dessert was a real treat as custard was reserved for special events, making an appearance only once or twice a year.

After we had all eaten and some of the neighbours had drifted away, prayers and singing were held in the lounge room to close the festivities. In other families that were less devoutly Christian, the evening would have continued with some music, singing and dancing. This would also have been accompanied by copious amounts of beer and the resultant drunken men declaring love for me and any other woman in proximity. While I missed the music, and the prayers would no doubt be long, there was certainly something to be said for the religious sobriety demonstrated by families such as ours.

The head of the household gave thanks for our visit and prayed for success in all our ventures in Australia. He prayed that we would make the family proud and inspire others to follow in our footsteps to improve themselves. At this point, everyone in the room broke into simultaneous personal petition, some in Setswana and others seemingly speaking in tongues. This cacophony of voices, with its meaning lost to all bar the petitioner, took some getting used to but by now I had seen it often enough not to be surprised. This night, I estimated that it went on for some thirty minutes or so, thinking it rude to check my watch midstream. Initially, I prayed about the things that were on my mind—Mello's papers and making it to Australia in time to register—then for each member of the family, and for a safe journey home in the morning. I went on to thank God for everything I had experienced in recent weeks.

After fifteen minutes or so, I ran out of things to say. Assuming that others would likewise dry up shortly, I sat and waited. I remember asking Khumo about the purpose of praying in this way, given that no one else could hear what you were praying for and pray with you. She said it was more to get lost in the moment of thanksgiving to God, letting it all pour out. I realised that growing up white and Anglican, I was not given to letting it all out and began to respect those who could. From the look of it, it seemed to do them a lot of good. So I waited for the family to let it all out, knowing there are precious few moments for this in most people's lives and plenty of hardships to bring to God's attention.

At the end of prayers, Teboho was asked to give a sermon. This was unsurprising, as his degree was in theology and sociology. With Willie sitting next to me translating where necessary, I listened to Teboho talk of God's love for us that is expressed through the love and hospitality of family, through His presence in suffering and in delivering us from evil. I felt he would have added 'of the apartheid system', had the audience not been so very apolitical. This part of the family, like many black South Africans, survived the cruelties of apartheid only through focusing on the glories of heaven to come. They purposefully avoided political involvement and put their faith in God to reward their long suffering in the next life. Mama was a little like this herself, not in that she believed political involvement was unchristian, just that she felt so disempowered to change things that she simply persevered while harbouring no bitterness, hoping heaven would be a kinder place.

It was almost midnight when the post-sermon singing finally died down. As they made their way to their beds, the older members of the family all agreed that it had been an excellent celebration. No doubt the stories of the day would benefit from retelling over the weeks and months to come. I was also looking for my bed by now and went over to the couch where Mello lay sleeping. She woke briefly as I lifted her onto my shoulder and carried her through to our room. As I walked down the dark corridor, I could hear the echo of Teboho's laughter outside. I wouldn't expect him any time soon.

I woke in the morning with Mello's hand tucked under my arm and Teboho fast asleep beside me. This time I was happy to stay put and enjoy the quiet. I lay listening to the rhythms of the local language and the birds, contemplating the extraordinary privileges presented to me through the choices I had made in my life, choices that at times also caused me a great deal of pain. However, in the balance of things, the opportunity to experience a life so apart from the one I had lived in Australia gave my days and nights a richness that more than compensated for all the things I had given up to be here.

I looked at the face of my husband, lying contentedly on the pillow next to mine. Perhaps feeling my eyes on him, he stirred. He rolled over to face me, asking if I'd had enough sleep. I rolled my eyes in Mello's direction and laughed. But I had not come for the sleep and told him so.

'Did you enjoy the visit? I know it was a bit strange this time', I murmured.

'I'm just happy to watch you getting so involved. I know we didn't spend much time together, but I had my eye on you most of the time', he replied with a smile.

'Did you now?' I said, eyebrows raised.

'That's my job as your husband, I believe.'

'That's true. And my job as a wife?' I asked.

'To stay with me, wherever I go. Even to the far corners of the country', he said grandly. 'Do you know, a few of the family told me how much it meant to them, to see you wanting to learn the culture and the language. I probably don't tell you often enough, but it means a lot to me too.'

'Thank you', I said with a kiss. 'But I'm not sure I deserve any praise on the food front. My family aren't very ambitious in the culinary stakes.'

'Only God is perfect, *Moratua*.'

We lay in bed for a time talking about the various members of the family I had met this trip and where they fitted into stories that I had already heard. We laughed about my visit to the witch. Teboho did not put much store in the power of witchcraft over him as he did not fear it. However, he didn't underestimate the impact it had on members of the family, nor did he scorn their beliefs. I respected his efforts to embody both the traditional and modern African cultures, embracing the value in both.

We knew it was time to get up when we heard Mama's voice in the kitchen. We had agreed to head back to Itsoseng straight after breakfast so we could avoid travelling in the heat of the day. After a meal of porridge, jam and bread, we packed and went to say our farewells. We stood around our car, embracing all the cousins and wishing them a wonderful year.

As we pulled away from the house, I saw the turkey scratching in the dirt, king of all he surveyed. In truth, I'm not sure who scared me more, the turkey or the witch. And as we drove off up the road I wondered if, in fact, the witch used neither zombies nor pumpkins for her night time escapades, as many of the family believed, but rather a certain evil bird that was readily to hand in the yard outside.

26

JANUARY 1994
ALL IN GOOD TIME

AFTER ANOTHER TWO WEEKS OF ANXIOUS WAITING, MELLO'S AND MY DAILY TRIP TO THE LETTERBOX FINALLY YIELDED THE LETTER WE WERE WAITING FOR. HER SOUTH AFRICAN BIRTH CERTIFICATE WAS READY AND WE COULD APPLY FOR A PASSPORT FOR HER.

We rushed to the offices as soon as they opened the next morning, stopping off in one of the mobile photo booths that surrounded the office like flies on a carcass. Once we had the photos and the birth certificate, we went straight to the queue for a passport application.

'Two to four weeks', replied the clerk coolly, after Teboho and I had explained our need for urgency. I nodded, knowing that this was the standard time taken to process a passport and that our plea had not moved him. I sighed and turned away from the counter.

'We've got five weeks at the most', I said, my earlier excitement at our progress having dissipated.

'Don't worry. There's still enough time', Teboho replied, ever the optimist.

'But we have to get the Aussie visa as well.'

'I know. We'll make it', he said with a kiss.

While we were both still working, we spent the following weeks sorting out our few possessions so that we would be ready to leave at the drop of a hat. Willie was going to look after most of our things, a windfall for him as he had just moved into a group house with other students from campus. Oxford Street had been sold just before Christmas, as Justin was also moving on.

One other important matter to take care of was Mello's third birthday party. Though she was born on 11 February, we thought our friends would forgive us if we celebrated a little early. It was to be the first birthday party she had ever had. Felicity and Tony offered their home for the party, which was also doubling up as a farewell. There were presents, speeches and tears, and a huge cake in the shape of a '3' that I had made with Felicity's girls. Teboho spoke on behalf of our family, thanking each person for coming, describing what their friendship had meant to us over the highs and lows of the last four years. He then led a chorus of 'Happy Birthday' for Mello, in English and Sesotho, as she stood beaming in front of the cake, ready to blow out the candles at a nod from me.

Three weeks later, we had Mello's passport in hand and were headed up to Pretoria to lodge her visa application. We had just two weeks before the registration for our Masters degrees closed. Standing in the embassy queue, I felt on the verge of tears. We were now so close and it had been so hard to get to this point, like wading through a river of mud with only desire to keep us moving forward. This was the final hurdle.

'G'day. How you going?' said the Australian official at the counter. I had to hold back a sob at the familiar accent.

I tried to keep my voice steady as I explained our situation: my husband already had permanent residence, both of us were accepted into Macquarie University and now all we needed was a visa for the little girl in my arms. She smiled and said, 'Let's see what we can do'.

Twelve days later, we were on the plane to Sydney. We had cut it fine, but we would make it. After months of paperwork, queues and waiting, it would come down to a matter of hours. Mum and

Dad were going to meet us at the airport in Sydney at 2 pm and we would drive straight to Macquarie University where registration for the academic year closed at 4 pm. Mum had let the university know about our last-minute dash, but their response was: 'Just make sure you're here before 4.00'.

After a stopover in Perth, we reboarded the plane for the final leg across the country. I sat reminiscing about our Jo'burg farewell. Just as with the send-off for our wedding, family and friends had been at the airport to wish us well: Mama and Ma Ellen, Caleb and the family as well as Moss and Khumo. My mind was focused on our return to Australia yet, as I looked at this group, my heart ached for what we were leaving behind. We planned to be gone for two or three years and though life would move on, I knew this large extended family would be waiting for us when we returned.

After almost seventeen hours travelling we were circling Sydney harbour, preparing to land. Keeping Mello entertained during the flight had taken the lion's share of our time, leaving little opportunity for Teboho and I to discuss how we felt about the next phase of our lives together. I hoped, now that we were about to arrive, he was as excited as I was. We had sat Mello next to the window so that she could see the city as we landed. As usual, she was full of commentary about all the wonders she saw. Peering over her head, I felt the tears prickle as I caught a glimpse of the familiar icons that exemplify home to all Australians who live abroad.

We struggled off the plane and through customs, with me carrying Mello and Teboho lugging our carry-on bags. At the carousel, both Mello and I grew impatient—Mum always jokes that I have a gift for being the last to come through the gates, and it was looking like my gift had not failed me. Finally, we loaded the trolley with our bags, perched Mello on top and emerged from around the barrier to a sea of searching faces. As soon as I spotted Mum, I grabbed Mello and ran forward to greet her. Mum's face was a blur through my tears—I was so happy to see her, so excited that she would finally meet Mello. After squashing her inside our mother-daughter embrace, I transferred Mello into her grandmother's waiting arms.

'Hello, Grandma', she squeaked, seemingly undaunted by all the commotion.

'Hello, sweetheart', Mum replied, shooting a look at Dad who was peering in over her shoulder to get a better look at his first grandchild.

'Hi, Dad. How are you?'

'We're doing alright now', he replied without taking his eyes off Mello.

'Hi, Mum. Hi, Dad', said Teboho, as he finally caught up with us, almost invisible behind a mountain of bags.

'We'd better get going', Dad urged. 'We're cutting it a bit fine.'

I shot a look at Teboho that said 'story of our lives' before turning to follow Dad as he headed towards the glass doors.

After a tense drive through traffic that was beginning to build for the early Friday peak hour, we pulled up in the parking lot on campus. Ever organised, Mum had collected a map of the university and had marked out where we needed to go. I took the map, having done work experience at Macquarie when I was fifteen, and sought to orientate ourselves. After agreeing to leave Mello with Mum and Dad, Teboho and I took off at a run, papers in hand, to the registration office.

We returned to the car thirty minutes later, a huge weight lifted from our shoulders. I finally felt the excitement of the two years that lay before us. Up until that moment, all the possible barriers had taken away the excitement of coming back—all I had felt was stress and fear. But now, with all the obstacles removed, I felt a rush of pleasure at the thought of living back in Sydney. Mum and Dad had offered to have us live with them in the two-storey, four-bedroom house that I grew up in, which was now a little big for my parents alone. They were also keen to do as much babysitting as possible while we were here, and living with them would give them all the access they wanted. In addition, Macquarie University was only a short bus ride away, making it an ideal option for all of us.

Once at the car, I looked around for Mum and Dad and Mello but they were nowhere to be seen. Then I heard a little voice from around the corner of the adjacent building saying, 'You a funny girl, Grandma'. At that moment, Mum and Dad came into view, having taken Mello for a walk to pass the time. She walked in between the two of them, swinging her arms and forcing them to do the same. Then she took a step back before leaping into the air, sending them all lurching forward as she giggled and my parents braced themselves to hold her up.

'I hope you're up for this', I called out.

'We've still got a bit of kick left in us, don't you worry', Dad replied, smiling from ear to ear. As I stood watching them, I suddenly felt jetlag grab hold of me and realised how very tired I was. It was time to head home.

Classes started almost immediately, as did our job hunting. I landed the second job I applied for, working in the state coordinating body for early childhood education three days a week. My classes were mostly in the evenings, leaving me almost two full days to do research and get assignments done. Teboho was not so fortunate. He ultimately applied for over thirty jobs, receiving rejection letter after rejection letter, never even making it to the interview stage. After a time, he shifted from applying for jobs that would suit his training in sociology and community work to applying for anything. After many months and much heartbreak, he found a job as a cleaner.

More than anything, I was embarrassed that my country could think so little of his skills and experience, or perhaps his heritage, that there was no other job employers thought he was fit for than one he would have been similarly assigned to in the past in South Africa. In selling the idea of us coming to Australia, I had said it would be a good break from the pressures of South Africa, where he was constantly judged by the colour of his skin. I felt now that he was still being judged—for being a foreigner, for being African—making it hard for him to find meaningful work. I began to think privately, as I suspect he did, that perhaps it wasn't such a great idea to have come. However, I wasn't in a place where I wanted to express such doubts and neither, it seemed, was he.

Mello was enrolled in the university's childcare centre four days a week and between the four of us, we saw that she got there and was picked up on time. Sometimes Mum would take her in the car but it was the bus trip she particularly liked. She felt it important to chat with the driver in her still broken English as we boarded the bus, and then to greet passengers as we made our way to her favourite seat in the back. She loved sitting high up in the clean, comfortable bus, commenting on the world passing by. Since living in Sydney, her daily exposure to English had risen dramatically, with only Teboho speaking to her in Sesotho. I overheard her one day, after a few months in the country, asking Teboho to stop speaking to her in Sesotho. 'I'm English now', she said with an exasperated sigh.

We had also noticed that Mello took a long time to warm to Dad. She had taken to Mum immediately but despite Dad's best efforts, turned to him only when there was no other option. On Fridays, when Mello was not at preschool, Dad began taking Mello up to the shops for lunch. He said it was 'their time' and the rest of us rarely received an invitation to join them. Initially, Mello was very reluctant to go with him but Dad persevered. He told the story of having to drag Mello across the street at the top end of the shops at Chatswood to get to the cafe with her shouting, 'I'm not your friend', thinking that at any moment someone would do a citizen's arrest on him for child abuse or kidnapping. Mello was not shy to voice her objections at being made to go to the cafe of Dad's choice, not hers. Mello also had a special look that she reserved for him at moments like that, a look that bore an unsettling resemblance to Dad's own 'evil eye'. On seeing it, Mum and I began to wonder if they were not somehow related after all.

But Dad persevered until those Friday lunches became hallowed ground. Basil, the cafe owner, held their special table for them near the kitchen where he and his wife could chat with Mello while they prepared lunch for the other customers. They both ordered the same meal each week, with a chocolate milkshake for Mello and a long black coffee for Dad. I think we all heaved a sigh of relief when the battle between them finally ended. Ironically though, Dad cherished a photo that Teboho took of Mello giving the evil eye in the early months of our stay. He had it by his bedside until he died.

On the morning of 27 April 1994, Teboho was up early. Hearing him get out of bed, I joined him and we washed and dressed with hardly a word between us. After breakfast, we left Mello with Mum and Dad and made our way up to the South African consular offices which, thankfully, were in Chatswood near where we lived. The streets were relatively quiet as the rush of the day was yet to begin in earnest. Teboho and I walked hand in hand as we came down the street towards the office. As we approached, we saw a camera crew on the steps. It seemed someone else had also worked out the significance of the moment. It was possible that Teboho could be the first black South African to cast a vote in a democratic election in the country's history. Today was the day we had all been waiting for and with the time zone differences between South Africa and the eastern seaboard of Australia, Teboho would be one of the first to vote.

We had a brief chat with the camera crew on our way in as they arranged an interview with him once he had voted. Unlike his countrymen and women who would be seen around the world queuing for hours in long snaking lines, patiently celebrating the moment for which they had waited a lifetime, Teboho went into the office alone. He cast his vote in private but there was no question, being an ANC member, as to whom he would be voting for. When the votes were finally tallied, over twelve million people did likewise. In the days that followed, almost sixteen million South Africans would also vote for the first time.

When he was done, I watched him stand over the simple box into which his vote had disappeared a moment before. He turned and lifted his clenched fist up to his chest and whispered, '*Amandla awethu*', Power is ours, the catchcry of millions as they protested against the cruelty of apartheid, a system which was now at an end.

Once he had voted and we were outside again, the quiet mist that had surrounded him like a shroud lifted and he was his flamboyant self once more. I hadn't wanted to pry into his thoughts that morning. One of the downsides of our leaving when we did was that he would miss this moment. I hoped it would still be a significant one and, given the smile across his face as I watched him being interviewed, his ANC T-shirt in full view, I had no doubt that he was still able to be taken up by the history of the moment.

We later heard from friends and family that the film clip was shown broadly across the South African media over the next few days, much to Teboho's delight. He was thrilled to have been a part of it somehow. We also read that he was, in fact, the second black South African to vote; a woman in New Zealand, who was claiming to be a relation of Mandela himself, had voted a few hours before. But it did not matter—Teboho had left his mark on history.

Mello was soon to join Teboho in a brief foray into the media. By now, we were used to being approached in public by people saying how beautiful she was, some even giving her small gifts. As an African child in Sydney, she stood out from her fair-skinned peers but she was also chatty and engaging, and as a child of rural Africa, readily talked to people she did not know. When we were approached by a woman doing PR for a modelling agency as we strolled around the shopping mall in Chatswood, I assumed she wanted to tell me how adorable Mello was. In fact, she wanted to recruit us for the agency. Mello was quickly seduced by promises of being on TV and so I reluctantly agreed to give it a try.

Within a few weeks, Mello had her first assignment. The commercial was for the United Nations, promoting the plight of refugees. We were asked to arrive at 7 am at Kurnell, a remote part of Botany Bay that was mostly windswept sand dunes. As soon as we arrived, Mello was taken to wardrobe and emerged shortly after dressed in muslin cloth wrapped around her small frame. The crew explained that Mello was to play the role of a refugee child in the deserts of Somalia. I was introduced to the woman who was to play her mother, easy to spot as she was by now similarly attired. As we moved across to where the cameras were set up, Mello's film mother was given a cloth bag supposedly full of their worldly possessions and asked to take Mello by the hand and trudge across the sand from one point to another, turning halfway to look back longingly.

While this seemed straightforward enough, the crew had also set up an enormous fan which was blowing across the two of them as they made their way along the sand. After a few takes, the director gathered us together and asked me to instruct Mello not to put her hand across her face. Before I could discuss this possibility with her, she replied, 'Just stop blowing sand at me', which seemed like a reasonable request to me. After a full day of filming on two locations, I discussed with Mello her impressions of life as an actor. She told me that she liked the food but not the sand.

I saw the footage only years later, over the shoulder of a newsreader as he spoke of a UN program for refugees. There was Mello standing alone in the desert, wrapped in her muslin cloth, looking for all the world like a Sudanese refugee.

Mello did two other commercials before I called an end to her brief career. She had been given each job she was put forward for but it was crushingly boring for both of us, with two minutes of filming every few hours. I also found I couldn't juggle work, study and Mello's career. Before I pulled the plug, Mello did an ad for UNICEF, where they needed children from different countries to say 'thank you' in different languages. Filming was in Centennial Park, just outside the centre of the city, where we waited for four hours so that she could say thank you fifteen times in Zulu, a language she didn't in fact speak, until the director was happy and let us go home. Her final ad was for the Department of Health. We were filming at a park on the South Head of Sydney Harbour. All the children were dressed in white calico dresses or shorts and shirts and they were to run around playing a game of tag. In post production, as each child placed a hand on the other, they were planning to superimpose a disease spreading from one child to the other. I believe it was an ad for immunisation and, given the requirements, one that Mello actually enjoyed shooting.

At the end of the first semester, Teboho and I had both done well and had enjoyed the stretch of the Masters level work. I was keen to take an extra course in the second semester, as was Teboho, given that his cleaning work wasn't fulltime. Despite our studies, there had also been time to catch up with old friends such as Nat, Pete and Anne, as well as for Teboho to form friendships with those who were yet to make it across to South Africa.

Outside of spending time with my friends, Teboho also sought to make new friends of his own. On campus he saw an African music night advertised in the inner city and was keen to go along. Through that and other such events, he built up a network of African friends. One of my friends, Gen, whom I had known for many years through St Andrew's, was also eager to join us when we went in search of African entertainment, having a keen interest in Africa herself. She would visit us several times in South Africa in the years to come, exploring much of southern Africa when she did. Before long, Gen and Teboho were also fast friends. In fact, given Gen was much more a night owl than I, the two of them went to some of the clubs without me. On those occasions, I would get a late-night call saying they were just dropping a new Ghanaian or Nigerian friend home before heading back to the northern suburbs where we lived. Given Teboho's experiences on the work front, I was delighted that he was able to make friends and feel socially accepted in Sydney, with few restraints on who he chose to be with and where. There were none of the 'no go' areas that existed in South Africa, where it wasn't safe to be seen in a mixed group or as a lone black person. For that at least, I was grateful to Australia.

Living back in my childhood home was easier than one would imagine. My parents were as involved as we wanted them to be, but happy to give us space when we needed it. Their lives were as busy as ours in many ways. Though they had sold the bookshop and retired, they still did a bit of work in the book trade with Dad's best mate, Abel. They were also avid golfers, playing two or three days a week, and Mum was down at the club an extra day for bridge. Each of them constantly had their noses in a book when they were at home, Dad always non-fiction, reading about politics, business or sport, while Mum loved a good novel or biography.

As the year passed, I continued to keep an eye on Mello's emerging relationship with Dad, which was now clearly based on winning and losing. While Mello won, she was happy to go along with Dad but if she lost, she cut him out. I wondered whether this had anything to do with growing up in a matriarchy, with Reggie having so little visible impact on her world. Teboho did not parent her with an iron fist but was playful and warm. I wondered whether the relationship with Dad was her first with a man who was more traditional in approach. Even at three, she didn't like being corralled.

Whatever the reason, Mello seemed to want a relationship with her grandfather on her terms. She seemed not to need or seek approval from him. To my surprise, Dad was devoted to Mello and in no way withholding, as I felt he had been with me when I was growing up. He adored her despite her fickle attentions and at times rampant disobedience. While I had heard that fathers are often completely different when they become grandfathers, given the passage of time and perhaps a touch of regret, I was genuinely surprised at the behaviour of my father in his new role. He was not at all who I had expected him to be. Though I didn't realise it then, I was also beginning to be jealous of the relationship between Dad and Mello. Had someone told me this at the time, I would have denied it as ridiculous—feeling jealous of my daughter's relationship with her grandfather? I would want them to bond. It was part of the reason we were so glad to be there. But it was true nonetheless, and this little crack began to grow and would one day leave a rift between Dad and me.

My relationship with my father had been a tempestuous one, particularly in my teenage years. We went to war over the smallest issue in order to prove who was right. It always felt as if there was a hazy mist between us, through which emotions and intentions became confused. Intellectually, I knew he loved me—but I never felt it on an emotional level. I never felt like 'Daddy's little girl', the one for whom he had a soft spot and would do anything. I wanted to feel like his princess—feel that he would go to war for me, not with me.

As it was, whether it was my fault or his, I felt inadequate as I grew up, always just short of what I needed to be for him to love me in the way I wanted. I didn't understand that, given the lack of love Dad experienced as a child, the fact that he loved me as he did was a huge step forward. He demonstrated his love by providing a comfortable and stable home, by loving my mother with a passion and by always being there for his family. While I can see this now through adult eyes, as a child I yearned for more personal demonstrations of affection. Without them, I oscillated between distancing myself from the family when I thought I could go it alone, and chasing after Dad for his approval when I realised I could not.

Tracing back through my childhood, there are numerous instances where I pursued interests that no one else in the family shared. The rest of the family would do something together and I would be elsewhere, casting out alone, making new friends, trying new things. In a way, my first trip to South Africa was part of this same pattern. Yet, in whatever I did, I sought to excel so that Dad would be proud. I won trophies in swimming, athletics, tennis; I excelled in all my studies; I put huge amounts of focus into whatever I did in order to do my best, all in the hope it would make me more acceptable, more like what he wanted. The yearning was never explicit or even conscious but it threaded through my childhood like a poisonous snake.

At the end of my Masters degree, in which I had received distinctions across all my subjects, I was still seeking his approval. I was twenty-nine years old, yet I waited for Dad to say he was proud of me. When he didn't, I asked him one night as we were putting out the garbage in the dark passageway beside the house.

'Can you say it now, Dad?' I said rather flatly.

'Say what?' he asked, genuinely at a loss.

'That you are proud of me, for getting my Masters with Distinction', I replied, exasperated, perhaps a little unfairly.

'You know I am.'

'I don't. Not unless you tell me', I said, before disappearing back into the house.

It was in Dad's last twelve months, as he neared the end of his race, that the mist between us finally lifted. Though dementia and frailty had overtaken him, I saw his eyes light up when I arrived in his room in the nursing home. He watched my face with delight as I told him stories from our past, hoping to give his sporadic memories some thread and substance. Then, as I told him it was time to leave and that I loved him, I saw tears in his eyes as he smiled and nodded, 'OK, I'll see you tomorrow'. Mum says that he told her stories about me after I had left, stories that had no roots in reality: a phone call from Adelaide, him protecting me from the police, me coming to fetch him on the train. But I know it meant I lived in his mind when I was not with him. I waited my whole life to feel that way, to have some tangible evidence of it. So strange that it should take the loss of his mental resilience to allow me to see and feel what has always lain beneath.

At the end of our first year in Australia, we hadn't seen any more of the country than Sydney itself, what with our busy lives. My mother's family all lived down in Tasmania and had invited us to visit for a few weeks before Christmas, an invitation we couldn't resist. We began our holiday in Burnie, a small town on the northern coast of the island, where Mum's sister Beb and her husband Jim lived. Two of my three cousins still lived in Tasmania—one in Burnie, one in Launceston—while the third lived in an ashram in India. We had a week in Burnie, enjoying my aunt and uncle's hospitality. They were also retired, my uncle having been somewhat of a media mogul in Tasmania during his career. One of Uncle Jim's hobbies was photography and during our stay, he gave Teboho the bug. It was wonderful to watch them deep in conversation, bent over a camera or a photography book. Teboho's love of cameras had begun when he took photos on the streets of Mohlakeng as a way of surviving. Now, he was able to return to that early love for the mere pleasure of it. Uncle Jim, recognising this passion, gave him one of his cameras when we left, an amazingly generous gift that Teboho always treasured.

While we were in Burnie, we travelled up to Cradle Mountain, still under snow in December, where Mello saw her first wallabies in the wild. She listened carefully to Auntie Beb as she named them for her, but ever after referred to them as 'wobbilies'. I was struck by the fact that Auntie Beb quickly developed a relationship with Mello that had a similar flavour to Mum's. They were soon thick as thieves, giggling and laughing at their own stories and jokes. I was so grateful to my family for making us feel at home, the cultural and racial differences never making interactions stilted or condescending.

After almost a week in Burnie and the surrounds, Auntie Beb offered us her car to see more of the island. We agreed that we would take a tour of the west coast and meet them in Launceston three days later at Carolyn and Phil's house. We struck out from Burnie, heading southwest to Queenstown, driving through some of the oldest forests in the world. The winding road allowed for breathtaking viewing, but also made Mello car sick all over Auntie Beb's car.

Queenstown is a memorial to greed and poor environmental management. It began to flourish in the 1880s after the discovery of minerals and gold, which led eventually to the area's ancient forest being demolished. The river is now stained an ugly copper colour and dead trees and tree stumps line its banks, giving it an eerie feel, as if their spirits still haunt the river, seeking revenge.

From Queenstown, we drove to Strahan, a picture perfect fishing village on the edge of Macquarie Harbour. We stayed at the Hampers Hotel, Mello loving the bunk beds that the rooms contained. With Strahan as a base, we were able to explore parts of the majestic Gordon-Franklin heritage areas.

When we arrived in Launceston, I realised that this short trip had been our first family holiday where the drama lay in the places we were visiting, rather than in people's reaction to our being together. It was a window of normality and wonder that has stayed crisp and fresh in my mind's eye all these years.

We spent two days in Launceston with the family, Mello making fast friends with Carolyn and Phil's two children, both just a little older than she was. They were fair-skinned and blonde-haired, as I had been as a child, in stark contrast to Mello's dark looks. If the three of them were an odd sight around the streets of Launceston, no one seemed to notice. Barton, Carolyn's youngest, was so taken with Mello that he asked her to come to school for show and tell. Putting aside the objectification of my child as a cultural relic, we all happily went to Barton's primary school and Mello bravely stood in front of the class and told them where she lived and what it was like. I watched Barton bursting with pride at having an African cousin.

Uncle Jim suggested that we go down south to Hobart and to Port Arthur for a few days, before returning to Burnie and our flight home. Carolyn thought Mello might like to stay with them instead of doing another car trip and to everyone's surprise but ours, Mello agreed, more than happy to stay with the cousins she had only just met. My family were unaware that she had been doing this kind of thing since she was a baby and saw nothing unusual in the suggestion.

We were to leave the next morning so Teboho was keen to go out and see some of the night life in Launceston before we left. He was much more of a night owl and big city person than I, and I suspect he had been missing the pace of the city. I was tired and knew we had an early start, so I was less than enthusiastic. Undeterred, Teboho suggested he explore the city on his own, which I was more than happy to agree to.

I went to bed early on a mattress on the living room floor but kept half an ear open for his return, only to wake up hours later to an empty bed. My first thoughts were that something had happened, an accident perhaps. How would the authorities know where to contact me? I lay there for perhaps half an hour, running gruesome scenarios through my head, before I heard him come creeping in. It was almost five o'clock. He told me he had been dancing at a few different clubs and had a great time, but when he realised how late it was, he had come straight home.

I lay there in the dark fuming. I felt he had embarrassed me in front of my family by behaving this way and I told him so. What would they think, him being out all night on his own at nightclubs? It was a rare moment when the anger I felt was the anger I spoke, not translated into a cold silence or taken inwards and held inside my body. After telling him how ashamed I felt, I rolled over, giving him my back.

A snake then rose up in the darkness, flared its hood, bared its fangs and struck. I had not known Teboho had this cruelty inside him, but it seems he would not allow me to speak to him this way, to emasculate him so.

'Do you know what it's like to be aroused all night?' he whispered into the darkness.

'What?'

'While I was dancing, while I was talking to a woman I met at the club.'

'What are you telling me?'

'I was turned on while we were dancing together. I danced with her at the first club and she followed me to the second. When I realised it was getting late, I told her I had to leave but she followed me outside. We kissed, then I left her there and came home. She gave me her phone number though.'

The snake's poison was travelling through my system now, making it hard for me to breathe. Dawn was beginning to break, pushing light into the room. The household would soon be up. No anger could be spoken now, for the house would shake if what I should have said left my mouth.

Psychologists speak about the 'necessity of betrayal', the moment that moves us from child to adult, the moment we understand that we live on this earth with humans, not heroes. My experience with Sizwe could be deemed my first betrayal, the experience of feeling alienated from ETHOS another. Perhaps I should have been ready for the next, or at least better able able to bear it. But those cruel words whispered in my ear left me in a state of shock.

Had I been stronger, less committed to the fantasy of my marriage and my ideal life in Africa, had I been able to do what needed to be done right there whether my extended family were witnesses or not, I would have taken him on, wrestled with him until we got to the cause of what he had done and said.

But I was neither ready nor brave and felt only numb, unable to process what had happened, unable to believe it was *my* husband who had said and done these things, my Teboho whose words were always like sunshine on my face, whose integrity and devotion were unquestionable. None of this resonated with the man I knew, with the life I had led up until that point, nor with the life I wished to lead. In a nightmare daze, I left it where it was and got up to prepare to leave for Port Arthur—a desolate ghost town to match my desolation. Teboho had also drawn into himself as we packed up, perhaps understanding that no more would be said between us for now.

That night, when Uncle Jim had gone to his room and I was sure he was asleep, I slipped outside into the open field in front of the motel, with only an old white horse for company. I wept loudly and bitterly over all the emotions I had been holding in during the day. I was still too upset to try and deal with what had happened and what it meant, still unable to reconcile the events of the previous night with what I believed to be true about Teboho. Great sobs racked my body—I feared something was broken that could not be fixed.

After a time, Teboho found me and put his arms around me, saying that it would be OK, that nothing had happened, nothing had changed. He begged me to come back inside and sleep, said he couldn't bear to see me this way. I don't remember if he apologised, but he did keep repeating that nothing had happened. It seems odd to me now. I think he meant that because he had not slept with her, nothing had happened and so no trust was broken—but that couldn't have been further from the truth. Stranger still, part of me wanted to make everything OK, put things back the way they were so that we could live the life we had planned. Is that what women do, when we are afraid, when we can't face reality? Do we compartmentalise what we cannot face and rationalise its existence? 'He's not like that when he's sober.' 'He promised he would never do it again.'

As we walked back to the small motel, I felt the space that had just been created inside me, one in which I had locked a piece of myself so I would not be quite so vulnerable in future. That smallest part of me that wasn't in denial knew Teboho could no longer be trusted in this regard. Perhaps the lesson for me was that I could not live my life completely trusting everyone around me; that to live in the world we need to hold something in reserve; that we need not only to acknowledge the capacity of those around us to disappoint, but also to acknowledge our own capacity for betrayal—humans not heroes. But these were things I was yet to understand as, in many ways, I was only in my adolescence at that time.

If my optimistic self thought this was a one-off event that would not repeat itself because Teboho had seen the pain he caused me, I was wrong. Later the next day, when Uncle Jim had stepped out of the car to take a photo, I asked Teboho to give me the woman's number.

'Why do you want it?' he asked casually.

'To destroy it', I replied, nonplussed.

'But I want to keep it. She's just a friend and I could give her a call some time. You said you wanted me to make friends.'

'But we won't be coming back to Tasmania and she's not your friend. Please give it to me', I said, almost begging.

'No, I want to keep it', he said, closing the conversation down as he turned to stare out the window.

Looking back, it is clear he was giving me a message, even if it was an unconscious one: 'I will not be contained and if you attempt to contain me, I will punish you'. Though I had no conscious understanding of this threat at the time, at a deeper level it was well understood. Unbelievably, we never spoke of these events again.

Perhaps I should not have been so surprised that Teboho knew how to inflict pain, whether he intended to or not. His life had contained more pain than security, more agony than love. And yet his actions were so unrecognisable to me that I separated them off as if they had been perpetrated by a stranger. I looked across the car at him as he stared almost contentedly out the window and knew, for the moment at least, that the man in the car was a stranger—one I hoped never to meet again.

Mello's first Australian Christmas was spent at my brother's apartment in the beachside suburb of Manly. Jon had returned to Sydney after three years in London and was now the CFO of a broking firm. Sadly, he and Helen had split up as she could not imagine a life in Australia and Jon did not wish to live anywhere else. He was living a bachelor's life once more, just a few steps from one of Sydney's most beautiful beaches.

Unfortunately, it was an overcast day, not the sublime beach weather that had blessed most of my childhood Christmases. Despite the weather, we celebrated being back together in Sydney and gave in to the pleasure of having a child with whom to enjoy the occasion. Mum and Dad gave Mello a huge teddy bear that was almost as tall as Mello herself. I was astonished when she named him Reggie, as she had never spoken of her father up until this point. Every photo from that Christmas has Mello clutching Reggie, beaming up at the camera, with each one of us looking as happy as she clearly was.

After we'd been in Australia almost a year, I noticed that Teboho's usual effervescence was becoming suppressed. We'd had a few conversations throughout the year about how he was adjusting, and we had both been hoping things would improve. But there was a disjuncture between the acceptance he felt socially and the rejection he felt in the workplace. Just before it was time to register for the new semester, he raised the issue of finishing our studies more quickly than anticipated.

'If we took a fulltime load, we could finish it by the end of July and then go home. I know we agreed to stay longer, but I just can't feel at home here.'

'I understand', I said, after a moment's hesitation. 'I've seen that it hasn't been good for you.'

'In some ways I've loved it, but not being able to find another job is wearing me down. I didn't come here to clean other people's toilets. If I'd wanted to do that, I could have stayed at home', he added with an uncharacteristic hard edge, his anger targeted at the situation, however, not at me.

I couldn't bear to see him being discriminated against, not after all the pain he had suffered in his life, and my heart went out to him. 'Of course we can. Why don't you stop the cleaning job? I can cover our costs with what I get and then you can focus on your studies.'

'No. I want to pull my weight.'

'Why don't you focus on finishing up? There'll be plenty of time for weight pulling back in Jo'burg.'

And so it was set. I told Mum and Dad about our change in plans. They were obviously sad, but understood. They had also seen heaviness about him over time and knew that it wasn't ideal for him here.

We had one more trip planned before we left. It was to drive down to Melbourne over Easter to visit Karen, a friend of mine since I was a teenager. Her father, Dave, was a youth worker and speaker who did a lot of work at my old church and Karen was his youngest daughter. I got on well with all three daughters but it was Karen with whom I developed the most enduring friendship. Over Easter, we were keen to see both Karen and Melbourne. We drove down with Dave, stopping in at the various Australian icons such as the Dog on the Tucker Box at Gundagai.

On our first day in Melbourne, Karen took the four of us for a tour of the city. We walked for several hours, seeing all the sights. When we stopped for lunch, I mentioned to Karen that I was feeling a bit strange in the stomach and would be giving lunch a miss, very unusual for me who, despite being slim, was always up for food. A week later, I discovered that the strange feeling was in fact the early weeks of pregnancy.

When my period was uncharacteristically late, I bought a home pregnancy test. I very much wanted to have a baby while we were in Australia so that I could have family around me. Teboho and I had been off contraception for over six months with no results, so I was attempting to keep my expectations in check when I went to the bathroom. I laid the test on the sink and then went to wake Teboho.

'Do you want to come and see the results with me? I'm a little nervous', I whispered towards his one slightly open eye.

'Sure', he replied, dragging himself from the warm bed.

We entered the bathroom gingerly, as if it was already a nursery, and approached the sink on which the test strip was perched.

'Two stripes for yes and one for no, right?' Teboho said, looking down on the two purple stripes.

'I'm pregnant', I squealed as we began to dance around the small bathroom.

As soon as we had finished jumping around, Teboho suggesting it might not be good for the baby, I ducked upstairs to wake Mum and Dad.

'Mum, guess what?' I beamed as I dropped onto the bed, waving the purple stripes in her face. 'I'm pregnant!'

'Are you sure?' she said, peering at the test strip. 'How reliable are these home tests? I wouldn't want you to get your hopes up.'

Mum had taken nine long years to fall pregnant with my brother, although a stream of doctors could find no reason for the delay. As a result, she had been cautioning me all along about not getting ahead of myself, that these things take time. Even now, with the evidence in front of her, caution borne of her own heartache still took centre stage.

'I don't think you should get too excited until you see the doctor.'

Holding back excitement isn't one of my core strengths, but I knew she was trying to protect me so I told her I would try.

After breakfast, I phoned Jon to tell him the news. It was no surprise when he repeated the identical advice Mum had given me: 'Don't get too excited until you've seen the doctor'. Growing up, they were always peas in a pod.

Later that day, during my visit with the family doctor, I tried to stifle a smile when he presented me with a pregnancy test kit identical to the one I had used that morning. I know Mum thought the doctor's method would be far more scientific. He did, of course, do a blood test, but the results wouldn't be back for a few days.

When I returned home with a smile from ear to ear, Mum felt confident enough to celebrate. I never told her what method the doctor had used to confirm the pregnancy.

As the months went by, I approached the changes in my body like a second Masters degree, reading everything I could get my hands on to describe my baby's inner life. Having done a medical-type undergraduate degree, I had all the basics of physiology and anatomy but as the months passed, I felt ready to sit an exam on antenatal development.

Mum worried that I was overly focused on the pregnancy. 'Don't forget you already have a child and she needs your attention too', she cautioned. I was unsure whether Mum was once more trying to protect me from the pain I would feel if I lost the baby or whether I was truly ignoring Mello. I knew two things at that point: firstly, it is my nature to throw myself completely into whatever I do; and secondly, I resented the suggestion that I shouldn't marvel at every moment of the pregnancy simply because I had a child already. I couldn't have articulated it at the time, but part of me resented both Mello and Mum for putting a dampener on the experience of my first pregnancy. I felt that if Mello hadn't been in the picture, Mum wouldn't have been pushing me to moderate my enthusiasm. But given my closeness to both of them, I couldn't allow those thoughts to find expression.

Dad ultimately gave me a target for these emotions when he casually passed a comment without realising the potential impact of his words. After telling me about his magic Friday with Mello, he said, 'I don't know if I could love another child the way I love Mello'. This could have become a philosophical discussion about the nature of love and the fact that, while it sometimes feels finite, it is not and can be endlessly stretched to include others. But given my current sensitivity and my history of sparring arguments with him, I took exception to his words and let them cut open a wound between us in which all my other emotions could fester. From that moment, I felt doubly protective of the small life I was carrying, determined to protect my baby from the same barbs I felt I had suffered. It was as if invisible lines had been drawn.

In the month before we were due to leave, Dad suggested that Mello should stay in Australia with him as she would not reach her potential if she went back to South Africa with us. I chose to read this as a vote of no confidence in my ability to parent her and lashed out at him. I believed he had come between Mello and me over the course of the year and I blamed him for the distance I now felt between her and me. In fact, it was more likely a result of the jealousy I felt about Mello being the apple of Dad's eye in a way that I had never been, combined with my resentment at being made to feel guilty about being absorbed in my pregnancy. I could not admit this to myself, nor could I feel anger towards my mother whom I loved dearly and never fought with. So Dad bore the brunt of my frustrations then and for years to come whenever I described the impact our time in Australia had had on my relationship with Mello. I believed he had spoilt her and had cast doubt on my own ability to parent her adequately. I believed it was my father's fault that my relationship with Mello now had an edge to it where only love had been. But perhaps ultimately Mum was right, because Mello seemed to be jealous of the baby even before it was born, somehow sensing that a change was to come that would shift her place in the family.

Teboho continued to see the African friends he had made in Sydney, sometimes having the families meet up for lunch but mostly going out at night to African clubs and bands. I was completely robbed of energy in the first four months of my pregnancy, especially having to juggle work, a Masters degree and parenting. So mostly Teboho went off alone on Saturday nights with his friends. Those nights were long and painful for me. Though I did not raise the events of Tasmania with him, perhaps for fear of a return to cruelty, they were large and fresh in my mind on those lonely nights. It felt as if there was a small wild animal inside my heart that was scratching its way out and my whole body was taut in an effort to keep it from breaking free. This pain would visit me again and again in the years ahead, haunting me like the silent approach of a torturer's hands.

When we left Australia in August of 1995, I was five months pregnant. Teboho was excited at the prospect of going home, not only to South Africa but home to Mohlakeng. I was also keen to leave behind an experience that had exposed a side to Teboho I had not seen before. The effervescence and optimism I loved were replaced in part by something I did not recognise and did not like. I suspect his inability to provide for the family had left him feeling emasculated and inadequate. Though he never said anything, I did wonder if he resented me for insisting we come and live in Australia for a time.

As we left, I knew that we would never live here again. I tried to think instead of what lay ahead back in Africa, a life that I had missed almost as much as Teboho had. And while I deeply appreciated Mum and Dad's generosity and hospitality throughout those eighteen months, I also felt I needed to get some space and try to rebuild my relationship with my daughter.

27
AUGUST 1995
THE PLACE OF REEDS

WITH OUR RETURN TO JO'BURG, I KNEW I WAS ENTERING A PHASE OF MY LIFE THAT WAS MORE ABOUT ARRIVING THAN ABOUT MOVING ON TO WHAT CAME NEXT. AFTER MANY YEARS OF WORKING TOWARDS OUR NEXT GOAL, WE HAD NO OTHER PLANS IN OUR MINDS THAN TO BE IN THIS PLACE, IN MOHLAKENG, THE PLACE OF REEDS.

We had borrowed a little money and bought some land across the road from Mohlakeng itself. The land had the foundations of a house already on it, though I could not say what stopped the previous owners from continuing. The white people who had lived in the area and were wealthy enough to move to a better place were selling up as the change in the country brought about an expansion of townships like Mohlakeng. Those who could afford no better, or refused to be moved, stayed on and had to cope with the changing social landscape. Some were bitter about it and others tried to ignore it, but change came creeping slowly towards them like the rising tide, powerful, inevitable and life altering.

Our new neighbours fell into the 'ignore it' category as we, and others families from Mohlakeng, bought land and sometimes houses. The plots were quite large, giving the area a semi-rural feel and appealing to large, black, extended families and those who wished to grow crops of mealies and the like. I later found out that this area was also home to the most conservative wing of South African Afrikaaner politics: one of our not too distant neighbours was caught harbouring a man who had slaughtered a number of black people in the name of his political party. After learning this I made sure I locked the doors at night, but slept no better.

In the first month after our arrival, we stayed with Moss and Khumo. Their house was now one of the largest in the township as they had added a second storey extension in our absence. It stood out against the rest of the dusty street with its two rows of identical township houses, placed one next to the other like a row of a child's Matchbox cars. As when I had visited in the past, Boggie gladly surrendered his room and joined his parents in theirs. Teboho and I shared our room with Mello, putting her on a mattress on the floor. My old friend Papi, Moss's father, was still well and occupying the bedroom next door. He was delighted to have me back, particularly in my pregnant state, and regularly broke with tradition by referring to it. He seemed fascinated by the concept of a mixed-raced child and was waiting anxiously for its birth.

Teboho had immediately applied for work when we returned and was snapped up into a good job at the South African Council of Churches, as the National Coordinator for their Human Rights Program. I think it may have reaffirmed his sense of worth as the old Teboho soon resurfaced and took centre stage once more. Mohlakeng was over an hour's drive away from the city. Fortunately, Khumo was also working at the Council of Churches, so Moss dropped the two of them off in the city on the way to his office a few blocks away. Back in Mohlakeng, I set about looking for a preschool for Mello, investigating local builders and seeing if I could find a house for us to rent while we built.

I was surprised that there were so few places to rent in the area, severely limiting our options. Ultimately, the only house I could find was through approaching a local bank to ask about repossession sales. It was in a suburb not too far from Mohlakeng that the bank was willing to rent a small house on a month by month basis, on the condition that we make it available for viewing by potential buyers with a few hours notice. I took down the address and found the suburb on the map. It was on the southwest side of Randfontein and only a short drive to Moss and Khumo's; it looked fine to me on paper. I bundled Mello into the car and set out to find it.

Like many towns outside the main city sprawl, Randfontein had a number of satellite suburbs that were scattered across the veld, like drops of mercury on a stone table. Each suburb was its own little enclave, joined to another only by a connecting road that crossed the expanse of veld that lay between. From the main road that joined Mohlakeng to Randfontein, I headed west to reach this house in the small suburb of Finsbury.

I pulled up in front of what was essentially a vacant lot with no fencing and no garden, just tufts of spiky grass and dirt. The tiny house stood there like a lost child. I took a deep breath before opening the car door, knowing that it was either this or impose on Moss and Khumo for months. I was also aware that Karen, my Melbourne friend who was with me when the first stirrings of pregnancy made themselves known, was coming over for a visit in a few weeks and it was not fair to ask Khumo to house her as well. With all that in mind, I climbed out of the car and opened the back door for Mello. Hand in hand we went up to the front door, the bank having given me a key to inspect the property. The house was a simple box shape: two bedrooms, one bathroom, lounge and kitchen. I entered the house through the kitchen door and in two steps was in the lounge. The rest of the tour was equally brief but given it was this or nothing, I told Mello this would be our new home for the next few months. At least she was excited.

Two weeks later, we were settled in. My daily routine started with taking Teboho across to Moss and Khumo's house in the morning for him to catch a lift to work. Mello and I then returned to Finsbury for breakfast before driving the twenty minutes to Krugersdorp where Mello was now enrolled in preschool in the same mining complex where Mama and Bophundlovu had lived many years before. After dropping Mello, I would head back to Moss and Khumo's house, put on a load of washing and make a few phone calls, as there was no phone in our Finsbury house. We had organised the builders to start in a few weeks and were hoping that enough of our own house would be built to allow us to move in before Christmas, when the baby was due. Once the phone calls were made and any grocery shopping done, I would return to the house for lunch and a short nap before driving back to Krugersdorp to fetch Mello. To save me the drive, Moss would drop Teboho home in the evenings.

Karen arrived when I was seven months pregnant. She planned to spend three weeks with us as well as going on a camping trip in Kruger National Park. There is nothing like the face of an old friend to raise your spirits and I was delighted to see Karen come through the arrival gates at the airport. I knew that her natural pragmatism and good humour would help me get through the current instability I was feeling. Now that I was pregnant, my capacity to go with the flow was much reduced. I was also having a few problems with Mello and hoping that Karen's close connection with her would help. My daughter and I were yet to recapture the closeness we'd had before our time in Australia, with Mello's behaviour and my response to it only driving us further apart.

I wrote several letters home to Mum regarding Mello's struggles to settle back into South Africa.

> *Mello had her two cousins, Katie and Mapule, stay over on Friday and Saturday night. She loves playing with them and it's helping her acclimatise. But she is terribly bossy, which is terrible, considering Katie is eleven and Mapule is eight years old. She also cries when she doesn't get her way. Katie told us that she whinges all the time and 'is going to be a stupid when she grows up'. So it seems like I'm not the only one who think she is behaving like a brat. I hope she will settle down and give it up soon.*

And later, after visiting her cousin Katie for an hour while I ran an errand, I returned to the township to find she had disappeared.

It turned out she had ducked out without anyone seeing her so that she could go to the shops with one of the kids from up the street. He had offered to buy her sweets, and the other rule of visiting her cousins, besides not leaving the house, is that she isn't to eat sweets and chips which all the other kids are constantly into. It turns out she went without Katie because she knew she would tell me what she was up to. Also, it wasn't the first time she's done it! She got a smack, lost her favourite Barbie doll to her cousins (which was the latest agreed punishment) and couldn't go to Katie's for two weeks. She later told Katie that she didn't care if she had her Barbie as she had five better ones coming from Australia. She then proceeded to scribble all over the doll with black Texta.

Mello's behaviour was deeply troubling to me. Despite doing everything I could to help her adjust, she seemed determined to prove herself better than the rest of the family, the rest of the community. Perhaps she no longer felt special, something I should have had more sympathy for.

Being heavily pregnant, my reserves were low and her belligerence was sending me over the edge. Each night, after she was finally asleep, I found myself rehashing the events of the day and panicking about how to resolve the dilemma. It was so bad at one point that I was beginning to get cramps and had some leakage of fluid. At the next antenatal check-up, the sister confirmed that my stress levels were not helping, but there was no major cause for alarm with the baby as these kinds of small ruptures of the membrane usually heal over. Truth be told, I think I also resented Mello during that period for putting me under such stress that it was affecting the baby; any sympathy I had for her iced over. So it was with great relief that Karen was now here to weave her magic with Mello, as I had often seen her do when we were living in Australia. In fact, there was something so special between them, something I could not give, that Mello to this day refers to Karen as her 'second mother'.

On Karen's first day, we went across to the plot where the building was about to begin. With the foundations laid and a steel frame construction, the house would go up quickly. I wanted to be moved in by Christmas which was just over two months away, so it would be an aggressive plan. At that point, I would have been willing to live in a warehouse as long as it was ours. After taking a good look around, we returned to the Finsbury house for lunch. As we sat at the kitchen table eating sandwiches, there was a knock at the door. The property was not fenced and our visitor had walked right up to the open door, giving us a start. He was from Mohlakeng and looking for work.

'Can I do your garden for you, Madam?'

'But there is no garden', Karen replied, holding back a giggle, 'only dirt and weeds.'

'Then I can pull up those weeds, Madam?'

Karen had to look away at this point, not wanting to laugh openly, so I told the man to wait and I would give him some money for lunch as we really didn't need a gardener. This was Karen's first experience of the peculiarities of South Africa, but there were more to come.

The next morning, I left Karen, Mello and Katie—who had come home with Teboho the night before to spend a few days with us—in Finsbury while I went to Moss and Khumo's to do a load of washing. Karen thought she would take the girls to a park she had seen a few blocks away. While it only consisted of a few swings in a vacant lot, it potentially provided more entertainment than staying at home or coming with me. So she locked up the house and headed off down the road with a girl on each side, all hand in hand. Karen noticed that she was attracting attention as the occupants of passing cars turned to look at the little trio. The interest was not only in the fact that they were together but also in the fact that Karen was obviously looking after them, as if she was the maid and the girls the children of her employer. Karen began to feel uncomfortable, but did not wish to be deterred by other people's reactions. Then she noticed one man who was so astonished by what he saw that he turned his head to watch them, and kept it turned as he drove on down the road and right into the back of a parked car. At this point Karen thought better of challenging stereotypes and turned the girls on their heels and ran home, not wanting to be around for the explosion of anger that would undoubtedly follow.

In Karen's first week with us, I was already seeing an improvement in Mello. Karen had made Mello her project and was spending hours playing with her, reading books and taking her out. I could not have been more grateful. When she left for her camping trip to Kruger National Park, I hoped that Mello would not relapse. For my part, I had promised to give Mello more attention, keeping the visits of the cousins to a minimum so as not to divide my time between them. I had come to realise that when the cousins were visiting, I favoured them over Mello because they had so little and Mello had so much. I wanted Mello to be a generous host—but she was just trying to hold on to what she felt she had lost.

Since our return, we had been attending antenatal classes and having regular check-ups at the hospital we had chosen for the birth. I discovered that South Africa had quite a high ratio of caesarean sections to natural births in the white community and was determined to make my own choices about the birth, as it had been a low risk pregnancy. We found a hospital in Jo'burg called Marymount that had a birthing unit as well as a labour ward. The birthing unit was staffed by midwives only, but if there were any complications with the birth, the obstetricians were down the other end of the corridor. They also had water birth facilities which I was interested in exploring for pain relief during the labour.

On my first visit to the hospital, I met Mona who was the head of the Active Birth Unit and also editor of one of the country's popular baby magazines. Each time we went for a check-up, we met with one of the midwives on the team—there were four of them—as we did not know who would be on duty on the day and didn't want to be attended by a stranger. I was very comfortable with all the midwives, though it was Sue who would ultimately deliver the baby.

All the check-ups had gone well, though I had only put on 6 kilograms in the pregnancy thus far. The midwife assured us that the baby was a good size and was unaffected, though I could do with a little less stress in my life. I bit my lip at the thought of building a house and moving in, all in the next two months.

Despite all the activity that was going on around me, I still took time out to enjoy being pregnant. While the first few months had been grim with morning sickness, from sixteen weeks onwards it had been a joy. The first few flutters had now turned into nightly festivals of movement. Karen, Teboho and I would sit on the couch and watch a foot roll across my belly, touch a little hand as it tentatively explored the boundaries of its world. I was in awe of the life inside, amazed that this was happening to me. While I knew it was the stuff of life and that women all over the world were falling pregnant each day, it still seemed like a miracle to me, a fragile balance of hope and loss, and one that I did not take for granted.

Teboho and I were enjoying the antenatal classes despite him being the only black person there. If the other couples were surprised or put off by our presence, they worked very hard not to show it. I appreciated Teboho coming along to class, remembering the family's attitude to Tshidi's pregnancy where no one had even mentioned the fact that she was pregnant. Not only were we mentioning it, we were watching birthing videos, studying anatomy and practising breathing techniques—definitely a departure from Teboho's own father's involvement in his birth.

After Karen returned from her trip to Kruger, we organised to have dinner with Willie, Teboho's younger brother and my favourite brother-in-law. He too was now in a relationship with a white woman, another Karen. She came from a very wealthy Afrikaaner family who did not approve of her choice in men. I remember going over to Willie and Karen's new home when they moved up to Jo'burg, a small inner city house that Karen's father had bought for her. Teboho and I went around to help them paint it. Willie, Teboho and I had popped out to buy more paint and in our absence, Karen's father arrived with the same intentions as we had. When we returned to the house, her father was up a ladder in the small entrance hall. We each filed through, introduced ourselves and shook his hand in greeting. Willie was bringing up the rear and, as he was yet to meet Karen's father, he also introduced himself. On hearing his name, Karen's father turned away and went back to his painting without a word. Change is slow when it involves your only daughter and a young black man.

We had agreed to meet Willie and Karen for dinner at a restaurant at Westgate, the largest shopping mall on the West Rand, or western suburbs of Jo'burg. By this time, the shoppers who frequented the mall were a mixture of all races, shopping side by side without a second look. However, our little party was still an oddity—two black men and three white women, one of whom was pregnant. From the perspective of the old South African mindset, there was just no way this mix could work out well. I was very accustomed to ignoring the stares, but our friend Karen was not; being the outspoken person she is, she stared right back or asked the starers if she could help them with something.

After an enjoyable dinner at an Italian restaurant, Willie and his Karen headed back towards the city while Teboho, Karen and I headed further west towards Randfontein. We were travelling along the dual carriageway between Krugersdorp and Randfontein when I noticed a police car behind us. The road was not well lit and there were no other cars along this empty stretch of road. Given my experience with police in the townships, I always felt they were as unpredictable and dangerous as wild animals so I was immediately on guard.

'Please make sure you don't go over the speed limit. Don't give them a reason', I urged Teboho.

'Relax, *Moratua*. We are just driving here', Teboho lulled in reply.

The police car slowly pulled up along side us, allowing each man inside to survey each of us in turn. After a few moments, they crept forward before changing lanes and settling in ahead of us.

'I don't like this', I said as I saw the policeman in the front passenger seat speaking into the radio handset.

The police car in front then slowed down, forcing us to do 50 kilometres in an 80 kilometre zone. I kept looking behind us, fearing the worst; before long another car dropped in behind and shortly after that, a third. I was in a panic, with one hand instinctively around my stomach in a useless attempt to protect the baby.

Once we were hemmed in on three sides, the police car in front screeched to a halt, momentarily making me laugh as I imagined these men thinking they were in a *Dukes of Hazard* movie. But the lightness quickly passed as we slowed to a stop, still a few kilometres from town.

'It will be OK. Just stay in the car, stay relaxed', Teboho said, as much to himself as to us.

The doors of the first police car opened and three policemen got out. One man came towards our car, the other two loitering behind.

'I want to see your licence and car registration', the man said in a stony voice, thick with an Afrikaans accent.

Teboho leant across in front of me and reached into the passenger's cubby hole for the papers. He handed these and his identity document, always carried next to his wallet, to the man standing with his hand outstretched.

The policeman flicked through the documents. 'Whose car is this?' he asked.

'It's mine', Teboho replied.

After a long silence, the man flung the papers back in through the window. 'Now get out of my town', he spat as he began to walk away.

I saw something in Teboho snap. He leapt out of the car, shouting at the policeman's retreating form: 'I gave you those papers in your hand. I expect you to hand them back the same way. I'm not a dog. I don't fetch'.

I felt my stomach clench in fear. I understood that this was 1995, there was a black government in power and Teboho should no longer be treated like this. But I also knew that we were alone on a dark road, surrounded by men who didn't care who the government in Pretoria was—clearly, around here, they were the law.

As soon as Teboho left the car, the policeman in the other cars were out of theirs and moving to form a circle around him and the first policeman. Without thinking, I pocketed my wedding ring and stepped out of the car after him. Karen, many years later, said that she watched me do this and still didn't understand why. But I knew these men needed no other reason to escalate the situation further. We were in this situation because they had seen us together. I didn't want to consider what would happen next if they realised this man was my husband and I was pregnant with his child. I also knew enough of this place to understand they were incapable of making such an impossible connection immediately.

I headed towards the crowd of men, Teboho and the officer standing in the middle, toe to toe, shouting at each other.

'This is not your town. I was born here and my father before me. This is my town and I will not be told when to come and when to go', Teboho was shouting defiantly.

'Who do you think you are?' the officer replied in a rage.

'The question is, who are you? I want your name and number.'

I stepped inside the circle of men, a few of whom had their hands to their guns by now. I placed myself in between Teboho and the officer, facing my husband.

'Let's go. There is no need for this', I said, trying not to beg.

After a few moments, he caught my eye, and perhaps seeing the fear rising there, he turned to go, pushing his way through the ring of men. As he did so, the officer called after him, 'Go on, get out of here'. I watched his back, afraid he would turn at the goading, but he kept on and headed back towards the car.

Once we were back on the road, the three police cars tailed us right through town and to the edge of the township—I had begged

Teboho not to go to the house in Finsbury. I saw that he was not afraid but angry, furious that he could still be treated this way without sanction. He resolved to lay a complaint against these men in the morning. Karen and I, on the other hand, were both left shaking and terrified. Even once we had reached Moss and Khumo's, my hands were still quivering with fear. On hearing the story Moss, like Teboho, was angry at the liberties taken and resolved to take up the issue himself. Moss, through his leadership in the black church, was a well connected advisor to the new heads of government. As we sat in the brightly lit kitchen, the dark night outside held at bay, I began to feel comfort that we at least had some recourse in 1995 that had not been available ten years before. However, I also knew we had been lucky to get away as lightly as we did, new government or not. For the next few weeks, I kept an eye out on the roads and in town for these men, but knew I would not recognise them if I saw them. I just hoped they would not recognise me.

My return to South Africa had not been as I had imagined it. I had hoped that I would see a change after the elections the previous year. In fact, change was happening, just not in the part of the country where we chose to live. But there was a visible change in our family at least. Teboho was delighted to be back home amongst old friends and all his family. It was as if his manhood was returning, having been lost along the way in Australia. Perhaps this was what the nightclub incident in Launceston was about, I don't know. Perhaps having a woman flirt and come on to him had given him a sense of manliness and power, one he chose to take advantage of when I tried to chastise him. In my seeking to rein him back in, he saw a threat to his newly affirmed manhood and he lashed out.

There is a strange and delicate balance of power when a black man marries a white women, given the inevitable social baggage of their union. I knew why I had been attracted to Teboho but I sometimes wondered what it was he saw in me. Could he separate out the colour of my skin and all it stood for and see the person beneath or is the package impossible to untangle, causing the reasonable to become suddenly unreasonable, the beloved to become the tormenter?

Back at home in the township, Teboho's happiness increased with each movement forward on the house, each milestone taking him closer to his dream. I knew he wanted a home that he could share with his extended family and friends, taking in those who needed somewhere to stay, just as he had done in his youth. He wanted to be available to the community, to help support those who were struggling, to spend time with people who needed someone to listen. And I loved and respected him for his generous, empathetic spirit. He also wanted a large family around him; with Mello, another child on the way and hopefully more to come, his life was finally coming together. As for me, I was relieved to see him so happy, glad to do whatever it took to make that happen for him. His reclaimed optimism seemed to deny the existence of that stranger in Tasmania with the cruel words and stony heart.

While I was finding the interaction in Randfontein intimidating, I was enjoying the opportunity to become part of the community in Mohlakeng. In my spare time, I was coaching some of the high school students I knew through church and had just volunteered to start a Sunday school. Upon our return to Mohlakeng we had, of course, joined Ebenezer Church where Moss was the minister. It operated out of the local school building and the congregation was continuing to grow. While I was the only white person there, I knew the vast majority of people quite well so I never felt out of place. While Karen was with us, she also came along to church and got to know the congregation.

The last weekend before Karen left, we drove up to a remote village called Bochum in the Northern Province, where there was a headstone raising for one of Mama's relatives. Mama explained that a second ceremony is held up to a year after the funeral—depending on how long it takes to raise the necessary funds—where a permanent headstone is placed above the grave of the person who has passed away. The family gathers once more and as with a wedding or funeral, a large feast is held over the weekend, culminating in the raising of the headstone on the second day. Mama, Teboho, Mello, Karen and I were to make the journey representing our branch of the family.

After many hours in the car, we arrived in Bochum just before lunch on the Saturday. The village was a mixture of traditional round rondavels made of wattle and daub with a thatched roof and corrugated iron shacks. There were also a handful of larger cement brick homes scattered throughout. These were all flat-roofed dwellings, painted white with a brown strip close to the ground so the mud that splashed up during the rain would not spoil the walls. The rondavels were similarly two-toned, with the brown strip coming almost as high as the top of the door frame. A number of family compounds were demarcated by a flimsy wire fence held in place by a collection of wooden and iron poles.

Our family's compound consisted of a white brick home with a semicircle of rondavels behind it. In the middle of the rondavels was a large concrete slab with a raised border perhaps two bricks high. I was unsure whether these were foundations for another home or built for a specific purpose but today, the area acted as an open air kitchen with five or six large pots boiling away like a cluster of witches' caldrons in one corner of the slab. There were a few thorn trees and oleander bushes scattered about the compound, but none provided much shade. The shadiest spot appeared to be on the veranda of the main house where a large pink bougainvillea had crept up the pillars like a swarm of hungry ants. It was from this cool haven that a number of female relatives emerged as we stood next to the car stretching after our long journey.

Festivities appeared to be in full swing and we were immediately whisked off to join in, the women to the open air kitchen and Teboho to where the men sat in a circle under a thorn tree across the way. I knew I would not see Teboho for a time, but ultimately he would break with tradition and make a lively appearance at the pots. Karen was keen to understand everything she was seeing and began flooding

Mama with questions. Mama had been through this process with me often enough to know that she simply needed to pass Karen on to the crowd of equally curious young women who stood shyly off to the side, allowing Mama to catch up on family gossip while Karen was shown around.

Given my late stage of pregnancy, I chose to sit with Mama while Karen disappeared with three teenagers who were to be her constant companions for the next twenty-four hours, despite speaking only patchy English. Karen re-emerged around the corner of the house forty minutes later, arms stretched out to the side, balancing a tin of water on her head. The women by the pots fell about in hysterics at the sight of her earnest concentration. I noticed the girls had been kind enough to give her a cloth ring to make the task easier (it provides a flat surface on which to balance the container). I had seen many white people attempt this feat without the benefit of the twisted cloth ring, failing miserably and wondering how black women can balance pots with such ease. Mama and the other women continued to laugh as they watched Karen inch her way past the pots, intent on learning this new skill. She eventually made it around the other corner of the house. It was another forty-five minutes before Karen returned again, this time with a baby strapped to her back. The women were cooking the traditional pap which required regular stirring, the task becoming more difficult as the pap stiffened. Karen was handed a large wooden spoon that stood as high as her armpit. Much to the delight of her fellow chefs she took the spoon and put her shoulder into it, baby still on her back.

Not long after, the drums started. Mama explained that this singing and dancing would continue through the night and into the morning until we everybody across to the family graveyard where the gravestone was to be raised. Passing the sleeping baby to one of its relatives, Karen and I went to see what was happening. Out in front of the house on an open piece of ground was a circle of older women. Two sat and a third stood next to three forty-four gallon drums with animal skin stretched over one end. One woman played with her hands and the other two held thick sticks with more skin wrapped around the ends. Moving in a relentless circle around the three were fifteen other women, each wearing a long string of rattles around each ankle. They appeared to be made from a type of grass or reed folded into triangles with a small rock or seed inside that shook when the wearer stamped her feet.

As the drums throbbed, the women shuffled forward, striking their heels into the ground as they went. In their hands were multicoloured beaded sticks with what looked like white raffia attached at the end. With each drum stroke, each step, they flicked the sticks and seemed to implore the heavens with moans rather than lyrics. Most of the women wore aqua garments over the clothes they had worn for cooking. Their arms and wrists were also thickly decorated with beaded bracelets and their heads wrapped in navy blue cloth. As this was not something I had seen before, Karen and I sat watching as if hypnotised by the rhythm and movement.

As the darkness closed in, the smells of roasting meat wafted across from where the men had gathered some hours before. Though I had not seen any slaughtering, no doubt a number of animals were required to feed this large crowd. I explained the routine to Karen and we soon had our plates on our laps piled high with lamb, pap and cooked vegetables. As we were in the middle of the bush, with the only light coming from paraffin lamps inside the houses, the stars pressed down on our heads, dense, heavy and glorious. I sat listening to the conversations around us and to the night sounds of the bush beyond, grateful as always for the chance to experience something that has been done for hundreds of years beyond the notice of the western world.

Around midnight, Karen and I were given a double bed to share. After finally managing to extract Mello from her distant cousins, the three of us retired for the night, the sounds of drums and shuffling feet pounding outside and echoing into my dreams. Teboho, like most of the other adults, stayed awake through the night talking, dancing and singing at intervals as the vigil continued until dawn.

I woke at first light with only a few hours of sleep under my belt. I had lost the ability to sleep through the night about a month before and now the baby's movements and my need for the toilet had me up a few times a night. Given the circumstances, I had ignored the call of nature but could not ignore my baby's acrobatics. I rolled over towards Karen and Mello to see if they had fared any better. Mello had, as usual, assumed the sleep position and was in possession of the majority of the bed. Karen was clinging onto what was left on the far side. Hearing me move, she opened her bloodshot eyes and stared at me with a pleading look.

'Between Mello and the drums, I don't think I slept a wink', she whispered over Mello's head.

I was under no illusion that Mello would wake anytime soon, so replied in a normal voice, 'Do you want to get up and see about breakfast?'

'Sounds like a plan.'

Breakfast was porridge that was already bubbling away in a few of the large three-legged pots in the open-air kitchen. We greeted all the women who were working there, including Karen's young friends from the day before, unsure if they had grabbed a few hours sleep or had kept the vigil all night. Karen was happy to stay and give the porridge a try but I went off in search of bread.

After breakfast, we popped in on Mello who was still fast asleep, before heading out to see the dancers. The same women were circling the drums, though they had all changed into matching purple outfits with blue and white trim creating geometrical designs on the bottom of the dress. Each woman was now wearing a white headscarf and carried two raffia sticks instead of one. I noticed a man emerge from behind the drums, wearing the same purple material made into a shirt and a white baseball cap in place of the headcloth. He stayed inside the circle rather than joining the line of women. As before, there was a crowd of onlookers, mostly boys and men. After a time, the crowd had grown to include many of the women who had been watching over the pots, giving me the impression that something was about to happen.

I began hunting around for Teboho who I was yet to see from the night before. Eventually I found him sitting a little way off under a tree with the older men. After the greetings and compulsory introductions that described in a long, complicated manner the relationship of each of these old men to us, I was able to ask what was about to happen. Teboho explained that we would soon be moving across to the graveyard to see the unveiling of the headstone. When the drumming changed and the dancers headed off, that would be a sign to follow.

As I made my way back to the circle, I spotted Karen on the veranda with yet another baby on her back and Mello by her side, looking like something the river had swept up after a storm. I went across and took Mello inside to wash her face and change. I had long since handed over the care of her hair to professionals and it was in need of some serious attention now. Mello has very tightly curled hair and lots of it, so the process of relaxing it to make it more manageable is a painful one. For the purposes of this trip, I had tied her hair into two little bunches and popped an Alice band over the front to keep the loose ends in place. On more than one occasion, a black woman would walk past her and 'tut tut' on seeing the condition of her hair. I braced myself for such condemnation today.

Once Mello was a little more respectable, we rejoined Karen on the veranda where we had a good view of the proceedings. Before long, the time had arrived: the dancers peeled off into a straight line and we joined the large crowd of relatives and neighbours who fell in behind. I was by now well used to the dancing motion that even the smallest child adopted as they made their way towards the fence line, though Karen kept her eyes on the feet of the person in front of her and attempted to copy the steps without tripping over. Soon a long line had formed and was snaking its way along the fence, down the dirt road and towards the open veld where the local graveyard lay. When Karen and I arrived, the minister was already in position by the headstone, along with the immediate family of the man who had passed away. After a long speech by the minister—I did my best to translate for Karen from northern Sotho, a language I did not understand beyond its similarity to Southern Sotho—the cloth that had been covering the headstone was removed.

The ornately carved granite headstone stood as high as the minister's shoulder and displayed the name of the deceased and his relationship to those he had left behind. It was also decorated with a wreath. The size of the stone and the nature of the carving communicated the respect the family felt for the departed; such stones cost many thousands of rands and all branches of the family, including our own, had been required to make a contribution towards it. After a short prayer and a song, the crowd broke up and quietly made its way back to the compound in groups of threes and fours.

We left Bochum after lunch as the heat and my pregnancy were making the day uncomfortable. Even with such an obvious excuse to depart early, it still took us over an hour to move around saying our appropriate goodbyes. Though we were all exhausted from lack of sleep, sweaty and dusty, I was so glad that this event had happened during Karen's stay and she was able to be a part of it.

Two days later, Karen was gone. As always, it was hard to see an old friend depart. She had been my constant companion for many weeks, one with whom nuances were understood, jokes shared and Australian sarcasm and slang did not require translation. Lonely days stretched out before me once Teboho was at work and Mello at school. As if sensing this, Mama sent word to say that she would be coming to stay, worried that I should not be left alone without a phone so close to my due date. Though I did not know it at the time, this would be a permanent arrangement and one that was to provide me with much companionship and support as I came to feel more isolated in our new home.

28

DECEMBER 1995
BROKEN WATER

BY THE BEGINNING OF DECEMBER, OUR NEW HOUSE WAS AS FINISHED AS IT WAS GOING TO BE. THE WALLS STILL NEEDED PAINTING, THE BATHROOMS TILING AND THE WOODEN FLOOR STAINING BUT WE HAD RUN OUT OF MONEY AND TIME. WE HAD DESIGNED THE HOUSE IN THREE SECTIONS, THE FIRST CONTAINING TWO BEDROOMS, A PLAYROOM AND A SMALL BATHROOM; THE SECOND, AN OPEN PLAN KITCHEN, LOUNGE AND DINING ROOM WHICH HAD DOUBLE FRENCH DOORS THAT OPENED OUT ONTO WHAT WOULD ONE DAY BE OUR GARDEN. THE THIRD SECTION CONTAINED THE MAIN BEDROOM, A STUDY AND A BATHROOM THAT AT THIS STAGE HAD NOT PROGRESSED BEYOND HAVING A TOILET. WE HAD ATTEMPTED TO BE AS ENERGY EFFICIENT AS WE COULD, THE HOUSE BEING NORTH FACING AND WITH CROSS VENTILATION IN EACH SECTION. IN FACT, IT TURNED OUT TO BE DELICIOUSLY WARM IN WINTER AND BLISSFULLY COOL IN SUMMER, NEVER REQUIRING THE EXPENSE OF HEATING OR AIR CONDITIONING.

When we moved in at the end of the first week of December, the house resembled our rental in Finsbury in that it was really just a house on a piece of land. There were a few wattle trees in the northeast corner but other than that, the land was covered in brittle tufts of grass, the same kind that is used to thatch roofs. As we had opted for tiles over thatch, the grass would remain untouched until I turned my attention to building a garden.

One of the reasons we had been interested in this property, outside its proximity to Mohlakeng, was the powerful bore hole that it reportedly contained. With the last of our money, we had paid a local contractor to erect a five metre water tower on which was perched a large water tank. A small pump drew the water from beneath the ground and up into the tank, then it was largely gravity that gave us water pressure in the adjacent house. True to predictions, the water was clean and strong and soon we had a plentiful supply of water for the house and garden.

The day of the move was an exciting one for all of us. I had packed up the Finsbury house many days ahead of schedule in anticipation. Though Mama didn't like to see me exerting myself so close to the birth, predicted to be less than four weeks away, I wanted no delays in getting us out of this mean little house and into our own home. Moss and Khumo and other friends from church were there to help, as well as Mello's oldest brother Joseph who was up in Jo'burg for the university holidays. So many hands made the move a quick one, though in reality we had very little to move: a couch, a double bed, a bunk bed which we had split into two single beds for Mama and Mello, two chests of drawers, a desk, a few prints for the walls and a rug for the floor. The rest of our possessions were packed into boxes: clothes, plates, pots, cutlery and Mello's toys. Moss and Khumo gave us their old dining room table and chairs as a gift, making our new home complete.

I had stayed at the Finsbury house to direct traffic until the last box was loaded, then squeezed myself into the front seat of our car next to Teboho for the short drive to the new house. As we pulled into the yard, I was overcome by the feeling of finally arriving after a long journey. I had a place to call home, a place where my child could be born. As I let my eyes run over the house and the surrounding trees, I saw a movement out of the corner of my eye. I turned my head in time to see the water tower buckle and surrender the tank's load onto the grass at the side of the house, spraying water in a huge arc as if some giant had just thrown a bucket of dirty water into our backyard. The water tank had cracked like an enormous egg and now lay in two pieces in the dirt.

Teboho screeched to a halt and leapt out of the car to assess the damage. I sat for a few minutes unable to move, pushing aside thoughts of what dreadful deeds I could have done to deserve this. Finally, I hauled my cumbersome body out of the car and went to join the crowd that had gathered as if around a grave to look at what was left of our water tower. It certainly felt like a grave to me. What would we do without water in the house? The tower and tank had been expensive and we had nothing left to pay for their replacement. I stood next to the pieces, willing myself not to cry.

A few days before, Teboho had driven me to the hospital with what I thought was the onset of labour, only to be told that it was Braxton Hicks contractions and that my body was merely doing a dress rehearsal. After checking the baby's vital signs and determining that all was well, they sent us home. I was afraid this disaster might send me back to the midwives if I didn't keep my emotions under control. So I left everyone else at the site of the crime and slipped into the house to begin unpacking. Twenty minutes later, Teboho found me in Mello's room to tell me that the foundations of the tower appeared only to be half a metre deep, set in poorly made concrete. The contractor must have been cutting corners to increase his profits. We would later sue him through the small claims court. After he was ordered to pay damages, he fled Randfontein but was discovered four months later in a small town a few hours to the west, claiming bankruptcy and therefore unable to pay. But as I sat amongst a jumble of boxes and toys, it wasn't justice I wanted—only water.

Thankfully the pump was still working and litres of fresh water could be sent cascading into waiting buckets with the flick of a switch. For the next five months, we joined the millions of South African households whose daily water supply was met by two large plastic water containers by the kitchen door.

By the following morning we were settled in. Joseph, Beans and Solly were all staying over to help paint the inside walls so that at least that would be done before the baby was born. The children's section was painted a practical white that could easily be touched up if necessary; the living room transformed to a cheery yellow; and lastly, our bedroom was painted a peaceful blue. These colours gave the house life and warmth that transformed it from house to home.

So we began our life in this new home in the way it would continue, surrounded by friends and relatives living in an extended family unit, not the small nuclear family arrangement that I had grown up with. This made our home vibrant and welcoming but it also meant that if I needed privacy, my bedroom was the only sanctuary. Thankfully the room was large and sunny and therefore a pleasant place into which I could withdraw.

In the week of the move, we had another late night false alarm. I felt for Teboho as he dragged himself off to work the next day, exhausted from a night at the hospital and the long drive home. Unbeknown to us, the midwives were now running a tab on the chances of me requiring a caesarean as I appeared to be tiring myself out even before the race had begun.

My waters broke in the morning, two weeks before the Christmas due date. Teboho had been up most of the night working on a document that needed to be submitted the following day. At about five o'clock, he woke me to come and edit his work, correcting the grammar in what was admittedly his fifth language, as we had done throughout his university career. I finished the edits and printed the document just as Teboho's lift arrived to take him to the city.

After seeing him off I was on my way to the bathroom, clearly misreading my body's signs, when my waters broke. Once I realised what had happened, I knew this would be no false alarm and was both relieved and slightly nervous. We had planned for this eventuality—going into labour when Teboho wasn't around. I phoned to tell him what had happened, grabbed my bag, and drove to the township where my brother-in-law's neighbour, Ma Phiri, was primed and ready. Ma Phiri was Caleb's only neighbour who knew how to drive a car and was usually at home. With these two essential attributes, she was signed up as part of the birthing back-up team, in case of just such an emergency.

Mama would accompany me to the hospital and we would leave Mello at Caleb's house where Nooi would watch her. Mama took Mello inside while I waited in the car taking deep breaths to keep me calm, though the contractions were yet to begin. Mama called Ma Phiri and the three of us headed into Johannesburg.

As we exited Mohlakeng we passed Toekomsrus, another township outside Randfontein, its tiny houses looking like strings of coloured popcorn as they laced around its dusty roads. Past Toekomsrus, a long road stretched towards the city, passing gold mines, flat empty fields and towering mine dumps as we travelled east. Eventually the road became a dual carriageway and veered left to skim the outskirts of Soweto. We passed the whole range of Soweto homes—rich and poor, permanent and transient, areas dominated by one tribal group or another—as we skirted around its southern border. With Soweto behind us, Gold Reef City loomed on the left. What was once a working gold mine had now been converted to a theme park. Like the now booming tourist industry in Soweto, this new icon of change drew all kinds of people to it, as if it has always been like this. Even I had been in the country long enough to remember that it used to be so different. Then we were on the freeway, driving beneath the skyline of Jo'burg. At the city's eastern edge, we took the off ramp towards the stadium and then to the hospital behind it—finally.

As we pulled into the parking lot outside the emergency entrance, I realised I urgently needed the toilet after such a long drive. I shuffled straight past reception, being chased by a panicked nurse who assumed I was confusing the need for the toilet with the need to push, and was actually about to deliver. I yelled at her over my shoulder that my waters had broken—again. Apparently the gait of a woman thirty-eight weeks pregnant and incontinent looks surprisingly like the gait of one who is crowning in the final stages of labour. Crisis over, we headed upstairs to the birthing suite with Ma Phiri, Mama and a midwife in tow. Once we settled into the room, the midwife on duty, Sue, explained how things would go.

We began with a quick check to see how the baby and I were progressing. We were doing well. My body, on the other hand, was yet to spring into action despite earlier positive signs. Sue decided to get things moving with the insertion of a small tablet and then we waited. It was just after ten o'clock.

Mona, the head midwife, popped in to see me while I was waiting for things to begin. She asked me if she could write an article on us for her magazine, the combination of a mixed race couple and a labouring in water being too good to miss. She asked me, as people often do, how I got here. I knew she meant: what is an Australian doing living in South Africa? as the reverse is the stronger trend. But even thinking about how I got there that day, the long drive past townships and mine dumps, tells its own story of how different my life has been from those of my childhood friends in Sydney.

At midday, the pains began. Mama and Ma Phiri were still patiently keeping me company while I was silently wondering where the bloody hell Teboho was. I had phoned him just after 8.30 and his office was only a short drive from the hospital. Mama sat by me and held my hand as the contractions ebbed and flowed over the next two hours. While I was reassured by her presence, since she had birthed six babies herself, I was a little embarrassed sharing these moments with Ma Phiri whom I hardly knew. While she was selected as part of the back-up team, I would not have described us as friends. She, however, found nothing odd in the arrangement. I suspected that this would make a good story for her friends back in Mohlakeng where Teboho and I were second-rate celebrities. (First-rate celebrities were successful soccer players and those with connections in the entertainment industry.) We had the distinction of being one of two mixed race couples in the area; the other couple split their time between South Africa and Canada. Attending the birth of our first child would no doubt keep Ma Phiri in demand for some time. I laid this cynical thought aside, knowing it was my husband who was the deserving target of my labour crankiness.

Mama looked up with a sigh of relief as Teboho entered the room just after two o'clock. Avoiding my eye, he was full of smiles and jokes, thanking the two women for doing a wonderful job in his absence. This was their cue, so they rose, hugged me and issued words of encouragement before they left for the long drive back to the township. As they left, Sue entered the room—my questions for Teboho would have to wait. Sue checked me again and told me I could jump into and out of the tub anytime I wanted. As I started to say that I was coping well, the first big contraction hit. I clung onto Teboho as it swamped me, taking my breath away. When it had passed, I stepped as quickly as I could into the tub. Sue had told me that the water acts as a pain reliever, and if that was the case, I wanted to have the next contraction floating in pain reliever up to my neck.

Sue settled me in and left again. I knew Teboho would have a story to tell me, one of people needing his help. I always found it so hard to stay angry with him once I'd heard where he had been, but not today. Our world was filled with people who needed help. He was hardwired to respond to them but he was not always hardwired to meet my needs, it seemed. As the pregnancy had reached its third trimester, I felt increasingly vulnerable and exposed. I had always been able to look after myself and everyone else and was not comfortable with needing other people as much as I did in this state. But today I had no problem with the neediness I felt, only with his lack of response to it. He told me that he had been scheduled to run a workshop in Pretoria that day, about an hour's drive from Johannesburg. In an effort to keep his commitments, he had gone without telling me, knowing I was in good hands with his mother until he could get away. It was only at lunchtime that someone in the workshop enquired about my health and he told them I was in labour. They chased him out of the workshop, saying they didn't need him that much.

His explanation cut me but as I had a rush of contractions to contend with, I decided to put the words away until later. I tucked the hurt and disappointment down, where it had good company with many other hurts hidden there. Being in a mixed marriage, I had tried so hard to be understanding of the cultural differences between us. I had learnt the language, embraced his family and their traditions, lived in a traditional extended family household and generally tried to be a good wife. Ideologically, I believed in the possibilities of the 'rainbow nation', and making our marriage work was part of my contribution. So I tucked it down. I tucked many things down for him, but one day, it would all have to come back out for me.

The next few hours passed with a certain rhythm—contractions, breathing, floating, checking, chatting, an occasional photo for the magazine. Mona had joined us for a while and as she and I chatted, she told me that today would be the day. Given the many false alarms of the previous weeks, this was just what I wanted to hear.

After my last false alarm, Sue had taken me to the nursery to see the newborns. I think she was trying to keep my eye on the ball. My baby was still an abstract at that stage, the outline of a foot that passed across my belly as I sat on the couch, staring down in wonder. Despite regulations, she had given me a baby to hold for just a moment, to remind me that this would soon pass and before I knew it, I would be holding my own baby. I remembered that moment and smiled, but declined to share my thoughts with Mona, just in case.

In between contractions, Mona and I discussed a bit more of our history together: where Teboho and I had met, the festivities of the wedding, my family's reaction. Teboho had taken a position behind me, leaning over the tub so as to cradle my back in his arms. But soon the chatting stopped and Mona, knowing that the interview was over, left the room and allowed Sue and I to do our work uninterrupted, Teboho looking eagerly on as the miracle unfolded.

By six o'clock, I feared my body would crack open like an egg into a mixing bowl. Sue later told me that the moment you question your very life it is a sign that you are there—I was completely there. I remember thinking that at that moment, somewhere, someone was having tea. I pictured them sitting quietly, watching the passing traffic as time slipped by unnoticed, utterly oblivious to my pain. Time for me was passing one painful centimetre at a time.

At 6.30, our son was born. Sue held him upside down as we all waited for his first breath. I could hardly make him out through my tears. He was no longer an abstract but a tiny dark-haired baby suspended over my belly. Sue gave him to me and I peered down at him in disbelief, trying to recognise him as my own. Sue was busy helping Teboho cut the cord while I continued to look until I found it—he had my feet, long and slender. Content, I passed him over to be checked and swaddled.

As with all African children, our son would be named after the circumstances of his birth—Puleng if born in the rain; Mojalefa, the last born, the one who inherits; Thabo for happiness, and so on. We named our son Dichaba which, in Sesotho, means 'nations'—united nations.

29
DECEMBER 1995
MAKING ADJUSTMENTS

AFTER DICHABA'S BIRTH, WE STAYED IN THE BIRTHING SUITE FOR A FEW MORE HOURS DEALING WITH THE MESSY AFTER EFFECTS OF BIRTH AND LATER LEARNING HOW TO BREAST FEED FOR THE FIRST TIME. WHEN ALL WAS WELL, I WAS TAKEN DOWN TO A HOSPITAL ROOM TO GET SOME SLEEP. IT WAS ABOUT 10.30 PM WHEN TEBOHO LEFT TO DO THE SAME.

In comparison to the drama of the birth, the next two days in hospital were very quiet. I had no visitors except for Teboho who popped in to see me briefly after work. He told me he had no leave left as he had used it up on numerous hospital visits and false alarms. I found myself incredibly lonely and starting to get a bit blue, so by the third morning, I asked to go home. They were keen for me to stay an extra day but I thought it would do more harm than good. The loneliness I was feeling at the hospital was an echo of the loneliness I had been feeling since my return, despite my optimistic disposition. In contrast to living in my beloved 'Maritzburg, I was now isolated in the far reaches of the West Rand, something I did not wish to deal with at that point. Late that afternoon, once Teboho had arrived, we checked out and went home—home to our half finished house, home to no running water, but still home.

In African culture, the mother of a newborn enters a period of confinement where she is looked after by female relatives, encouraged to rest and simply concentrate on producing milk and feeding the baby for the first weeks or even months. If it is her first child, she will often go home to her mother who will teach her how to look after the new baby. I've heard of instances where a mother can be gone for as much as two years without the father having seen the child. Teboho used to joke that during this time, the woman was to 'take a rest' from her husband, so it was not only a way to have support from her mother but also a form of birth control. I was also told that during this rest period, the husband was free to sleep with other women so as to have his needs met. While Teboho and I used to joke about there being no 'rest period' allowed in our marriage, the shadows of Tasmania played on my mind.

Going home to Mum was not an option but Mama was keen for me to stay put on the couch and rest, insisting she would look after me with young Katie's help. At that stage, I was struggling to put Katie back in my good books after an awkward welcome home from her: Dichaba was still in the car with Teboho when Katie turned to me in surprise and said, 'Ragadi, I thought you had the baby already'. No one had told me, either, that your belly stays distended well after the birth, forcing you to stay in maternity clothes just when you are dying to finally get back into your jeans. With time I forgave her, but I have never let her forget.

Mama also insisted on no visitors to the house in the first week and later when they did come, they were forced by her, a woman who rarely insisted on anything, to jump over a broom in the doorway. When I asked Teboho what was going on he explained that this was to prevent evil spirits entering the house and affecting the baby. It had not occurred to me that evil spirits might piggy-back on friends and family as they came to visit, but the irony of them jumping over a broom—a symbol of witchcraft in my culture—brought a smile to my face as distinguished men like Moss leapt in through the French doors.

I loved the idea of a supported confinement period as I knew many young mothers in Australia, left alone with a newborn, felt exhausted and unsure how to respond to their baby's insistent cries. However, in reality, I found it difficult to sit on the couch and watch Mama doing housework and preparing meals. Once again, I did not wish to be one of those women who had 'no hands'.

I sat on the couch watching Mama and feeling guilty. I had spent many years working against that stereotype, always wanting to be the first to get my hands dirty, and was having a very hard time sitting still. I was literally chased out of the kitchen on a number of occasions when Mama discovered me making food for myself once her back was turned. 'You must ask me and I will get something for you', she roused. Exhausted as I was, it was guilt that drove me off the couch again and again, until after a week, Mama finally gave up. But she insisted it was too soon for the baby or me to leave the house, as birth would make us both vulnerable to witchcraft. Out of respect for her, I didn't argue the point for another week or two, by which time I was going completely stir crazy.

Dichaba wasn't much of a sleeper—if he woke only three or four times a night, I considered myself lucky. Most nights, he was up eight or nine times. Each time as I put him down, I would mutter a heartfelt prayer: 'Please God, just an hour, I just need an hour'. I seemed to be making every mistake in the book, letting him fall asleep on the breast so that he was neither burped nor being taught how to settle by himself. He had no routine—I was so delighted when he finally went to sleep, I didn't care what time it was. As a result, he slept more during the day than he did at night. I remember one occasion when he had been asleep for five hours, with me repeatedly checking to make sure he was still alive. Eventually, I picked him up and virtually held him upside down to wake him—I was afraid he might be in a coma. First time mothers should come with a warning label.

While my baby was catching up on sleep during the day, or at least trying to, I rarely felt able to go and take a nap myself. If I could do it over again, I would be more gracious about accepting help and would certainly sleep as much as possible instead of trying to be a supermum. As it was, I was almost hysterical with exhaustion every day. I tried to keep Dichaba awake at night after his bath, delaying his feed until after eight o'clock in the hope of him sleeping at a time when I could join him. This usually resulted in two hours of screaming each evening which did nothing to improve my state of mind.

When my confinement ended, I took the baby out to Westgate shopping centre so I could feel a little normal again. I remember a number of white women coming up to me and cooing over the beautiful little baby in the pram. I found myself thinking they would not be so enthusiastic in their praises of his fine dark looks if they knew he was mixed race. In my mind's eye I could see them turning distastefully away as if insulted by a foul smell. Though the thought of this amused me, it also reminded me of how outside the norm I was, how my choices had isolated me and potentially my son.

After a blissful hour of shopping, Dichaba started to cry for a feed. I had never noticed until that moment that I had only ever seen black women breastfeeding in public. It was not something white women did in this conservative society with its deep Calvinist roots. Yet in 1996 there were no mothers rooms, nowhere that I could go and feed him. In utter desperation, I entered a shoe shop where I had been browsing earlier and explained my dilemma. They kindly offered me a chair in a quiet corner of the shop to sit and feed the baby. Afterwards, I limped home discouraged to lick my wounds, my first outing hardly the glamorous return to society I had hoped for.

Since Dichaba's birth, I had also been observing my daughter's behaviour. Karen's visit had certainly worked wonders. Mello's obstinate behaviour slowly dissipated and she returned to being the child I had known before. I also noticed, though, that it was not a peaceful transformation but more of a defeat. I suspect the birth of a biological child undermined Mello's confidence about her place in the world. And yet she only had rare moments of taking it out on

Dichaba physically, as first-born children are often seen to do after the birth of the second child.

There is one photo, still displayed in my mother's kitchen, that was taken when Dichaba was six or seven months old. I am sitting cross-legged on the floor of our house with Dichaba in my lap. Mello, after much encouragement from Teboho and me, entered the photo at the last minute and is standing behind me wringing her T-shirt in her hands, her shoulders turned as if she is about to walk out again. She was only five years old at the time. That is the photo I find most heartbreaking in our whole collection but if I'm honest, it's the one that most captures how Mello felt much of the time. There are also photos of her clowning around, drama queen that she was, trying to grab attention from all around her. But it was this photo that captured what was really going on. Although I saw it, perhaps less clearly then than now, I had little energy to do more than take care of her physical needs. Had I acted more decisively, more compassionately then, I might have saved her much torment and doubt in years to come.

The first few months passed in a haze. Besides all the usual baby adjustments, we were still without running water; carrying buckets over our yet to be sealed wooden floors was a daily worry. When Dichaba was a few months old, Teboho suggested I take the kids and spend a week in 'Maritzburg so that he could sand and stain the floors, something he was reluctant to do with a baby in the house. Margie had just given birth to her third child, also a boy, and was very keen to have us come and stay. 'Come down and we can sit in the garden and feed babies together', she implored. So it was decided. I packed the kids into the car and made the five-hour drive down to my old home.

We spent a blissful week with Jacques and Margie. They were as gracious in their hospitality as they had always been and our friendship seemed once more close and warm. There was always the dark zone of Steve but we silently agreed never to go there. Jacques and Margie's place was a graceful old house with wooden floors, high pressed ceilings and verandas all round, just down the road from ETHOS. They also had a large back yard that Margie and the gardener tended with much care. Stephanie, their eldest daughter for whom I had always had a soft spot, was now at school and all grown up. It was the first time I had met Rebecca, their second daughter, who was fair-haired, unlike the rest of the family, and adorably naughty and strong-willed. If I had been her mother I may not have found her strength of character charming, but certainly as a friend, it was a delight to watch her engage with the world. Dominic, Margie's new son, was dark like Stephanie and seemed to me to be an angel. He slept well, fed well and rarely cried. As my little family found its way into our host's routine, I discovered that Dichaba himself was far more settled too. The extra sleep quickly allowed me to recover the ability to hold a decent conversation and I was inordinately grateful to Margie for that.

One day, as we sat rocking babies on our laps in the garden while Mello and Rebecca played on the swings, we suddenly heard a heart-wrenching wailing coming from the street. Margie quickly handed over Dom, leaving me with one baby in each arm, and rushed out the front to see what was happening. After a long time the wailing subsided but it was almost an hour before Margie returned. She had found the neighbour's maid sitting in the street, hysterical. The woman appeared unable to talk, so Margie sat down in the gutter with her and simply held her hand. Once she had calmed down, she explained to Margie in a mixture of English and Zulu that she had just received news that her husband and son had been killed several nights before in an attack on her homestead near Henley's Dam, just above Edendale Valley where I had lived a few years before. It had taken days for her sister to get to a phone and tell her the horrible news. This call had come through at the woman's employer's house, much to the employer's irritation. After a short while, the employer had asked the woman to take her noise outside, as the crying was starting to annoy her. Margie had never had a good relationship with the woman next door, who constantly frowned on all the black people coming and going at Jacques and Margie's house, but this level of insensitivity took her breath away. As Margie relayed the story to me, I was stunned that the killings were still happening two years after the elections. Margie, for her part, had given the woman some money and offered to drive her to the bus stop in town once she had collected her things.

South Africa had taught me that death is a companion to life, that they go hand in hand. I was not hardened to the impact it had on those left behind, but the possibility of death was ever-present and therefore no stranger. Some in South Africa had taken that knowledge and assumed that it made life cheap, but others of us knew it made life both precious and fragile. After spending time back in Australia, I realised that the Australian lifestyle did not carry with it a knowledge of the presence of death. In her book, *Lost in Translation*, Eva Hoffman describes it well. She and her family migrated to Canada when she was a teenager after surviving the holocaust in Europe. She struggled to learn English until she realised that Canadians spoke only in 'high notes'; they lacked a 'base note'—something her childhood had taught her was a constant in life. The base note is the presence of suffering and death that counterbalances the joys of life, allowing for lows and highs, shadow and light. It was not until she understood that there was no base note—no lows—in the language in Canada that she could learn to speak it.

For me, South Africa had a base note and I had learnt to speak that language, so that when I returned to Australia the dialogue sounded somehow insubstantial. Perhaps countries, like individuals, experience a loss of naivety, a movement from childhood to adulthood, only as they recognise the existence of a base note. What is interesting about Australia is that we moved from being a harsh penal colony where transportation from England was equivalent to a death sentence, to become 'the lucky country'—and somehow we forgot the suffering, our often idyllic lifestyles drowning out those earlier memories. So when Margie and I heard the base note in that woman's wailing, we held our babies more tightly, the garden suddenly seemed greener and we went about finding ways to help.

While I was at Margie's house, a number of my old friends dropped by: Fiona, Tony and Felicity and Justin, who was now back in town. We also went out to an event on campus where I was able to catch up with many others. All in all, the week in 'Maritzburg was like a healing balm, leaving me feeling more like myself and back in my skin after all the recent stresses and strains. I realised that it was actually akin to coming home, a home which far too soon I would have to leave.

Back in Jo'burg, the floors were now done, giving the house a real facelift. I was less panicky about carrying water across the room. While our trip had not converted Dichaba into a baby who slept through, it had taken the edge off my exhaustion, allowing me to cope a bit better. So I settled back into life in Jo'burg with our full house and our many visitors, all the while missing the peace and connection I had felt in the green gardens of 'Maritzburg.

Since returning to South Africa, but particularly since Dichaba's birth, my relationship with Teboho had felt quite functional: building, shopping, child care, moving. He was busy with work during the week, sometimes staying on in the township when there was a need. On weekends, he seemed to be called off on one issue after another. When he was at home, he was upbeat and happy, loving our extended family setup and his role as the generous patriarch. However, I was finding when we were alone that the sullenness I had seen in Australia would sometimes return. The intimacy between us seemed to have dissipated—though whether this was due to the suspension of sexual intimacy after the birth or something else as well, I did not know. What I had noticed in most of the township families around us was that the married women seemed to find their companionship with other married women, while the men kept company with each other.

While I understood this peer dynamic from when I lived in Caluza among those who were yet to marry, I had assumed our marriage contract was similar to the one I had grown up with: the first level of intimacy is with your partner, followed by your children and then your friends and community. Our marriage had operated this way in 'Maritzburg and in Australia, but there seemed to be something about Teboho's return to the township where he had grown up that allowed him to switch the way he lived, perhaps even without his own knowledge.

In Sesotho, the word for wife is *Mosadi*, meaning literally, 'the one who stays'. It struck me that this was a good description for how I was feeling. I was staying still while he orbited around the home, around me, sometimes closer, sometimes further away, but always out of reach. He seemed to be finding his intimacy with his old childhood friends Beans, Solly, Daddy, Dennis and the others, perhaps needing less from our relationship as a result. I have no doubt that he felt very grounded by having me, his mother and the kids to come home to, but he seemed to need home a little less because he knew it was waiting there for him. I saw many other township men operating in a similar way.

My own observation of marriages in Australia had been so different. Watching my parents, I understood that their allegiance was to each other first, particularly on my father's part, as he clearly adored my mother, and that we as children came next. I believe this is what saw them through fifty-five years of marriage. Without ever articulating it, my own expectations were shaped by this. I had not considered what Teboho observed as a child—his mother a widow from his earliest memories and then in a reluctant marriage of convenience where she kept to her children and where his own presence was only just tolerated by his stepfather. What I hadn't anticipated was that when we were back on his home turf he would begin, perhaps unconsciously, to shift.

But it was not only Teboho who was holding back. I knew I was as well. His arriving so late for the birth had hurt me badly. For me, it was the ultimate example of him putting the needs of others above my own and I could not set aside the disappointment I felt.

This was compounded by the loneliness of the first few days after the birth when I needed him and he wasn't there. I had every intention of addressing this with him afterwards, but lacked the energy in those first few sleep-deprived weeks. With the words unspoken, the emotion festered away like a hidden sore.

I was also beginning to feel quite cut off, living in Randfontein. It was over an hour's drive from where other friends such as Barry and Rags were now living. The only person I felt a real connection with was Khumo. Ironically, she told me she was in a similar situation to my own. She had grown up in Soweto and was part of a large and connected family that was engaged at many levels in the life of Jo'burg. When she married and moved out to Mohlakeng, she also felt the kind of isolation I was suffering from. Many Mohlakeng locals rarely left the area, limiting their experiences and aspirations. Khumo felt cut off from family and friends with whom she had much deeper connections than with her neighbours and even church members in Mohlakeng. Moss, in his own way, was like Teboho—he responded to each and every community need, as ministers do. Khumo was constantly called on to share her house, her possessions and her finances with any and all who came to ask for help. While Khumo is a generous person, she knew her own limits better than I and was able to draw a line in the sand. However, I also saw that Moss and Khumo had an intimacy and a partnership that Teboho and I no longer possessed. I suspect this sustained Khumo to a certain degree, as did the growing closeness of our relationship.

The other person I had to lean on was Mama. Though I couldn't unburden to her in the same way I could to Khumo, she was a constant kindness in my life and our love for each other crossed over our language barriers. She had a way of being present without imposing herself on how I wanted to run my home or raise my children and I found her extraordinary in this regard. With this gentle acceptance of who I was, the daily sharing of household chores and child raising knitted our lives together and built a relationship that was both profound and long lasting.

Perhaps these two relationships created my own circle of intimacy from which I excluded Teboho, I'm not sure. Certainly, I felt cut off and a little resentful about the relocation of our lives so far from where I had a possibility of creating one of my own. I blamed our lack of intimacy, both emotional and sexual, on my exhaustion after many months of sleepless nights and the many other demands of motherhood. But the reality was that I was beginning to pull away, a little disillusioned with the dream.

When Dichaba was six months old, Mum and Dad came to stay with us for a month. We made this arrangement when we left Australia, thinking that by then Dichaba would be more active and interesting than if they had come out for the birth. While this seemed like a practical and logical arrangement, a few weeks before the birth, when I realised I needed my mother, she had tried everything but could not get a flight over because of the Christmas holidays.

So it was that they arrived in July to a very warm and loving welcome. We had no plans to travel around beyond a short trip to Blyde River Canyon, near Kruger National Park in the country's east, a province they were yet to visit. Both kids loved having three grandparents doting on them each day and I took the chance to catch up on some sleep, often grabbing an afternoon nap. This trip was also an opportunity for Mum and Dad to get to know Mama, as it was the first time that they had met. They found her as gracious and endearing as I did and despite limited communication in Mama's faltering English, a bond was created between the three of them that has been as long lasting as my own. Mum and Dad were delighted to get to know their first grandson, with Mum spending many hours on the floor playing with Dichaba when Mello was at preschool. Mello was still the apple of Dad's eye, and I also saw that he found her easier to relate to than a small baby. While he delighted in watching Dichaba play, he rarely got on the floor himself.

Halfway through their visit, we took our trip to Blyde River Canyon. We left on a Friday, driving Mum and Dad's hired car through to Lydenburg, where Teboho was planning to meet up with us on his way back from a field trip a few hours to the south. We arrived in Lydenburg at lunchtime, having agreed to meet Teboho at two o'clock at the tourist information centre in the main street. We took the kids for lunch at a nearby restaurant while we waited. By three o'clock, Teboho had not arrived and though I had tried to contact him, his phone was switched off. We filled in time by browsing through the art and craft shops on the main street. Mum told me much later that she couldn't believe how relaxed I was about him being late. Although I was indeed outwardly calm, I was still angry that he was making not only me wait, but also my parents, regardless of the reason. Just before five o'clock, Teboho breezed into town with stories of how he had been held up in a community meeting but I was only half listening to his explanation, more concerned with getting to the resort where we were staying over the weekend. We were still an hour and a half from where we needed to be and it would be getting dark soon.

After getting a little lost in the dark, we finally found our way to the resort and checked in, with a few strange looks from the clerks behind the desk, mentally querying the composition of our family group. The resort consisted of close to forty chalets spread out over a large parkland area. There were common facilities such as playgrounds, swimming pools, trampolines and barbecue areas that could be shared by all residents. We had booked a large three-bedroom chalet for four nights, though Teboho would be going back to Jo'burg early Monday morning.

On our first morning, we didn't rush to get going, allowing ourselves as much of a sleep-in as two small children would permit. Mello had taken Chaba through to Mum and Dad's bedroom as soon as she heard them wake. Not long after, I gave up trying to get back to sleep amidst all the chatting and giggling and joined them, leaving Teboho still in bed. After about half an hour of playing with the kids, I suggested breakfast and went through to the kitchen to start unpacking the box of groceries we had brought with us. As I headed down the corridor towards the kitchen, to my everlasting horror, I walked straight into a large male baboon. On seeing me, he stood up on his hind legs, as much in shock as in aggression, then simultaneously we both flung our arms into the air, screamed, turned and ran. I'm not sure who was more surprised by the encounter, me or the baboon, but we kept the kitchen door firmly locked from that moment onwards.

When we left the chalet just over an hour later, we saw what was most likely the same baboon go up to the stable kitchen door of the chalet opposite and fling himself at the top half in an attempt to gain entry and find food. This at least answered the question of how he had found his way through what I had thought was a bolted door—the bolt secured only the bottom half.

We spent the next few days exploring the area, seeing such wonders as Burke's Luck and visiting the small pioneer town of Pilgrim's Rest. We also went to a cheetah research and breeding centre near Kruger National Park. After driving around for a few hours, we made for the Vulture's Restaurant on the map we had received when we passed through the gates, all of us starving by now. I cannot describe the disappointment we felt as we rounded the corner, only to find it was literally a restaurant for vultures, the ground littered with rotting meat and carcasses. By this time, we were almost in tears for lack of food, so we headed straight back to the gate where we ate a late lunch of chocolate bars and chips.

The month with Mum and Dad flew by and it was soon time for them to leave. We had spent an idyllic time together and I felt that some of the stresses from the end of our stay in Australia had dissipated. Both Mum and Dad had bonded with Dichaba and I felt no criticism of the way I was parenting either child. We parted on a positive note, expressing the hope that we might be able to visit Australia the following year.

I had been at home for eight months now and it was clear that we could no longer afford for me not to work. We had finally saved enough to replace the water tower, but the kids' bathroom—the only operational one—was still untiled. We had no built-in cupboards, only a pine chest of drawers in each room; no garden, with only a dirt trail where the car drove in to break up the thatch grass; and absolutely no savings. Somewhat reluctantly I contacted an agency to enquire about looking for work.

With all its pains, I had adored being a stay-at-home mother. I hung on every new thing that my son learnt to do. Despite not sleeping, he was a gentle-natured, happy child who was always affectionate and quick to smile and I knew from the beginning that he was the love of my life. It was also clear that Mama felt the same way. Knowing she would be taking care of him was the only thing that allowed me to wrench myself away and go back to work. Still, I yearned for his heart-shaped face and almond brown eyes, the smile that seemed to reach from hairline to chin, his soft brown curls, the curve of his forehead and his kissable olive skin.

I went for just one interview and was immediately offered the job. It was with a small consultancy called Palmer Development Group, run by two brothers, Richard and Ian. Richard, who would be my boss, was the younger of the two and displayed all the playful risk-taking characteristics of a last born, with Ian the responsible and wise older brother. They employed only half a dozen consultants in each office—one in Jo'burg and the other in Cape Town—each person brilliant and an expert in his or her own field. They focused exclusively on public sector work, particularly on large scale water and sanitation projects, domestic energy, education and local government—all the elements of a national development program.

I was delighted to be offered a position there and they suggested an immediate start. In South Africa in 1996, returning to work part-time wasn't even a consideration; it was a full-time job and I gladly accepted it. There was just one thing I had to do before I could start, and that was to get Dichaba to sleep through the night.

I had heard about controlled crying but it was not part of an African approach to child raising, so we had not tried it up until this point. However, with only a few days to sort things out, I was willing to give it a go. After Dichaba's night time bath and feed—he was still breast fed at this point—we put him down for the night in his cot in our bedroom and left him. He howled for thirty minutes until I relented and put him in the bed next to me, but other than that, I did not pick him up again and did not feed him. He screamed for another forty-five minutes until finally falling asleep from sheer exhaustion. By this time my nerves were completely frayed and I felt as if my heart had been ripped from my chest—but he was asleep. Both Teboho and I made the most of it and went straight to sleep, ready to wake soon and repeat the process. When I did wake, it was not to the sounds of my baby crying, but only as the light crept in through the windows with the dawn. It was the first full night's sleep I'd had since I was seven months pregnant. I lay there and watched my child's chest rise and fall—he was still deeply asleep—the same movement echoing in Teboho's chest behind him, almost breath for breath. To my utter amazement, Dichaba has slept through the night ever since. As it turned out, it was only one night of torture in exchange for the reward of restorative, mind altering, blissful sleep.

And so it was that I turned up for work the following Monday, wide awake and eager for the next adventure to begin.

30

August 1996
Fast Forward

GOING BACK TO WORK WAS LIKE OPENING A DOOR ON A MUSTY ROOM. I FELT CONNECTED INTO A BROADER LIFE ONCE MORE, OUTSIDE OF MY HOME AND, IN PARTICULAR, OUTSIDE OF RANDFONTEIN. THE OFFICES WERE LOCATED IN A CONVERTED HOUSE IN THE NORTHERN SUBURB OF RANDBURG—EVEN THOUGH IT TOOK ME WELL OVER AN HOUR TO DRIVE THERE EACH MORNING, I FELT INVIGORATED. IT WAS ALSO REFRESHING TO FEEL NO JUDGMENT ABOUT MY LIFE CHOICES. THEY WERE INTERESTING TO MY NEW COLLEAGUES, BUT NOT A SOURCE OF REPULSION SUCH AS I HAD EXPERIENCED FOR THE LAST YEAR IN RANDFONTEIN. IN FACT, THE OFFICE WAS A MIX OF RACES, RELIGIONS AND SEXUAL ORIENTATIONS, SO I SEEMED TO FIT RIGHT IN.

I was also excited by the work that Palmer Development Group, or PDG as everyone called it in South Africa's love affair with acronyms, was doing around the country. By applying the minds of bright people to difficult social, infrastructure and financing problems, they were helping to create a country where services were available to everyone. It sat well with me ideologically and challenged me intellectually, as well as meeting my need for social interaction outside the small community in which I was living.

My first task, and the one for which Richard had employed me, was to project manage a solar energy study funded by the German government to the value of six million rands, working in collaboration with the South African Department of Minerals and Energy. It was a massive project of which the first phase—a two-year longitudinal field study—was about to begin. The test sites had been chosen and some local fieldworkers employed. The Germans were on their way in four weeks to take part in a week of fieldworker training, followed by a week in the field visiting the chosen communities, all of which I would be responsible for organising.

I did notice that Michael, my colleague who had been looking after the project before I arrived, heaved a considerable sigh of relief once he had finished the short handover session. Only later did I understand that, as an economist, field research was not really his cup of tea. At the time, I took that sigh to be an indication of the amount of work he was happily avoiding in the next month or two. Despite this, I plunged into the job, as is my way with all things I take on.

There was a joke at PDG that the probation period was known as 'sink or swim'—the Palmer brothers had the tendency to throw new recruits into the deep end. It was no different with me. In my first week, I met with the various people on the project team. Richard and I would work closely together on this project from the PDG side. Then there was Tony, our client in the Department, Paul the sociologist from one of our project partners, and Marlett who was an independent energy consultant (I didn't know such a profession existed prior to this project) and had worked for the Department for a number of years before heading out on her own. Karl, our German technical expert, would contribute scientific depth and research rigour to the project. And Colleen, who was introduced as a gender expert, was to train the team in investigating the implication of gender in our research. Each one was to become an important person in my life over the next two years of the project, but none more than Colleen who would become my friend and mentor for the next ten years.

The weeks prior to the German funders' visit were a flurry of activity. In the rush, I didn't have time to find out how to claim expenses, only how to rack them up. This led to the particularly embarrassing experience of having my credit card turned down when I was buying groceries, juggling my two small children and a full trolley. I went through to the office, unable to believe there wasn't some simple solution. The bank confirmed the supermarket's decision, suggesting that perhaps I should simply cut the card in half and call it a day. I made a mental note as I shuffled out of the shopping centre empty-handed, to speak to Richard first thing on Monday morning about reclaiming all my project expenses.

The week of the training workshop, I made the drive through to Pretoria early on the Monday morning. The young fieldworkers had arrived the night before and were staying at a budget hotel in the city which, according to Marlett, they thought was a palace compared to their own township family homes. It was not lost on me that the Germans were staying at a five star hotel across town. One of my tasks in the setup was to review a few of the nicer hotels in Pretoria and choose the one that most closely matched the Germans' requirements.

The five-day workshop was a combination of technical and sociological training. The fieldworkers and the project team needed to be able to understand the working of each type of solar cooker in the study, and be able to repair them if necessary. They would also interview the families who were testing the cookers, make their own observations and record information. Our German technical advisor, Kurt, was thorough and demanding but by the end of the week, we felt technically competent. Marlett and Paul did the sociological training, taking us through all the information we would need to make this an internationally valid piece of research.

The workshop also gave us a great opportunity to get to know all the fieldworkers. They varied in age from nineteen to twenty-eight and were from either the coloured or the black communities that we would be working with. We had found them through the local youth organisations, with tremendous competition for the positions as jobs were so scarce in these isolated communities. We had also been aware that the salaries they were to receive would most likely change the dynamics in their communities, in essence making them rich and powerful, not only as salaried employees but also as people having strong connections with national and international development agencies and government bodies. It was a heady experience and we wanted to keep a close eye on the fieldworkers during the first two years of the project. If we played our parts well, we hoped many of them would be able to use this job as a springboard to a career in development.

The fieldworkers spoke a mixture of English, Afrikaans and Setswana so between Marlett, who was Afrikaans speaking, Paul and myself, we hoped to be able to work with them effectively on a monthly basis. Our job was to visit each of the sites, collect the data from the fieldworkers, make our own observations and provide whatever support was needed. There were three sites that we were monitoring, each with household users and institutional users. For the duration of the first phase, households would rotate through four different household cookers and the schools would test the three larger industrial sized ones. The test sites were all in the northwest part of the country, which was largely desert and had the highest number of days of sunshine per year.

The first test site was in Vryberg in the North West province. We had twenty test households in the large urban township called Huhudi, just outside town. There were also two township schools in the study, one preschool and one primary school, both of which were participants in the government's feeding scheme. As well, there was a multiracial high school a few kilometres outside town that Richard had a long history of supporting; as a boarding school, it was ideal for the largest of the institutional cookers.

When we were dealing with schools, not only did the principals, government officials and teachers need to be on board with the project, but we also had to train the cooks in how to use the equipment and this was often where the greatest resistance was encountered. For the school, there were great financial savings to be made that meant funds could be invested elsewhere, but the cooks were being asked to change habits learnt over many years, as well as to overcome their scepticism that the stoves could actually work. Many schools employed local women as cooks to prepare food they were now receiving under the new government's feeding scheme.

The other two sites were in deep rural areas where the primary source of cooking fuel was wood collected from the surrounding veld, supplemented by the more expensive paraffin and coal. One site was just outside Kimberley, the home of diamond mining in South Africa. The nearest town to the site was Barkly West, about 30 kilometres to the northwest of the city, with the village we were targeting accessed off a loose dirt road that seemed to head off into nowhere. The only assurance that visitors were on the right track was a large sign explaining that a solar project was being undertaken in the area, sponsored by the Department of Minerals and Energy and the German Government.

Organising for the signs to be erected was one of the more painful parts of my first few weeks in the job. Sections of the road were no more than quicksand, as I learnt by trial and error on my first foray. At the end of almost a kilometre, it opened out into a large clearing that housed the quiet rural community. Many of its residents still used donkey carts to move around, living in simple houses made of mud and tin. The area was the site of the first diamond discovery in South Africa, and many of the village residents were prospectors or descendants of the original pioneers. Being in the village felt like stepping back a hundred years. The area was so intriguing that Marlett and I later used it as a site for a second piece of research on the emergence of small black mining companies.

The last site was by far my favourite and the most difficult to get to. It was located deep in the Northern Cape on the border with Namibia. We flew from Kimberley to Upington and then drove the two hours west to Pofadder, a quirky little desert town boasting the famous Pofadder Hotel where we spent many pleasurable nights during the course of the project. Pofadder can get hot, with temperatures in the low forties being commonplace. The heat tolerant residents of the town of Pofadder referred to our test site as 'the front stoep of hell'. Frankly, I wondered why we were testing solar cookers there as I felt sure it would be possible to fry an egg on your head if you stood in the sun for long enough.

The test site was at Onseepkans some 50 kilometres to the north of Pofadder, though we were also testing the institutional cookers at the mission school in Pofadder. Onseepkans is a border post into Namibia and a small farming community on the fertile banks of the Orange River. Essentially, the community supplied workers to the local farms. There was also a mission in Onseepkans, established by the same Catholic priest who ran the somewhat famous one in Pofadder. In Onseepkans, the coloured residents only spoke Afrikaans, so Marlett took the lead. I soon developed an Afrikaans vocabulary that related to food, cooking, wood collection and other daily chores. The journey to Onseepkans was a dry one, but over time I began to appreciate the enormous beauty of the mountain ranges, the stark, magical quiver trees and the breathtaking colours of the desert as we made our monthly pilgrimage.

The solar project itself had come about via a number of retired German inventors who for some reason were very interested in solar energy, though interestingly Germany isn't blessed with a great deal of sun. They invented a number of prototypes and pressured parliament to find avenues for commercial distribution, particularly in third world countries where deforestation is an enormous problem.

After discussions in parliament, funds were allocated through the Department for Technical Cooperation, or GTZ, an aid-type wing of the German government that sponsors projects in developing countries, particularly those than can be addressed by some form of German technology. The German government set up an agreement with the South African government, allowing the Department of Minerals and Energy to commission a research project to test the viability of solar cookers in South Africa. Given PDG had done a great deal of research in domestic energy, the Department contracted us to do the research.

It was this chain of events that saw me flying out to Kimberley with Kurt, our German technical consultant, Tony from the Department, three German donors and Marlett after only four weeks in the job, hoping like hell the signs were up in each of the sites when we arrived.

The plan was for me to do the first two days of the trip, flying back after visiting Barkly West, and for Michael, my colleague who had managed the project up until now, to handle the other two sites over the next three days. Richard had made this arrangement out of respect for the fact that I had a baby at home whom I had never left overnight before. My boss, thankfully, was a man who loved his family deeply and understood the need to balance work and home.

The night before we were due to fly out, Michael phoned to tell me that he had just arrived at the hospital with suspected encephalitis and wouldn't be able to replace me halfway through the trip. Though I was upset that I would now have to spend five days away from my little boy, I was also worried about my friend, as this could turn out to be very serious. What I didn't know was that, besides being a very talented economist and having a brilliant mind, Michael was also a bit of a hypochondriac. As it turned out, he did not have encephalitis but rather a bad case of sinusitis, a fact that no one in the office, especially me, would let him forget for years to come.

The trip began with check-in at 5.30 in the morning at Jo'burg airport, an auspicious moment I nearly missed, what with an hour and a half's drive from Randfontein and getting lost trying to find the long-term parking turn-off. As I raced around the corner to the departure gate a few minutes before boarding closed, there stood an anxious Marlett and Kurt, plotting a plan B in case I missed the only flight to Kimberley that day.

We arrived after a short flight, gazing like all Kimberley's visitors into 'the Big Hole'—the deepest open mining pit currently on the earth's surface, so we were told. It was only a short drive from the airport to Barkly West and when we reached the turn-off to the village, there in all its glory was the solar cooker sign. The Germans were so delighted that they insisted we all pile out of the kombi and take a photo. We were soon back on the dirt road, Marlett offering to manoeuvre the kombi along its treacherous length. But before we had gone too far, we spotted Cecil, one of the fieldworkers, waiting for us under a tree. He was eagerly welcomed into the front of the van where he skilfully navigated us through the deep sand drifts.

When we first arrived at the village, we went directly to the house of the headman and his wife. The headman was not at home, as he owned a small trucking business and was often on the road, but his wife and grown sons were and they welcomed us into the cool of their living room. This was to become our routine on every visit—we would announce our arrival and be given permission to work in the village. Cecil mentioned that the other fieldworkers would meet us here shortly, no doubt having already heard about our arrival on the grapevine. True to his word, just as a tray of cool drinks was being placed before us, there was a timid '*ko ko*' coming from the doorway. The other two fieldworkers joined us in the now crowded room, standing awkwardly pressed next to the wall. I suggested to the Germans that we drink up and get going, before thanking our hosts for their hospitality and 'asking for the way'.

Outside, the heat was already bearing down though it was still early. We asked Cecil if the container had arrived; he nodded and began to lead us off in the direction of the school. As we left the compound, I noticed a public phone in the yard. I was just thinking that being headman has its perks when Cecil caught my eye and explained that people would come to the house day and night with their problems and requests for help, so the headman had the public phone installed in an effort to allow people an avenue to sort out their problems direct.

At the school, we were greeted warmly by the principal and students, all eager to see what was inside the container that had dramatically appeared a few days before. I had no idea how a truck bearing such a weight would have made it down the dirt road to the village, but before I could ask Cecil and the others about it, the crowd of people erupted as the container was opened and the first cooker was brought out. A large shiny dish made of interlocking reflective panels that spread out like a dancer's fan—the cooker that most reminded me of a spaceship—was being placed delicately on the ground. It was propped up on a steel frame which extended into the middle of the contraption so that a pot could be placed into the centre. Though it was very light, it was so large that it took two people to move it safely.

The next cooker to emerge was a box with a perspex lid and three reflective panels that spread out like wings from three sides of the box. With this cooker, the pot was placed lidless inside the box with its reflective internal panels directing light into its centre. Once closed, the perspex lid of the box also became the lid of the pot itself.

The third cooker was the simplest, the cheapest and the only South African cooker to be included in the study. Richard had given me one of these to take home on the day I joined and I had been doing a field test of my own with Mama, to see if she would cook with it in preference to the stove inside the house. This cooker was simply a black plastic trapezium-shaped box with reflective panelling stapled inside and a piece of perspex that slapped down on top at a forty-five degree angle. It was small, light and easy to lift and store and came with two black pots, one large and one medium-sized, that could be placed inside the cooker.

Soon the container had been completely emptied and an array of strange looking contraptions filled the school yard with over a hundred curious school children dying to handle them but instead shyly standing back. The noise of the school children had soon drawn the neighbours to the school as well and before long the yard was full, with half the community joining the festivities. It took the principal and Cecil almost half an hour to sort people into test families and others, so that the cookers could be properly assigned.

From there, we split up so that each member of the team went home with a family and a cooker, ticked off against the schedule that Kurt had diligently drawn up weeks before.

I was assigned to help a family that lived on the far side of the village, allocated the heaviest cooker, the box with the wings. As I waited to be introduced, a thin shy woman in her forties stepped forward once her name was called. Unlike all the others gathered there, she was alone. The community spoke a mixture of Afrikaans and Sesotho, but from her features and her darker skin, I took a punt that she was Sotho speaking and greeted her accordingly. She responded in kind and we began to find out a little about each other as we lugged the cooker away, taking almost twenty minutes to reach her home. She lived right on the edge of the village, as if shunned by it. I found out she was a widow with two school-aged children. Her husband had died in a work accident some years before and she struggled to make ends meet. Other families employed her to fetch wood and collect water, with her children helping after they returned from school. She also took in a little washing, but I had the feeling that it was all dependent on the kindness of neighbours and their own ability to pay for such chores to be done.

Those families with even the most modest means bought paraffin or coal from the store rather than spending up to six hours a day searching for wood in the increasingly barren surrounds. And while no family in the village had a washing machine, there seemed to be an abundance of unemployed young women who earned their keep in the family home by washing and cleaning. I understood why Cecil had included this family in the study, as any saving they could make in time or money might mean more food in the pot. I also knew that I could justify giving her food to cook as part of the field study without offending her, as we wanted families to test the cookers with different staple meals. With this in mind, I excused myself and went to the community store, explaining that the cooker came with supplies which I had forgotten to pick up. In all my visits, I made sure to spend time with this family, always bringing extra food, but in the two years of the project, little changed for them. I watched the children continue to go to school without shoes and in uniforms that were too small.

We returned to Kimberley just before dark and headed to the Holiday Inn. The city was full, but it was only when we reached reception that I realised why. We had arrived in Kimberley in the middle of an international rugby tour and all the faithful had arrived for the match to be played at the local stadium. After sharing this piece of information, the young man at reception went on to tell me that they had unfortunately given our rooms away, as they were unsure whether we were coming and had other visitors begging for rooms. I was irate as it was only seven o'clock and I had an international delegation that was now without accommodation. Realising his mistake, he promised to phone around but couldn't promise anything.

After twenty awkward minutes in reception, he called me back to the desk to inform me he had found a new guesthouse that was willing to take us in, given that everything else was full. When we arrived at the guesthouse a short distance away, I quickly realised that it was not a guesthouse, but the home of a large family who had sent their children off to the relatives and given us all the spare bedrooms in the house. I didn't know whether to be grateful for the beds or angry that some family friend of the receptionist was charging each of us hotel rates for sleeping in their children's bedrooms. Despite being offered a home-cooked meal by our hosts, we declined and made our way to what we had been told was one of the few decent restaurants in Kimberley. It was to become our regular haunt on our monthly trips to the city.

Sitting in the restaurant that night, I couldn't help but be struck by the contrast between the elegant surroundings in which I now sat and the poverty I had seen during the day. While I had lived and worked in both towns and townships for many years, I sometimes found the transition from township to town difficult. Working on this kind of project meant we didn't only encounter people in community meetings, in the schools and halls. It was a far more intimate exchange when we entered people's homes, talked to them about what they ate, how they prepared it, how they managed to meet their basic daily needs. Knowing what it took for the families to prepare even a simple meal, then to later sit down in an expensive restaurant and dine with our funders, discussing the technicalities of the project design and management, made the food stick in my throat.

Early the next morning, we were up and off to the airport for the flight to Upington. After many hours of travelling, we finally arrived at the Pofadder Hotel, already weary though it was not yet lunchtime. Because we were on a schedule, we dropped off our bags, grabbed a packed lunch and began the drive to the Namibian border and our next test site of Onseepkans. The scenery became more mountainous as we approached the border and after almost 50 kilometres of hot flat road, we were relieved to enter the oasis of green that surrounded the Orange River. We turned left just before the border post and headed west towards the village, hugging the river's edge, passing a number of farms and an old derelict shop on the way. Marlett told me she had plans to buy the shop and convert it into a house where she would come and spend the winter. I soon realised that she was only half joking, easy as it was to fall in love with this remote, enchanted place.

Our fieldworkers, Doreen, Nola and Ezekiel, were to meet us at the Mission in the afternoon. We had considered agreeing on a particular time, but knowing the distance we had to travel and the concepts of time in deep rural areas, we simply agreed on the afternoon. We also knew that we would be the only hire car driving into the village that day and that the fieldworkers would be alerted to our presence within minutes and would make their way across to the Mission. Who needed mobile phones really?

As we approached the village, I saw that the houses were made of what seemed to be reeds rather than the wattle and daub I was used to. Marlett explained to us that many of the homes were built this way to allow the breeze to cool the house; even in winter, Onseepkans reached temperatures typical of a European summer. We threaded our way through the village until we saw the Mission just ahead. Pulling into the courtyard, we found the priest already waiting. The Mission was multipurpose in the community and we were planning to place an institutional sized cooker in their school. I heaved an enormous sigh of relief when I saw that the large container full of solar cookers had arrived safely and was now tucked away against the eastern wall of the courtyard. We made our greetings and introduced our international guests. The priest was delighted to be taking part in a project such as this and while interest from the outside world was not as uncommon as you might think, this project had potential to save the community time and money if it could work, rather than simply providing data for policy makers in the nation's capital.

Not long after our arrival, our three fieldworkers entered the Mission compound and made their way over to the container. The priest had been given the keys when the container arrived and we had just opened it and were peering inside when they appeared. There were twenty-five solar cookers for households, five of those being spares in case of damage and five more to be tested at the school here and at the Mission in Pofadder. Our plan was to help with the distribution of the cookers to the families and then to put the larger cookers in the schools. Kurt was on hand to ensure everything was in good working order. We spent the rest of the afternoon going from home to home, speaking with families as one of the fieldworkers explained how to use the cookers. Families appeared to be cautious though curious enough to agree to participate. We set up each cooker with a pot full of water before moving to the next home, promising to come back once the water was boiling. Marlett and Tony from the Department were kept busy translating the questions of the Germans to the families we visited, particularly the women who for the most part were taking custody of the cookers.

I hit the wall at about four o'clock, having been up well before dawn two mornings in a row, but it wasn't until dark that we finally climbed into the kombi and made the drive back to the hotel. Despite desperately wanting to go straight to bed, protocol insisted that we once more have dinner with our guests before calling it a night. I was also aching for home and my baby, who was still breastfeeding morning and night. Many times in the last few weeks, I had flown through the door at the end of a long day and swooped him up for a feed, relieving the pain of the last few hours. Without him now, there was nothing for it but to jump in the shower, express the milk away and change for dinner.

The Pofadder Hotel was run by a husband and wife team, though it was Mrs Pofadder, as Marlett and I called her, who dealt with the guests. She owned two pets that she seemed more inclined to introduce than her husband. Going with her wherever she went was her small white poodle that Marlett and I would have liked to boot into the hotel pool after its first attempt to snap at our ankles. Her other pet, one more to our liking, was a colourful parrot who had the auspicious name of Vicegrip. He spent most of his time in the office on his perch, squawking happily at all passers by.

We shared a fine meal at Mrs Pofadder's table before being introduced to Hendrick the barman, who kept our group supplied with one nightcap after another. As a non-drinker, I struggled to keep up with the Germans, all seemingly well-practised after dinner drinkers. But it was Marlett who was the surprise packet. She later told me that after a bout of alcohol poisoning at university, she seemed immune to the stuff and could drink any man under the table, a talent sure to impress and infuriate in patriarchal South Africa. Knowing the local side was well represented, I made my excuses and snuck off to bed.

We spent the next morning at the Mission in Pofadder, setting up the institutional cooker there with Doreen's help. She had come back with us the previous night from Onseepkans and stayed the night at the Pofadder Hotel with the team. In all her twenty-four years, she had never had money or cause to stay at the hotel. We left Doreen at the Mission, telling her that Marlett and I would be back in four weeks to see how things were going, before making the long drive to the last site in Vryberg in the North West Province. I drove for most of the way, occasionally splitting the driving with Marlett, hurrying our visitors back into the kombi whenever we made a pit stop. I was anxious to get to Vryberg—the sooner we finished there, the sooner I could get home. So obvious was my desire for speed that Kurt and Marlett gave me the nickname of 'fast forward' on that trip, one that stuck for the duration of the project.

The North West Province has a completely different feel to the deserts of the far Northern Cape. Gone were the dramatic ochres, mountain peaks and lonely trees. The North West, where many of my own relatives lived, was a flat landscape dotted with gum trees and acacias over a sea of ruddy shrubs and grass. The reds and oranges of the desert were replaced by pale green and dusty brown.

Tiger Kloof school was on the road into town and it was with a great sense of relief that we pulled into the driveway after many hours of monotonous driving. Having announced ourselves at the office, we were taken to the principal's house for tea.

Like many fine schools in South Africa, Tiger Kloof was originally a mission school set up by the London Missionary Society in 1904. It boasted beautiful stone buildings, a chapel, workshops, boarding houses, classrooms and stables. In the 1930s and 1940s, it was educating 600 to 700 Setswana speaking students and student teachers, including Seretse Khama, the first President of Botswana, Ketumile Masire, its current president, Ruth Mompati, now the leader of the ANC in the province, as well as many other leading politicians and businesspeople in Southern Africa. Back then, Tiger Kloof not only produced black intellectuals but also had a trade program producing craftsmen of such high calibre that their student efforts were funding their own fees and making a profit for the school.

Then in 1954, under the jurisdiction of the Bantu Education Act that limited the opportunities of study for black students beyond those subjects that would prepare them to be 'hewers of wood and drawers of water', Tiger Kloof was closed and sold for a fraction of its worth to the new apartheid government. It was run as a government school for a few years, with a dramatically diminished curriculum, but was finally closed under the Group Areas Act as the farm was declared a white area on which no black person could reside. Verwoerd, the President at the time, appeared to so hate what Tiger Kloof stood for that he ordered it razed to the ground. However, after only one building was destroyed, the property was sold to the Dutch Reformed Church where it briefly became a holiday camp for boys.

In 1988, the property was declared a national monument and given the costs of its upkeep under these new standards, it was once more sold. In 1995, Tiger Kloof was finally reopened as a school, with the help of the Anglo American and De Beers Chairman's Fund, the Independent Development Trust, the Open Society, the Genesis and Solon Foundations and a number of local Vryburg businessmen and alumni.

The reopening of the school was a lavish affair, attended by President Masire of Botswana, Ruth Mompati, Popo Molefe, the Premier of the North West, Desmond Tutu, whose mother was once a student there and three thousand others, including the local white community from Vryburg. David Matthews, the new principal and my boss Richard's dear friend, had been the principal of the famous Maru a Pula school outside Gaborone in Botswana. This school is one of the most remarkable in Southern Africa and has its own proud history producing graduates who go on to attend the top universities in the US and UK. David hoped to restore Tiger Kloof's heritage of excellence and add to the already impressive list of 'old tigers'. But David also saw that Tiger Kloof needed to respond to the current market conditions and sought to prepare pupils for a variety of careers in the trades, hospitality and catering as well as professional careers. It was the hospitality focus that led David to be involved with our project.

This astonishing history was explained to us by David as we toured the grounds, the stone buildings as impressive as any I had seen in the top private schools. What was so extraordinary was that most travellers would simply have driven past, longing for the comforts of even a small town such as Vryburg after hours of nothingness on the road. What other stories lay hidden in remote parts of the country, if only one would stop and listen?

We ended our tour in the large kitchens of Tiger Kloof. Near the side door, the now familiar container stood, ready to be opened and its contents examined. The size of the kitchens gave us a unique opportunity to test the monster of all cookers, so large it needed to be fitted into the wall. The solar panels were positioned on the outside of the building and the cooking surfaces inside. It was also the only cooker that could store energy, allowing the cooker to work at night and on a cloudy day. A team of students had been briefed about the installation and were anxiously waiting outside the container, ready for a first glimpse.

We had spent a few hours at the school when the fading light reminded us that we still needed to head into town and check into the local hotel. We would return in the morning to train the catering staff and students on the use of each of the cookers, before heading to the township to meet the families there.

Huhudi was less exotic than the two other sites, being more akin to the urban townships I had been working and living in for many years now. Hearing the familiar rolling tones of Setswana in contrast to the predominance of Afrikaans spoken in the other locations, I was glad to be able to communicate once again. Veronica was one of our fieldworkers and as a well known youth leader in the township, she was able to open many doors for the project. As in each of the other locations, the fieldworkers' own families were often part of the study; in Huhudi we took the first solar cooker to Veronica's mother's home. Once that was delivered, we began the slow process of visiting as many families as we could to distribute cookers before dusk sent us once more back to the hotel.

As we were dropping Veronica back home on our way out, she mentioned that she believed there were relatives of mine living in Huhudi and if we had time, we would pop in on them tomorrow before we left for Jo'burg. I never ceased to be amazed at the networks that operated in black South Africa. They were the first questions you asked when you met someone: 'Where are you from? Do you know such and such a family?' In the townships, no one had an interest in what you did for a living, only in who you were in relationship to others. There is a word often used in South Africa that describes this: '*ubuntu*'. It means that we are only human through other human beings, and can only express our humanity through our relationships and dealings with others. In isolation, we cannot be truly human. Upon hearing that I had relatives in this community, I knew it would change the way I was viewed, giving me an entry and a belonging that the others in the project team would not be able to achieve.

Sadly, in a few years time, I would join the community to mourn the deaths of Veronica and four other youth leaders, killed in a car accident when they were on their way to a youth summit in Mafikeng. I would sit with Veronica's family in the church and when it was time, stand before those assembled and, in Setswana, tell of all her achievements as a fieldworker and youth leader, passing on our condolences to family and community alike.

We delivered the remainder of the cookers to the families, unaware of future events and the cloud they would cast over the project team. As they entered each home, our funders asked their now well-oiled questions about cooking, fuel choices and household arrangements. We finished with the last family at midday and, with tremendous gratitude on my part, loaded up the kombi and began the four-hour drive back to Jo'burg. At the time, I didn't fully appreciate the experiences this project would afford, the places I would now regularly visit and soon come to love deeply. On this trip, rushing through it as I was, I caught only a glimpse of what was to come.

Coming home after five long days on the road was exquisite relief. I leapt straight from the car to where Mama was waiting by the door with Dichaba in her arms. I held him close, smelling his hair and neck in deep thirsty draughts. I then heard a long squeal from inside the house that sounded like an approaching siren. Mello burst through the doors and wrapped herself around my legs. It was so very good to be home.

That night, when Teboho was back from work, we sat around the dining room table for a rowdy family dinner and I recounted stories of my trip and all the wonders I had seen.

31

1997
CHOICE AND COMPROMISE

THE FIRST MONTHS IN MY NEW JOB WERE INTENSE AND CONSUMING AND, DESPITE THAT FIRST WEEK AWAY, I WAS ENJOYING THE STIMULATION. AS WITH EVERYTHING I DID, I THREW MYSELF INTO THIS NEW CHALLENGE WITH VIGOUR, WANTING TO SUCCEED, NEEDING TO PROVE MYSELF BACK IN THE WORKPLACE. BUT I WAS ALSO BEING FED BY THE FRIENDSHIPS WITH MY NEW COLLEAGUES, ESPECIALLY MARLETT WITH WHOM I SPENT UNTOLD HOURS DURING OUR MANY FIELD TRIPS AND PROJECT MEETINGS, AND LATER JEREMY, WHO WORKED IN THE OFFICE NEXT TO MINE. THOUGH JEREMY AND I NEVER WORKED ON A PROJECT TOGETHER, HE WAS A CONFIDANTE AND A SOUNDING BOARD FOR ANY SUBJECT I BROUGHT THROUGH HIS DOOR. JEREMY, AS A GAY MAN, UNDERSTOOD THE DYNAMICS OF DIFFERENCE, STILL THE UNOFFICIAL SPORT OF OUR CHANGING NATION. WE OFTEN FOUND OURSELVES EXCHANGING HORROR STORIES AND THE NAMES OF PLACES WHERE YOU COULD GO WITHOUT FEAR OF HARASSMENT.

It was still surprisingly difficult to travel around the country on holiday without feeling watched or under threat. Despite a growing understanding of Afrikaans through my work, I remained reluctant to learn the language properly as I did not wish to know what was being said to me when people spat and swore at me in Randfontein.

I remember one occasion where I was with Moss and his son Boggie. We had gone to the roadhouse in town early one evening to fetch takeaway for both our families. As the tirade began, Moss urged me to respond so that they would hear that I was a foreigner.

'They are angry because they think you are betraying the race with a black man', Moss explained. 'If they hear your accent, they will just think you're a bleeding heart foreigner who doesn't know any better', he said with a chuckle.

Though Moss refused to be intimidated, I felt that crowd pressing in, my fear rendering me unable to speak. At these times, I was grateful for my friendship with Marlett for without her, I would surely have written off all Afrikaaners as a cruel and heartless people.

Though Jeremy's experiences and mine were different, he understood the everpresent threat of violence and intimidation that still wafted around the country like a bad smell. He understood the habit of constant vigilance. But he also understood the need to laugh at the situation and make light of it so that we should not accept it as the norm.

My life felt richer now that it was no longer confined to the far West Rand. My experiences and relationships in the township were balanced by my friendships at work. At home Chaba, as everyone now called him, was becoming a little boy. His gentle, playful personality blossomed like wildflowers on the roadside. Despite the conflicts of the world around him, he had a generosity of spirit that radiates only from those who feel completely loved and safe. Mello had started pre-primary at a nearby school in Greenhills and was growing wings. The school was newly integrated but the teaching staff were surprisingly committed to creating an open environment, even in the suburbs of Randfontein.

On weekends, we all laboured together to make a garden, Teboho and I first laying a large lawn on which the kids could play. Slowly I planted one garden bed after another around the house, then a large vegetable garden which produced the tastiest food to pass across our table. I made use of our extended household with Joseph, Mello's eldest brother and many others who came to stay, working long hours digging up and replacing the barren topsoil. Within a year, the garden had become a place of rest as well as toil, and a place to play when we finally bought a swing set for the kids, all of it making the house more of a home.

To the world around us, we must have appeared to be a happy family: two beautiful children, a house full of family and friends, Teboho and I both with good jobs and the opportunity to travel. Surely there were those who envied us our lives together. Yet there remained an emptiness that rattled round our house like pebbles in a tin. Gone was the treasured closeness of our years together in 'Maritzburg, where we spoke of all things, big and small; where we loved and cared for and protected each other. Our interactions now were merely functional, pragmatic: what, where, when, how, who—never why. It was too easy to engage with the many other people who lived with us—children, mothers, brothers, nieces, nephews, friends—and both Teboho and I rose to the occasion, seldom withdrawn or moody in front of others.

Teboho was an adoring father, playing, joking, tickling, and lavishing them both with affection and love. While he could be a disciplinarian when the situation required, his return from work each day triggered laughter and joy in both our children. I sometimes wondered, however, whether Chaba in particular became the recipient of the tenderness that we could have been giving to each other. Sex between us, once tender and frequent, was now mechanical and irregular, at times little more than a marital obligation. I felt that what we once had was slipping away, like water dripping from a broken tap, one missed opportunity at a time, becoming a memory of what once was.

While the exchange between us that morning in Tasmania could quickly have grown into something that destroyed us, it did not—it blunted our relationship but did not break it. I suspect I unknowingly called upon my mother's legacy to get past this wounding: accommodate, adjust, accept. While I was rarely this way in the world, I had unconsciously learnt to be this way in my relationships with men. And yet, there was never a repeat of the cruelty he had dished out to me that day. Never again did he hurt me so unashamedly, blatantly throwing another woman in my face. As soon as we left Tasmania, he once more became the husband I knew. Sometimes, it was as if it was someone else's story, not my own. I wonder if he put it aside himself, forgetting, denying that it had ever happened.

And yet, I now knew that he was capable of betrayal and one day soon I would find out, to my complete surprise, that I was too.

You could reason that we were no longer close, that I suspected he was unfaithful and wanted to settle the score. You could say that I was lonely, that Teboho wasn't paying me enough attention and if he had, it never would have happened.

You could say all of these things and yet none of them would adequately explain why one day, a man I knew through work flirted with me yet again and I flirted back. It simply felt good to do it. Though I felt no strong obligation of fidelity towards Teboho given what had happened in Tasmania and possibly since, in reality I wasn't thinking about anyone else—about revenge, about what it could do to my marriage, my own sense of honour, my faith. I wasn't thinking.

After months of being on a slow boil—a word, a look, a gesture, yet nothing returned to which he could attach a promise of more—I took a single step across the line that kept it a simple flirtation, fun, harmless. I decided to go down this road with him, to follow him back to his apartment, to kiss, to caress, to reciprocate. I put my mind on hold and found a momentary freedom on the other side of that line, one I was raised not to cross—by my family, by the church, by society. Yet I didn't flinch, nor did I find myself wracked with guilt.

In many ways, I had been in a state of inaction in my marriage for years, letting things go, overcompensating for our differences by embracing his life, his culture, his community. This step felt like a movement in the opposite direction, a step back towards myself. I also found that on the other side of the line, I could be more expressive and adventurous than ever before, feeling present not only in the decision to be with this man but to be doing something that was for me alone—not husband, not family, not community.

Each encounter with him was complete in itself; there was no promise of a future together, no questioning what it meant for us. It was all it needed to be in that moment, all I needed. I had no words for these feelings at the time, but understood that my lack of guilt suggested something beyond a simple affair was happening. Had I allowed myself to remember my own fear of the torturer's hands, the possibility of pain to come, I would not have put Teboho through it. And knowing what I know now, I would never choose to go down that path again. But this was one time when I was not thinking about him, about his pain, his wounds; I was thinking only of my own life, attempting to still my own restlessness.

Over the few months of our affair this man, who was in many ways more friend than lover, began to challenge me about where I was in my life that I would even consider an affair. He admitted that in all the months of flirtation, he had felt sure I would not reciprocate and so flirted unashamedly. By taking things further, and essentially calling his bluff, I had caught him off guard. After the initial thrill of intimacy, he could not help but wonder why I was doing something so out of character. He encouraged me to think about what it was that I really wanted, rather than what others expected of me.

'It seems to me that you spend your weekends attending weddings and funerals of people you hardly know, just to do the right thing by the family. What would you do on the weekend to relax, if it was completely up to you?' he asked me one day.

'Do you know I've never actually thought about that?' I replied, astonished.

'Never?'

'No. There are things on and we are expected to go. I usually enjoy it, but sometimes work is so draining that I wish I could have stayed at home.'

'You should try it next weekend. Just once, do whatever it is that would make you happy.'

As strange as it sounds, I was so used to communal living that I had never taken a weekend to do only what pleased me. Of course, I had spent time gardening and the like which brought me great pleasure, but I had always done what was expected of me as a *makoti*, a bride, a *mosadi*, a wife. As I began to think through how I would like to spend my time, I longed for friends, movies, restaurants, music, things we did a little of but only within the confines of the conservative West Rand, amid stares and derision from those white people around us.

I longed to go to places where I would not stand out, places where change was happening faster. I knew Barry and Rags lived in a more integrated part of Jo'burg with their son and their adopted black daughter. I knew they lived a vibrant life, full of the things that suddenly seemed important. Initially when I thought of the things I wanted to do, I felt the need to do them without Teboho, to strike out on my own for a time. But I also knew that the desire to be alone was a temporary one. The more I sat with this, the more I knew that I wanted to find a way to be happy with my family intact. I wasn't ready to break our family apart, of that I was sure. As this knowledge emerged, I knew it was time for the affair to end. I also knew that this was not a pattern I wished to repeat, then or since. While my feelings for this man did not disappear—in fact, I felt more for him as he patiently helped me work through the issues—the decision was made to end it. I also made another decision at that time—I wanted to talk to Teboho about moving away from the township.

'Can we talk?' These three small words echoed around our bedroom.

'About what?' Teboho replied cautiously.

'I want us to think about moving. As much as I love this house, I'm finding it increasingly difficult to live here.'

Teboho did not respond, but looked off through the window into the garden. I took a breath and continued on.

'I feel very cut off from friends, living so far out. No one comes to visit. It takes forever to get to friends. Even getting to work and back is two and a half hours a day.' I let these reasons fall and resonate like a broken string of pearls.

After a long silence, Teboho finally spoke: 'But this was our dream, to build a home here, to build a life as part of this community. I feel like you're breaking a promise you made to me'.

His words hung in the air, the truth acting like helium, suspending them.

'That's true, this was our dream. I've tried to live this way, but I can't.'

'But you have friends here. What about Moss and Khumo? What about Beans, Dennis, Daddy, Solly and all the others from church? They are all your friends.'

'Khumo is my friend, and Moss. But the others are your friends. And most of the people from church need our help in some way. They're not *friends*. There's a difference. I need something more.'

'What are you saying?' he said, a thread of fear in his voice.

'I'm saying that I want us to move closer to Jo'burg. I want some middle ground if this life is going to work for both of us.'

Silence filled the room once more, making the sound of my breathing seem like an intrusion. Finally, in a whisper he said, 'This is the life I want. It's here that I was born and it's where I belong. I don't want to leave'.

I almost took it all back. Despite everything, I still flinched at the thought of hurting him, of making his life harder than it had already been. I knew that the only time he had not lived here, apart from our brief stint in Australia, was when he had gone away to study in 'Maritzburg. I knew it was his home.

'I don't want to make you unhappy. I really don't. But I'm not sure I can be happy here. It feels like it costs me so much to hang in. I know it's not what we planned, but I just don't think I can do it. I'm sorry.'

He slowly got to his feet, leaving me sitting on the edge of our bed. 'Let me think about it', he said, as he moved quietly out of the room.

After several weeks of deliberation, Teboho agreed to move. He felt that if it was no more than a thirty minute drive to the township, he could make a compromise and, anxious to move, I agreed. I will always be grateful to him for this decision. It wasn't what he wanted, but he did it because he loved me. After all we'd been through, after all the distance of the last few years, he still loved me and was willing to give up what he wanted to make me happy. It was no small thing.

We began looking at properties a few weeks later. While the thought of moving closer had me on a high, I soon realised that a thirty minute radius still had us in the West Rand, still with potentially conservative neighbours, still one of the few black families in the area. Despite this, I deeply appreciated Teboho's willingness to compromise and was determined to find a place that would meet our needs.

We ultimately found a house five minutes away from Westgate, the shopping mall where I had taken Chaba when he was only a few weeks old. The area is perched on the edge of a long escarpment that cuts a line from Krugersdorp through to the Jo'burg ring road, a six-lane concrete highway that circles the city, dividing the inner suburbs from the urban sprawl beyond.

The views from the edge of the escarpment were breathtaking and we managed to find a three-bedroom thatched house on the edge of a swell of hills, set just back from the escarpment itself. The house had two bedrooms, a bathroom, kitchen, dining room and lounge room downstairs and the main bedroom, ensuite and study set inside a large attic area. The upstairs walls were less than waist height, meaning that most of the walls were made up of the sloping thatch of the roof, giving the rooms the smell of the open veld. Behind the house, the land sloped up sharply before flattening out at the very top, from where one could catch panoramic views of the northern suburbs if you were willing to make the climb. In front of the house was a paved courtyard into which the dark creosol beams that supported the thatched roof pierced the ground like spears. In between the beams were a series of planters that were overflowing with annuals, cheering the surroundings like vases of fresh cut flowers. Having braved the steep driveway and the stairs up to the house, arriving in the courtyard was akin to entering a sanctuary. After one visit to the house, I knew this was the fresh start we were looking for.

We put our old house on the market, enrolled Mello in the local primary school and within a few months, were packing up the swing set and all our memories on our way to a new home.

Mama moved with us as she was so much a part of the family that there was never of question of her staying behind in Mohlakeng. However, given we were no longer as accessible as before, visitors only stayed for a short time. The exception was Joseph who would often spend university holidays with us and so stay a little longer. Mama had one of the bedrooms downstairs and the kids shared the other. As I had done for Mello's room at the old house, I painted a mural around the new bedroom, this time using a circus theme with the stripes of the big tent and carousel ponies. Though the kids shared the room during the day, Chaba slept cuddled up next to Mama most nights, taking his turn for a time as each grandchild had done before him.

Soon we were settled down into a new rhythm with Chaba, now two and keen to mimic his big sister, going to a local nursery school a few mornings a week. Mello was happy at her new primary school, quickly making friends in our street and joining a weekly ballet class at the dance school across the road. Teboho and I both had a much shorter commute to work, meaning we left later and got home sooner. And while I was sure the whole neighbourhood was talking about the new family that had just moved in, mixed marriages still being so rare, there was no open hostility and for that I was grateful.

One of the biggest changes to our family was that we now saw little of my favourite niece Katie. Soon, however, we were to have a new house guest in the form of her older sister Tashia. Tashia and Nooi, Caleb's two eldest daughters, were close friends and confidantes, both quiet and respectful in the presence of adults, yet they ruled the house with an iron fist when their parents were not at home, organising the younger siblings and the array of visiting cousins in the house at any given time. Since the girls reached puberty, they had been regularly lectured by Caleb and Ousi on the risks of pregnancy and the implications that a moment's carelessness could have on their lives.

The number of teenage pregnancies in most South African townships is very high. One reason for this is the lack of recreational options for young people. Traditionally, boys start playing soccer in the streets long before they are old enough to play in an official team. While the girls can join netball teams, the sport cannot match the popularity of soccer. But by far the most popular pastime in the townships is to go walking the streets with a group of friends and see who you meet along the way. Given that most families in the township don't own a car, you are almost guaranteed to meet up with your friends as they, too, have nowhere else to go. It becomes more difficult to contain when the strolling around also happens after dark, which is the usual practice for meeting up with a boyfriend or girlfriend. Parents do not welcome their daughters bringing boys to the house, as it's seen as disrespectful to them, and this drives relationships out of the home and into the night.

The second reason was surprising to me when it was first explained, in the light of the conservative stance on teenage girls and boyfriends. Given the importance of children in an African marriage, many girls choose to demonstrate their fertility by bearing a child in preparation for a marriage proposal. It should also be said that some girls, like their peers all over the world, may also try to secure the affection of a particularly favoured boy by having his child. Either way, the parents of the boy would be required to pay damages and then continue paying to maintain the child as it grows.

Whatever the reasons, teenage pregnancy is very common and this includes church youth. All of Caleb's kids attended church youth group, with Tashia and Nooi being the only two of their female peers who were yet to fall pregnant. This is something Caleb was proud of. He hoped that seeing the burden of single parenting by their girlfriends would continue to act as a deterrent to them having unprotected sex, or sex at all, if Caleb had his way.

Teboho and I were aware that both the girls had boyfriends and would find an excuse to slip out to see them on weekends. Teboho had more than one word with them about it, urging caution. AIDS in South Africa is as high as one in four in many areas and young black women are most at risk. Many black men mistrust condoms, sometimes seeing them as a western plot to limit the growth of the black population. From the outside, this sounds quite paranoid. However, with the amount of social engineering that went on during the apartheid years, it would not seem too far fetched for many black South Africans.

To say that Caleb was unhappy when Tashia finally confessed her pregnancy after almost six months would be an understatement. He was so furious that he threatened to kick her out, as often happened in such circumstances. While I understood Caleb's distress, I also held him partly responsible. Despite his and Ousi's ground rules on boyfriends, they spent many evening away from home visiting with friends of their own, having a drink or two, leaving the girls to babysit the others on their own. In many ways, it was only a matter of time before someone was caught out, given the lack of parental supervision.

Because of this, and the fact that we knew Caleb's anger would eventually subside, we offered to have Tashia come and live with us until after the baby was born. I was also keen to have Tashia with us to keep an eye on her nutrition and medical care in the lead-up to the baby. Under normal circumstances, the kids' diet included more chips and sweets than fruit and vegetables and I was sure Tashia had not deviated from this habit in the first months of her pregnancy, given her still waiflike physique. It was clear that she was also yet to see a doctor. The family agreed to the new arrangement and inside of a week, Tashia was living with us.

Tashia was a beautiful, kind-hearted girl. She resembled a dark-skinned pixie and was as shy as one. Living with her gave me an opportunity to get beneath her usual polite greetings and conversations and get to know her a bit better. She was in a steady relationship with the father of her baby and hoped that having his child would not ruin things between them. We had met him when the parents came to pay damages. I was unsure of the exact amount that had been negotiated, but it was enough to cover the costs of antenatal care, the birth and the baby's immediate needs. The young man's family seemed as distressed about the turn of events as Caleb and Ousi. Events such as this could sometimes ruin the chances for the boy to study beyond high school, as he would have to earn money to support his new baby.

Tashia soon found her place in our family routine and seemed to relax around us and open up a little more than she did in Mohlakeng. Her being around when Mello got home after school allowed the two of them to get closer. Despite the pregnancy, I felt that Tashia was a good influence on Mello. Tashia, like all young women her age, had long since taken responsibility for the maintenance of the household: cooking, cleaning, washing. Mello would have taken on a similar role had she stayed with Tshidi and as Teboho and I didn't want her to stand apart from her peers any more than she already did, we had instigated chores that she was responsible for. Mama also tried to keep her honest in doing these household duties while we were at work. Mello, however, perceived this to be a form of child slavery and was happy to tell anyone who would listen. Tashia's presence and willingness to do her share made Mello at least slightly more inclined to participate without lodging a complaint to the Human Rights Commission.

It was also good for Tashia to spend more time with her grandmother through the last few months of her pregnancy. Tashia, Mama and I spent many hours in the evening discussing pregnancy, good nutrition, labour and looking after a newborn. However, I should say that Mama never ceased to be amused, and at times horrified, by my candour. I told them that in Australia, you may even put an announcement in the paper to announce the pregnancy and that there was a particular pecking order of who should be told first when it was considered safe to announce. They both looked at me in astonishment at the strange cultural practices of white people.

While Tashia, out of her own fear of the unknown, was willing to take as much information as she could get, Mama had grown up old school, similar to my own mother who also had no idea what was happening to her body until it happened. In fact, when my mother got married, my grandmother was still insisting that babies came out of your belly button. This was quite a concession, however, as she told Mum all through high school that pregnant women were actually sick and babies came from the cabbage patch. Mum had prepared me for womanhood somewhat differently and I was keen to equip Tashia with as much information as possible.

After about six weeks with us, Tashia was looking healthy and beginning to put on some weight. I think her fear and concealment had kept her weight dangerously low. She had hidden the pregnancy so well up until that point that even her mother had no idea. Mama was now taking Tashia to the local clinic for regular check-ups and all was progressing well.

As Caleb had no insurance that would cover the costs of the birth, Tashia was to have the baby at a local government hospital. A hospital that served a nearby coloured community was chosen. I hadn't heard good things about this hospital, or any other government hospital for that matter. It was really only private hospitals in South Africa that could boast first class care. I remembered Nonsi, from my home in Caluza all those years before, talking about her training as a nurse. She had chosen nursing because it was the only professional option outside teaching open to young black women at the time. She admitted to having no calling or even interest in caring for the sick. Her training communicated the same laissez faire style she seemed to have developed, with her supervisors telling her that it was fine to simply check a patient's temperature every second day and then average it out on the chart. It didn't fill me with confidence for Tashia's care.

To my delight, Tashia asked me to come with her when it was time and support her at the birth. The rest of the family was happy with this arrangement. The concept of a birth partner was not a common one, neither was having the father of the baby there. I'm not sure why she thought to ask; I was just glad that she did, knowing what I did of the hospital system.

When Mama woke me in the middle of the night several weeks later, I was ready to pack Tashia up and get her to the hospital. She had been having contractions for about four hours and had said nothing. Ultimately, she became quite frightened by the intensity of it all and woke Mama who was sleeping in the next room. The three of us sat in the lounge room and began to time the contractions but given Tashia's distress, I thought it best just to take her to the hospital and see what pain relief we could get for her there.

It took about twenty-five minutes to drive to the hospital and during that time, Tashia's pain seemed to have worsened. Once we arrived, I took care of the paperwork while they took care of Tashia. Hospitals are often, by their very nature, soulless institutions. However, this hospital was particularly so. The corridors seemed dark and dingy, both patients and visitors looking drawn and hopeless.

They had taken Tashia through to the labour ward where she sat surrounded by seven other black or coloured women in various stages of labour, all of whom were much older than Tashia and all of whom were on their own. My presence, as usual, was creating a bit of a stir. However, this time it wasn't only the colour of my skin drawing unwanted attention. Some of the other women did have family floating about, but none appeared to be sitting with them and talking them through contractions. At this stage, Tashia was looking like a deer caught in the headlights, her eyes wide and pleading. While I knew we still had a long way to go, she clearly thought death was imminent.

Over the hours to come, nursing staff came and went, checking on the progress of the various women in the ward. Some left to move on and deliver, others remained with us, still having more work to do. Tashia herself was progressing very slowly. It was hard to judge the actual strength of the contractions as she had clung to my hand

and cried through each contraction since we arrived. However, things changed by late afternoon. By about five o'clock she seemed to have lost all control. She virtually crawled onto my lap to be held as the pain swept over her. She sobbed with each wave, leaving my shoulder wet from her tears. It was hard not to see her for what she was—a child who was terrified of what was still to come.

I asked the nurses once more for some pain relief for her, but continued to be told she had to wait until the doctor came to check her. She was now not progressing and I suspected they wanted to review options. By ten o'clock that evening, the doctor had been and agreed that if she still failed to progress, they would do a caesarean section. Tashia had been in labour for twenty-four hours.

At five the following morning, we were entering the operating theatre. They had taken some convincing, but given I was her aunt they let me come with her. I stripped down and put on the hospital greens and was soon waiting with Tashia in theatre as the contractions kept rolling in. She was back in my arms, exhausted with the labour, hysterical with pain. I told her she only had one or two more contractions before she was finished, as the anaesthetist was preparing the epidural. The greatest difficulty at that point was to extract her from my arms so he could do the procedure. But once that was done, the operation was extremely fast. Within five minutes of the first cut, the baby was out and being held up for Tashia and me to see—a boy. Tashia didn't tell me until much later, but when she looked at her son all she saw were white spots from looking into the theatre lights, so she thought he was albino—not an easy life for a child in Africa. She was so horrified by what she saw that she hardly spoke for hours.

After showing us the baby, the nurses took him across the room to be checked and then down to intensive care for six hours, as was routine. I felt that Tashia needed to have the baby with her. Given the trauma of the whole event, I was concerned about bonding. I repeatedly asked for the baby to be brought to her and was repeatedly told that this was procedure. When they finally brought the baby through and gave him to Tashia, she had managed some sleep and I had been home for a shower and change of clothes and brought Mama and Teboho back with me. When Tashia saw her son, she burst into tears. I asked her what was the matter and she told me about the white spots. I assured her that the baby was perfectly normal as I lifted him into her cautious arms. Despite the joy and relief of that moment, she lay back on her pillow and told me she was never having sex again. I was sure Caleb would be relieved to hear that.

After visiting with Tashia and the baby for a while, we left her to sleep. I was in need of a nap myself, so we headed back home. I left the rest of the family downstairs and dragged myself up to bed. I think I was asleep before my head hit the pillow. Back downstairs, there was a flurry of happy phone calls to the family. Ousi and Caleb were both thrilled with the news of a grandson and promised to bring the rest of the family to see her in the morning.

Mama and I went back for the evening visiting hour and as we entered the ward, Tashia appeared to be doing much better, sitting up in bed, new baby on her lap. We told her that the family all sent their love and would be in to see her tomorrow. When the hour was up, we left Tashia attempting to breastfeed her new son.

That night I slept long and hard and was the last to wake up in the morning. When I did, the house was unusually quiet. I came downstairs and Teboho caught my eye and asked me to join him on the couch. He held my hand and told me that Caleb had phoned to say Ousi had died during the night. She appeared to have had some kind of epileptic fit in her sleep, chocked on her tongue and suffocated. Caleb, who was in the bed next to her, didn't even hear her. It was a terrible shock for all of us. Ousi was in her early forties. But it was her daughter Tashia I was most concerned about. Teboho told me that Caleb had requested I tell Tashia only the next day, to give her time to recover from the birth. He asked the family that I be the only one to visit her in the meantime. I wasn't sure this was a burden I was ready for.

When I went to visit Tashia that day, she looked well and happy. She was up and dressed and had lost that haunted look from the days before. The baby was there beside her bed, fast asleep. Tashia asked me where her parents were. I lied and said that they couldn't get transport but were trying everything they could to come later. As they didn't have a car and it was fifty minutes to the hospital from Mohlakeng, I think Tashia accepted this excuse. She stared down at her son and asked me if I thought he was beautiful. I did. She then told me she had decided to call him Lesego, meaning lucky. I smiled and told her that was a wonderful name for him.

The next morning, I went to tell her what had happened to her mother. When I entered the ward, her eyes told me she was anxious as no one else had been to visit. I sat down on the bed next her and took a deep breath, faltering before I could finally get the words out. It was one of the hardest things I had ever had to say. I tried to tell her how Ousi had died, but quickly realised that my long-winded, nervous explanations were falling on deaf ears. She turned to the wall and was silent until, slowly and quietly, she began to cry. I sat on the bed next to her feeling useless, wondering what one does in circumstances like this. After a time, with Tashia still weeping and moaning, rocking herself backwards and forwards, I got up to go and speak to the doctor to explain what had happened, asking if I could take her home. It was agreed that I could take her home that afternoon. In the meantime, Teboho had arranged for Nooi to come and stay at our house for a while to be with Tashia.

When we arrived home, Tashia was still looking stricken. She didn't say a word, just handed Lesego to Mama and went to her room with Nooi, not resurfacing until after dark. We made her eat something for the baby's sake. Tashia struggled through the next few days, oscillating between sobbing and silence. Thankfully, taking care of Lesego was a welcome distraction but also a reminder of life. Mama and I made sure we took him after his feed, allowing Tashia to sleep. Nooi kept her company and they spent hours together with Nooi catching Tashia up on what her friends had been doing in her absence.

Nooi stayed with us until the funeral the following Saturday. Hundreds of people turned out at the church in Mohlakeng that morning. There were prayers of thanksgiving, songs, a few words were spoken of her life, her children, her new grandson whom she had not ceased telling the neighbours about on the day of his birth. I was glad that she had died after hearing he and Tashia were both healthy, that she had died so very happy.

After the church service, people formed a procession of cars and kombis, following the hearse to the graveyard on the other side of the township. Phuti, Teboho's father, was also buried here. Each vehicle turned its headlights on as the procession snaked its way through the dusty streets. Other cars pulled over as we passed, children stopped playing and waited respectfully by the side of the road. We arrived at the gate of the cemetery and parked the car. I walked with Teboho, Mama and the children to join the growing circle of people at the graveside. A marquee had been set up to provide some shade from the hot mid-morning sun. There were perhaps 500 people there by the time the minister addressed the crowd. Once he had finished, he gave the nod for the funeral attendants to begin lowering Ousi's casket into the freshly dug grave.

During the minister's brief words, Tashia had been deeply upset and was held up by Nooi as her heartbroken sobbing made it hard for her to stand. Now, she moved slowly and calmly to the graveside and said her final farewell. We each stepped forward in turn, gathered a handful of dirt and flung it into the grave with a prayer. I always found this part of a funeral distressing in its finality and as I stood looking down at Ousi's casket, now partially covered with dirt, tears streamed down my face. I cried for Ousi, gone so suddenly; I cried for Caleb, now with five children to raise on his own; but mostly I cried for Tashia. I was aware of the many pairs of eyes on me but had ceased to care.

Tashia stayed with us for another six weeks after the birth, before finally returning home to Mohlakeng.

I saw Lesego recently, now nine years old. I paid a visit to Caleb's house and found Nooi taking a pair of clippers to Lesego's head, with a few of the other cousins watching, waiting their turn. As I looked at him, I thought it strange that I was the first one to see him when he was born and now I could barely recognise him.

But life had moved on in many ways. Nooi now had a baby of her own, yet still seemed responsible for all the children of her father's house. Caleb had remarried—his third wife—and she came with five children of her own, the youngest being about Lesego's age. Katie was still there, now a young woman of twenty. She also had a child, Lerato, three years old, but told me that the father had passed away of TB a year ago, having died in prison. I battled to imagine Katie falling for someone whose life would end this way. I also wondered if it was AIDS that killed him, but decided not to ask.

I asked Katie where Tashia was, but she looked sideways at Nooi before replying, 'She doesn't really stay here anymore. She's running around now and we don't see much of her. She pops in from time to time to see Lesego but she sleeps wherever a friend will give her a bed'. My mind cast back to that frightened little girl who clung to me with each contraction, afraid that the force of this new life wanting to be born would swallow her whole. I struggled to picture her now. Perhaps she would be as unrecognisable to me as Lesego had been.

The township can be a vortex of complacency into which the majority of its young people disappear. The most pervasive form of poverty there is not financial: it is a poverty of aspiration and desire. Most young people fail to imagine a future beyond the borders of the township and if they do, lack the desire to drive through the many barriers that stand in their way. Most of them give up well before they are able to create a life for themselves; the kind of life their parents were prevented from having.

I often wondered what was different about those who managed to pull themselves out of the vortex. I knew Khumo had. Though she and Moss still lived in the township, they were able to operate on a bigger stage. Her upbringing had mirrored that of so many around her so I could only guess that it was something inherent, an intelligence both intellectual and emotional, that had given her wings. But perhaps this was also combined with the sense of purpose that her faith and her values gave her, allowing her to rise above the life that the government predestined for her and her kin.

Whatever these rare qualities were, I wondered if Teboho possessed them as well, so that we could find a place to be that didn't compromise us both out of existence.

32

1998 AND 1999 RETREATING

THE FIRST PHASE OF THE SOLAR COOKER PROJECT HAD COME TO AN END AND PHASE TWO WAS BEING PLANNED. FROM OUR TWO YEARS OF RESEARCH WE HAD LEARNT SOME FASCINATING THINGS THAT WOULD BE INVALUABLE IN THE SECOND PHASE, THE PRIMARY PURPOSE OF WHICH WAS TO MANUFACTURE SOLAR COOKERS FOR COMMERCIAL DISTRIBUTION IN SOUTH AFRICA AND POSSIBLY THE REGION.

We were not surprised to find that families had preferences for one cooker over another, but our western upbringings had not prepared us for their reasons. Overall, there was a strong preference for the smaller more manageable cookers, as it was often women who were responsible for cooking. Though the introduction of solar cookers had resulted in more men and boys taking an initial interest in cooking, this had soon waned. It was the women—from teenage girls to grandmothers—who were carrying the cookers out into the sun each day.

We were fascinated by the unfavourable response to what was, technically, the most efficient cooker. This was the one with a perspex lid that came down directly onto the pot, aluminium wings outstretched, allowing for a tight seal and direct sunlight on the food. This cooker was large enough to hold a number of pots but still light, with its aluminium frame. The families explained that if the contents of their pots were on show to the neighbours, they soon found that there were more visitors on the day they cooked meat than on the days without. Culturally, it was impossible to refuse visitors a plate of food if they arrived at mealtimes and so this had created a very awkward dynamic in the community, putting unwanted stress on the important social networks that poor communities used to sustain themselves.

We knew that families borrowed when times were tough, not from banks but from other families. These families were happy to oblige, as it created a social insurance policy for them when the tables were turned. In this way, families within communities wove a sophisticated web of indebtedness that somehow managed to sustain them all. Our project had added a variable into that fragile web, causing it to strain and groan. The number of times a week a family could afford meat was an indicator of relative wealth in many poor communities and to place this on show for any passer-by to see was not desirable for families and simply too tempting for their poorer neighbours. We were fascinated by this dynamic and reluctantly put a black mark against that model of cooker, despite its superior technical performance.

Despite all the sophisticated German technology and inventiveness, it was the simple South African design that the majority of families—including my own—preferred. It was light, easy to use and had no complex parts that would be difficult to source and repair. Unbeknown to the families, it would also be the cheapest to manufacture and distribute. The fact that it took a little longer to cook the food did not outweigh its other benefits in the minds of its users. Although they were time poor in terms of tasks that required their daily attention, preparing food an hour or two earlier than normal was no burden, especially in light of the saving in time and money.

Richard and I flew out to Frankfurt armed with this information and our bulging reports to work with the Germans to plan phase two.

We flew economy class to Europe knowing, as the large man on my right who had already colonised the armrest and half of my seat began snoring, that the Germans had flown out to Africa business class.

When we arrived bleary-eyed after the overnight flight, our two German colleagues were there to meet us, waving enthusiastically at the gate. I wished for nothing more that a shower and a bed, but was told with great excitement that they had managed to secure a visit to the Solar Research Centre only a two-hour drive from here and we would be able to visit a large open cut mine on the way back. Richard, who appeared to be able to sleep standing up, responded with the required enthusiasm while I slipped in behind him out of view of our hosts, knowing my face was an open book and likely to betray me.

When we were finally dropped off at our hotel nine hours later I dragged myself sulkily to my room, only to discover that it was so small that if I wanted to unpack, I would virtually have to take my bag into the hallway to open it. I had cruel and ungrateful flashbacks to searching the hotels of Pretoria for the most comfortable accommodation for our funders just over two years before. I grudgingly reminded myself that they had flown us out here at the project's expense to allow us to influence its next phase and I should be glad for the opportunity. While this was all true, I still found the politics of aid an eye-opener.

We spent the next five days in intense discussions with the Germans, developing a plan for phase two. Their government favoured a planning tool called the logical framework, a template that required the intellect of a laser physicist and the patience of a saint to implement it. I remember having to take deep and purposeful breaths on more than one occasion when I ended up in a cul-de-sac of an argument with a German member of the team over the semantics of an English word. I wanted to scream, 'I've been speaking English for thirty-three years; I think I can judge the appropriateness of that word with more authority than you'. Richard, seeing I was about to blow, would often step in to negotiate an alternative wording lest I destroy the funding relationship altogether.

We ate lunch every day in the nearby cafeteria which was a large, standard affair with seating for a couple of hundred bureaucrats. On our fourth day, I queued up to select my meal as I had every other day, before making my way, full tray in hand, to the table where our party sat. On this day, whether there was water on the floor or whether my shoes were at fault I don't know, but I felt myself suspended momentarily above the hard tile floor, each ingredient of my meal airborne, with all eyes upon me. A heartbeat later, I lay sprawled across the floor, my food scattered about like a Salvador Dali painting. After a few seconds, the silence that had hung about me like a cloak disappeared and everyone went back to their lunchtime conversations without really skipping a beat. I lay there for a moment, trying to take in what had happened. Then my dear Kurt suddenly appeared at my elbow and helped me gingerly to my feet. My hip and elbow stung as if they were on fire, but it was the humiliation that really burnt me. If it weren't for the reaction of those around me, I would have laughed after falling flat on my face in a crowded cafeteria. But I saw that everyone was wishing the embarrassment away, ignoring both me and my misadventure as if we did not exist.

In that moment, I wanted to go home. I felt that in Africa such a thing would never have happened, that I would have been surrounded by a thousand helpful hands ready to lift me to my feet, apologising that such an event had occurred, whether it was their fault or not. As I pondered this, Kurt reappeared with a replacement of the meal I had so inelegantly lost and led me to the table with my other colleagues.

After a week in Germany, I was very glad to be home. We had finally agreed to the structure and funding for the next phase of the project and a contract engaging our services for phase two would follow shortly.

Richard and I had other projects that also needed attention. We had been working together for several months to evaluate a water and sanitation project in rural schools out near Kruger National Park. The test schools had only pit toilets for their students and relied on water delivered by government trucks sent from the provincial capital, Nelspruit. The problem was that the drivers often sold their load to households on the road to the schools for a few extra rands, leaving the schools at a distance from Nelspruit without water, sometimes for months on end. We were evaluating a project that sought to address this problem by installing rain water tanks. We were also testing a pit toilet design with improved ventilation in these schools.

I had another water project, this one run by a non-government organisation called Mvula Trust. We were experimenting with incorporating 'rural participatory methodologies' into the design and implementation of water projects; the solar cooker project had taught me the importance of accurately mapping the complex relationships between families, communities and natural resources.

I was also delighted to be working with Colleen again. She had made a huge impact on me with her coaching work during the solar cooker project and a strong friendship had emerged between us. I realised she was becoming the mentor Fiona had been when I lived in 'Maritzburg—a clear and steady voice on whom I could rely for both wisdom and the hard truth. Colleen had also become a sounding board as I thought through the issues in my marriage. A few years earlier, she had divorced a man who was well known and loved in the development community in southern Africa, causing everyone to question her actions. But of course, marriages are private and complex affairs and those on the outside of them can never really know what happens behind closed doors. Colleen and I talked a great deal about the dynamics between husbands and wives: what we give, what we take and why we stay. Not surprisingly, we saw similar patterns play out in the communities whose dynamics we were being asked to study.

Richard had also given me another project from the Department of Minerals and Energy. They wanted to understand the value chain from manufacture through to point of sale of all non-electric stoves in the country. This project saw me visiting factories and remote retail outlets in every corner of South Africa, noting down prices, mark-ups and distribution mechanisms of paraffin, coal and gas cookers. It was with some pride that I said I knew more about this topic than any other person alive; the obvious question from my colleagues was: 'Who, outside policy makers, would want to?' This project won the 'short straw' award in the office for two years running and was, as Richard liked to point out, designed to keep me humble.

Work was full of travel, laughter, challenges, friendships and hard work and I was still enjoying every moment of it. Teboho had left the Council of Churches and was employed as a sociologist in the same engineering company that had partnered with us on the solar cooker project. Paul, who often travelled with Marlett and I to the test sites, had now become a colleague and close friend of Teboho as well.

My favourite story from Teboho's social impact assessment work with his new company was about a housing project in the Northern Province. A mine had commissioned alternative housing to be built for a community in compensation for a new mining project on their land, yet they were refusing to take ownership of the homes. Teboho was sent in to help the company understand the issues and shift the gridlock. While it would obviously have been preferable to have made use of his skills prior to the building of the houses, he was quickly able to get to the bottom of the problem. He explained in a meeting with the project managers that the corridors weren't wide enough.

'They don't want to accept brand new homes because the corridors aren't wide enough?' asked an exasperated executive.

'That's right. They say that they were very clear about what they wanted, but the building contractor didn't meet the specifications', Teboho replied calmly.

'Why do they need such wide corridors anyway?'

'For coffins. When a family holds a funeral, they have to be able to move the coffin in and out of the lounge room. Funerals are always held in people's homes, with the coffin there for the vigil the night before. It's an important part of community life and because the corridors are too narrow, they can't accept the houses.'

The development and reconstruction process in South Africa was going to take some time. It was a new phase in our country's history and everyone was learning, after generations of separation, how to get along.

One of the agreements Teboho and I had made with the move to the thatched house was to spend more time doing things together as a family. With this in mind, we bought a tent and took the kids to a few of the game reserves within a three-hour drive of Jo'burg.

My favourite trip was to Pilanesberg National Park, just next to Sun City. Camping is a popular pastime in the Afrikaans-speaking community and we knew we would be putting ourselves under the microscope again—but we were unwilling to let their attitudes stop us from enjoying the country. Nevertheless, we chose a camping spot in a secluded corner, far away from other campers and the amenities but providing us with a little shelter from staring eyes. As it was the first time we had pitched the tent, it took us well over an hour to work out which pole went where until the tent finally stood, resembling a new born antelope, as it quivered before finally finding its feet and deciding to stay up.

Chaba and Mello were incredibly excited, running in circles around our new campsite. Mello, keen to get the adventure started, was offering to set up our kitchen table and fetch sleeping bags, so Teboho channelled her energies into tasks that she could manage. Soon everyone had a job and the campsite took shape just as darkness fell. Not long after, the welcome smell of meat and onions on the *braai* swept across us as Teboho got supper going. We sat balancing plates on our laps while the last of the wood burnt away, and I felt cocooned by the night in one of the rare moments we had shared together as a family of four. Later, in the tent, with sleep escaping me in the humidity, I allowed the flavour of contentment to roll around in my mouth like a favourite sweet, as the sounds of our sleeping children accompanying the crickets.

The next morning, we were up before dawn. We wanted to be the first through the gates at six, having been told this would allow us the best game viewing of the day. As we drove slowly down the road beyond the main gate, the park opened out, offering a dozen different directions to explore. We stayed on the main road, the only car in sight, having decided to head down to the lake in the hope that the game would make the same decision.

I was awestruck by what I saw—a scene surely akin to the garden of Eden. There were herds of zebra, buck, giraffes, warthog, rhino and, as we rounded the bend, elephants, all making their way down to drink. I have never before or since seen animals congregate in such numbers, as if this was how they behaved in the absence of humans. Wherever I turned my head, my vision was filled with animals on the move, the early morning light intensifying the richness of the browns, oranges and greens all around. Though it felt as if time was standing still, the moment didn't last and within twenty minutes, the animals had disappeared back into the bush. Even the colours returned to their normal hues as the sun rose higher and struck the valley below. This was the Africa I had dreamt of as a child and while the reality had proven to be much richer than my own imaginings, I was deeply grateful to have been given this moment in which my childhood fantasy came to life.

With the move to the thatched house, a few other things changed. I had stopped going to church, choosing instead to join a home group that Rags and Barry were part of. They met each week in the home of one of the members, just as we had done in 'Maritzburg several years before when I was still part of Sizwe. I felt I now had bigger questions to ask, ones that were not addressed in the course of a church service or the minister's sermon each week. Home group allowed me to grapple with these issues via a dialogue, rather than the monologue that the church provided.

While we joined the home group as a family, Teboho continued to go back to Mohlakeng each Sunday, taking Mama to church there but also attending church himself. Initially, he would be gone until lunchtime but as time passed, he and Mama would only return in time for supper, Teboho needing or wanting to spend the whole day in the township. Sometimes the kids went with him but as the time away from home extended, they chose to stay with me.

I found his absences confusing. When we were together he seemed to resent the fullness of my life, claiming that I neither needed him nor loved him enough. Yet when he was away, it was as if he did not need us, or perhaps me. I wanted him home more; I wanted him to be there when he promised to be. I had lost track of how many times we arranged to go somewhere and I was left standing, waiting, not knowing whether to go on alone. It felt as though the magic of our family's weekend trips away was trickling like water through my fingers.

I could see that our marriage had become an art of compromise. His concession was to live away from the township, this home in the suburbs less of a refuge for others than our home had once been; mine was to allow him time to do what he wished to do, to continue to love and support his extended family, to raise the children as Africans, not encouraging them to be white and middle class.

In terms of giving him space, I was not naive enough, particularly in the light of my own actions and the events in Tasmania, to think he might not be seeing other women. But there was nothing concrete to confirm that he was. One day I asked him if he had ever slept with anyone else, not in an accusing tone, but with an intention of telling him about my affair, hoping to make the conversation more one of coming clean to each other and moving forward. After a hesitation, he told me he'd had several one-night stands, mostly out of need during the many months of celibacy after Chaba's birth. He had sought out sex as a release rather than turning to other women for intimacy. He told me that these one-night stands included sleeping with someone from work while I was down in 'Maritzburg during the sanding of the wooden floors. While I was taken aback by his confession, I was suddenly gripped by the realisation that he had slept with another women while I was breastfeeding our son.

'Did you use protection?' I asked fearfully.

'It wasn't planned, so no I don't think I did', he replied cautiously.

The intention I had held to tell him my own truth, forgive him his mistakes, hope he could forgive mine and move on was suddenly subsumed by such ferocious anger that I could barely speak. What if he had HIV, had given it to me and I had passed it on to Chaba?

'You need to have an HIV test and you need to do it now', I said coldly, before standing up and walking away. The next few weeks were like living in a world frozen by a witch's spell; all conversations, all thoughts hung in mid air until the answer to the only question that mattered was known.

Mum and Dad, Jon and his new wife Androulla arrived to spend the December holidays with us, just in time to celebrate Chaba's third birthday. We decided to go all out and do a theme party, with Peter Pan being Chaba's first choice. We invited Moss and Khumo who brought their son and two cousins; Marlett and her daughter; Jeremy and Mmathabo from work; as well as a few of Chaba's friends from school and down the street. Chaba was dressed as Peter Pan, Mello was Wendy, I was a mermaid and Jon was Captain Hook, with all our guests dressed as pirates, Tinkerbell or Lost Boys.

We had done up the courtyard as the various locations in the story: the swings became the pirate ship, we had the Indian village and the home of the Lost Boys. Just before we cut the cake, Wendy was captured by Captain Hook, sending Peter Pan scuttling off to the pirate ship to save her. Once Peter Pan had put a sword through Captain Hook and he came tumbling to the ground, all our young guests took it as their cue to leap on top of him and keep him there. Teboho was the designated photographer, capturing all the precious memories on the same camera that Uncle Jim had given him in Tasmania.

After Chaba's party, our whole clan headed off down to Cape Town and the Garden Route on a ten-day holiday. While the HIV tests had come back negative for myself and Teboho, there was now a chasm between us fuelled by my simmering anger at his thoughtlessness. The family holiday was overflowing with happy memories, yet the tension must have been obvious to all. I remember with some shame taking it out on Mello at one point, as she stood too close to the edge of a cliff for my comfort, despite her uncle and aunt standing nearby enjoying the view. When she refused to move back, I went over and grabbed her roughly by the arm and told her to do as she was told, before yanking her away. I saw that I had both hurt and confused her, but in my anger, I was unable to take a step back myself. I also knew that I would never have been so rough with Chaba. To my shame, my frustrations were more easily vented with Mello, compounding the rocky journey of our love.

I was diverting my anger rather than addressing the real issues with Teboho. I don't know if I was afraid of a repeat of the exchange in Tasmania, or whether I felt that if I tried to take it on, the whole house of cards would come tumbling down.

All too soon, the holiday was over and Mum, Dad, Jon and Androulla left to go back to Sydney. Mama returned from Mohlakeng where she had been for the last five weeks, allowing us space to host my family. Teboho and I went back to work and things remained unsaid.

Several months passed before I realised how very tired I was with all the deadlines, travel and strain. Colleen phoned me and said she was going to splash out and spend a week at a spa in Stellenbosch in June. She asked me to join her. Teboho, with a look somewhere between that of a beaten dog and a hopeful child, said he had no objection. Was he thinking that a break would do us good and I would come back refreshed, or was he afraid that this was another step towards a different life for me? With that look, I knew that despite all that had passed between us in recent months, he still loved me and wanted things to change.

Stellenbosch is wine country, less than an hour's drive east of Cape Town, with sharp peaks and plunging green valleys. It's an area that exudes rest and relaxation, regeneration and pleasure. We had stopped there briefly on our trip with my family in December, but this would be the first time I stayed here. My holidays had always consisted of visits to family in rural areas far from tourist attractions such as Stellenbosch; my luxurious room at the Hydro was in sharp contrast to the wattle and daub homes or tin shacks that were my usual accommodation. While I initially felt guilty for leaving the family behind and spending money just on myself, I knew I needed something dramatically different to shift me out of the state I was in. I was most grateful not to be making this journey alone.

Colleen lived in Cape Town, though she had grown up in Jo'burg. She had been to university at Wits, moving in circles with the likes of Ruth First, Joe Slovo and Steve Biko, people who to me seemed like famous characters from a novel or history book rather than ordinary people who were once studying for a degree, just as I had. During those early years, she found that the principles of communism, of equity, of sharing, and the intellectual analysis of a society that she had observed from the window of a white working class house, resonated with her and felt like home.

At university, she came to know others who heard a similar tolling of the bell and was soon in organisations that put her on the wrong side of the political divide. She and her circle of friends were arrested before they could finish their degrees, held and tortured in solitary confinement before fleeing into exile. Many ended up in London, but Colleen and her then husband returned to Swaziland as members of the ANC, where they worked to safely exit ANC members from South Africa. Ultimately the South African government's raids stretched like reaching fingers beyond its borders and into Swaziland, forcing Colleen, her husband and their two small boys to move to Zimbabwe. Colleen and her family lived there for many years, working in development and politics, writing, publishing and researching, before finally returning home to South Africa after the elections in 1994. My life felt bland compared to hers, and though I would not wish for the hardships she suffered, I valued the wisdom they had generated.

Colleen and I arrived at the Hydro, both in need of repair. Colleen needed rest, a place to give up smoking and the discipline and good food to shed some weight. I, however, needed to put on weight as the demands of work and a strained marriage had caused me to shed pounds unintentionally. Our daily routine was breakfast in our rooms followed by a hydro treatment, a massage and an afternoon activity of our choice. We could exercise in the pool or at the tai chi classes, or we could choose another treatment such as aromatherapy or reflexology. The grounds also drew us outside for long leisurely walks on many afternoons, allowing us to talk through all the thoughts that were surfacing. Coming from a long line of vivid dreamers, I started a dream book that week in an effort to try to understand what was going on for me in my life. On our afternoon walk on the second day, I recounted one of my first dreams.

'Last night I dreamt that Mum and Dad moved out to South Africa to be with me', I began.

'Interesting', said Colleen. 'I always imagined that you had moved here to start a life away from them.'

'Well, I couldn't have got further away if I'd tried. Any further and I would have started coming back. I've often wondered about that, but I don't think it was the issue. I think I was running towards something, not away. But in this dream, the only place that Mum and Dad could live was in a rural village, somewhere near Itsoseng. When I went to see their place, it was a three-roomed shack made of wooden planks with a mud brick floor. Mum told me she was doing some part-time work to try and earn money, but Dad couldn't work because of his dementia and the Parkinson's disease.'

'Does your father's dementia affect him all that much?' Colleen asked.

'No. At the moment it's just an occasional episode, but the doctors are telling Mum that he will decline in the years to come', I replied. 'But in the dream he couldn't really leave the house and so Mum had to take care of everything. I became so distressed with their standard of living that I began counting the wooden planks and the nails in each plank, as if that would somehow show them how impoverished their lives had become. Eventually I convinced them to go back home, though I was very upset that they were leaving. Mum then said that she was actually relieved as she had felt so cut off from the world living in Africa.'

'How fascinating. The life of the woman in your dream is impoverished because she has chosen to live in South Africa and when she is finally convinced to leave, she feels relieved. She realises she has been in denial about how cut off she was. Who do you think the dream is about, your mother or you?' she asked.

'I think I've been financially impoverished, working for peanuts and supporting the extended family whenever I have been earning some money. But I certainly wouldn't say my life has been impoverished overall. I think it's been rich with experiences I wouldn't have otherwise had', I responded, perhaps slightly defensively.

'But on an emotional level, you've been quite cut off in order to stay with it. Even sexually, you've been cut off.'

I had told only Colleen and Marlett of the affair. Since then, Colleen and I had talked about how differently I viewed myself sexually after that. Something of the early repression had been lifted, though I still felt constrained in my marriage, unable or unwilling to open up, particularly since Teboho had spoken about his having unprotected sex.

'I think emotionally that's true, but perhaps the sexual restraint had nothing to do with being here. I think I brought that with me. I think a lot about what attracted Teboho and I to each other. Perhaps we somehow recognised the emotional immaturity and idealism in the other and it felt welcome, familiar.'

'I think you're right', Colleen agreed, looking out at the valley below as we topped the rise of the hill we were slowly climbing. 'I believe we are attracted to people who meet our needs at that time. The question is, can you grow together over time as those needs change?'

'I reckon Teboho is a bit threatened by where my life is taking me. I know I've changed. I want more now for myself than I did before. I think he believes I've broken a promise.'

'He fell in love with the woman ferrying children out of a township during the Seven Day War. He thought you were a soldier who would fight with him in his cause: capable, brave, self-sufficient, someone who he wouldn't have to take care of, someone who could take care of herself.'

'I think taking care of others makes him feel better about himself, as if it diverts attention from having to look at his life, his history. Sometimes I think of him as Peter Pan, collecting Lost Boys', I reflected, my mind casting back to Chaba's birthday party. 'Then he meets Wendy, who he is in love with but also wants to be mothered by. I fell in love with Peter Pan—who wouldn't?—but it's been ten years now', I said, my voice trailing off. 'I think, like Peter Pan, he doesn't want to be constrained, even by his own shadow. He wants to be free to fly away whenever he wishes, off to his Lost Boys, off to fight pirates.'

After a long silence, broken only by the sounds of our footsteps, Colleen finally asked: 'Do you think he can partner you—strong, powerful you?'

'I want him to. I'm not prepared to give up on us, on our family. If I walked away, then I'd be saying that mixed marriages don't work. I want to believe that they can.'

'That's a lot of pressure on two people.'

It was my turn to pause and look out over the valley, green and fertile. I could just make out the vineyards from where I stood, knowing that generations of families had made their lives here, tending these vines.

'If I walked away I would feel like such a failure', I said at last.

'It's not about failure, it's about what you want, what will be enough to sustain you and enrich you. Some people are able to work through infidelity and come out the other side, knowing they aren't perfect, knowing that betrayal is always possible, but choosing to have a life together anyway.' Colleen turned to face me, her kind smile opening up her face while her eyes pinned me down. 'It's a choice, Sandy, to stay and make it work, knowing what you know. But staying without taking it on is not a choice, it's just avoidance.'

We turned then, as if by sudden mutual consent, and headed back down towards the Hydro, lost in our own thoughts for a time.

After a week at the Hydro, detoxed and relaxed, we drove down into Stellenbosch for our new start. Colleen was caffeine and nicotine free and I was armed with a list of things I needed to do differently in my life to achieve better balance.

I wasn't ready to walk away from Teboho. I wanted us to evolve into a new stage in our marriage, one in which we were no longer adolescents—ideological, impulsive and afraid—but mature adults.

33

October 1999
The End of Time

MY RETURN HOME FROM STELLENBOSCH WAS A JOYOUS REUNION, AS WAS OFTEN THE CASE FOR US AFTER A LONG SEPARATION. I COULD SEE IN TEBOHO'S EYES THAT HE WAS NERVOUSLY AWAITING THE OUTCOME OF MY TIME ALONE, MY TIME TO THINK. I SHOWED HIM MY DREAM BOOK, TALKED HIM THROUGH WHAT I HAD BEEN THINKING, WHAT I FELT WOULD MAKE ME HAPPY IN OUR LIFE TOGETHER. HE LISTENED PATIENTLY TO THE WORDS THAT FELL FROM ME LIKE DROUGHT-BREAKING RAIN. I SPOKE OF THE NEED FOR BALANCE AND HEALTH, FOR TIME OUT AS A COUPLE SEPARATE FROM TIME OUT AS A FAMILY. I SPOKE ABOUT THE NEED TO PULL THINGS BACK AT WORK AND STOP TAKING ON SO MUCH THAT I HAD TO WORK ON WEEKENDS—ABOUT ASKING FOR HELP TO GET THINGS DONE.

But I lacked the courage to speak about how we would move forward, knowing that neither of us was perfect; knowing that we could not live up to our own expectations of the world, of each other, of ourselves. Idealistic as we both were, could each of us accept our own imperfections and love the humanity in the other, rather than just the dream? Could we face up to the details of where our lives had taken us, step through the minefield of broken promises, and emerge intact?

I had considered the consequences of opening up all the baggage our marriage had packed away, especially in the last four or five years. The thought of picking through it piece by smelly piece made me turn away in fear. But I also knew that unless we did this, we would never be able to move forward into a different type of relationship, one based on truth and a mutual respect for each other's boundaries.

Contemplating the possible failure of the marriage was another kind of nightmare for me. I imagined the look on Teboho's face if I said, 'I can't stay with you anymore', and the thought of the pain I would cause made my legs buckle. I still did not want to be the one to inflict pain. I did not want to be the one to say, 'Our marriage isn't working, the dream is over'. And underneath all that, I was deeply afraid of the stigma of failure bestowed by the title 'divorced woman'. Somewhere in my childhood, I had come to believe that where there is failure, there is no love.

For all these reasons, I spoke only of making resolutions for better health and work-life balance, more time together—as if that was all it would take.

Whether Teboho saw through my long list of superficial changes or not, I knew he was also trying to pull things back together. I knew he felt the distance between us and mourned what we had lost. Yet I also knew that the township, and his need to be needed by those without hope, were powerful forces that kept pulling him in, allowing him to feel worthwhile and whole in service to others.

I knew he was making a huge sacrifice by living in the white suburbs where he could never feel at home. His personality was loud and boisterous and the suburbs quiet and peaceful; like oil and water, they would never blend, despite all the stirring and shaping on my part.

I also knew that until we acknowledged what was really going on, there was no hope of emerging from the deep hole we had fallen into.

A few weeks later, I suggested we go to couples therapy to get some support as we worked on our marriage. Teboho had been to see a therapist a couple of times in 'Maritzburg before we met. Although he found the experience helpful, it also opened a Pandora's box of past hurt and trauma that could not easily be closed up at the end of the hour. After a few sessions, he just stopped going back. When he agreed to go to counselling with me now, I was reminded once more that he still loved me.

We were referred to a marriage therapist by Rags and Barry—a woman who lived in the northern suburbs, a forty minute drive from our home in the west. We had a nine o'clock appointment and left early to allow for peak hour traffic. What we hadn't allowed for was a major accident that meant we arrived almost forty minutes late. The long drive served only to heighten my fear of speaking the words that needed to be said and by the time we got there, all I was capable of doing was sobbing in this stranger's office. I cried for all that was at stake, for all that had happened, for what we had already lost and what else could possibly disappear if the truth were spoken. As the therapist had another appointment, she guiltily sent us away, with me still quietly weeping, unable to get control of myself.

The drive home was long and silent. I'm not sure that before this Teboho realised how close to the edge we were. He knew things weren't as he would like them to be, but my outburst had really spooked him. Perhaps he believed I had been through so much in my life in South Africa that my shoulders were broad enough and my back strong enough to bear anything. I know that's what I wanted to believe, but I also accepted that the space that had opened up in me in Tasmania had continued to grow. It was no longer a matter of whether I could bear it, but whether I chose to bear it.

We arrived on time for our second session and the therapist was able to get a coherent download of our history. If she was at all surprised by the events we outlined, she was professional enough not to show it. At the beginning of our third session, she wanted to focus on why we had come and what we hoped to get out of therapy.

She listened patiently to our half-hearted explanations before launching in as if to lance a wound.

'Sandy, I believe what you really want is help to end this marriage', she said flatly, as if her eyes were like an ultrasound, able to bounce off the space inside me that held the truth even I was afraid to see. 'Teboho, I'm not sure that you're in the same place.'

I forced myself to look at him in the heavy silence that followed, though I could feel his heart breaking into pieces like shattered glass. I stole a glance and saw that he was looking into his lap, tears in his eyes. In that moment, I wanted to take it all back, make it OK again. I wanted to say it wasn't true, that I still was committed and wanted to work it through. But I knew this was the legacy of my mother's generation once more: adapt, accommodate, accept. My real self said, 'Yes, maybe it's that. I'm afraid to go there, but it might be true.'

Teboho turned at last and in a barely audible voice said, 'Why? I thought we were happy', then turned his face to look at the wall so I could not see what emotion was written across it. Sorrow, anger, blame?

I suddenly remembered another dream I'd had at the Hydro a few months before. In it, I was driving down one of Cape Town's steep hills with Mello in the car, my foot heavily on the brake, barely in control, feeling as if at any moment the car could get away from me and send us both over the edge. That same feeling choked me now: everything was out of control, there were no brakes I could apply, and the edge of the cliff was very near.

'I was happy, but it's been harder and harder to stay that way. I can't trust you to be there for me, to choose me over other people because *I'm* your wife. I know other people need you, but I need you too. I've been so incredibly lonely', I said, almost pleading.

'But you have more resources than the other people, more ways to cope. They have nothing, you have it all.'

I had often wondered how Teboho reconciled marrying a white person, someone who symbolised everything he was denied while growing up. I know he appreciated the fact that I was willing to share what I had, willing to use my influence to help others. I know he loved me. But perhaps a subliminal resentment of what I represented lay alongside that love.

As he said these words—'they have nothing, you have it all'—I wondered if his actions were a subtle punishment for being white. His making me wait, putting others' needs in front of mine, keeping promises to others but not to me, his love affairs with black women—countless memories flooded in. I knew he had a powerful rage against the white society that had kept him impoverished, divided his family. Is it possible to sleep with the enemy and never once take up arms against them?

'I think we have both made compromises to be together, to find common ground, but I'm afraid we may have compromised our relationship out of existence. I think you're very angry with me for asking you to move away from Mohlakeng', I said, tentatively stroking a subject that had not been raised.

'It's not what I wanted, no', he replied firmly, 'but if it's what makes you happy, then I'm OK with it.'

'I think you want to be OK with it, but you're not and you take it out on me in other ways.' I watched him think for a moment, then dismiss the idea like shrugging off an old coat.

'What other ways, Sandy?' the therapist interjected. 'Be more specific.'

'OK. When it's suppertime during the week and I don't know where you are. Your phone is off so I phone the office and Paul says you have left two hours ago. When you do come home, you breeze in full of laughter and light, play with the kids, tell a few stories around the table, make everyone laugh, but say nothing to me about where you've been. I feel as if I'm being punished; I want you at home, so you do the opposite.'

'I often make a few stops on the way home, nothing important. If it's only about getting home earlier, I can do that.'

'It's more than that', I replied, frustrated by his desire to put my feelings back into a box when it had taken so long to get them out.

'Well, what exactly?' he said, suddenly attacking.

'It's trust', I spat out, close to tears again. 'I don't trust you to put me first, to choose me. I don't trust that you will be faithful. I don't trust you to keep your promises to me. I don't trust you to understand me and what it is I need.'

'Well, if you don't trust me, then there's nothing more to be said', he stated icily, as if shutting a steel door in my face.

I was suddenly afraid. I had been struggling with being in the marriage for a number of years now, but I had always felt it was my choice to stay or go. I had suspected Teboho wasn't faithful, but I never thought he would leave. Suddenly, I saw it was possible that he would pull back and be the one to end it. I felt out of control once more, careering down a steep hill, feet pumping useless brakes.

Perhaps seeing the panic in my eyes, the therapist took control of the conversation. 'Trust is important, but it can be rebuilt if both parties are committed.'

'Is it what you want, Sandy? I think you've given up and just want to walk away, clean and easy', Teboho said accusingly. 'How could you do that? What about Mello and Chaba? What about our family?'

I felt the tears spill from my eyes, although I was trying to hold them in, to keep calm. I had to stop myself thinking about the kids—what a divorce would do to them. I knew it was a distraction at this moment, a barb meant to hurt me.

'I don't think we want to jump to any conclusions just yet', the therapist said calmly. 'Let's call it a day for now. Let's agree that no decisions are made while we are still in this process. We are working together to understand how each of you feel before any action is taken. Can you both commit to staying with the process for now?' she asked, as I sat wondering how it had come to this so quickly.

I didn't feel ready to put a stake in the ground about what I wanted or didn't want. I felt that the discussion had leap-frogged over my intention and now Teboho had placed himself in opposition to me, on the other side of a fence that hadn't existed an hour before.

The therapist was still looking at us both searchingly, waiting for a response. 'OK', we said in unison. 'Can I also suggest', she added as we stood, 'that you don't discuss this during the week. We'll talk again next week, but just take a break until then.' We nodded our agreement and left the room quickly, eager to get away from the words that hung in the air like threads of a spider web, sticky and clinging.

We did as the therapist suggested, almost finding relief in returning to the day-to-day. We both worked a little longer in the evenings, found a reason to be busy over the weekend and generally kept things above the line. All the while, I was challenged by what the therapist had said. Was the suggestion of therapy really a way to get help to end it; to allow a professional to diagnose a fatal flaw, saving me from being the one to call it? I knew it was possible. But I was oscillating between wanting a return to the way things had been in 'Maritzburg, yet feeling we could never get that back, and that what we had now was not enough.

The following week I was in the kitchen preparing supper when the phone rang. Mama was watching Chaba in the bath and Mello was in her room changing into her pyjamas. I knew Thabo, the man on the other end of the phone, as the partner of one of Teboho's female friends at work. Thabo and his partner had been together for many years and had a six-year-old son. He was phoning to tell me that they had broken up. As Thabo and I had never met, I was struggling to understand why he would phone me to tell me this. But suddenly a bell chimed inside me and I went on the attack.

'Why are you telling me this?' I demanded.

'We broke up because she is having an affair with your husband', he said calmly, without venom.

'Thabo, I don't think you should be phoning me like this, making trouble', I said, failing to convince even myself that I could hold the high ground here.

'Think what you like. I just thought you had a right to know', he said roughly, before the phone went dead.

I walked back over to the stove and continued with supper, weighing up what Thabo had said as I added beans to the stir-fry. It might be true, it might not. It didn't really matter. I knew from my own experience that an affair was an empty promise, like searching in the wrong place for what has been lost. I also knew that I could not judge, having made my own mistakes in the past. So there was no raging at the possibility of another infidelity—just a quiet knowing that for me, the marriage was over.

Perhaps, for Teboho, loving me was enough. His mother had chosen to stay, to invite Ma Ellen into her home because she loved her husband. The love between them was strong enough to survive even his relationships with other women. But I was not like Mama. I was not willing to live that life, not anymore.

I knew Teboho loved me, loved me the best he could, despite the difficulties our love presented. I knew he was making compromises to hold onto that love. I knew the fact that he came home each night was, to him, a daily testimony of his commitment. I knew he was doing the best his shattered childhood, his abandoned adolescence, would allow. I knew he was giving all he had to give and that this had led him to ask, genuinely, 'Why? I thought we were happy?'

And though I loved him too, with his Peter Pan ways and boyish charm, I also knew that this life and this love were no longer enough for me.

It was only a few weeks until Christmas and we had long planned to spend the holidays in Cape Town, travelling down on the train to celebrate the new millennium at a party in the foothills of Table Mountain. Rags and Barry and some other friends from home group were going and had invited us to come along. Colleen had offered to share her home for the week we would be down there.

The kids, now nine and four, were almost vibrating with excitement at the thought of an overnight train trip. They loved the idea of us all sleeping in the fold-down beds, eating at the restaurant and watching the world go by, while still being able to run around on the train. Though I was looking forward to a holiday, I also knew I couldn't let things go on and it was time to have a conversation with Teboho. It was this thought that weighed heavily on me as we waved goodbye to Moss who had dropped us off at the train station in downtown Jo'burg.

Juggling suitcases and backpacks, we jostled our way towards the compartment. The kids rushed through the door and quickly began investigating each moving part, each secret panel, but were finished too soon, I thought, with a twenty-four-hour journey ahead of us. The compartment was a standard size, but the words I needed to say filled up the space as if a large stranger had entered behind us and was now making himself comfortable.

Soon we were under way and the hours began to flick past as quickly as the open expanse of the highveld. Darkness settled down like a dog for a nap, circling until suddenly it dropped to the ground. Our family card game of crazy eights continued, pausing only as Teboho stood to switch on the lights. Teboho and I had spent the hours focusing on entertaining the children—but the time was approaching when they would sleep and we would be alone together, all distractions removed.

We took the kids through to the dining carriage, allowing them to choose from the menu. Though I was uninspired by the selection, Mello and Chaba hungrily ordered hamburgers and chips, delighted with the idea that by the time the food was brought to them, we would be miles from where they had ordered it. We shared a lively family meal, full of tales of travelling adventures had by Teboho and me before the kids were born. We spoke of Namibia, Zimbabwe, Botswana, France and London. They took turns telling us of memories from their favourite family holidays, longing to add Cape Town to the list. The knowledge that this would most likely be our last family holiday was packed away for now like the folding table in our compartment, making space for other, more important things.

After supper, we made our way back to the compartment, feeling like novice sailors on a rolling ship, casting from one side of the corridor to the other as the train sped along. Teboho took the kids to the bathroom while I made up the beds. As it turned out, it was not practical to make up only two, allowing us to send the kids to bed before us, as the lowering of the bunks made it impossible to sit comfortably on the seats. So by nine, we were all four of us tucked up in separate bunks, allowing the movement of the train to rock us to sleep like a mother's hand on a cradle.

We arrived in Cape Town in the late afternoon, Colleen waving enthusiastically at the barrier, her youngest son Thomas by her side. I had always had a soft spot for Thomas, who was like a kid brother to me. He had his father's compact good looks and his mother's enquiring mind, yet perhaps in the shadow of two powerful parents always seemed to hesitate, unsure which was the best path. I think it was this hesitation that made me want to take him under my wing, be a big sister and a friend.

It was Colleen's birthday the following day and Thomas took us aside to let us in on the secret plans. He and his brother Kezia were planning a party at Colleen's new house, which would be both birthday party and housewarming. Our job was to get her out of the house for the day so he and Kezia could arrange their gift for her. They were building a large Indian love bed in the sunroom that opened out of the living room. The boys had attached five single bed mattresses together under one large blue cover and were having a carpenter come to build the platform on which they would rest. They had asked each guest to bring a cushion as their birthday/housewarming gift, to be placed on the love bed until it was full, each cushion telling the story of those Colleen loved and held dear. It was a wonderful plan and we were happy to be a part of it. Dutifully, we asked Colleen to take us to Kirstenbosch Gardens the following day.

As planned, we returned from Kirstenbosch at 5.00, allowing time to shower and change for the party. When we arrived at the front door, Colleen submitted to being led through to the living room, eyes firmly shut, one hand on the outstretched arm of each beloved son. As she opened her eyes and saw the transformation, she sighed and held them close, having always wished for a love bed but never having the place to put it.

From this night, the love bed would become the heart of this welcoming home, drawing to it all sorts of dear friends who, without a word, would kick off their shoes and climb up, wine glass in hand and settle down to an evening of conversation. The love bed's magic was to draw out what was normally held inside—as friends reclined gracefully on the cushions, mouths and hearts seemed to open and souls find comfort.

But this was all still a dream as we stood in front of the new love bed, with only two cushions yet there, one from each son. I had slipped off to the gift shop in Kirstenbosch to buy a third and now produced it from the backpack I was carrying. So the evening began, with each guest arriving bearing food and a cushion. Soon there were too many guests for the living room and they began to flow out through the kitchen onto the back veranda where couches and low wooden stools awaited.

On the second to last day of 1999 in the warm Cape Town evening, we celebrated another year with Colleen, the start of her new life in this home and the soon to be finishing millennium.

The next day, Teboho was keen to help Colleen with a few odd jobs that needed doing around the house so he disappeared to hunt around the nearby hardware shops, sourcing what was needed. Not long after he left, Thomas arrived for brunch, after which we all retreated to the cool of the pool. By mid-afternoon, Teboho had still not returned. With Thomas playing with the kids, Colleen was free to ask me what was going on.

'I don't know where he is. He'll come home when he's ready', I said in a resigned tone.

'You know, it feels as if you brought your family down here to show me, to show me your beautiful children, to show me the distance between you and Teboho, to show me how hard it is for you to decide what to do.'

'I have decided', I said in a whisper, as if afraid that speaking it out loud would make it real. 'I need to tell him. I love him, but I can't live this life anymore. It's too lonely.'

Colleen said nothing, but squeezed my hand as we watched Chaba leap from the edge of the pool and into Thomas's outstretched arms.

Teboho returned late afternoon with no real explanation of where he had been all day. It seems we both found ways to get by. He finished the jobs for Colleen in time to change and head into town with me for the New Year's Eve party. Colleen had offered to look after the kids; one party was enough for her. She was reading them a story on the love bed as we left for the night.

We made the short drive along the freeway before taking the turn-off towards Table Mountain and the suburb of Oranjezicht. We finally found the address, parking the car well down the street as every second house seemed to be hosting a party. The city had planned fireworks at the harbour front as well as a laser show from Table Mountain. From Oranjezicht, you could see both.

Though we were among the first to arrive, I could hear Rags's laughter pouring out through the front door like escaping balloons, lifting up into the night. Up the steep stairs, there was a level grassy area in front of the house, and other guests stood on the lawn in small groups. Rags came through the front door carrying a bowl of chips in one hand and a dip in the other. Barry followed closely behind with a tray of drinks. As they reached the lawn, they separated and circulated amongst the early arrivals, eager to get things started. I made straight for Rags, with Teboho following behind. We had hardly spoken in the car, words falling short of the distance between us. 'Sandy!' Rags shouted as she spotted me coming towards her, before giving us both a kiss, hands still full of edibles. 'Paul and Tracey are inside and Peter should be here any minute', she said as she moved to the next cluster of guests.

We stood awkwardly together, not knowing whether to meet new friends or seek out old ones, but also unsure if we would do it together or alone. We were both facing Table Bay with the city stretched out before us. The view was impossible to ignore and so we stood in almost companionable silence for a moment, taking it all in.

'The end of a thousand years of human history', Teboho said ponderously. 'And the beginning of the next.'

'Also the end of a century, the end of a decade', I replied.

'A decade together', he said.

'Yes', I whispered, not sure I wanted to be drawn into the subject with other couples standing a few feet away. 'Where were you today?' I attempted, not wanting it to sound like an accusation.

'I just drove around mostly. I couldn't be there. I couldn't watch the kids having such a great time, feeling the way I do. And I couldn't watch you opening up to Colleen when you are a closed door to me.'

Guilt and regret possessed me, churning my stomach like a grinder. Despite everything, the thought of hurting him still undid me. 'I'm sorry. Can we talk about this tomorrow?' I suggested, needing some privacy from the raw emotions I was feeling.

As if he hadn't heard me, Teboho continued, 'It's so hard for me to be here now, watching you happy and smiling, looking so beautiful, but not beautiful for me.'

His vulnerability pierced me, making me wish there was another outcome we could craft instead of this inevitable coming apart.

He took my hands in his and looked into my face, searching for the words I lacked the courage to speak. 'OK', he said, 'not tonight', before he turned away and walked towards the beckoning light of the house.

I realised then that he knew the decision was made and though it wasn't what he wanted, it was made nonetheless. We spent the rest of the evening celebrating the New Year in a strange companionship, as if missing each other already and wanting to stay near, wanting to hold onto what we'd had in the protected greenhouse of our lives in 'Maritzburg, in Oxford Street, in Tony and Felicity's garden cottage.

The party had become too much for the hosts just after midnight and the guests, as if feeling the change in temperature, drifted off to find other parties that would see them through to dawn. We followed our friends to another house but the spell was broken, leaving Teboho and I feeling suddenly awkward in light of the knowledge revealed by my face. What had been possible in the torchlight of the garden lamps was chased away now as we sat in the well-lit lounge room. We made our apologies and left shortly after, despite pleading from Rags and the promise of some decent music to dance to, which had been missing up until now. Though that would normally have been enough to make us stay, neither Teboho nor I could face the thought of dancing together to the sensual African rhythms.

We made the short drive home in silence after agreeing that we would take time on the train trip back to Jo'burg to talk through what needed to happen next. Until then, we would try and make the remaining few days memorable for the kids. This was something we both managed to do, as if a pause button had been pressed on the anger and bitterness that was to follow, allowing us all to make the most of the time that was left.

After warm farewells to Colleen and Thomas, we made the slow journey back north. At one point, Teboho asked me to take a photo of him and the kids. As he gathered them close, one under each arm, I watched him struggle with tears, instead bending down to kiss his son gently on the head. I struggled with tears of my own, seeing what the consequences of my decision would be. After the photo, he took the kids for a walk up the train, leaving me to my thoughts. We'd had a few brief discussions about me moving out, what could be taken, what would stay, all as clinical as a surgeon's knife.

This was not the ending I, the holder of dreams, had imagined. My dreams were always big dreams, nearly impossible dreams, dreams that few else wanted. Now, I would have to let this dream go.
The train that was taking me north would carry me to new beginnings: a women's consulting group in partnership with Khumo

and Rags; a new home for the kids and me where friends were frequent guests. There would be tumultuous years with Mello where she worked through her shattered identity, leaving us both broken and torn, and there would also be a drawn-out, painful divorce. Dad's continuing decline into dementia would ultimately call me back home to Australia, but not before I found a new love.

As I sat alone in the carriage, all this was still before me. I knew that soon I would put aside the security of my wedding ring, jewellery many women wore to show that they were loved. I would soon have to stand alone in the new world I had created where different things would define me. Gone were the idealism and naivety I had brought with me to Africa, the political allegiances that allowed me to take a stand, and the husband and the lifestyle I chose to prove that I could. All that remained was the woman who lived inside a small space that had been created in a dark field one night in Port Arthur, Tasmania.

That was all I took with me. Laying all the other props aside, I turned my mind to what was to come, shedding the stages of my life as a snake sheds its skin before moving onto the next incarnation, longing for something more.

ACKNOWLEDGMENTS—TO THE PEOPLE WHO HOLD UP MY SKY

In October 2005, I was having breakfast with one of Australia's most extraordinary athletes, John Maclean. I had invited him to speak at a Westpac conference I was hosting and we were in the middle of a morning-after debrief on his session. The conversation drifted towards our ten-year plans. I told him that ours was to work in Sydney for another ten years and then do a 'tree change'—we would get a few acres out of the city where I would have the time and space to write a book about my years in South Africa. He raised his eyebrows and asked why I wasn't planning to start writing now, if it was genuinely a passion of mine. Then he looked me straight in the eye and said, 'If you're really serious, I will introduce you to my editor, Hazel Flynn, at Murdoch Books. But you really have to want it'. I returned his stare, wondering if you could tell a guy who has done the Hawaiian Ironman three times and swum the English channel twice—without the use of his legs—that you were too chicken to make a dream into a reality, just in case you couldn't pull it off. I decided against it, took a deep breath and said, 'OK'.

Two months later, Hazel was giving me a contract to sign and eighteen months after that, with much encouragement along the way from John, I was submitting the manuscript for publication.

Dreams are heady things when you actually chase them down—and John, you are the dream maker.

At that same conference was Li Cunxin, author of Mao's Last Dancer, whom I had asked to speak on the second day. Over lunch, I mentioned the conversation I'd had with John and asked Li for his advice. He not only encouraged me on the day, but continued to support me over the next two years, freely offering advice on and contacts for all aspects of the writing and publishing process. His example is an inspiration to me.

Despite the image of authors as solitary creatures, writing a book is a team effort. I would firstly like to thank my managers at Westpac, Heather Miles and Ilana Atlas, for agreeing that I could work flexibly and still hold down an exciting role at the bank. Both have also been role models of high achieving women who are able to maintain vibrant lives outside of work.

This book would not have been written without my magnificent editorial team of Diana Hill, Desney Shoemark and Hazel Flynn, women who have coaxed the best out of me as we walked the corridors of my history together. Thanks also to the very talented Reuben Crossman for his beautiful design work which captured the essence of my years in South Africa and the way I wanted the story told. Murdoch Books have made a wonderful contribution through the establishment of Pier 9, a list that allows the stories of many fascinating Australian women and men to be shared and enjoyed. I am honoured to be part of their number.

I would also like to thank my faithful friends who, particularly in the early months of writing, spoke with such enthusiasm about the draft chapters that I began to believe I really could pull this off—namely, Tanya Kruimink, Heather Matejka and Colleen Crawford Cousins. And a special thank you to Grace O'Chee, with whom I have been friends since I was six years old. She kept all my Sizwe newsletters and every letter I ever wrote to her, which were invaluable in piecing together the details of those years.

Thank you to my children, Chaba and Mello. To Chaba, who every single day makes me proud to be his mother. He is an angel child who touches the heart of everyone he meets with his thoughtfulness, insight and lightness of spirit. And to Mello, who is becoming a bold woman in the world. In her sixteen years, she has dealt with more difficulty than most of us have to endure in a lifetime, yet she is sure of who she is and brave in holding her own line. To Mum, thank you for being the place I go to. I would be lost without you. And lastly, to my beloved husband Shaun, with whom I have undertaken a new journey. He understands that it is through imperfection and uncertainty that love finds its soul.

Mello and Chaba, Pilanesberg Game Reserve

First published in 2008 by Pier 9, an imprint of Murdoch Books Pty Limited

Murdoch Books Australia
Pier 8/9
23 Hickson Road
Millers Point NSW 2000
Phone: +61 (0) 2 8220 2000
Fax: +61 (0) 2 8220 2558
www.murdochbooks.com.au

Murdoch Books UK Limited
Erico House, 6th Floor
93–99 Upper Richmond Road
Putney, London SW15 2TG
Phone: +44 (0) 20 8785 5995
Fax: +44 (0) 20 8785 5985
www.murdochbooks.co.uk

Chief executive: Juliet Rogers
Publishing director: Kay Scarlett

Commissioning editors: Hazel Flynn and Diana Hill
Project manager and editor: Desney Shoemark
Concept and design: Reuben Crossman
Production: Kita George

To contact Sandy Blackburn-Wright, go to www.wrightings.com.au

Back cover and cover flap photographs: Getty Images
Photographs on the front cover and page 519 are from the author's personal collection.
Quoted material appearing on pages 161–163, 165, 171–172, 174–175 and 176 has been sourced from the Truth and Reconciliation Commission Hearing Transcripts, Pietermaritzburg, 18–21 November, 1996.

National Library of Australia Cataloguing-in-Publication Data

Blackburn-Wright, Sandy.
Holding up the sky: an African life / author, Sandy Blackburn-Wright.
Sydney: Murdoch Books, 2008.
ISBN 9781921208232 (pbk.):
Blackburn-Wright, Sandy. Community development personnel - South Africa - Biography. Apartheid - South Africa. Blacks - South Africa - Social life and customs. Country life - South Africa.
361.0092

A catalogue record for this book is available from the British Library.

Printed and bound in China in 2007 by Imago.